THE
WARRIOR
IMAGE

THE WARRIOR IMAGE SOLDIERS IN AMERICAN CULTURE FROM THE SECOND WORLD WAR TO THE VIETNAM ERA

ANDREW J. HUEBNER

THE UNIVERSITY OF NORTH CAROLINA PRESS

CHAPEL HILL

Set in Scala and Campaign types
by BW&A Books, Inc.
Manufactured in the United States of America

The paper in this book meets the guidelines for permanence
and durability of the Committee on Production Guidelines for Book
Longevity of the Council on Library Resources.

Library of Congress Cataloging-in-Publication Data
Huebner, Andrew J.
  The warrior image : soldiers in American culture from the Second
World War to the Vietnam era / by Andrew J. Huebner.
       p. cm.
  Includes bibliographical references and index.
  ISBN 978-0-8078-3144-1 (cloth : alk. paper)
  ISBN 978-0-8078-5838-7 (pbk. : alk. paper)
    1. United States—History, Military—20th century. 2. United
States—History, Military—20th century—Pictorial works. 3. Soldiers
—United States—History—20th century. 4. Soldiers—United States
—History—20th century—Pictoral works. 5. Soldiers in art.
6. Soldiers in literature. 7. Soldiers in motion pictures. 8. United
States—Civilization—1945– 9. United States—Civilization—1945
—Pictorial works. 10. Popular culture—United States—History
—20th century. 1. Title.
  E745.H84 2008
  306.2'7097309045 —dc22   2007027989

A version of chapter 4 appeared as "Kilroy Is Back: Images of
American Soldiers in Korea, 1950–53, *American Studies* 45, no. 1
(Spring 2004): 103–29. © 2004 by the Mid-America American Studies
Association. Used by permission. A version of chapter 6 appeared as
"Rethinking American Press Coverage of the Vietnam War, 1965–68,
Journalism History 31, no. 3 (Fall 2005): 150–61. © 2005 by the E. W.
Scripps School of Journalism, Ohio University. Used by permission.
Acknowledgments of permission to reprint other copyrighted material
appear in a section preceding the index.

12 11 10 09 08   5 4 3 2 1

In memory of
Doris Hultgren Huebner
and John L. Thomas
And for Mom, Dad, and Min

War is not nice. War is something else.

—WILLIAM EASTLAKE, *The Bamboo Bed* (1969)

CONTENTS

FIGURES

ACKNOWLEDGMENTS

In the course of writing *The Warrior Image* I benefited from the accessibility, kindness, and support of several mentors. First and foremost, I was fortunate to have James Patterson as my thesis adviser at Brown University. From the beginning, Jim was the model of a superior teacher, scholar, and friend. His careful editing, probing questions, and moral support have made this book immeasurably better, and I thank him as well for his continuing guidance and generosity. Howard Chudacoff, Karl Jacoby, and Elliott Gorn were all extraordinarily gracious and encouraging readers, and this book was much improved by their unique contributions. Tom Gleason was also extremely supportive and helpful in myriad ways. And I cannot overstate the influence of the late Jack Thomas, who not only read the manuscript and improved it with his insights, but was also a dear friend throughout my years in graduate school. Had Jack lived to see this book come out, I'm sure it would have joined the works by his former students that he proudly stacked up in his living room.

I am deeply grateful to John Bodnar and Marilyn Young for their perceptive critiques of the manuscript in its draft stages—both of them were especially helpful in challenging me to clarify the book's aims and arguments. For similarly helping to sharpen my thinking I am indebted to John Baky, William Chafe, Edward M. Coffman, Zac Coile, Nancy Huebner, Mike Majoros, Kurt Piehler, Woody Register, Rob Riser, Jim Sparrow, Travis and Kristin Stolz, and Josh Zeitz. Several colleagues, friends, and relatives read some or all of the chapters: Jan Brunson, Robert Fleegler, William Gillis, Morgan Grefe, Jim Huebner, John Huebner, Wendy Huebner, Brendan Schriber, and Paul White. As the project took shape Robert, Morgan, and Jan offered me constant encouragement, curiosity, and intellectual energy, and later in the process Paul was similarly generous with his time and ideas. At UNC Press Chuck Grench, Paul Betz, Katy O'Brien, and Liz Gray have been genial and supportive throughout the publishing process.

I could not have completed the research for this book without the help of staff members at the John F. Kennedy Library in Boston, the National Archives in Maryland and Washington, the Wisconsin Historical Society in Madison, the Museum of Modern Art Archives in New York, the La Salle University Library in Philadelphia, and the John Hay Library in Providence.

For help tracking down and securing permissions for poems, I owe a debt of gratitude to Jan Barry, W. D. Ehrhart, Robert Hedin, Larry Rottmann, William Childress, Rolando Hinojosa, Stan Platke, Earl E. Martin, Charles Purcell, Margaret Nemerov, Maureen Sylak, and Ruth Wantling. Merrily Harris and Jessica Lacher-Feldman generously provided much-needed assistance with acquiring image permissions. At the University of Alabama, the William G. Anderson Endowed Support Fund helped offset the costs of those permissions. Two graduate students in Tuscaloosa, John Mitcham and Charles Roberts, graciously aided me in the process of proofreading. And I thank David Douglas Duncan for speaking with me about the project and granting permission to reproduce his haunting photographs.

Looking further back into my own past, it is evident that I never would have become a professional historian without the early encouragement of Jim Huebner, Lee Huebner, and Mike Naylor. And for all their love and support, my deepest thanks go to the best people I know—Mom, Dad, and my brother Min.

THE
WARRIOR
IMAGE

INTRODUCTION
BEYOND TELLING
OR IMAGINING

Reflecting on more than two decades of experience covering conflict, the eminent war correspondent Martha Gellhorn wrote in 1959, "War is a malignant disease, an idiocy, a prison, and the pain it causes is beyond telling or imagining; but war was our condition and our history, the place we had to live in."[1] Gellhorn's words suggest that capturing the sorrow of war is something like the journalistic quest for objectivity—rarely, if ever, attainable but always worth the attempt. Despite her own belief that war was "beyond telling or imagining," Gellhorn told readers about warfare and helped them imagine its consequences for six decades, from the Spanish Civil War in the 1930s to the American invasion of Panama in 1989. She and other American correspondents, filmmakers, painters, radio personalities, poets, photographers, and television reporters of the war-ravaged twentieth century endeavored to convey some small sense of battle to the reading, viewing, and listening public—and many of them were skeptical, like Gellhorn, of their own ability to do so.[2] Yet if they failed to convey the nature of war, they succeeded in doing something else: illuminating the culture and values of their own societies. Consequently, by the late twentieth century scholars were treating war as a cultural event—an opportunity to examine the beliefs and attitudes of human beings through their depictions of warfare.[3]

This merging of military history and cultural history—one something of a pariah in the American academy, the other the heir apparent to the "new social history" emerging from the 1960s—is particularly suited to studying America in the years beginning with World War II.[4] There are few periods richer in war imagery than the four decades in the United States following the Japanese attack on Pearl Harbor in 1941. In these years portraits of combat became more vivid and widely consumed than ever before in human history. Advancing literacy and technology—along with declining federal control over image making and the press—brought increasingly unvarnished images of war to millions of Americans. The popular press, novels, newsreels, magazines, museum exhibits, photographs, radio shows, television broadcasts, government films, and Hollywood movies carried portraits of war to the American home front during and after three major overseas conflicts: World War II (1941–45), the Korean War (1950–53), and the Vietnam War (1964–73). In this book I will be concerned specifically with American cultural representations of *soldiers*, forming the architecture of what I call the "warrior image" from the 1940s to the late 1970s.

Of course the warrior image has had a long and varied history. From ancient times to the twenty-first century, and in all the world's cultures, people have felt the need to make sense of, glorify, or lament this most disturbing of human practices—war is, after all, "the place we had to live in," according to Gellhorn. In the many centuries before World War II, artists and writers depicted and remarked upon the nature of warfare through the principal cultural forms of the day: stories, drawings, paintings, murals, tapestries, poems, sculptures, memorials, and songs. Throughout history people have created images of soldiers ranging from the heroic to the pitiful, and in doing so have said much about their own societies.[5] A brief survey of this immense body of cultural output helps frame the issues of emphasis in my own study of modern American war imagery.

In the seventh century B.C. Greeks wrote down the tale of *The Iliad*, an epic account of the Trojan War that mourned the slaughter of thousands in the city of Troy. An unknown Roman sculptor carved the *Dying Gaul* in 240 B.C., depicting a mortally wounded enemy barbarian with surprising sympathy. In the same era Chinese artists sculpted thousands of life-size clay horses, chariots, and soldiers, some deployed in poses of hand-to-hand combat (all of it found in 1974 in one of the grandest archaeological discoveries of modern history). Several hundred years later and across the Pacific Ocean, a sixth-century A.D. Mayan temple mural showed pitiful captives supplicating before resplendent warriors.[6]

One of the grandest premodern images of warfare appeared in late eleventh-century Europe, just a few years after the Battle of Hastings in 1066. Across 230 feet of embroidered fabric, the *Bayeux Tapestry* (1070–80) vividly depicted that momentous clash between Norman and Anglo-Saxon warriors, in what art historians have called "a kind of distant anticipation of modern pictorial [war] reportage."[7] Thirteenth-century Japanese painters produced a similar work in the Heiji Scroll, a panoramic rendering of the great battle in 1159 between the first two prominent samurai clans.[8] Several centuries later William Shakespeare described the legendary Battle of Agincourt of 1415 in *Henry V*, giving theater-goers of 1600 (and later movie audiences) a bloody yet glorified view of combat in the king's St. Crispin's day speech:

> From this day to the ending of the world
> But we in it shall be remembered,
> We few, we happy few, we band of brothers.
> For he today that sheds his blood with me

Shall be my brother; be he ne'er so vile,
This day shall gentle his condition.
And gentlemen in England now abed
Shall think themselves accursed they were not here,
And hold their manhoods cheap whiles any speaks
That fought with us upon Saint Crispin's day.

To the literary critic Yuval Noah Harari, these simultaneous themes of blood and glory also resided in Renaissance war memoirs. Soldiers emerging from European military aristocracies forged their identities through honor—and combat, though deadly, offered the ultimate opportunity to perform honorable deeds.[9]

In the nineteenth century Eugène Delacroix's painting *Liberty Leading the People* (1830) celebrated armed revolution in France while also showing the casualties of war. Darker was the theme of Francisco Goya's painting *The Third of May, 1808* (1814), which depicted the execution of several Spanish civilians during Napoleon's intervention in Spain. Without glorification—or "mercy for the viewer's sensibilities," as two art historians have put it—Goya showed "the horrors of war." Blood drenches the earth as some victims cower in terror, while the main subject bravely invites death.[10]

Americans, whose very independence arose from war, were just beginning to contribute to the depiction of armed conflict in the nineteenth century. Emanuel Leutze's dramatic painting *Washington Crossing the Delaware* (1851) glorified the resolute Gen. George Washington leading American revolutionary troops in 1776. The British attack on Baltimore during the War of 1812 provided the inspiration for Francis Scott Key's poem, "The Star-Spangled Banner," which circulated widely in American newspapers in 1814 before being set to the tune of an English drinking song. Like Shakespeare's *Henry V*, the last verse of the original poem looked forward to the war's legacy, though this time in national, not personal, terms:

O, thus be it ever when freemen shall stand,
Between their lov'd homes and the war's desolation;
Blest with vict'ry and peace, may the heav'n-rescued land
Praise the Pow'r that hath made and preserv'd us as a nation!

Steadily increasing in popularity, "The Star-Spangled Banner" became the American national anthem in 1931 and a fixture at sporting events thereafter during the twentieth century.[11]

Not long after the penning of the future anthem, a new figure was changing the face of combat imagery: the war correspondent. With the proliferation of newspapers in the United States and Europe in the 1840s, a small handful of journalists began visiting combat zones and sending back reports to their home offices. One scholar has identified the *New Orleans Picayune*'s George Kendall, who reported the Mexican War of 1846–48, as the world's first professional war correspondent.[12] From that conflict emerged the first daguerreotype photographs of warfare, though the poor marketing efforts of the cameramen prevented anyone in the public from seeing them.[13] Several British and American journalists traveled to the Black Sea region to observe the Crimean War in the 1850s, issuing vivid reports on the suffering of wounded English soldiers. The high incidence of needless deaths in that conflict—reported by William Howard Russell of the *London Times*, among others—eventually led to Florence Nightingale's attempts to reform the military health-care system in Great Britain. The British government, meanwhile, countered such imagery by producing its own staged photographs of cheerful soldiers—not the last time that official image makers would wage battles against the popular press.[14]

By the eve of the American Civil War, a spreading network of newspapers and telegraph services in the United States ensured that the looming conflict would be the first in human history to be widely covered by journalists. The growth of railroad lines and the development, in 1844, of the magnetic telegraph allowed reporters to submit their dispatches faster than ever before. Once the war began in 1861, an increasingly literate American population consumed war news from about five hundred correspondents reporting in relatively new publications such as James Gordon Bennett's *New York Herald*, Horace Greeley's *New York Tribune*, and Henry Raymond's *New York Times*. Not all of the press originated in New York; of the 2,500 American newspapers in circulation in 1860, one-third were in the South, including 80 of the 373 daily papers. Complementing these publications (almost all of them linked closely to a political party) were three major illustrated journals: *Harper's Weekly*, *Frank Leslie's Illustrated Newspaper*, and the *New York Illustrated News*. Reviving the old technique of woodcut illustration, publishers used converted drawings to show combat, burial of the dead, and the war's impact on civilians.[15]

The advent of combat journalism did not hinder the production of war-related artwork, poetry, novels, memoirs, songs, and photographs. The Civil War inspired the tune "When Johnny Comes Marching Home," as well as a trove of battlefield artwork.[16] Ambrose Bierce's stories, Stephen Crane's novel *The Red Badge of Courage* (1895), and Walt Whitman's poems such as "The Wound Dresser" were only the best-known works of an immense literature emerging from the conflict. Despite the graphic nature of some of these works, to the historian David Blight "romance triumphed over reality" in most writings about the Civil War, as scores of veterans' accounts, short stories, and periodical pieces submerged battlefield horrors beneath tales of martial nobility and camp life minutiae.[17] Among the grimmest Civil War images were Mathew Brady's photographs of the dead at Antietam and elsewhere, though few Americans ever laid eyes on them at the time. Without the halftone process, patented in 1881, publishers were unable to reprint photographs in the popular press.[18]

In 1898 images and words about an impending conflict in Cuba splashed across the front pages of American newspapers. Joseph Pulitzer's *New York World*, and even more so William Randolph Hearst's *New York Journal*, used images of Spanish treachery, often announced in screaming headlines and vivid cartoons, to help push the country into the conflict.[19] Once war came after the sinking of the U.S.S. *Maine*, between three and five hundred print correspondents, including the *World*'s Stephen Crane, headed to the war zone. Also there was the dashing Richard Harding Davis, perhaps the best-known war correspondent in American history to that point. Accompanying Davis was the famous American pictorial artist Frederic Remington, to whom Hearst allegedly wrote, "You furnish the pictures and I'll furnish the war."[20] The first, albeit small, contingent of photojournalists also traveled to Cuba and the Philippines. Though censorship of the press was heavy, grainy photographs of combat appeared in some American weeklies, including *Harper's*, *Leslie's*, and *Collier's*. And from the Philippines, journalists publicized American atrocities against local guerrillas and civilians.[21]

When the Great War broke out in Europe in 1914, tight censorship of the media severely limited correspondents from Great Britain, France, Germany, Austria, and Italy. The United States, when it joined the war in 1917, also joined this collective endeavor to control the news. Moreover, still prevailing in American culture was what the historian David Kennedy has called an "irrepressibly positive and romantic view of war," and amid strict mobilization of public opinion this view suffused popular imagery. Few grisly photographs of the trench fighting reached American audiences. Instead, "countless posters depict[ed] Dame Columbia or some other drapeaued goddess," Kennedy has written, "benevolently shepherding doughboys into battle." Popular films such as *Pershing's Crusaders* and the song "Over There" also pushed an upbeat, patriotic message.[22] Such imagery celebrated traditional soldierly virtues of duty, honor, and manliness. To paraphrase Shakespeare's fictionalized Henry V, combat was an adventure—a chance to prove one's manhood.

Such chivalric imagery of warfare, bound up in older, even medieval, battle practices, could scarcely withstand the screaming shells and machine-gun fire of World War I. Some observers of the conflict—maintaining an age-old view of war stitched across the more glorious one—depicted the shattering impact of combat on soldiers. A rich trove of poetry from the Great War, for instance, showed the helplessness and suffering of individual troops and veterans. Particularly moving were the words of Wilfred Owen, an English soldier who suffered from shell shock in the trenches and eventually was killed in the last week of the war. Owen captured the new dreadfulness of mechanized warfare in his apocalyptic poem "Anthem for Doomed Youth":

> What passing-bells for these who die as cattle?
>   Only the monstrous anger of the guns.
>   Only the stuttering rifles' rapid rattle
> Can patter out their hasty orisons. [23]

After the war British memoirists Siegfried Sassoon, Robert Graves, and Edmund Blunden kept the conflict alive in accounts of their "unforgettable military experiences of outrage, fear, pain, and comedy on the Western Front," in the words of literary critic Paul Fussell. [24] The German novelist Erich Maria Remarque's *All Quiet on the Western Front* (1929), a withering critique of modern warfare, also drew on the author's experiences in the trenches. A movie adaptation in the United States earned the Academy Award for best picture in 1930. In their literature of postwar alienation, American authors Ernest Hemingway (*A Farewell to Arms*, 1929) and John Dos Passos (*Three Soldiers*, 1921; *1919*, 1932; *The Big Money*, 1936) wrote against official wartime images of unified and efficient armies marching off to make the world safe for democracy. Instead, these and other observers portrayed a military afoul with excessive authoritarianism and arbitrariness. [25] Such imagery may have resonated with an alarmed American public when several thousand World War I veterans, seeking their army bonuses, were forcibly expelled from Washington, D.C., by federal troops in 1932. [26]

In the 1930s the Spanish Civil War generated more grim combat imagery. Pablo Picasso's mural *Guernica* (1937) depicted in Surrealist fashion the awful consequences of the German bombardment (on Gen. Francisco Franco's behalf) of the Basque capital. In the painting grotesque figures represent combat's innocent victims. [27] Equally striking was a legendary photograph from the war zone. Among the journalists who covered the Spanish Civil War was photographer Robert Capa, who went on to snap dramatic images during the D-Day invasion of 1944 and would die in a Vietminh mortar attack on assignment in Indochina ten years after that. In 1936 Capa took perhaps the most famous war photograph in history, "The Falling Soldier." Whether it was posed, or was in fact a shot of a man simply stumbling down a hill-side, has been debated. Yet it shocked viewers around the world, who saw it first in the influential French publication *Vu* and later, in 1937, in *Life* magazine above a caption announcing the dominant interpretation: "A Spanish soldier the instant he is dropped by a bullet through the head." Some readers recoiled at the violence. As one of Capa's biographers has put it, "No such image had ever appeared in the homes of Middle America."[28] Newsreels, which had originated in the 1890s and appeared sparingly amid censorship in France and England during World War I, played an increasing role in delivering scenes from the Spanish Civil War to theater audiences, particularly in Britain. Before the age of television, these were among the first moving pictures of combat and its aftermath in the twentieth century.[29]

Those who witnessed the Spanish Civil War left a rich literary record of it in later years.[30] Hemingway, who had covered the war as a journalist, published a fictionalized account of his experiences, *For Whom the Bell Tolls*, in 1940; and in 1959 his former wife Martha Gellhorn published her dispatches from Spain and elsewhere in her collection *The Face of War*. George Orwell fought in the Spanish Civil War, enduring a grievous wound but living to tell about it in *Homage to Catalonia* (1938).[31] Several movies in Europe and America also took the conflict as their subject, including *The Last Train from Madrid* (1937), *Blockade* (1938), and *For Whom the Bell Tolls* (1943).[32] By 1943, of course, American attention had turned to the colossal bloodletting in Europe and the Pacific.

Despite this long history of war imagery, it was during World War II and thereafter that *mass* audiences away from the front lines, particularly in the United States, began to glimpse the nature of armed conflict. Although World War II has been labeled "the censored war," it introduced millions of Americans to combat and the foot soldier as never before.[33] A freer press than in 1917–18 brought the fighting into the living rooms of home-front audiences, while hundreds of Hollywood war movies played on the silver screen. Radio executives, as well, produced myriad programs about Americans fighting in Europe and the Pacific. After 1945, as the United States entered two major wars in Korea and Vietnam, the warrior image spread across the landscape of American culture. Popular magazines, government films, museum exhibits, photographic collections, literature, and television programming carried depictions of soldiers and veterans—in words and pictures—to the American public.

My book tells *a* story—surely not the only one—about this extensive imagery of warriors in Cold War culture. By "imagery" I mean visual depictions as well as written material. I will use the terms *soldier, veteran, warrior, serviceman,* and GI rather broadly, to include members of all military branches. I have limited my study of soldiers and veterans in this period to *males,* since they dominated popular imagery of war. Women in uniform were routinely excluded from most military roles, war films, news accounts, and benefits packages extended to males.[34] Also, with some exceptions I have limited my study to foot soldiers, rather than airmen or seamen, partly for reasons of space but also because much war-related culture in this period featured the infantry. For the same reason I have focused on combat troops, rather than support personnel and other forces in the rear—though it should be remembered that the large majority of veterans in the United States did not engage in combat during their time in the service. Lastly, space and time limitations compelled me to end my study with the spate of Vietnam War films of 1978. It would require several additional books to cover cultural representations of Vietnam in the 1980s, debates over the three national war memorials erected between 1982 and 2004, media coverage of the conflicts with Iraq, and the rejuvenation of World War II nostalgia and image making in the 1990s.

As surely as historians and archaeologists have used ancient and premodern portrayals of warfare to explore societies of the past, scholars can learn a great deal about American culture, politics, and values from the vast body of war-related imagery produced after 1941. I have asked two general questions of this material: How did images of warfare and soldiers evolve or change in American culture between the 1940s and 1970s? What do such changes and continuities tell us about American ideals and values in these four decades?

Although many writers have asked such questions of combat portraiture over this period, few have stretched their analyses across boundaries of either time or media. A thriving yet compartmentalized literature on World War II imagery has come forth from film theorists, literary critics, journalists, and historians.[35] The Korean War, not surprisingly, has garnered little attention in terms of war imagery.[36] Cultural representations of the Vietnam War, like World War II before it, have inspired a rich body of scholarship, but once again individual works tend to focus solely on novels, films, media coverage, or some other form of expression.[37] These studies of World War II and Vietnam collectively posit a precipitous decline in sentimental images from one war to the other, with portraiture of the Korean War GI somehow lost in the muddle. As Daniel Hallin and Todd Gitlin have expressed it, "After World War II an extremely positive, romantic image of war came to dominate American culture. It was modified significantly by Vietnam, as one can easily see by comparing war films from the Vietnam period with those from World War II and the Korean War."[38] I find, instead, multiple continuities and *gradual* shifts in military imagery across the Cold War era, with the Korean War playing a crucial role in generating cynical and critical depictions of the armed forces.[39]

My inquiry focuses on depictions of soldiers and veterans in (mostly popular) cultural forms of the day.[40] Of course, these changed between the 1940s and the 1970s. Depending on the years in question, these images might have come from radio shows, films, newsreels, television broadcasts, museum exhibits, poems, novels, or, during the Vietnam War, antiwar demonstrations. Some works were more widely consumed than others, yet on the whole I have selected a mixture of well-known and more obscure texts about each war to demonstrate the ubiquity of the meanings I find. A book of this sort naturally invites readers to ask why their own favorite war movie, novel, or television show is not included—but I have chosen to stress thematic patterns across genres rather than comprehensive coverage of any particular one. Throughout these chapters I have anchored my analysis with depictions of soldiers and veterans in the popular media. Archival material has helped me dig below the surface and learn what was *not* shown—often as significant as what *was* shown.

On occasion archival resources have helped explain the motivation for propagating one image or another, but generally both the *producers* and *consumers* of war imagery play much less prominent roles in this book than do the depictions themselves. In other words, this is neither a study of public attitudes toward war nor a behind-the-scenes account of how war imagery was created—undertakings that would require wholly different sources and methodologies. Rather, it is an extended interpretation of martial imagery consumed by large numbers of Americans, tracing specific themes across a wide range of cultural forms. Finally, I am cautious about saying the meanings I find *dominated* war imagery in this period (though they did so at times among some media), preferring to say they were highly *prominent* ones. Other scholars might easily discern narratives contrary to or complementary of the story I have to tell, and I welcome the dialogue that such studies would provoke.

In my interpretation of this material, architects of "war culture" between 1941 and the late 1970s, as in the preceding centuries, freely mingled romanticized depictions with realistic ones—the warrior image was in fact dynamic and complex. Yet amid two brutal wars in Asia, declining federal control over the press, and increasing public cynicism about federal authority, realist imagery increasingly eclipsed sentimental imagery, long before the start of the Vietnam War—often marked as the conflict that smothered romantic views of warfare in post-1945 America. [41]

For many scholars of war-related culture, however, part of this story is controversial—the notion of federal control over the press—and addressing that issue here helps frame my broader assumptions and conclusions in this book.

In the growing literature on war and the media, spurred on in large part by Vietnam and, later, the Gulf War of 1991, a debate has developed over the relationship between the press and the state in times of war. On one side have been government officials, military leaders, and some journalists and scholars who argue that the press, most obviously in the case of the Vietnam War, delivered bloody, pessimistic, and ultimately misleading dispatches to the home front, thus "losing" that conflict for the United States. War correspondent Robert Elegant formulated the classic expression of this view in 1981, writing disapprovingly, "For the first time in modern history, the outcome of a war was determined not on the battlefield, but on the printed page and, above all, on the television screen."[42] A few journalists and peace activists have assigned the press similar power during the Vietnam War, but have *applauded* it, arguing that crusading correspondents and editors rightly convinced the American public that the war was unwinnable and also not worth winning. [43]

A wide range of scholars have argued quite the opposite regarding both the Vietnam era and the more recent war on terror. These thinkers suggest that far from being an opponent of the government, the media is a mouthpiece for it. In this view journalists simply reproduce the viewpoint of the administration, of military leaders, or of a broader "national community" or "nation." As the sociologist Richard Kaplan put it in 2003, "The press, now as in the past, is intrinsically tied up with narratives of the national community, and, more specifically, with stories of the USA in combat with enemies abroad as it goes about the business of constructing empire."[44] This charge was particularly common in the aftermath of the terrorist attacks of September 11, 2001, when some scholars vilified what they saw as a "partisan, cheerleading media" abetting the American war on terror. Since 9/11, according to a proponent of this view, "The press has remained generally in the thrall of the executive branch."[45] Other observers, most conspicuously Noam Chomsky, have argued that earlier conflicts of the twentieth century saw similar collusion between the media and federal authorities. Particularly during World War II and the Vietnam War, these scholars have suggested, the press sugarcoated American wars as part of their devotion to or reliance on mainstream values, corporate parent companies, advertising revenues, or official military sources.[46] (Historians of the Second World War have claimed similarly that Hollywood propagated sanitized or state-sanctioned versions of the conflict.)[47] For some of these observers the stakes of war reportage are quite high, as they charge that one of the foundations of American democracy—a free press—may in fact be a farce.

These media critics have offered a vital corrective to long-standing claims that the press "lost" the Vietnam War and have continued to subvert the government and military. They are quite correct to point out that the media, particularly in the early part of the Vietnam War, have often embraced the initial premises of American intervention overseas and shared with the public a desire to see the United States "win." (Of course, such a characterization applies easily to the entire span of World War II and to the beginning stages of the Korean War.) Yet in my view, both sides in this polemical debate oversimplify a tremendously complex web of images, meanings, and viewpoints delivered by the mainstream press—preoccupied, as they tend to be, with identifying and condemning the biases of the media.

This book shows that whether the creators of a publication (or movie or novel, for that matter) supported a particular war or not, the most salient aspect of war imagery was *sympathy and identification with the soldiers,* and not necessarily with the war effort itself. As Hallin and Gitlin have put it, "The primary role of the media in wartime in the Anglo-American world has long been to maintain the ties of sentiment between the soldiers in the field and the home front."[48] Perhaps no individual embodies this tradition more than the World War II correspondent Ernie Pyle. Yet as we will see, his dispatches, as well as many other films, photos, novels, and articles over the years—whether inherently "antiwar" or not—shared a preoccupation with the attitude and physical condition of the individual GI. More importantly, after World War II reporters forging these ties of sentiment with the soldier came to imply that he was a *victim* of his government, suggesting a far less cozy alliance between media and officialdom than is commonly described in recent scholarship. In the decades after 1945 Americans confronted an increasing number of frustrated, disillusioned, isolated, and embittered soldiers and veterans across different forms of culture.

So while in some ways the mainstream press, Hollywood filmmakers, and other image makers may have served the purposes of administrations, in other ways—in the depiction of soldiers—they often have undermined or challenged the government's war efforts. Journalists, for their part, seem to feel an affinity for the soldiers and a responsibility to broadcast the horrors those troops face, particularly when wars come into question, though not exclusively at those times. Moreover, renderings of war are not always simple or straightforward things. News reports—or films or novels or photographs—may contain a broad range of meanings, tones, and implications, beyond whatever grand theme or message they appear to be advancing. Postmodern theorists have rejected the idea of a monolithic media injecting a pliable public with information and opinions in a linear process. Rather, in the words of media scholar Susan Carruthers, news audiences—and I would add audiences of movies and novels and other media—"can resist intended, surface meanings and find instead subversive interpretations, uses or 'gratifications' from the media they consume."[49]

What were some of these meanings? To reiterate, journalists, filmmakers, novelists, poets, and other American observers of war between the 1940s and 1970s exposed the suffering of individual soldiers, GIs' attempts at overcoming their suffering, the forms that overcoming took, and, increasingly, the possible victimization of American troops not only by war itself but also by politicians, diplomats, and military leaders. More and more, designers of the warrior image stressed the plight of the individual over the cohesion of the collective; the damaging rather than the edifying consequences of battle; the isolation of the soldier instead of the enveloping presence of the military leadership, the government, and the home front. These elements, in turn, increasingly fueled implicit and explicit critiques of the nation's military commitments overseas—long before most Americans had ever heard of Vietnam.[50]

THE
WORLD
WAR II
ERA

CHAPTER 1
HERE IS YOUR WAR, 1941–1945

Walking through New York City's Museum of Modern Art (MoMA) in the summer of 1942, visitors would be sure to see the exhibit Road to Victory, a photographic account of the American people's reluctant entrance into the Second World War. Beginning with serene pictures of the American West and small-town life, the sequence took a dramatic turn with a large photograph of the attack on Pearl Harbor just months earlier. Nearby was a photo of Japanese emissaries to the United States laughing at some unknown joke; placed alongside images of the explosions in Hawaii, the Japanese seemed to be snickering at the American dead. From there viewers saw pictures of the great factories and farms that kept the war machine rolling, as well as large renderings of American soldiers. Along the way poetic captions explained the images. "Country boys, big city lads, home town fellers," one placard read, "they're in the Army now." One otherwise fierce GI smiled confidently at onlookers from behind his bayonet. Pictures of American families underscored the simple origins and ideals that shaped the greatest warriors in the world, "Trouble-shooters in the first round-the-world war."[1]

Opened five months after the Japanese attack on Pearl Harbor, Road to Victory appeared at MoMA from May to October 1942, drawing over 100,000 visitors. (Despite the show's title, Allied victory was anything but guaranteed that summer, with the Germans penetrating deep into the Soviet Union and Africa, and the Japanese on the offensive in the Pacific until the Battle of Midway in June.) Lt. Edward Steichen, an acclaimed photographer of the First World War now employed as a chronicler of the navy, filled the exhibit with photos culled from the archives of the army, the navy, the Agricultural Adjustment Administration, and other alphabet agencies of the Depression years. The poet Carl Sandburg, Steichen's brother-in-law, penned the accompanying captions. In 1943 and 1944 smaller versions of the exhibit took to the road under the sponsorship of the Office of War Information (OWI), the new propaganda arm of the federal government. The exhibit attracted tens of thousands of visitors in Cleveland, Chicago, St. Louis, San Francisco, Honolulu, and smaller venues such as Providence, Rhode Island; Davenport, Iowa; Brookings, South Dakota; Northfield, Minnesota; and Carbondale, Illinois.[2]

Press reaction around the country was enormously favorable. The *New York Times* labeled Road to Victory the "supreme war contribution." In Cleveland journalists touted the exhibit's "dramatic dignity" and role as an effective "morale builder." The *Chicago Sun* called Road to Victory a "smashing presentation of modern American art, as well as a reflection of the country and the times." In Wisconsin a reporter noted the "fine and mighty climax" of the exhibit, a "mural 12 feet by 40 feet of armed marching men," while the *St. Louis Globe-Democrat* found it a "fine and high spirited exhibition."[3] The director of St. Louis's City Art Museum reported that the show "was received with great enthusiasm on the part of those who saw it" there.[4] Scores of large and small publications around the nation announced their approval of Road to Victory, many merely reproducing MoMA's written description of the exhibit for their own papers.

A few observers were not so impressed, however, and their dissent hinted at issues that would surround the warrior image throughout the conflict. Eleanor Jewett of the previously isolationist *Chicago Tribune* acknowledged that she and her editors were a "minority of one" but that they did not share the "tremendous enthusiasm" surrounding the show. Drawing their criticisms were the sanitized images making up most of the exhibit. Jewett charged that the display was "government propaganda" and that "sugar had been spread rather thick." Alongside general praise for the show, another Chicago paper partially agreed with Jewett, admitting that the exhibit "tells nothing of the actual fighting." Yet Jewett's position broke sharply with much of the national reaction. Most observers agreed with a California paper that warned the faint of heart, "There has been no minimizing of the gravity of war."[5]

Eleanor Jewett and the *Tribune* had a point. The photographs for Road to Victory had been selected from a limited and censored body of images and included no pictures of combat, wounded soldiers, or the dead. During World War II federal and military authorities exerted tight control over the dissemination of photographs, making what one scholar has called "the most systematic and far-reaching effort in its history to shape the visual experience of the citizenry."[6] Road to Victory was one of the first expressions of that effort, representing obvious, uncomplicated propaganda. It suggested that American soldiers were capable, proud, eager participants in a conflict strangely devoid of bloodshed. The exhibit gave viewers no reason to think, moreover, that combat would have any negative effect on American servicemen, boys reared in the heartland and steeled by a mighty resolve. On the contrary, war would transform a generation of American youths into *men*.

The *Tribune*'s cautious dissent hinted at two larger questions: How should soldiers (and later, veterans) be portrayed, and what role would the federal government play in the shaping of those images? The job of presenting the American fighting man to the home front fell to a diverse and inchoate group of journalists, government propagandists, mental health experts, Hollywood producers, politicians, and some soldiers and veterans themselves.

People who endeavored to portray a "typical" American GI or veteran faced an impossible task. More than 16 million men and women served in the armed forces between 1941 and 1945. The vast majority were white males (of various ethnic backgrounds), but there were nearly a million African American troops, mostly in service units but some fighting in segregated combat outfits. The famed Ninety-ninth Fighter Squadron, or Tuskegee Airmen, for instance, flew missions over North Africa and Europe. Although thousands of Japanese Americans were confined to internment camps in the United States, their brethren fought as well, most famously in the 442nd Regiment operating in Europe.[7]

Overall, 405,400 Americans died during World War II (battle and non-battle deaths); 670,800 were wounded; 139,700 were captured; and about 1.3 million suffered debilitating psychological disorders.[8] Around a million—one in sixteen U.S. soldiers—saw extended combat, while the majority of American military personnel never saw an armed enemy soldier.[9] The rest worked to supply the troops, cook food, fix jeeps and tanks, service airplanes and warships, build bridges and repair roads, police occupied cities, give care to the wounded, and carry out countless other jobs, big and small, required to keep an army of 16 million men and women operational (inductees were put into one of three categories: technical, clerical, and infantry).[10] More than 2 million soldiers returned home *during* the war. These "previctory" veterans were mainly physical and psychiatric casualties, but others came home for disciplinary reasons, age, illiteracy, or ineptitude.[11] The rest returned after the war in one of the largest military demobilizations in human history.

Despite its reputation as "the good war," World War II offered diverse horrors to those who *did* see combat.[12] This grand clash of governments and ideologies played out in localities—in arctic and tropical climates, in cities and jungles, on beaches and in trenches. For individual soldiers and support personnel, the scope of experience was smaller, with millions upon millions of unreported moments of drama, heroism, and tragedy. Stitched together over a four-year period, these individual performances and ordeals made up the fabric of American military experience in World War II. Those landing on an enemy-held shoreline confronted mines, machine-gun fire, and the threat of drowning under the weight of their own gear. Soldiers told to storm a beach routinely vomited, soiled themselves, or broke down emotionally. In land warfare one might go temporarily or permanently deaf from the awful din of artillery fire. Detached body parts, typically excluded from

Hollywood depictions of combat, often littered the battlefield. The decks of ships might become flooded with human detritus during a bombardment or kamikaze attack. And wafting over a war zone was the almost unbearable stench of dead bodies. Added to all this were the miseries of life in the field—poor food, unsanitary conditions, shortages of water, the constant struggle to sleep. Pilots often enjoyed a more refined existence on land, but once airborne they faced antiaircraft fire, dogfights, and the perils of ejecting over hostile territory. The famed flier-poet Howard Nemerov wrote of the experience:

That was the good war, the war we won
As if there were no death, for goodness' sake,
With the help of the losers we left out there
In the air, in the empty air.[13]

Decades later scholars were to complicate "good war" mythology by illuminating these and many other harsh elements of combat in World War II, though of course veterans had long understood them.[14] Some of these writers, most notably the World War II veteran and literary critic Paul Fussell, have framed their work as a corrective to roseate imagery in the popular media of the 1940s. The radio and film industries, for instance, cooperated readily with government officials in packaging the conflict and GIs for the public; they showed little blood, little psychological breakdown, and plenty of patriotism, good will, teamwork, and camaraderie.[15] Various critics have similarly charged the press corps of World War II with willingly delivering a sanitized version of combat to the public.[16]

It is true that throughout World War II, the tone set in Road to Victory continued to dominate coverage of the conflict. Amid strict censorship of words and images from the combat zone—and with a press corps that tended to believe deeply in the war effort—portraits of simple, heroic, humble American GIs abounded.[17] These virtuous individuals had responded when Japan viciously and unjustifiably attacked the United States, an opening salvo of violence that would in turn lead the public to sanction monumental retaliatory violence against the Japanese—reluctantly delivered by the modest American soldier. In this imagery, war and the military positively transformed the soldier from a *boy* into a *man*, with many of combat's sinister realities submerged. Government propagandists and journalists alike participated in painting such portraits. Road to Victory was just an early example of much collaboration between federal agencies and private citizens in the business of presenting the warrior image to the public.

Yet as the war ground on, some depictions of warfare, the GIs, and returning veterans grew more complex. Censorship of grisly photos of the dead and wounded slackened when government officials sensed a growing public complacency about the war, and some media coverage of combat became grimmer.[18] Almost before it took hold, the mythic image of the sturdy, war-hardened American GI began showing cracks.

———

At the center of the propaganda effort during World War II was the Office of War Information, established by executive order in June 1942. Like its predecessor in World War I, the Committee on Public Information (CPI), OWI was charged with helping to win the war by mobilizing public opinion and clarifying American war aims. The agency euphemistically described its own project in 1945: to issue information "on as broad a scale and as quickly as possible in order to assist the public to an understanding of some wartime problems."[19] George Creel's CPI had gone too far in this regard in 1917–18, stimulating a virulent hatred of the Germans (sauerkraut was renamed "liberty cabbage") and characterizing World War I as a crusade to "re-win the tomb of Christ." When Woodrow Wilson's vision of the peace settlement collapsed at Versailles, the CPI's histrionic language suddenly seemed over-wrought. Remembered by many Americans for stirring up hate, hysteria, and unrealistic hopes, wartime propaganda had a poor reputation going into World War II.[20]

OWI struggled against this background, but the agency had other problems as well. As World War II rumbled on, American political and military leaders moved away from a lofty defense of democracy (OWI's specialty) toward a pragmatic effort to end the war as soon as possible. Once again, the propaganda wing of the government found itself out in front of the administration. Initially committed to the Four Freedoms and the democratic ideals of the Atlantic Charter, Franklin Roosevelt proved a less idealistic and more flexible president than Wilson. FDR preferred to focus on winning the war, and propagandists issued appeals to conserve resources and buy war bonds. In 1943 a frustrated Arthur M. Schlesinger Jr., in fact, joined a great exodus of writers from OWI who remained committed to the war's ideological roots.[21]

The agency also languished under the disorderly and contentious system of wartime information management. Early in the war a slew of federal agencies fought turf battles within the two major areas of public relations: censorship and propaganda. Soon after the creation of OWI in June 1942—itself a move toward consolidating the national flow of information—something of an agreement was reached when OWI officials signed a pact with the Office of Censorship. The latter was to quietly tell journalists what *not* to say, while OWI was to gently suggest what they *should* say. Yet OWI continued to operate in a world of overlapping jurisdictions and ambiguous chains of authority. The armed services had their own censorship bureaus and could exercise influence in Hollywood by withholding technical assistance from filmmakers who sent the wrong message—a weapon outside of OWI's arsenal. In short, the flow of information and imagery during the war followed no simple, overarching pattern. There were internecine conflicts in OWI, battles between agencies, and ad hoc arrangements governing the proliferation of imagery.[22]

These limitations did not prevent OWI from commanding a large audience through its authority in the press, in Hollywood, and among radio executives, as well as its coordination of information management among all other federal agencies.[23] Through its influence on the portrayal of American troops and the readjustment of veterans, OWI directly and indirectly reached millions of Americans throughout the war.[24] Yet OWI's suggestions, particularly for the media, were not always followed to the letter, despite subsequent observations on the controlled and monolithic nature of information management during the war. A look at some OWI guidelines for the press, and contemporary images of soldiers and veterans in the media, reveals an untidy picture.

In late 1944 OWI officials started work on a set of recommendations for how journalists should present GIs and returning veterans to the public. Chief among OWI's goals, in addition to educating vets on how to redeem their GI Bill benefits, was addressing the matters of wounded vets, neuropsychiatric vets, and the potential for a postwar clash between ex-soldiers and civilians. . In February 1945 the agency published a guide, the *Veterans' Information Program*, to be distributed to media outfits around the country. The booklet was a demonstration of OWI's role as the coordinator of government information, representing the "consensus of the several government agencies dealing with the problem"—the War Department, Veterans Administration, Department of Labor, and the navy, just to name a few.[25] OWI's text consisted of suggestions, not orders, for journalists; if censorship of photographs was strict, the printed word featured a freer exchange of views on soldiers and veterans. Nonetheless, the document revealed the desires of several federal agencies regarding the portrayal of soldiers and veterans, which many journalists in fact followed to the letter.

The OWI booklet came at a key moment in the selling of the war. In 1944–

45 wounded and neuropsychiatric veterans were attracting ever-increasing attention in the media, thanks in part to broader disclosure of the conflict's costs. In 1944 the Roosevelt administration manipulated the casualty figures it released each month to *accentuate* American losses and thus confirm that the United States was pulling its weight in the face of enormous casualties on the British and especially Soviet sides. This practice had the collateral benefit of preparing the American public for the anticipated "casualty surge" of 1944, with offensives planned against mainland Europe and Japanese holdings in the Pacific. When that surge came, though, the administration began worrying about the psychological impact of these high numbers, and by the end of 1944 it had reversed its policy of disclosing more inclusive casualty figures. Yet no amount of doctoring in 1944 and early 1945 could mask the enormous human costs of striking the Axis in Germany, the Marianas Islands, the Philippines, Iwo Jima, and Okinawa. For the remainder of the war the Roosevelt administration performed a delicate balancing act, attempting to soften the news of high casualties by statistical manipulation, but also preparing the public for greater losses in the future—especially as it planned the invasion of Japan in 1945.[26]

owi's instruction booklet for the press, then, arrived in February 1945 as part of this effort to manage the public's reaction to casualties. The document had strong messages on the portrayal of the wounded. The veteran's "readjustment may be somewhat difficult," owi officials cautioned, "but a strongly affirmative approach to this problem [of being disabled] will be much truer than one which continuously paints him as an object of pity." The booklet asked that the print media give the following advice to civilians: "When meeting the disabled, the disfigured, or the seriously ill, allow no horror, sorrow, or revulsion to appear in face or manner. . . . What a man looks like matters little. One of the most cheerful and pleasing personalities is often carried about in the twisted and deformed body of a hunchback." owi authors surrounded this language with case histories of successful disabled people, warnings about treating the handicapped as dependents, and condemnations of "shameful" civilian attitudes.[27] In short, owi wanted journalists to discourage overt pity toward wounded veterans.

Some federal officials were equally aware of the large number of psychologically wounded veterans returning from the war—but tended toward a policy of "complete silence" on that subject, according to one scholar of wartime imagery.[28] As early as August 1944 a field worker for the Veterans Administration reported back to his supervisor, "I have noticed that a majority of the cases who have applied for vocational rehabilitation up to now have either been psychotic or psychoneurotic."[29] Frank T. Hines, administrator of the Retraining and Reemployment Administration, lamented the many soldiers whose "war-torn nerves could stand no more."[30] George Roeder has discussed how the Office of the Surgeon General administered a secret study of the effects of combat on the individual GI and found that rather than hardening him, extended warfare could be expected to break his spirit.[31]

Yet OWI officials counseled the media to send just the opposite message, that warfare transformed the soldier into a better, more mature, and more productive citizen. A directive for radio broadcasters suggested, "Avoid invidious comparisons between servicemen and civilians. . . . Any suggestion that [the veteran] is better than a nonex-serviceman should be avoided. Rather, it should simply be stated that the veteran is a better man and a better potential employee than *he himself* was before he entered service."[32] OWI's *Veterans' Information Program* for print journalists suggested that treatment of the "neurotic veteran . . . can easily receive over-emphasis. Constant informational activity on the problems which the men and women in these groups face and on their care may create the impression that all veterans are changed markedly, and such an impression would react most unfavorably on all veterans, normal and otherwise." Many print journalists would put forth material in harmony with OWI's view that "the largest number of veterans will be normal."[33] The term "normal" in those days signified emotional stability.[34]

Aside from worries over disabled and neuropsychiatric vets, OWI officials harbored concerns over the interaction of civilians and returning servicemen, and more generally, over the impact that nearly 16 million returning soldiers would have on American society. Agency analysts seemed well aware of the animosity many soldiers and veterans felt toward civilians generally and sought to minimize that anger by conditioning the media on how to portray the home front. "Certainly the word 'sacrifice' in connection with anything the civilian has done," the booklet warned, "is woefully inept and inaccurate when compared with the immensely greater contributions of the fighting men."[35]

OWI's directives for radio broadcasters underscored these concerns.[36] Agency officials instructed radio personalities on how to direct veterans toward employment, health insurance, and educational benefits. But some of the strongest language concerned disabled vets, neuropsychiatric vets, and the feared postwar friction between soldiers and civilians—the same concerns that informed OWI's guide for the print media. OWI officials firmly did *not* want emotional readjustment discussed on the radio. In its *Background Material on Veterans' Readjustment*, OWI told radio broadcasters in March 1945: "Perhaps the most effective way to deal with the subject [readjustment] is through the development of typical homecoming experiences and situations in plots of dramatic programs. *Do not, however, depict in an emotional way the efforts of a veteran to readjust himself—nor particularly the problem of so called 'psycho-neurotic' or 'shock case' veterans. This can be most detrimental."* [37] Another OWI directive to broadcasters put the matter even more starkly: "Radio messages should deal only with veterans in general, without regard to physical or other disabilities." [38] OWI felt that the subject of emotional readjustment would require "delicate handling" on the radio because of "the special nature of the medium." It was best to avoid depicting veterans in an "embarrassing" fashion or in a way that would give them an alibi for an "anti-social attitude." *"It is especially important,"* OWI cautioned, *"not to create a picture of marked maladjustment."* Officials justified this approach by citing the fact that most veterans (75 percent, the agency believed) were perfectly "normal," and thus to fixate on disturbed veterans would be misleading to the public. [39] For one official of the War Department, "psychoneurotic" was even a "vicious word." [40]

Toward the end of the war OWI attempted to broadcast its own preferred vision of the American fighting man by producing a short film on returning vets. [41] Throughout late 1944 and early 1945, OWI's Bureau of Motion Pictures worked on a film alternately titled *When I Came Home* or *When I Come Home* to address the problems of returning servicemen. The script went through a bewildering number of revisions based on the comments of several government agencies and outside readers, and the project seems never to have made it out of the script-writing stage. Yet the exchanges over content reveal the typical veteran OWI members and other federal officials sought to project.

An early version arrived at OWI from screenwriter Paul Trivers. The story unfolds as Joe, a "fine-looking American boy," returns home from the war. Quickly, as Joe interacts with his family, some of the problems of readjustment become evident. Joe's narrative voice asks, "Why did mom keep looking at me so funny?" Worried, she asks Joe why he seems different. "Well, I been through a war," Joe responds. When he gives his kid sister a dead German soldier's hat, his mother reacts badly: "Oh, Joe, how can you be so cold-blooded!" In the scenes that follow, Joe and his mother clash as she hovers over him, reminding him to wear his galoshes and be home early. "Those first couple of weeks were murder," Joe grumbles. The prototypical "bad" veteran, Joe drinks too much and loafs around the house. In the margins of the script, an editor from OWI marked his displeasure with these narrative elements by penciling an "X" next to each of them.

The tone of the script changes when Joe is reunited with his boyhood friend, Bill, who represents the good returning veteran. Bill is missing a leg but is far more confident than Joe, volunteering to fix his mother's fence and chiding Joe for feeling sorry for Bill's amputation. "I'm not sorry. I'm glad I'm around," Bill says in response to Joe's sympathy. Joe's narrative voice-over tells readers, "It didn't take me long to see that Bill had a different attitude toward things than I did. He was feeling great and so was his Mom." Bill's character implies that there is no reason for him—or other disabled vets—to feel discouraged. After some time with Bill, Joe overhauls his attitude, makes amends with his mother, takes a job at a factory, and ends up reunited with his old flame. As in many wartime depictions of vets, the pretty girl is the reward for a positive outlook. [42]

As happy as that sounds, the Trivers script was not happy enough for OWI officials. In September 1944 Taylor Mills of the Bureau of Motion Pictures suggested that the film end with a "flashback show[ing] Joe at his work and later that evening taking his girl to a dance for a happy ending"—promoting the implied sexual payoffs of readjustment. Yet Mills also thought the script should show more sensitivity about Joe's attitude, rather than just maligning him as the bad veteran. Mills wanted the script to make clear that Joe suffered from memories of "strenuous combat conditions," leaving him "mentally injured." Mills's comments on the script offered a clear expression of OWI's stance on those mental injuries. "Many of [Joe's] experiences he wants to forget if he ever can forget them." Yet a narrator should tell the audience, Mills wrote, that Joe "is a capable and responsible person and has a place in this world." The moral of the story should be "how [Joe's] family helped him get over what was apparently a very serious physical defect and how quickly he found himself and how he could be of service to his community." [43] Mills appreciated the severity of psychological difficulties, but he also wanted OWI's movie to characterize those problems as remediable through quick, easy steps.

Perhaps because of Mills's comments, the Trivers script quickly fell out of favor with OWI officials. A version dealing more directly with combat wounds arrived at OWI in March 1945 from the well-known Hollywood writer Dore Schary, just as American marines were sustaining heavy casualties in their victory on Iwo Jima. As per wartime conventions, a montage of soldiers with diverse white ethnic names (Morelli, Wilenkiewicz, Levy, Smith) serves as the framing device, speaking with one voice as the collective sufferer of physical and mental injuries. "And then after a time I'm on my way out of the hospital," the composite narrator tells viewers, "with an Honorable Discharge, a clear picture of all my rights, and a pretty good hope for the future." As this mythic soldier heads home on a train, his narrative voice implores viewers not to stare or ask too many questions but essentially to ignore the disability. Then a shell-shocked ex-GI chimes in: "I've got it tough because too many civilians don't really know what battle fatigue is. Too often they think I've cracked up for a silly reason. Silly reason? Get a load of this . . ." Now Schary calls for a volley of artillery fire "tremendous in volume," machine-gun and rifle shots, and mortar explosions meant to rattle the audience. It continues unabated until the voice-over asks, "Loud, aren't they? Multiply that. Ten times, fifty times, one hundred times, one thousand times."

At this point the neuropsychiatric vet describes a flashback episode he might suffer and tells viewers how to handle it. "Leave me alone. I know how to sweat these things out and I'm going to be all right—in time." Here Schary offered a frank treatment of a relatively common occurrence among World War II veterans. Yet the OWI official who read the script crossed out the entire flashback sequence, including the line about feeling "all right—in time." Much like Taylor Mills's revisions to the Trivers script, these edits suggested that OWI wanted to portray battle fatigue as a temporary and curable ailment. Intent on balancing the script, the official scribbled in the margins, "Insert section on normal guy."[44]

In April 1945 OWI sent the Schary script to the War Department. A cover letter explained, "Of course, prefacing the introduction of this material [on the readjustment of veterans] would be a statement to the effect that the large majority of men will be coming out like this, perfectly normal, and if changed at all, changed only slightly through maturity and as a result of the rigorous life of war." The letter went on to apologize, almost, for the current state of the script, which spent too much time on the maladjusted veteran. "We propose," Robert Hutton of OWI wrote, "to have more than one-third of the film devoted to . . . the treatment of the perfectly normal veteran." In spite of this pledge, the War Department official wrote back that his agency would not want such a film circulated "in the very near future."[45]

Days later, the Department of the Navy weighed in with its view of the Schary script. Before sending its impressions of the film off to OWI, the navy circulated an internal memorandum on April 9, 1945. The document made one of the most concise expressions of how veterans should be portrayed by the government and military: "Would it not be appropriate to develop the thought that the veteran is a normal individual who has been away, who has been injured, who wants to be treated as a normal individual, who wants to resume a normal life, and whose personal affairs should be no more the subject of curious inquisition than those of a civilian[?]" The navy did not go as far as the War Department, which wanted the film suppressed. Rather, navy officials thought the movie should remind viewers that most veterans were different but urge them not to say so or to treat them as such. These agencies were tiptoeing around the matter of disabled vets, if dealing with it at all. The navy memo also offered a clear response to material then circulating in the media that harped on a "veteran problem": "It would be unfortunate to further build up the all too prevalent idea that the veteran must be treated differently than other individuals simply because he is a veteran."[46]

As it turned out, the views expressed in this memo would predict the tone of many of the government films that followed. Three other official motion pictures from 1945 that made it to production—*Welcome Home, The Returning Veteran,* and *Peace Comes to America*—offered roseate depictions of war's impact. According to *Welcome Home* the U.S. soldier had "changed in many ways, but they're good, sound ways" (though the short did contain the wartime rarity of a GI weeping).[47] Another film, *He Has Seen War* (1944), likewise indicated that the ex-serviceman would be transformed by his combat experiences, though not for the worse, according to scholar George Roeder.[48] Meanwhile, *When I Come Home* got bogged down in the script-writing stage and never seems to have appeared as a film.

Yet the project revealed much about the way some federal agencies wanted soldiers and veterans to be portrayed. It was no accident that "GI Joe" and "GI Bill" were the two main characters in *When I Come Home.* American soldiers often appeared as generic versions of the real, live soldiers they were meant to represent. The stickiest problem for OWI to deal with, at least in regards to the images it offered, was the mental and physical readjustment of veterans. The producers of *When I Come Home* never could settle a variety of issues: how to depict rehabilitation, how many "normal" men to show, how vividly to portray psychological disintegration. Faced with the worries of many Americans about the postwar world, propagandists in OWI sought to reassure the public. In doing so, they minimized some of the difficulties facing returning veterans.

———

During the war many social scientists, psychologists, journalists, and other commentators turned their attention to the soldiers still in combat overseas, the vets already back home, and the future demobilization of nearly 16 million men and women who put on the uniform between 1941 and 1945.[49] They asked the same questions that animated OWI's efforts to influence coverage of the American soldier: What effect was combat having on the individual GI? How would wounded vets assimilate into the workforce? Would they wallow in self-pity? How should relatives cope with disabled vets? Could neuropsychiatric soldiers resume normal lives? Would civilians welcome home the ex-GI with appreciation or trepidation? Would 16 million trained killers unleash a crime wave in postwar society?

As OWI counseled, many pieces in stateside periodicals discouraged Americans from pitying the disabled veteran. *American Mercury* ran a piece in January 1944 entitled "Case History of a Casualty." A grenade had landed near Cpl. Irvin Sheedy of Green Bay, "causing a compound fracture of his left leg, a simple fracture in his right leg, fifty-seven shrapnel wounds, a shattered nerve in his left forearm, and considerable damage to his left ankle bone." The piece went on to describe in detail Sheedy's wounding and recuperation and discuss other gravely injured soldiers convalescing at Walter Reed Hospital. Yet for all of their gruesome wounds, most of the patients were resolute and heroic, even handsome, in their "dashing maroon pants" and hats worn at "rakish angle[s]." These were fallen warriors, not men to be pitied. Sheedy said, "I've seen men with guts, but nothing like we've got here. There are fellows who can just barely get around in wheel chairs, but raise holy hell if anybody tries to help." Complainers were portrayed as a tiny minority and anathema to the other men. "Somebody started complaining the other morning," one vet told a reporter, "and practically everybody yelled at one time, 'Pipe down!' and he piped down."[50]

A piece in *Ladies' Home Journal* in July 1944 concurred: "The rule must be that sentimentality is barred. Men allowed to pity themselves will, in time, be disqualified from normal life and will end their days in veterans' hospitals." Readers should not feel sorry for wounded vets and should expect speedy recoveries. An article in *Life* told the story of a disabled marine from Binghamton, New York, who failed at several careers before settling on a desk job. "Now he is leading a normal, happy life again." The most important thing, the piece went on, "is not to show grief or pity" toward wounded veterans. An article in *Rotarian* in 1945 described an almost impossibly optimistic casualty of the war: "Billy is from Brooklyn, never finished high school. He will spend the rest of his life in a wheel chair. He is cheerful about it, too."[51] For this author anything less than a positive attitude would have been unusual, even un-American.

Working in concert with such texts were photographs of disabled exservicemen. In late 1944 *Newsweek* ran a photo of an amputee smiling as his doctor proudly fitted him with a prosthetic arm. An issue of *Time* in August 1945 featured a picture of a smiling serviceman in bed, playing a portable electric piano. "This happy pianist is 21-year-old Aviation Machinist Mate

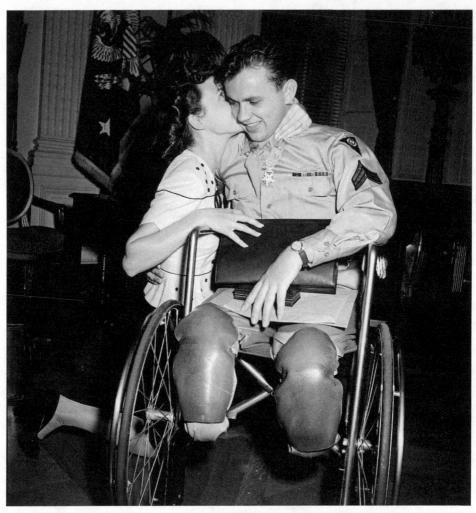

FIGURE 1. *Jean Moore kneels and kisses her fiancé, Congressional Medal of Honor winner Ralph Neppel, Life, September 3, 1945. This typical wartime image reassured the public that the wounded were resilient and optimistic, with the affection of a woman the visible payoff for such attitudes. Courtesy of Time & Life Pictures/Getty Images.*

3/C Alan Wagner," the caption read, "who was seriously injured six months ago." Wagner had lost the use of his legs, so he spent hours "making boogie-woogie" for the other patients at St. Albans Naval Hospital in New York. A month later *Life* ran a large photo of Ralph Neppel, double amputee, grinning in his wheelchair while his fiancé kissed him.[52] (See figure 1.) Apparently wounded vets might not lose their virility or attractiveness to women because of injury, a reassuring message that was to resurface in postwar portrayals of the returning GI.

Advertisements in popular magazines conformed to such conventional images of wounded ex-servicemen. *Newsweek* ran an ad for the Nash-Kelvinator Corporation in March 1944 featuring two soldiers carrying a wounded, bloody comrade on a stretcher. Though injured, the man was smiling slightly, with determination in his eyes. His words told why: "I never thought I'd go home like this. But whatever comes next, I'll take in my stride because . . . in *my* America, you can't keep a good man down!" Advertisements for Pullman sleeping cars showed wounded soldiers on trains. Waited on by attractive nurses, the disabled vets often beamed at viewers from beneath their bedclothes.[53]

Late in the war grittier images of the wounded occasionally appeared in the national media. In June 1945 *Life* ran a series of horrific paintings depicting the marine landing at Peleliu. One showed a dying marine taking his last step, his arm and face a mangled, bloody mess. (See figure 2.) A ghastly picture appeared in *Life* two months later, just at war's end, depicting a wounded man feeding ice cream to a horribly burned sailor, his "head weirdly encased in white bandages." (See figure 3.) The change to more graphic images did not go unnoticed among contributors to the "Letters" page of *Life*. One reader wrote to the magazine, "Congratulations on Tom Lea's paintings of wounded marines, etc. on Peleliu. . . . We can't have too much of stark reality." Three servicemen felt differently, comparing the editors unfavorably to the Nazis, who in all their brutality would not show "such a picture." Others agreed. "There are so many gruesome pictures of death in horrible forms in the recent issues of Life," wrote another reader, "that it really seems to stink. . . . Why must [these images] be thrust before the eyes of the public in all of the bloodiest details?"[54]

Why indeed? As George Roeder has shown, officials in OWI sensed complacency about the war effort among the American people as early as 1943, and also sensed a diminishing tolerance for sanitized images of the war. They began releasing more grisly photos to motivate the public, photos that had previously been consigned to the War Department's "Chamber of Horrors" file. OWI even requested that advertisers begin using images of

FIGURE 2. Tom Lea, "The Price," Life, June 11, 1945. Tom Lea's paintings of marines at Peleliu, like this one of a man taking his dying steps, were some of the most graphic and disturbing images of the war. Courtesy of the Army Art Collection, U.S. Army Center of Military History.

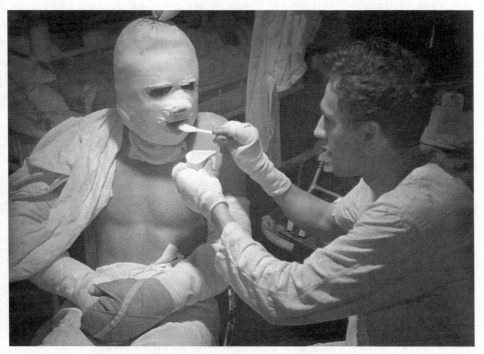

FIGURE 3. *Burned and bandaged men aboard the* USS Solace, Life, *August 20, 1945.* *These men were badly injured when their ship was hit by a kamikaze attack. Images* *such as this one revealed the dreadful effects of combat on individual servicemen, reflect-* *ing a shift away from more sanitized depictions of war and its participants. Courtesy of* *National Archives.*

American dead, released for the first time late in 1943, for the Third War Loan drive that fall. Pictures of fallen warriors challenged renderings of manly invulnerability put forth by Road to Victory and other World War II iconography. As Christina Jarvis has put it in her discussion of wounded soldiers, "War produces alternative or 'abject' masculinities that exist alongside and in opposition to dominant cultural representations." Despite the dominant sentimentality of wartime culture, Americans also confronted alternative, and sobering, visual portraits of war and the men who waged it. [55]

Many writers also expressed concern over the problem of neuropsychiatric vets—a matter OWI thought should be handled with the greatest care. Some observers denied that psychoneurosis would be much of a problem at all among ex-servicemen. Lt. William Best wrote in the *Saturday Evening Post* in April 1945 that veterans "must have help and consideration. But that many of them need elaborate psychiatric treatment, I strongly doubt. . . . The veterans I am talking about are men who have come back to civilian life and have settled down to normalcy. They are no different from the boy of ten years ago." Another writer, a marine, agreed that the problem of neuropsychiatric vets was exaggerated, but conceded that ex-GIs were changed for their experiences. David Dempsey complained bitterly that all the fuss over vets' mental health was threatening to turn mothers and wives into "kitchen psychologists determined to 'cure' the veteran—even at the expense of his sanity." Yet he also admitted, "It is only reasonable to expect the soldier to be changed when he returns." R. L. Duffus of *Nation's Business* also downplayed the problem of battle-fatigued soldiers, arguing that neuropsychiatric veterans would be few in number and their ailments "more curable than a shattered leg." Duffus and Dempsey articulated a view common in the periodical literature, especially among ex-servicemen themselves: The ex-GI would certainly be changed by his time overseas, but only a small percentage would be irreparably damaged emotionally. [56]

Major weekly and daily publications also tended to minimize the problem of neuropsychiatric veterans. An early treatment of the subject appeared just before D-Day, 1944. *Time* ran a small piece on the first neuropsychiatric casualty among American pilots in Europe. The unfortunate flyer, "H.P.," came across in the article as an oddity, part of the "small percentage" of airmen disturbed by combat missions. Tail gunners, who might have been expected to crumble emotionally in the face of their terrifying duties and high casualty rates, were actually "sound, cheerful and proud." *Newsweek* ran an advertisement in March 1944 that neatly summarized the dominant characterization of battle nerves. An ad for Hammond Organs showed a soldier and chaplain laughing heartily above the words, "I feel so much better, Chaplain." The copy explained what had happened: "It was mostly that he felt alone . . . completely lost. . . . And now he's facing something big . . . a lot bigger than ever before. But he'll be all right now . . . he's right on the beam." An ad in *Life* for a radio company echoed that claim. Beneath a picture of a smiling GI recuperating from wounds with "the sounds of war beat[ing] through his head," the copy read: "Today he smiled for the first time. . . . Yes, there's power in music . . . a power to heal, a power to relax, a power to give men fresh courage and hope." A little talk with the chaplain or some soft music could cure the darkest worries, these ads suggested. [57]

Like images of the wounded, however, renderings of neuropsychiatric soldiers became more graphic in the last two years of the war, alongside continuing efforts to minimize the problem. Henry Pringle, a staffer at OWI, wrote in *Ladies' Home Journal* in the summer of 1944, "Readjustment will be hard enough for the man who is wholly normal. It will be more so for the one who is suffering from the shocks of war." The *New York Times* reported on New York's statewide rehabilitation plan in early 1945. Of "especial interest" was the plan's section on neuropsychiatric soldiers, who, it was hoped in the article, could be restored to a "normal outlook." One pair of mental health experts in the army air force warned in 1945 that some flyers returning to civilian life would do so "in a peculiarly dissatisfied and often disturbed state of mind." [58]

In February 1944 *Time* magazine covered a psychiatric conference in Chicago that addressed the military's handling of battlefield breakdown, revealing draconian methods. Though field psychiatry far outpaced that of World War I, when commanders were notorious for sending shell-shocked doughboys back into combat, emotionally spent soldiers were still returned to battle with very little counseling whenever possible. [59] A lieutenant colonel in the army delivered a disturbing report before the conference in early 1944. The army used two approaches: the old, World War I practice of "forget-it" counseling, and the newer "catharsis" program, whereby soldiers were made to "spit it out," with or without the use of drugs. The old-fashioned method was by far the more common: "The anxious soldier is given rest, sedatives, food and psychiatric pep talks. These are usually given so that all the world may hear—only the most personal part of the discussion is *sotto voce*. The question is asked repeatedly: 'You want to go back and try again, don't you?' The man is led to think that giving up is dishonorable." Only men who failed to respond to this "forget-it" approach received more advanced care in which they were permitted to explain their anxiety. Col. Roy Grinker, later the coauthor of the mental health book *Men under Stress*, reported that the "forget-it" method yielded success in about 60 percent of cases. The only thing to recommend it, he said, was speed. It was not clear whether the 60 percent of GIs who rejoined their units (the definition of "success") were effective in combat. More apparent, however, were the long-term effects: "The end result in many cases of repressed anxiety will be a mental problem after the war, if not before."[60]

Visual images of psychological breakdown could be as troubling as those of the wounded. In June 1945 *Life*'s montage of paintings documenting the Peleliu invasion included a haunting, full-page portrait of a battle-fatigued marine, known as "That 2,000-yard stare." Part of the caption read, "He half-sleeps at night and gouges Japs out of holes all day. Two thirds of his company have been killed or wounded but he is still standing. So he will return to attack this morning. How much can a human being endure?" (See figure 4.) Some advertisements in popular magazines likewise exposed the psychological costs of war. *Newsweek* ran an advertisement in 1944 for the Red Cross showing a downtrodden soldier above the words, "Is your boy out there . . . in the land that God forgot?" Another widely circulated ad from the Bell Telephone Company featured a terrified marine cowering in a foxhole, calling for artillery support on a field telephone.[61]

Mingled among concerns in the print media over wounded and neuro-psychiatric veterans were anxieties over the potential clash between veterans and civilians—also one of OWI's central worries. The best-known book on veterans, Willard Waller's *The Veteran Comes Back*, appeared in 1944 with a telling first chapter: "Veterans—Our Gravest Social Problem." "All too often," the sociology professor at Columbia wrote, the veteran "is a problem because of his misfortunes and his needs, because he is maimed, crippled, demented, destitute, cold and enhungered." Waller went on to warn that unless the veteran was "renaturalized," he would become "*a threat to society.*" A small piece in *Time* reported in the spring of 1944 that the head FBI agent in New York had predicted a major crime wave upon the return of "ten million veterans trained to kill" and was doubling the enrollment at the FBI's Police Academy that summer to prepare for it. Other commentators thought *civilians* would be the problem. *Nation's Business* said in April, "Soldiers who have lost a leg, an arm or an eye . . . bitterly resent the rudeness and stupidity of civilians who gape at their handicaps." In September *Time* quoted a soldier on furlough in the States: "A lot of us are damn glad to be going back overseas. What they should have prepared us for was the shock of coming home. . . . I saw people jamming the bars and hot spots and movies. Their way of life hasn't really changed a damn bit. They are a million miles

FIGURE 4. Tom Lea, "That 2,000-Yard Stare," Life, June 11, 1945. Late in the war some representations of battle fatigue became more haunting, such as this one from Tom Lea's Peleliu series. The caption read, in part: "He half-sleeps at night and gouges Japs out of holes all day. Two thirds of his company have been killed or wounded but he is still standing. So he will return to attack this morning. How much can a human being endure?" Courtesy of the Army Art Collection, U.S. Army Center of Military History.

away from the sufferings of the war."[62] Scores of other articles were similarly glum on the prospect of future relations between vets and civilians.[63]

A wave of more optimistic literature soon countered these gloomy views in 1944–45, heeding OWI officials' wishes that the media reassure Americans about the postwar world. Much of this material argued that returnees had changed little or for the better. Donn Layne of *Nation's Business* charged doomsayers with believing that "our fighting men were all recruited from the dregs of society and that, changed by war into merciless hoodlums, they will either come back with itchy trigger-fingers and a yen for slitting throats or as indigent cripples or hopeless neuropsychiatrics." Cpl. Peter Allen agreed in a long, impassioned letter to *Ladies' Home Journal*, printed in its January 1945 issue. "Some changes there will undoubtedly be," he conceded, "but pretty generally we'll come back much the same as we went away." A writer for *Rotarian* thought GI Joe would come home changed, but in purely positive ways. "If he has served aboard a warship worth millions of dollars," the author's argument went, "he will have a new respect for keeping things neat and shipshape." If the soldier had worked with internal combustion engines, the veteran would be able to fix the family car. "The *boy* who went away will return a *man*."[64]

Some advertisements promoted this vision of a smooth reintegration of soldiers into society. An ad from the *Saturday Evening Post* in July 1945 proclaimed that the veteran was "an abler, more aggressive and resourceful citizen than the boy who went away." Many ads reminded civilians of why certain resources or services were scarce, attempting to stave off frustration toward servicemen and the war effort. An ad for the Pennsylvania Railroad showed a proud soldier—"180 pounds of bone, muscle and fighting energy—a fine specimen of American manhood"—evoking a common wartime link between masculinity and military service. If travelers were finding rail service not all it used to be, they should remember that "military needs must come first, as all Americans would have it."[65]

Wartime observers rarely agreed on the social and psychological implications of the conflict. Some people felt that battle would have little effect on soldiers' mental states, others thought it would have a terrible impact. Some believed that a great postwar struggle between vets and civilians awaited the country, others predicted a smoother transition. Some described wounded soldiers as confident, productive citizens, while others, especially toward the end of the war when government censorship eased, revealed a starker vision of their pain and anxieties. Such "negative" images were still outnumbered by portraits of confident, patriotic, masculine, heroic American GIs, and much of the real fretting about the veteran problem circulated within a community of intellectuals. Nonetheless, Road to Victory's early version of the warrior image was beginning to show cracks.

The tensions coursing through wartime coverage—between optimism and pessimism, cheeriness and grimness, confidence and cynicism, realism and idealism—materialized before millions of Americans during World War II in the work of Ernie Pyle and Bill Mauldin. No one did more to shape the public image of the American GI than these two figures. And although both Pyle and Mauldin supported the war effort, that did not keep them from showing the gloomy effects of combat on the individual GI. In fact, as Pyle became more cynical about the war, his sympathy with the fighting man held steadfast or even intensified.

By April 1943 Pyle's dispatches from the war were appearing in 122 newspapers, with a total circulation of 9 million; after D-Day in June 1944, his audience approached 40 million Americans. All of Pyle's columns were published in three popular books: *Here Is Your War* (1943), *Brave Men* (1944), and *Last Chapter* (1946). Mauldin's cartoons, meanwhile, ran in *Stars and Stripes*, the popular newspaper for soldiers of the U.S. Army, until they were syndicated nationwide in the middle of the war. One of his drawings appeared on the cover of *Time* magazine in 1944, and the next year he won a Pulitzer Prize. Pyle had won his own in 1944. Mauldin's cartoons appeared in his books *Up Front* (1945), which spent a year and a half at No. 1 on the *New York Times* bestseller list, and *Back Home* (1947).[66]

The two men who would mold the public's vision of the American soldier had little in common at the outset of the war. Mauldin, hailing from New Mexico, was just nineteen when he joined the army in 1940. Soon Mauldin's artistic talents landed him a job as the cartoonist for *Stars and Stripes*. Pyle, in his forties during World War II, was already established as a journalist when he traveled to Europe in 1940 to cover the German bombardment of England. The Indiana native had joined the *Washington Daily News* in the 1920s, later distinguishing himself as a travel writer during the Depression. His column appeared in the *Daily News* and other papers of the Scripps-Howard chain until his death in combat in 1945. Unbeknownst to most of his readers, Pyle suffered frequent bouts of depression, stemming both from his tumultuous marriage to an alcoholic and from the horrors of war he witnessed for several years.[67]

Whatever their differences in age and experience, Pyle and Mauldin developed remarkably similar visions of the American GI. The cartoonist relied on humor, the correspondent on an eye for poignant detail in showing readers "what I see." Their work merged to create a distinctive cultural hero for home-front audiences. Pyle's GI and Mauldin's "dogface" or "doggie" was a selfless team player, willing to suffer his lumps for the good of the guy next to him. He was not a super-patriot; he labored for his comrades more than for "democracy" or America itself. Mauldin's soldiers in particular, the irascible Willie and Joe, griped incessantly about officers, the mud, and combat itself, but usually with good humor. Pyle found in his GIs the dogged determination—and cynicism—etched in the weathered faces of Willie and Joe. Pyle also wrote rather freely of the GI's fears, his needs, his sacrifices, and his sorrows. So if the two men combined to portray a sturdy and virtuous American soldier, that did not prevent them from showing his rough edges.

Pyle and Mauldin, like their counterparts throughout the media and in government censorship offices, did withhold graphic images of dead, wounded, and neuropsychiatric soldiers. Mirroring the dictates of OWI, Pyle marveled at how quickly, even exuberantly, GIs recuperated from physical and psychological wounds. "Those still recovering were anxious to return to their outfits," he wrote from North Africa in 1943, when he was still relatively new to combat reportage. "I inquired especially among the wounded soldiers about this, and it was a fact that they were busting to get back into the fray again. Morale was never higher." He went on: "Although wounded veterans by then, and alive only by a miracle, those patients were just the ordinary American boys they had always been, friendly and enthusiastic and sensible. Only occasionally was there one who seemed affected by his experiences. . . . But on the whole they were just as normal as if nothing had happened." Several months later Pyle wrote from Italy in similar tones of amazement at the recovery of battle-fatigued men: "And yet to me it's one of the perpetual astonishments of a war life that human beings recover as quickly as they do. For example, a unit may be pretty well exhausted, but if they are lucky enough to be blessed with some sunshine and warmth they'll begin to be normal after two days out of the line. The human spirit is just like a cork."[68] Officials at OWI could not have written it any better themselves. Pyle's message neatly captured the images of resiliency, strength, and recovery abundant in much World War II iconography.

Yet as Pyle saw more and more combat, he became increasingly aware of its dark impact on the soul of the infantryman. It was also true that his own spirit, unlike the cork he spoke of from Italy, was sinking by 1944. He had tried to write a column about battle fatigue in Africa earlier in the war, but military censors stopped it, driving him nearly to tears, according to a friend. From Africa he went on to Italy, and from Italy to France. By 1944, after the D-Day invasion at Normandy, Pyle was finding scores of broken men fighting among the hedgerows of France—and by now the censors, perhaps seeing his name atop the columns, were letting descriptions of such GIs slip through. One of them was Tommy Clayton: "The worst experience of all is just the accumulated blur, and the hurting vagueness of being too long in the lines, the everlasting alertness, the noise and fear, the cell-by-cell exhaustion, the thinning of the surrounding ranks as day follows nameless day. And the constant march into eternity of one's own small quota of chances for survival. Those are the things that hurt and destroy. And soldiers like Tommy Clayton went back to them, because they were good soldiers and they had a duty they could not define." Pyle might have been describing his own feelings. Though he was privately becoming deeply cynical about the war, Ernie still honored the selfless individual soldier for enduring. As Pyle biographer James Tobin has described it, this was the "downtrodden G.I. as suffering servant."[69]

Bill Mauldin won his Pulitzer Prize for a cartoon depicting that sufferer. The drawing showed tired, haggard American dogfaces escorting tired, haggard German prisoners through a driving rain. "Fresh, spirited American troops," the caption sarcastically read, "flushed with victory, are bringing in thousands of hungry, ragged, battle-weary prisoners." (See figure 5.) Besides mocking the naive buoyancy of headlines in the United States, the cartoonist suggested that war, not the Germans, was the enemy. In the same spirit of revelation Mauldin's words in *Up Front* echoed Pyle's description of Tommy Clayton: "The endless marches that carry you on and on and yet never seem to get you anyplace—the automatic drag of one foot as it places itself in front of the other without any prompting from your dull brain, and the unutterable relief as you sink down for a ten-minute break, spoiled by the knowledge that you'll have to get up and go again—the never-ending monotony of days and weeks and months and years of bad weather and wet clothes and no mail—all this sends as many men into the psychopathic wards as does battle fatigue." Though Mauldin did so in this case, neither he nor Pyle needed to use the words "battle fatigue" to convey the misery and exhaustion that warfare brought. Another Mauldin cartoon showed an exhausted GI, his head down on the muzzle of his rifle—a haunting image that was to reappear with regularity during the Korean War.[70]

Though Pyle became cynical about the military brass, he never wrote about it. When Gen. George Patton slapped two battle-fatigued soldiers in Sicily in 1943, Pyle was incensed. "Ernie . . . hated Patton's guts," a friend said later. For whatever reason—perhaps partly a consciousness of the censors—Pyle preferred to glorify a modest general such as Omar Bradley

*"Fresh, spirited American troops, flushed with victory, are bring-
ing in thousands of hungry, ragged, battle-weary prisoners . . ."*
(*News item*)

FIGURE 5. *Bill Mauldin, "Fresh, spirited American troops . . . ," from* Up Front, *1945.
This cartoon, which earned Mauldin a Pulitzer Prize in 1945, suggested that war was
the enemy of all men, victors and vanquished alike. Copyright 1944 by Bill Mauldin.
Courtesy of the Mauldin Estate.*

rather than criticize a blustery one such as Patton (he wrote in August 1944 of the military's "magnificent top leadership"). The cartoonist Mauldin had no such compunction, even though he actually worked within the army bureaucracy. When Patton wanted to censor Mauldin's drawings, Gen. Dwight Eisenhower, supreme commander of Allied forces, told him that *Stars and Stripes* was a soldier's paper, not a general's. With that freedom, Mauldin made officers and generals frequent targets of his wit. In one infamous sketch a group of GIs and brass hats entered a liberated French village to the delighted cries of the townspeople. As the French threw flowers and kisses at the doggies, the doggies threw tomatoes at the generals. Patton thought Mauldin was trying to start a mutiny with cartoons like this and wanted to "throw his ass in jail."[71] Eisenhower's support of Mauldin probably saved him from such a fate.

The dogmatic and uncaring officer continued to be a staple of Mauldin's work. In various cartoons throughout the war, the young artist poked fun at military bureaucrats who listed as "safe" areas that were not, at the "totalitarian" army hierarchy, at the vast gulf between the facilities and comforts of soldiers and officers, at harsh regulations governing life away from the front lines, at officers who underappreciated medics, and at officers and generals who never seemed to appreciate the hard, miserable work of the dogfaces.[72]

Through these words and drawings Mauldin hinted at an idea that would take hold much more firmly in war-related culture in decades to come: The individual GI was a nameless victim of more powerful forces above him.[73] This notion had limits; Mauldin usually made a joke of it and often suggested that GIs had the last laugh at the expense of officers. As Mauldin put it, his philosophy was to draw "an army full of blunders and efficiency, irritations and comradeship. But, most of all, full of men who are able to fight a ruthless war against ruthless enemies, and still grin at themselves."[74] If Mauldin himself declared the limits of his cynicism, his work nonetheless lamented the trampled-upon individuality of American soldiers in a way that much wartime imagery, such as the Road to Victory exhibit, neglected entirely.[75]

Officials at OWI who feared a postwar clash between civilians and veterans might have been concerned by Mauldin's work. Deep resentment of the home front coursed through the army of Willie and Joe. In Mauldin's drawings and text GIs griped about American newspapers sugarcoating their sacrifices with talk of "victorious, cheering armies"; about Americans who wrote letters about how tough gasoline shortages were; about fickle or unfaithful girlfriends and wives; about civilians who thought of combat deaths as statistics; about cost-cutting companies at home producing "faulty" equipment; about rosy advertisements that used the GI's sanitized image to sell products. Mauldin, in fact, covered many of the major and minor gripes later associated with American soldiers in Korea and Vietnam.[76]

Yet like many other observers in wartime America, Mauldin scoffed at the idea that veterans would be a postwar "problem." As he wrote in his book *Up Front*, "The vast majority of combat men are going to be no problem at all. They are so damned sick and tired of having their noses rubbed in a stinking war that their only ambition will be to forget it." Along with wartime ads and periodical pieces, Mauldin suggested that the best thing for battle fatigue was to move on, "forget it," and get back to normal civilian life. Ernie Pyle's dispatches on the swift recovery of wounded and tired soldiers sent similar messages. Yet elsewhere, Pyle was more guarded, writing from France in August 1944, "Thousands of our men will soon be returning to you. They have been gone a long time and they have seen and done and felt things you cannot know. They will be changed. They will have to learn how to adjust themselves to peace."[77]

Media coverage of the Second World War, Pyle's and Mauldin's included, has drawn criticism over the years for its sentimentality, its censored blandness, and its reliance on official sources. Adhering to journalistic conventions of the day, Pyle and Mauldin usually did not describe wounds and death in grisly detail, nor did they dwell on neuropsychiatric casualties of war. And in their totality, the dispatches of Pyle and the cartoons of Mauldin *did* paint a picture of stoic GIs fighting bravely. Mauldin summarized the soldiers that he and Pyle gave readers: "Their nobility and dignity come from the way they live unselfishly and risk their lives to help each other. They are normal people who have been put where they are, and whose actions and feelings have been molded by their circumstances. There are gentlemen and boors; intelligent ones and stupid ones; talented ones and inefficient ones. But when they are all together and they are fighting, despite their bitching and griping and goldbricking and mortal fear, they are facing cold steel and screaming lead and hard enemies, and they are advancing and beating the hell out of the opposition." Yet as this passage suggests, it cannot be said that Pyle and Mauldin offered a thoroughly sanitized or "official" version of war. As Pyle wrote in August 1944, "For me war has become a flat, black depression without highlights, a revulsion of the mind and an exhaustion of the spirit."[78] The fact that Mauldin and Pyle saw the necessity of the war and thus "supported" it did not prevent either man from laying bare the miseries of combat and the fears and cynicism of the GI, or stop Mauldin from lampooning the ineptitude of the military brass. These were bleak features of the warrior image that were to reappear with greater regularity and intensity over the decades to come—especially, but not exclusively, when journalists questioned the wisdom or management of American wars.

For all their cartoons and dispatches on the American GI, Mauldin and Pyle joined most other producers of culture during the war in their near-exclusion of black soldiers. Although African American troops made up between 5 and 10 percent of the armed forces during World War II (depending on the service), they found themselves largely absent from popular imagery of GIs. Critics of that myopia cheered in 1944 when the War Department released a film entitled *The Negro Soldier.*

American society—and much of the U.S. armed forces—still bore the mark of segregation and discrimination during the war. Most blacks in the military worked in service roles, carting around supplies, cooking food, and in general doing the dirty work required to equip millions of soldiers far from home. One black sergeant remembered, "We serviced the service. We handled food, clothing, equipage. We loaded ammunition, too. We were really stevedores and servants."[79] (See figure 6.) Even worse, some prominent white Americans questioned the resolve of those blacks in uniform. In a well-known and shameful incident, Senator James Eastland of Mississippi said before the Senate, "I state that the conduct of the Negro soldier in Normandy, as well as all over Europe, was disgraceful, and that Negro soldiers have disgraced the flag of their country."[80] In the South and in former border states, prisoners of war from belligerent nations were often accorded better treatment than black GIs. In early 1945 Lena Horne performed before Nazi prisoners in Arkansas, while African American troops were excluded from the show. Meanwhile, near St. Louis a white lieutenant ordered several black soldiers to give up their seats—in the front of the *black* car—for fifteen Italian POWs being transported by rail. [81]

With African American soldiers engaged in a worldwide fight for freedom, many black activists and advocates now reacted more angrily to this sort of treatment. The writer Langston Hughes captured the incongruity between the war and home-front oppression, as well as the persistence of white racism, in his poem of 1943, "Jim Crow's Last Stand."[82] In 1944 the *New Republic* aired the views of an African American soldier who spoke menacingly of how returning black GIs would react if the war did not, in fact, kill off Jim Crow as Hughes imagined: "A new Negro will return from the war—a bitter Negro if he is disappointed again. He will have been taught

FIGURE 6. *The Negro Seabees training near Norfolk, Virginia, ca. 1942. The Seabees were members of Naval Construction Battalions, segregated by race like the rest of the military during World War II. Courtesy of National Archives.*

to kill, to suffer, to die for something he believes in, and he will live by these rules to gain his personal rights."[83] To be "disappointed again" referred to the dark days after World War I when returning black soldiers were met not with appreciation or new rights but with heightened resentment and, in some cases, lynching.

Historians often see World War II as a key moment in the march toward civil rights, yet at home the conflict often had the effect of stilling organized dissent. There had been angry demonstrations in 1940 and 1941 against racial segregation in the armed forces and discrimination in the defense industry, leading to A. Philip Randolph's proposed march on Washington in 1941. But much changed after Pearl Harbor. In a nation mobilized for total war, many black leaders sponsored "Good Conduct" campaigns to prove the loyalty of their constituents. "Mr. President, Count on Us," proclaimed the black press in December 1941. When blacks rioted in Detroit in 1943, activists were terrified. An NAACP official in January 1945 called for a "New Year Resolution" among blacks to eschew "ugly" behavior and disruptive "public conduct."[84] Whereas Randolph's earlier proposal for a march on Washington had garnered widespread support in the African American community, a poll in the middle of the war suggested that 71 percent of blacks now opposed a similar measure.[85]

A partial exception to this quieting of militancy concerned black reaction to war coverage. Federal officials did little to advertise the contributions of black soldiers, and activists routinely protested the exclusion of African Americans from newsreels and war reporting in the press. An editorial in the February 1944 edition of the *Crisis*, the NAACP's newsletter, cited two specific cases of Hollywood newsreel producers, Pathé and Paramount, deliberately cutting black troops from war footage. Thus "the movie-going public, estimated at 75 million people weekly, sees no films of Negro soldiers."[86] Many African Americans wanted their loyalty broadcast, so in a sense this form of protest mirrored the anxiety about rioting; many activists thought that the exclusion of blacks from newsreels tarnished the reputation of black patriotism.

In February 1944 black leaders brought this complaint to the desk of OWI's Bureau of Motion Pictures. An official of the NAACP sent a letter accompanied by a petition signed by 1,053 persons "protesting the action of the five news film agencies and the O.W.I. in excluding pictures of Colored American troops from their releases. . . . One tenth of the men and women in our armed forces and in our culture are Colored Americans and by the laws of chance they should appear more often in your releases."[87] Taylor Mills of OWI responded that to his knowledge, no efforts had ever been made to exclude black troops from government newsreels. He directed the NAACP official's attention to *The Negro Soldier,* a production of the War Department on black contributions to the war effort.[88] "We are sure," Mills wrote, "that all members of the Negro race will have reason to feel proud of this outstanding motion picture."[89]

There was indeed much for black Americans to relish in *The Negro Soldier.* Directed by Academy Award–winner Frank Capra (who had made several other films for the government, including the *Why We Fight* series), the film highlighted black contributions to wars and American society in general since 1776. Yet in keeping with the tone of other government productions, *The Negro Soldier* described black GIs and the experience of African Americans in sanguine tones. Capra suggested that throughout American history blacks and whites had worked together to build a great democracy. After World War I, the movie suggested, blacks "came marching home" to screaming crowds and victory parades, while in reality they returned to virulent and sometimes violent racism. The film made no mention of segregation in the armed forces of the World War II era. If *The Negro Soldier* had a central African American character, it was an *officer,* suggesting disingenuously that it was common for black soldiers to achieve that rank. Viewers of the film saw blacks as full and equal participants in the war effort, not as the "stevedores and servants" which many of them actually were.

Nonetheless, *The Negro Soldier* broke from other government films in important ways. In addition to showing female members of the armed forces, the movie portrayed blacks in a positive and heroic manner—much like films showing white soldiers. In this sense government propagandists were consistent in their manipulation of the GI's image, now incorporating blacks into the universe of martial heroism. Indeed, the NAACP, which had been active in protesting the exclusion of blacks from war films, sang the praises of Capra's work. "This is by far," an editorialist wrote in the *Crisis,* "the best film about Negroes and their part in America and in the American army that has ever been made."[90]

Yet whatever the film's merits, it is not clear that *The Negro Soldier* filled the void that had rankled the NAACP.[91] Officials in OWI initially decided to release the film only to "non-theatrical" distributors, that is, for the 16mm projectors in civic clubs, churches, schools, and other public locations. Although OWI believed these centers served 7.5 million viewers per month, agency officials were doubtful that white distributors would request prints of a film on "this subject."[92] Not surprisingly, the vast majority of requests for the picture in 1944 came from African American organizations. It received almost no attention in popular magazines such as *Time* and *Newsweek*, and only a lukewarm review in the *New York Times*.

The next year the film began to play to slightly bigger audiences. By February 1945 it had run in 1,800 public theaters and was still circulating out to others (these were still paltry numbers—most short films produced by OWI played in at least 13,000 of America's 16,000 commercial movie houses). Taylor Mills, the OWI official who had assured the NAACP that all blacks would be proud of *The Negro Soldier*, now began to develop reservations about the film. Many white audiences were ambivalent about *The Negro Soldier*, which was essentially "out and out propaganda," according to Mills. He suggested in a letter to the War Department that in the future, the black soldier be portrayed "like any other soldier," rather than as the feature of a whole film.[93] After running in few commercial houses in 1944, the film was cut to twenty minutes—a more suitable length for showing before a feature presentation—and eventually played in about 5,000 theaters in that form.[94]

In the final analysis, *The Negro Soldier* failed to alter dominant representations of American military personnel.[95] The warrior image remained a white one. If World War II in some ways helped to pave the way toward the civil rights revolution of the 1950s and 1960s, in this instance racism wavered little. As John Blum has argued, meaningful recognition of black sacrifices came "almost exclusively from Negro correspondents writing for Negro audiences."[96] Regular photo essays in issues of the *Crisis* did more to publicize black soldiers than any other news organ, but for a largely black audience. A writer in *Phylon*, a journal on race and culture, said late in 1945: "In many sections of America, one would hardly know that Negroes fought and died in this war."[97]

––––––––––––

With the fall of Germany in May 1945 and the defeat of Japan three months later, America's greatest overseas war was finally over. Around the world *Life* correspondents found elation. GIs formed conga lines in London, were "jubilant" in Berlin, danced in Paris, and tore about in jeeps in Manila, blaring their horns.[98] *Time* used pastoral imagery to celebrate the return of veterans to America: "Soldiers who had cheered Manhattan's towers when their ships docked now strained their eyes for the half-forgotten tree or turn of road which would mean the real end of their long journey home."[99] Many Americans extended open arms to these men. Joseph Goulden has written of the many ways citizens welcomed home the boys: colorful banners in shop windows, discounts on magazine subscriptions, countless local memorials and monuments, and the provisions of 1944's historic GI Bill.[100] They were also met with laudatory depictions of themselves in the media, on radio, and in films.

If Road to Victory had helped inaugurate wartime image making in 1942, Norman Corwin's famous radio script, "On a Note of Triumph," helped conclude it. Aired on V-E Day, May 8, 1945, and read by narrator Martin Gabel, the program received such a positive response that it aired again five days later. A German translation became mandatory listening for every prisoner of war from Hitler's vanquished country. "On a Note of Triumph" contained a great deal of chest thumping about the victory over Nazism but also a nod to the simple American boys who had gotten the job done: "Far-flung ordinary men, unspectacular but free, rousing out of their habits and their homes, got up early one morning, flexed their muscles, learned (as amateurs) the manual of arms, and set out across perilous plains and oceans to whop the bejesus out of the professionals. . . . Seems like free men have done it again," Gabel intoned with his signature brusqueness. Now, returned from the war, the American veteran became a sturdy male hero, reminiscent of so many other model veterans portrayed since 1942 in the media, on radio, and in film. In Corwin's vision the returned veteran was "a fighting man—glad to be alive, a little tired, but in good shape."[101] The "home town fellers" who had marched off to war in the photographs of Road to Victory were finally back, and no worse for wear.

With strict military censorship of war reporting and extensive information management on the home front, the preponderance of wartime imagery echoed Road to Victory and "On a Note of Triumph." That is not to say that there was no variety. The prospect of returning veterans drew the histrionic worries of social scientists even as it inspired the vapid cheeriness of magazine advertisements. Yet most imagined warriors were specimens of soldierly virtue—honorable men who were better for their time in the service, would be more productive citizens in the postwar economy, and were fit fathers and husbands. Although Ernie Pyle and Bill Mauldin encouraged Americans to sympathize with their fighting men—and offered grimmer images of war than is commonly believed—they pulled up short of making them seem victims. The GI of most imagery during World War II invited gratitude and admiration, not pity.

Such near-exclusion by the media of pitiable veterans may have fulfilled the "wartime psychological needs" of Americans, in the words of John Blum. Images of heroic servicemen "gave the American people exactly the symbol with which they could easily identify, the brave soldier in whom they could see themselves and in whom they could take personal pride." There is no doubt that images of the positive, heroic serviceman fitted into and advanced a much wider story of American recovery, strength, and masculinity in the aftermath of the Depression. On the occasion of his homecoming in 1944, one soldier told a reporter that people "didn't want to hear what men have to endure. They wanted dime-novel stories of adventure. They didn't understand what I was trying to say." John Kennedy wrote in 1943 that as a participant in World War II, the papers from home showed him "how superficial is most of the talking and thinking about [the war]." World War II veteran Ed Stewart remembered how his stories of combat also had to suit a preconceived notion about the war. "They wanted the embellishments, the glory, the success, the survival," he recalled, "but not the raw experience."[102]

More and more of that "raw experience" had crept into public images of the GI by the end of World War II—a trend that was to continue apace after the war. During the war, though, such experiences seemed to make the serviceman a fitter postwar citizen, not a victim of trauma or disability. Much wartime culture pictured the collective endeavor of military service as an edifying rite of passage for the American boy-turned-GI, not something that trampled upon his individuality. The notion of victimhood, however, implied at the margins of mainstream depictions of the soldier, would soon come into sharper relief.

CHAPTER 2

LITTLE GUYS WITH GOLDEN EAGLE BADGES, 1945-1950

By the fall of 1945, the euphoria of America's triumph in World War II was receding behind a host of acute national crises. Simmering labor disputes, rising racial tensions, a housing shortage, and the enormous task of demobilization, all repressed by the war, finally boiled over. In late 1945 a heated battle raged in Washington over who among the military brass had been responsible for negligence leading up to Pearl Harbor.[1] A *Newsweek* headline in October proclaimed, "Peace on Earth! Its Magic Light Is Dulled by Riot, Strike, Dissent." The article began, "The dancing was over. The cheers had died away. Last week there was nothing but a wistful memory of the wild rejoicing that victory had brought nearly two months ago. Americans had been told to expect a hard transition to peace, but few had listened. . . . Wherever they looked—from the streets of Saigon to the picket lines of Detroit—the theme was trouble."[2] Many contemporary observers noticed a palpable if inchoate deflating of the national spirit. As the cultural historian Warren Susman later wrote, "This moment of triumph was accompanied by something disturbing: a new self-consciousness of tragedy and sense of disappointment." For some observers, there now seemed to be "severe limits to what human society could be," according to another scholar.[3]

The citizen-soldier of World War II had concerned many sociologists, psychologists, and members of the media during the war. Now, the actual return of millions made the matter more immediate for the general public. As the historian David Gerber has argued, Americans received World War II vets with a "divided consciousness"—one that combined appreciation for ex-GIs with fear of their return.[4] *Harper's Magazine* articulated the mixed feelings of early 1946: "A specter is beginning to haunt the American scene—the specter of the little guy with the Golden Eagle badge [issued to WWII vets] on his lapel. Showered with fulsome praise by welcoming committees as he staggers down the gangplank . . . the citizen-soldier turned veteran soon discovers that though the country loves him it doesn't quite know what to do with him."[5] The veteran did not always know quite what to do with himself, either. After enduring maddening delays on the journey home, many veterans had trouble readjusting to civilian life. One ex-soldier wrote in late 1946, "I was discharged from the Army in April of this year and I am still not working. I haven't even tried to get a job. I'm trying to figure out why. I'm worried about it."[6]

Other veterans had a different worry. Cpl. John Bartlow Martin, writing in *Harper's Magazine* late in 1945, felt that civilians too readily accepted sentimental images of martial life. "They must never have known," he wrote, "never have known anything about it at all. The advertising agencies, the cheerful radio announcers, sold them a bill of goods." Now, Martin believed, the same sanitized tone was permeating postwar images of veterans. Particularly frustrating was a radio interview with blind ex-GIs. "The prepared script was jolly, the veterans had few cares in the world," Martin complained. Another veteran, Edgar L. Jones, wrote in *Atlantic Monthly* three months later that most ex-GIs harbored a "bitter contempt for the home front's abysmal lack of understanding . . . and its nauseating capacity to talk in patriotic platitudes."[7] These men desperately wanted a more honest accounting of the war and of those who fought it.

Such demands would be partially answered in the years between 1946 and 1950. Images of soldiers and veterans in the realms of film, the media, and novels were not simply "jolly"—instead, they reflected the overriding postwar duality of triumph and tragedy that Susman was to describe forty years later.

In 1945–46 the nation was turning its attention to those veterans and their reentry into civilian life. From October 1945 to February 1946, three-quarters of a million men and women were discharged *each month* from the service; by the summer of 1946 over 12 million veterans had returned to civilian life.[8] From late 1945 through the end of the decade, depictions of the returning GI spilled forth from books, films, periodicals, newsreels, and newspapers. At the same time, some vets were finding ways to shape their own image.

By the time Charles Bolté's book *The New Veteran* appeared in 1945, efforts to depict the 16 million veterans of World War II had been under way long enough to produce multiple warrior images. Bolté, a war amputee and writer whose work appeared in the *New York Times*, *Harper's Magazine*, *Mademoiselle*, and the *Nation*, lamented the many caricatures of servicemen already in use at war's end: "GI Joe, mythical darling of the advertising copy writers, has had more nonsense written about him than has ever been set down concerning any other American folk hero with the possible exception of Davy Crockett." He went on to condemn several adaptations of the imagined soldier then in common usage: "simple-witted boy," "trained killer," "mental case," "bitter and cynical man," "starry-eyed idealist," and "hopeless incompetent."[9] Meanwhile, in the fall of 1946 the authors of an article in *Public*

Opinion Quarterly argued quite the opposite—that the public conversation on postwar America *lacked* adequate variation in its portrayal of veterans. "There has been an evident disposition," they wrote, "to speak generally of 'the' veteran—the veteran thinks this, the veteran feels that, the veteran wants this." Social commentator Benjamin Bowker agreed, writing, "'The veteran' does not exist. . . . What we have is a group of several million individuals . . . with a few things in common."[10] If observers differed on *how* veterans were being misrepresented, most agreed that wartime forecasts about veterans—and postwar images of them—needed correction.

During the war numerous public intellectuals had predicted that veterans would form a lawless band of trained killers running rampant across America. A great wave of crime never materialized, though there were isolated cases of violence. Veterans rioted in Athens, Tennessee, in August 1946 against a corrupt local political machine. Progressive periodicals such as the *Nation* spoke glowingly of the GI rebels—"Young men who did not come home to be robbed of the rights they had been told they were fighting for"—but the *New York Times*, for one, offered a more alarmed account.[11] "Scores of war veterans" helped storm a jail where other vets were held hostage, using "tommy-guns, rifles, shotguns and pistols." The mob ultimately killed a deputy sheriff, and a month later the mayor fled the city for his own safety. Finally, by the end of September a new election peacefully replaced the officials "ousted by GI guns."[12] Scores of local stories documented berserk veterans committing crimes of all varieties. Former tank gunner Howard Unruh killed thirteen people and wounded three others in a twelve-minute rampage in Camden, New Jersey, four years after the war's end. "You a psycho?" police asked him. "I'm no psycho," Unruh answered calmly. "I have a good mind."[13] Other commentators saw more diffuse disillusionment among vets. An article in *Collier's* discussed the "appalling loneliness and bitterness" and "dangerous cynicism and frustration" of many veterans, reviving the widespread worry of the war years that disillusioned ex-soldiers posed a threat to American society.[14]

When attached to African American veterans, such images could have sinister consequences. In the South portrayals of "uppity," gun-wielding black vets accompanied a spike in postwar racial violence and intimidation. Many progressive observers remembered the lynching of some African American troops returning from World War I and hoped for better treatment after *this* war, focused as it was on defeating a racist enemy.[15] Yet the events of 1945–46 resembled the dark experiences of 1918–19. In a harbinger of things to come in the civil rights movement, trouble began when black World War II veterans tried to vote in the wake of *Smith v. Allwright*, the Supreme Court decision of 1944 that outlawed the white primary. Emboldened by that ruling—and by their combat service in Europe—a group of black veterans in Decatur, Mississippi, sought to exercise their right to vote in the Democratic primary of July 2, 1946. Panicky newspapers had warned potential black voters to stay away from the polls, but Medgar Evers and the other vets ignored the advice. More convincing were heavily armed mobs of white men at the polling stations, and the black ex-GIs of World War II were driven away without voting.[16]

African American veterans in other southern states endured violence and intimidation away from the ballot booths. On the day of his honorable discharge from Camp Gordon, Georgia, Isaac Woodard took a bus to South Carolina, only to be arrested, beaten senseless, and blinded after an altercation with the driver. The police chief of Batesburg, South Carolina, admitted to crunching Woodard's eyes out as he lay on the ground but was later acquitted of the crime. In Monroe, Georgia, a mob of whites killed black veteran George Dorsey, his friend Roger Malcolm, and their wives. Fishermen on Dorcheat Bayou in Louisiana discovered the body of John C. Jones, an African American army corporal, who seemed to have been literally whipped to death. *Time*'s story on the lynching (which misidentified the victim as John Johnson) reported that although he had been a soldier in Europe, local whites considered him "a 'bad nigger;' he got drunk and was uppity."[17] Protesters marching for a federal antilynching law carried a sign through Monroe, the Georgia town where Dorsey perished: "Guadalcanal '42. North Africa '43. Germany '44. Okinawa '45. Monroe, Ga., USA '46. We veterans are still being killed by fascists." The NAACP's magazine, *Crisis*, reported anecdotally that in two out of three instances of violence against blacks the victim was a veteran.[18] All in all, the Tuskegee Institute counted six lynchings in 1946; but according to John Egerton, at least four times that number were reported in local southern newspapers.[19] The northern press covered these cases with great interest, and the Woodard case earned international notoriety. Meanwhile, the crimes of 1946 convinced the NAACP to renew its campaign for federal antilynching legislation.[20]

Despite these events, the vast majority of soldiers peacefully reentered society, thanks especially to the generous and unprecedented GI Bill. *Time* magazine reported in April 1946 that after all the wartime fretting, all the histrionic projections, all the worrying over violent veterans, peace was in fact proving peaceful. "The great transition was taking place without violence," the author wrote. "Across the land, veterans of World War II tried to make the best of this best of all civilian worlds."[21]

If most veterans were neither criminally inclined nor dangerously cynical, millions of former soldiers did experience the difficulties of readjustment. In a manual on counseling veterans, published in 1946, two academics spoke for a silent GI Joe: "What if people knew how uncertain I feel? Do I want to go back to the old job or not? Do I want any job? I feel so changed, I'm not sure I could make the grade. And if I had a job, could I hold it? Funny the way folks suppose that just because you lived through the Normandy beachhead you will be able to cope with anything. Never felt so uncertain in my life, nor so queer." These scholars went on to claim, "It is the rare citizen who does not know a serviceman who is facing real problems of adjustment."[22] These hurdles included securing an education, employment, and housing, and coping with the problem that could exacerbate all of those—being wounded in mind or body. Fortunately for veterans of World War II, Congress had enacted a comprehensive series of reforms with these problems in mind. Nevertheless, in the public discussion of vets and the GI Bill, yesterday's heroes often seemed like today's victims.

The Serviceman's Readjustment Act of 1944, or GI Bill, was at its most generous in providing for education, though scholars have long debated exactly what effect that provision had on higher learning in America.[23] What is clear is that millions of veterans used the bill to obtain postsecondary education. Title II of the legislation guaranteed that every honorably discharged veteran with at least six months' military service was entitled to one year of college or technical school at the expense of the government. Federal funds also covered books and other supplies, and provided a $50 monthly stipend for living expenses ($75 for married ex-GIs). If the veteran successfully completed that year of study, he could stay in school for an additional year for every year he had spent in the armed services. The student-veteran's entire time in college could not exceed four years. After the war, Congress expanded the GI Bill further, doing away with limits contained in the original legislation on age and the length of time after the war during which vets could pursue a federally funded education. Meanwhile, the Veterans' Vocational Rehabilitation Act of 1943 helped disabled veterans improve their employment chances with vocational training; it was also liberalized after the war. Scores of state and local laws supplemented the federal entitlements.

All in all, more than 2 million World War II veterans attended college under the auspices of the GI Bill, while 3.5 million pursued technical training or correspondence courses. Female veterans were largely left out of this educational bonanza, although women who had served in auxiliary military roles and had been injured could obtain an education thanks to a special amendment to the Vocational Rehabilitation Act of 1920. Male veterans who belonged to minority groups were entitled to the same educational benefits as whites, but de facto and de jure discrimination often limited their ability to gain admission to colleges and universities. [24]

Despite the extension of higher education to white, male veterans, journalists uncovered all sorts of vet-related crises at American colleges and universities. The intertwined problems of overcrowding and poor facilities received broad attention in the media, and also from embittered veterans themselves. Early in 1946 several student-veterans reacted angrily to yet another visit from photographers documenting GI education. "Why do they always take all the pictures in that fancy upholstered Sloan Room?" one vet asked a reporter from the *New Republic* who was visiting the unnamed school. "Sometimes they ought to take a few [pictures] in our dumpy little classroom. People ought to see how badly it needs a paint job and some good lighting." *Time* magazine reported two months later that 41 percent of veterans were crowding into just thirty-eight schools in the United States. At the same time *Newsweek* reported that 70 percent of American colleges were pressed for veterans' housing. "Living is cramped and studying difficult," announced a headline in *Life* the next year. [25]

Other observers grumbled in 1946 about the high cost of education, which exceeded GI Bill allotments. At the University of Iowa, where 6,000 veterans composed 60 percent of the student body, student-vets were asked by a *Life* magazine pollster early in 1947, "Can you get along on your GI money?" Ninety-nine percent answered no. According to the counselor for veterans at Harvard, just 5 percent of ex-GIs at that school were surviving on their GI Bill money alone. Students at the University of Chicago and UCLA complained about stingy allotments. An article in *Time* magazine on these gripes reported that most veterans were grateful for the help they received, yet "many a vet at college still felt that the Government had promised to underwrite the whole cost of his education." With the same sense of victimhood, a caption under a photo of cramped housing asked, "Did the U.S. promise more?" [26] In the face of such inquiries, Congress raised GI educational stipends with some regularity in the late 1940s.

But complaints persisted. *Time* magazine took the occasion of graduation day, 1947, to visit the "first big batch of veteran graduates" on thirty-eight campuses around the United States. The resulting article painted a dark picture of GI education. To have graduated by 1947 meant that these particular ex-soldiers had been "jerked from college" before the war, returned to school to be "crammed in crowded Quonset huts," and generally endured a "grim experience" at college. Their main concern upon graduation, the article reported, was "me and mine." One veteran responded bitterly to charges that ex-GIs were rushing their educations: "We're all trying to get where we would have been if there hadn't been a war." Even darker were forecasts about the postwar world, revealing "disillusionment" and "resignation." A student-veteran at Western Reserve fretted, "Everything seems to be on the brink of destruction. I feel I should be doing something but I don't know what." Some felt the United States was headed for socialism; others worried about a new depression; still others agonized over a potential war with the Soviet Union. Student-veteran Thomas Whithorn of Georgia Tech told *Time* reporters cryptically, "I'm disgusted. Our leaders have let us down."[27] Veterans' bleak views of the future, it seemed, were matched only by their bitterness over a cramped, delayed, and rushed higher education.

Media coverage of student-GIs made them seem victims of circumstance, but resourceful ones. Scores of articles in popular periodicals lauded the seriousness with which veterans handled their studies, making a mockery of the notorious worries of university presidents James Conant (Harvard) and Robert Hutchins (University of Chicago). Those educators had believed that student-vets would corrupt the intellectual life of the university and viewed the GI Bill's provision for education as a crass way of staving off mass unemployment.[28] In fact, the great majority of veterans studied hard under difficult circumstances—though they did tend to prefer skills training over fields such as philosophy, English, and history. Winston Churchill, receiving an honorary degree from the University of Miami in 1946, hinted at the bitter-but-resourceful reputation of American student-veterans. "Millions of young men have had their education interrupted," Churchill said in his fifteen-minute speech. "I have been cheered," however, "by the tremendous efforts which are being made . . . to make up . . . what they may have lost."[29] Charles Bolté, now the head of the American Veterans Committee (AVC), probably spoke for many veterans when he wrote in 1947, "For many of us bitterness against a world we'd never made was translated into the conviction that we must make a better one for ourselves."[30] Such characterizations suggested that World War II veterans had much to complain about at college but tolerated the problems with the same resolve that had carried them through the misery and privation of war. Here, once again, were Willie and Joe, Bill Mauldin's popular cartoon dogfaces of the war years. Now they were off to college, still grumbling, but still muddling through.

The postwar depression that many observers expected never materialized. Unemployment rose a bit after the war, but only in contrast to 1945, because wartime production needs had kept such figures unusually low. After double-digit unemployment percentages during the Depression, the number dipped to a low of 1.2 percent in 1944, then rose to 3.9 percent in 1946, and by 1950 had hit 5.3 percent. [31] Thanks to a series of laws enacted during the war and immediately afterward, most veterans had a relatively easy time finding employment in the booming postwar economy. The most important vocational benefit for veterans was the U.S. Employment Service (USES), an agency that set up hundreds of local offices to help match ex-servicemen with appropriate employers. Nonetheless, job-related problems lingered below the surface and were covered by the press around the nation. Like the stories on GI education, this coverage painted some veterans as victims of their military service.

One problem for returning GIs was the matter of seniority. What would businesses do with veterans who had lost their places in lines of promotion? In Boston more than four hundred World War II vets returned to their jobs as clerks, carriers, and mail handlers in the Boston Postal District. These men had taken the Post Office Civil Service Examination in 1937 and qualified for future promotions. But when war came, they lost their positions in the Post Office hierarchy to employees who had avoided induction into the military. Upon the vets' return, many upper-level positions were filled with these replacements, some of whom actually had scored lower on the Civil Service exam yet were now earning more than the World War II vets. In short, the Post Office seemed to penalize the veterans for their service overseas. [32]

The *Boston Globe* called the vets "the almost forgotten men." "Naturally they are grieved," the paper said, but unfortunately a bill to correct the situation seemed lost in Congress, jeopardizing the prospect of the vets getting "the places they deserve." [33] A piece in the *Boston American* used more forceful language: "So Uncle Sam's long arm reached out and grabbed those [postal workers] that were physically fit and rushed them, willy-nilly, to the four corners of the global compass where they suffered hazards and hardship. . . . More than 400 eligibles *found themselves pawns in the game of political Parcheesi*, being put back to the start [of the postal ladder] without favor or preference." [34] Veterans, in this rendering, were powerless victims of a bureaucracy that failed to reward their great sacrifices of the war years.

Such controversies over seniority replayed across the country. In some places, veterans demanded that they occupy positions *higher* than those they had left, a practice known as "superseniority." A case receiving widespread attention was that of Abraham Fishgold, a welder from Brooklyn, New York, who had been inducted into the army in 1943. After his honorable discharge from the military Fishgold returned to his job at the Sullivan Drydock and Repair Corporation in August 1944. Soon thereafter Fishgold's company laid him off temporarily while (nonveteran) welders above him were retrained and kept on the payroll. Fishgold argued that he should occupy a position on the seniority escalator comparable to where he would have been without the intervening war. The case went back and forth between rulings by the district court in Fishgold's favor and counter-rulings in favor of the local union, which argued that Fishgold's demand to leapfrog over welders hired after his departure conflicted with collective bargaining agreements.

In early 1946 the Supreme Court heard Fishgold's case, ruling six to one *against* the notion that veterans were entitled to superseniority. Justice William O. Douglas declared that veterans should rejoin their companies at the precise position they had vacated before induction into the armed forces. Douglas granted, however, that the ruling should be liberally interpreted, to benefit "those who left private life to serve their country in its hour of great need."[35] According to experts testifying before a Senate committee on the matter, the Supreme Court ruling directly resulted in many veterans losing their jobs to nonveterans with greater seniority.[36] For the next two years, members of Congress would seek to soften the blow of the decision with legislation ensuring various reemployment rights for veterans in certain jobs and workplaces—airports, civil service, and the merchant marine in 1946, District of Columbia fire fighters and police in 1947.[37]

Other problems were industry specific. Returning postal workers in particular seemed hard hit by the low pay scales in which they were stuck. Several postal employee vets wrote to *Time* magazine in 1948, summarizing many of the well-publicized gripes of veterans in the immediate postwar period: "Imagine the plight of us World War II veterans who chose the Postal Service for a career, and at the bottom grade pay of $2,100 a year must somehow support our growing and frequently evicted and homeless families. Under present Postal Regulations it will take us ten years to reach the $3,100 level, if we manage to hang on."[38] Other vets had trouble getting jobs for which they felt eminently qualified. Airmen organized the Association of World War II Pilots to campaign for employment in the civilian aviation sector. At a rally in early 1946, led by their dashing leader, Chick Logan, the pilots picketed at an airport for jobs with air-freight companies. A newsreel commentator spoke of the "thousands of veterans, now on the outside looking in at the aviation industry." The men in the newsreel footage carried picket signs proclaiming their victimhood: "30 Seconds Over Tokio [sic]—30 Years Without A Job"; "America Recognized Us in War—How About Now?"; "We Saved Civilization—Help Us Back in Aviation"; "America Needs Us! We

Need America!"[39] Other veterans drove their taxicabs from Chicago to Washington, D.C., to protest a law regulating the number of cab licenses doled out in that midwestern city.[40] Coal miners in Pennsylvania, wielding banners reading "Welcome Home for What?" picketed for the jobs they had lost during the war to "outsiders."[41] In these instances, veteran-protesters were helping shape their own images as victims—a minor foreshadowing of what would come from antiwar vets toward the end of the Vietnam War.

Despite the strong postwar economy, unemployment remained a problem for some vets. Agnes E. Meyer, writing in *Collier's* late in 1946, imbued jobless ex-GIs with victim status: "The vast majority of these 2,000,000 unemployed veterans are floating in a vacuum of neglect, idleness, and distress which is as harmful and dangerous to them as it is to the country." The *New Republic* reported in the spring of 1947 that several veteran-submitted short stories on the ordeal of finding a job "show an enormous concentration of resentment."[42] If most veterans were making tangible advances in readjusting to civilian life, others were having serious trouble.

Unemployed veterans in particularly dire straits did have a safety net. Part of the GI Bill's employment program was nicknamed the "52–20 Club," a provision for unemployed ex-GIs to receive twenty dollars a week for fifty-two weeks, as long as they were actively looking for work. *Time* reported in August 1946 that more than 6 million veterans had drawn an average of two months' benefits and that the number of vets in the 52–20 Club and their length of time in it were both increasing each month. Omar Bradley, the head of the Veterans Administration, "had sharp words" for those taking advantage of the government's generosity and thought the public would not tolerate such bilking.[43]

A long piece in the *New Republic* in March 1947 suggested that not all the men in the 52–20 Club could be charged with taking advantage of the system. At an unemployment insurance office in Los Angeles, a few were indeed deadbeats, "the small rotten handful . . . who gave a bad name to the whole setup." The majority, however, lacked the skills, youth, or physical abilities—not the work ethic—to hold down a steady job. The result was a demoralizing cycle: "A vet would take a job, quit, come back for his unemployment checks, take another job, quit. They'd do that until they found something they liked to do, something with security and a living wage and a future." The men mired in this spiral felt a sense of shame and bitterness. One vet withheld his name from reporters. "He still had some pride left, he said. 'Not much, but some.'" Another could barely suppress his anger over the way the country had welcomed him home as a hero but then allowed him to sleep on the beach and go penniless. That was only the beginning of his troubles: "My wife left me. I've got a four-year-old kid I've never seen." Shuffling through the 52–20 line in the pouring rain, most of the men said little; the others "talked in question marks." When the program was discontinued in 1949, *Time* called it "a kind of caboose on the G.I. gravy train."[44] In tones reminiscent of Depression-era stories, journalists suggested that most of the 52–20 men were honest characters simply going through tough times—but now, as veterans, they could also seem the victims of a particularly harsh and ungrateful neglect.

––––––––

Meanwhile, veterans were central figures in the most severe predicament of the postwar years—the housing crisis.[45] Enabling veterans to obtain housing had been a key aspect of the GI Bill. Title III of the legislation had offered loan guarantees of up to $2,000 for veterans, with a cap on interest rates of 4 percent. Ex-servicemen could also take advantage of Federal Housing Authority (FHA) loans, which had rekindled home buying during the Depression. Many returning veterans, however, lacked the capital to purchase homes, either because they were young and poorly paid or because they were enrolled in college. Student-veterans barely earned enough to make ends meet, let alone buy a home. Ex-GIs who did have money, often those who were older than their college-going compatriots, found a severely limited housing market.[46]

America's housing shortage reached crisis proportions in 1946, but the origins of the problem were deeper. The residential construction industry had languished during sixteen years of depression and war, averaging fewer than 100,000 new homes per year (before 1946 the peak year for construction had been 1925, when 937,000 units were built, according to the *Nation*).[47] Tens of thousands of new dwellings had been constructed for migrant defense workers, but this housing was largely temporary.[48]

After the war "doubling up" in small living quarters was common practice, particularly for young veterans who had shared prewar homes with their parents. In October 1945, when a mere 20 percent of American soldiers were home from overseas, the government estimated that over 1 million families were already doubled up; this figure would reach 6 million by 1947.[49] A mother grumbled to President Harry Truman in 1946, "For the past year and a half, I have been trying to build a house so I may have room for my son, returning from service in May. . . . I have had quite a struggle."[50] The great number of ex-GIs attending college created a similar crunch on campuses. In 1947 the University of Minnesota enrolled more than 30,000 students, fully 60 percent of them veterans. Six thousand of these student-veterans were married, and many of them vied for the 674 family units in the school's Veterans Village.[51] In Chicago veterans who were living with in-laws or their own families decided to squat in a newly built housing project. An article in *Time* reported that police left them alone for a while, since they were "deserving 13th ward boys," but eventually some were arrested. "Who wants that medal of mine?" said bitter ex-GI Paul Principato. "They can have it."[52]

To confront the housing emergency, in 1946 President Truman appointed Louisville mayor Wilson Watkins Wyatt to a new post—housing expediter, or "housing czar," as it became known. "Make no little plans," Truman instructed Wyatt.[53] The new housing czar, a liberal, brought an enormous amount of energy to his job, speaking before newsreel cameras in January 1946: "I will vigorously pursue the task of providing adequate houses for our people, especially for our returning veterans, just as speedily as it is humanly possible to do. . . . The country in general, and the veteran in particular, are entitled to get action on this gravely pressing national problem, and they will get action."[54] The sense that veterans were *entitled* to good housing drove Wyatt's efforts. Since the position of housing expediter fell under the auspices of the Office of War Mobilization and Reconversion, Wyatt intended to use wartime powers to hold down the prices of building supplies and homes, keeping rents and home costs within the range of America's poorer ex-GIs. After a month of meetings with veterans' organizations, real estate officials, labor leaders, and experts on the housing industry, Wyatt proposed the Veterans' Emergency Housing Program (VEHP). The plan would control the prices of building materials, keep rents artificially low, and limit the cost of a new house to $10,000, while pledging to build 2.7 million homes within two years.

Real estate interests and critics on the right excoriated the bill for its allegedly socialist character. Other opponents simply thought the plan would not work, but reiterated their philosophical support for veterans' housing. Said Republican Walter Judd of Minnesota on the House floor, "Any costs incurred in getting homes built rapidly for veterans is a legitimate part of the cost of the war"; but Wyatt failed to convince him that VEHP would be effective. Judd understood the political cost of his position: "I realize fully that a vote against this program will be labeled by some as a vote against the veteran." Indeed, supporters of VEHP shot back that real estate boards were greedy for profits and indifferent to the needs of veterans. Why did veterans deserve decent housing? Democrat John McCormack of Massachusetts answered his own question: "We took these young men from civilian life because our country needed their services in time of danger." Now rewarding them with affordable housing was "the first job we have to do."[55]

From the left, some critics charged that the VEHP did not go far enough (only a few veterans had $10,000 for a new home), but made pleas similar to those of more moderate supporters of the bill. A former administrator of the U.S. Housing Authority, writing in the *Nation*, maligned real estate officials for victimizing veterans: "I believe that they do not appreciate how men feel who discover that while they were risking their lives to protect us, we were doing nothing to protect them and their families. Millions of ex-service men are bitterly resentful that we have provided no place for them to live but a miserable slum dwelling."[56] In spite of such support, Republicans and conservative Democrats in the House of Representatives stripped the bill of much of its teeth. In the Senate, long-time advocate of federal housing Robert Taft restored the elements that the House had removed, including the price ceilings, and shepherded VEHP to passage over conservative opposition in that chamber. Thanks to pressure from veterans' groups and the Truman administration, the resuscitated VEHP returned to the House and passed in the spring of 1946. Truman signed the Veterans' Emergency Housing Act on May 22.[57]

Meanwhile, other observers and lawmakers favored more long-term solutions. The day after it passed VEHP, the Senate commenced debate on the Taft-Ellender-Wagner Bill (TEW), an ambitious plan for replacing half the inferior housing in the United States by facilitating the assembly of 1.5 million new homes a year for ten years.[58] While supporters of VEHP intended to service the immediate needs of ill-housed veterans, advocates of TEW called their bill "the most comprehensive housing program ever prepared."[59] In April 1946 TEW passed in the Senate but died in the House Banking and Currency committee. The same opposition to federal housing that had threatened VEHP would keep TEW mired in Congress for years.

Once passed in the spring of 1946, Wyatt's VEHP met with mixed success. *Time* reported in August 1946 that of the 1.2 million homes Wyatt had insisted would be built in that year, only 225,000 were complete, half of them started in 1945. Many of the new homes were already falling apart: "They had been put up with green lumber, ersatz plumbing and slapped together by careless carpentry. Worst gripes came from Mineola, L.I. [Long Island], where walls cracked, cellars flooded, rafters warped." One house in Mineola saw daily floods of sewage in its basement.[60] *Collier's* reported that fall, "To visit almost any veteran's family, whether employed or unemployed, is to start upon an endless chain of woe. As you sit in overcrowded rooms, both wife and husband refer you to other relatives who are enduring similar or worse conditions."[61] Such language deemed the veteran a victim of government neglect. Hundreds of thousands of veterans continued to "double up" with relatives, rent substandard dwellings, and crowd into Quonset huts on college campuses. National coordination of building materials fell far short of what Wyatt had envisioned, thanks in part to major postwar strikes in the steel, lumber, and railroad industries. More damaging to VEHP, however, was continuing political opposition to price controls. The November 1946 elections that gave the Republicans control of Congress signaled the end of most price ceilings such as those in VEHP. Wyatt resigned late in 1946.

Nonetheless, under VEHP housing *starts* in 1946 topped one million for the first time in history. By 1947 a million veterans had received home loans, and indistinguishable houses were going up in the suburbs at an explosive rate. Many scholarly accounts of the postwar housing emergency end here, with testimonials on the success of the Levitt brothers and their prefabricated dream homes.[62] Because this period saw such unprecedented growth in the suburbs, some historians have downplayed the continuing housing crisis among poorer Americans, including many veterans. One important history of the period has even suggested that the housing shortage "disappeared" by 1947.[63]

In fact, many veterans' groups, members of Congress, civic organizations, and figures in the media perceived a continuing crisis in 1947 and well afterward—and one in which veterans were the central sufferers.

A piece in the *Commonweal* in March 1947 included striking accounts from ex-GIs on the housing shortage. One veteran, tongue firmly in cheek, accused the government of harboring two secret plans for veteran housing. "Operation X" would sterilize veterans and solve the long-term housing problem. "Operation Y" was the short-term solution: "We put the Belsen gas chambers in operation," the former GI explained, "run veterans' families through—no more housing problem."[64]

Veterans' organizations united amid the persistent crisis in housing after 1947, a rare instance, indeed, of consensus among these contentious groups. The conservative, old-guard organizations—the American Legion and the Veterans of Foreign Wars (VFW)—initially lukewarm on the issue of housing reform, had switched sides and thrown their weight behind TEW by early 1948. Speaking before the House Committee on Veterans' Affairs in January, a VFW representative lobbied for the measure, calling housing "the No. 1 headache and problem facing the majority of veterans of World War II."[65] The liberal American Veterans Committee (AVC), which arose in direct opposition to the old-line organizations and had been working diligently for veterans' housing since 1946, took out a full-page newspaper advertisement in February blaring, "My Kingdom For a House."[66]

By early 1948 other voices were joining the campaign for better veteran housing. The young congressman and VFW member John F. Kennedy told reporters in March, "We veterans have scattered our forces and have not concentrated on housing, which is our greatest need." The *Washington Post* mused, "All in all—excepting housing—Uncle Sam has done well by his GIs," joining a host of other papers from around the country that condemned government efforts to secure housing for veterans.[67] One official of the American Prisoners of War even claimed with bitter hyperbole that American POWs had been better accommodated in enemy prison camps than in stateside housing.[68] President Truman himself called the housing shortage "almost a fatal one" in May 1948, while as late as 1949 a Paramount newsreel showed veterans' families living in slum conditions in New Jersey.[69]

Disgruntled vets channeled their frustration into the National Veterans Housing Conference, convened in Washington, D.C., in February and March of 1948. Aware of their special authority as veterans, conference planners sent out notices to local organizers on how to influence the press in its coverage of the meeting. These read, in part, "Get local housing experts, city, state, and federal, to release to you and to the press and radio the latest dope on housing in your area. Get pictures of sub-standard dwellings. Start letters to newspaper editors. . . . Get radio interviews with veterans who have not been able to find a decent place to live. *These and other sources can be exploited to tell a startling story.*"[70] In addition to invoking the victimhood of ex-servicemen, conference planners also succeeded in marshaling all the major veterans' groups behind passage of TEW. "Veterans usually have the last word on veterans' legislation," the *New Republic* had predicted in 1946, "if they shout loud enough."[71] In this case shouting loud enough meant shouting with one voice.

The consensus among veterans' groups helped dislodge TEW from the legislative gears in which it had been stuck since 1946. Public housing appeared on the agenda again in 1949—for the third consecutive Congress, which was now controlled by Democrats. By this time, however, the House had adopted a crucial rule change, the "anti-blockade" rule of January 1949, partly with the public housing bill in mind. With committees no longer able to consider (and reject) legislation, the latest version of TEW finally reached the House floor after passing the Senate for the third time since 1946. Voting on the measure for the first time, the House passed TEW easily, 227–186. After four years and over 9,000 pages of hearings, TEW became law on July 15, known to history as the National Housing Act of 1949.

The sweeping law contained important veteran-friendly provisions. First preference for new low-rent public housing would go to families displaced by slum clearance, starting with wounded vets, then families with deceased servicemen, then to all other vets, and finally to other families displaced by such clearance. Families *not* displaced by slum clearance came next in the hierarchy, with all vets of the two world wars coming at the head of that group as well. Households not displaced and not containing a veteran had the last shot at low-rent federal housing.[72]

After five years of patchwork legislation—and more importantly, explosive building in the private sector—the housing emergency abated by 1950. Central to lobbying efforts for housing reform was the use of the veteran's image. As in the coverage of crises in education and employment, veterans often appeared as powerless victims of sluggish federal programs and lawmakers who somehow were not providing what these men deserved.

Most veterans returning to the United States in the late 1940s were unharmed physically, but great numbers bore some imprint of their time in the service. More than 670,000 Americans were wounded during World War II.[73] Diseases took a great toll on soldiers overseas, and many returned to the United States with the lasting effects of illness. Many also suffered from varying degrees of mental breakdown. All told, one historian of military psychiatry has estimated that 1.3 million servicemen developed debilitating neuropsychiatric disorders during World War II.[74]

Some vets believed these casualties ought to be more publicized. John Martin, the veteran who wrote bitterly in *Harper's Magazine* about wartime advertising and radio, worried that a sanitized warrior image stifled awareness of combat's psychological toll. "People should never be allowed to forget," he wrote. "They should never be allowed to forget the mud and the boredom and the uncertainty and the nervousness."[75] An ex-GI writing in *Atlantic Monthly* in February 1946 believed that "all of us, not just the battle-enlightened GI's, should fully understand the horror and degradation of war before talking so casually of another one. War does horrible things to men, our own sons included. It demands the worst of a person and pays off in brutality and maladjustment."[76] Just as these veteran-observers were worrying about public amnesia, there were newer, more graphic images of combat, the wounded, and battle fatigue appearing in the popular media.

Several pictorial documentary books on the war offered glimpses of this darker side of combat. One of the most well known of these, *Soldiers' Album*, was published in 1946 by two public relations officers of the Supreme Headquarters, Allied Expeditionary Forces (SHAEF). The book contained some of the most graphic and horrifying images seen in the immediate postwar period, far surpassing anything viewed widely during the war. Taken both by civilian and military photographers (including some Germans), many of the pictures would not have made it past wartime censors in the United States.[77]

Soldiers' Album documented the Allied Expeditionary Forces' drive from the beaches of Normandy to the heart of Germany. Some images of Americans in the volume testified to the dreadfulness of combat wounds; others documented the severe emotional strain of war. An American tank driver is shown hurled from his vehicle, his leg blown off as two comrades rush to his aid. Another photo depicts weary, surrounded American soldiers resting in a barn during the Battle of the Bulge. As one reviewer of *Soldiers' Album* put it, "Even without the caption, it would be quite obvious to the reader that the men shown were counting on being dead reasonably soon after the picture was taken."[78] Massacred American prisoners lie ignominiously in the snow in Belgium; others appear terrified during fighting in the Ardennes; the dead sink into mud as German soldiers ransack their gear; the American attackers of D-Day lie dead, wounded, and encrusted with mud. Rarely before had the price of victory been so clear.

Yet a brighter message hovers over these bleak portraits. *Soldiers' Album* documents the great degree of cooperation and coordination required for the drive to Berlin. Indeed, the book is essentially an account of how teamwork, good will, ingenuity, and resilience defeated barbarism and treachery. American military engineers, transportation coordinators, and supply quartermasters appear steadfastly alongside the troops. Scores of photographs record the friendly relationship between American GIs and the liberated civilians of France. Conversely, German atrocities receive ample attention, particularly those committed against Americans and against civilians in Nazi concentration camps. In short, the book tells a triumphant tale but does not shy away from the horrors of war. The final photograph features a lone American soldier—he could have been Bill Mauldin's Willie or Joe— trudging through the forest above the bold caption, "Please, God, don't let this happen again."[79]

Meanwhile, an article in *Atlantic Monthly* of late 1946, "The Wounded Still Fight," gave readers a rare, detailed glimpse into the lives of casualties after they left the battlefields of Europe and the Pacific. When Edgar Jones first visited a hospital to interview wounded soldiers for the piece, he expected that as a veteran himself, he would be able to relate to the men. As it turned out, nothing in his experience as an ambulance driver in Europe prepared him for what he found. There was a man called "the Nose" because he lacked one, a man named Freddie whose head had been reduced to the size of a fist by an explosion, a former mathematical genius whose neurological injuries rendered him barely able to count to ten. The Nose, whose real name was Hal and who had been accepted to Harvard, liked to read and write poetry, until a gruesome procedure changed him: "To allow time for a flap of skin to take hold around his mouth, Hal had to keep his head bent against a shoulder for six weeks, and that got him out of the habit of reading and talking." Despite such horrors, outwardly the veterans seemed "as cheerful as a pack of Pollyannas." "We put on quite a show," an impotent vet named Dougherty said, "with all this sweetness and light." In reality, many of the vets felt neglected and forgotten. According to Jones, "There are no more cheers and parades for the vets, they say; it's moans and groans now about what to do with them all." The final lines of the piece mocked the more idealized picture of recovery dominating wartime culture: "Instead of going boldly back into society, they will seek out the dark corners which do not throw too much light on the scars that no one has had time to fix up."[80]

Though such postwar representations of injured ex-GIs were increasingly graphic, some magazine articles suggested that wounded veterans still found coverage of their condition overly sanguine. In early 1946 an ex-GI responded crossly to a photographer who posed a picture of amputees dancing, telling a *New Republic* reporter, "They danced just long enough for the photographer to take his shot and then they hurried back on their crutches. But the photographer wasn't interested in that; *he'd got his phony picture.*" "Why do they have to take all these pictures anyway?" another ex-soldier asked the reporter. An older veteran, dripping with sarcasm, interjected an answer: "They want to show us looking happy so that the public will know how wonderful America is treating its disabled heroes."[81] Several Universal newsreels in 1946 portrayed wounded ex-servicemen with similar fluff: "Maimed Vets Play Golf"; "Amputee Drives a Mercury"; "Blind Vet Gets His Land." Though images like these remained sanitized, many postwar media representations of disabled veterans surpassed wartime images in their vivid portrayals of suffering.

Postwar depictions of psychological trauma among veterans also were a bit more explicit than before but still usually stressed speedy recoveries. A piece in the *Saturday Evening Post* in the spring of 1946, "Brash Young Man," told the story of James Harry Bradley, a wounded veteran who was "making up for lost time with the girls." Did Bradley suffer from psychological problems? "Jim, for all his distinguished war record, shows no outward effect of his war experience." He could speak freely of combat, killing "Japs," and his dead friends. Deep into the article the author admitted, "There are some psychic scars which persist: restlessness, impatience, a quickness of temper. But time, best of all healing agencies, has helped him to forget the fearfulness of the war. . . . He no longer, as his mother says, yells in his sleep or gets up in the middle of the night." Now, Jim was a specimen of manly strength—"sturdy, heavily muscled"—and, despite wounds to his legs, was "physically perfect and is rated by the Ford doctors as able to do any type of job."[82] Jim's clean bill of health as a potential worker connected him to—or even made him the embodiment of—the national recovery from depression and war ongoing in the mid-1940s.

In the same vein *Time* magazine, in the summer of 1946, described neuropsychiatric vets filing through New York's mental hygiene clinic. The afflicted ex-GIs seemed like broken machines on a conveyor belt: "The psychiatrists worked swiftly and efficiently. By nightfall 180 troubled veterans had spilled their principal worries, [and] trooped out." According to the article, postwar emotional trauma was no small problem. "In addition," the piece went on, "many a soldier who stoically endured the war has cracked up since." But all in all, the difficulties were serviceable—and in fact, one psychiatrist believed, were actually attributable to the tumultuous home front. A Dr. Brown argued that most soldiers with battle fatigue would have recovered "easily" and "without treatment" in the absence of postwar worries over "home and job." The housing crisis in particular bore much of the responsibility for neuropsychiatric vets' readjustment troubles. That shortage "forces jittery veterans to live with jittery relatives."[83]

A tale of psychiatric recovery appearing in the *New Republic* in early 1947 revealed the somewhat tenuous balance struck in postwar culture between idealism and realism. The article described the ways doctors in Peoria, Illinois, were handling anxious veterans. An ex-GI described his nocturnal experiences: "'Every night I wake up screaming—every single night—got to help me, doc. . . .' Doc usually does. Often his psychotherapy is simply common sense." Despite much-touted advances in psychiatry, sometimes it appeared a simple talking-to could help a vet out of his troubles. And fortunately, according to a local psychiatrist, psychological problems were scarcer than wartime projections had forecast.[84] Yet the veteran woke up screaming *every night*. It is debatable which is more striking in this passage: the pain of the ordeal or the ease of the recovery. In embryonic form, here was a message embedded in World War II imagery that would stretch forward through time to the film *Saving Private Ryan* (1998): Americans should revere the "greatest generation" not only for victories secured, but for the suffering they worked to overcome.

In postwar accounts of veterans' affairs and the war itself, images of GIs were becoming increasingly heterogeneous. Joining the wartime portraits of the veteran as a hero, provider, and family man were newer ones: Veterans might be victims of government neglect, of insensitive civilians, of the housing shortage, of debilitating physical injuries, of haunting wartime experiences. Frequently they came across as highly resentful about some or all of these problems; indeed, the word "bitter" appeared in scores of article titles of the period. Occasionally veterans seemed like complainers, deadbeats, "bilkers," or "chiselers." Some observers worried that GI benefits were making "bums" out of America's vets, but even that notion imbued the exserviceman with a sort of victimhood.

Yet this more "realistic" imagery did not depart entirely from wartime messages. Many descriptions of vets remained highly optimistic and portrayed hardy ex-GIs whose manliness, capability, and, significantly, employability had been bolstered by their experiences in the military. These exservicemen symbolized the nation's swift recovery from the dislocations of World War II, a wider story told often in popular media of the day.

Such tales of resilience may have had an adverse effect on vets who were *not* able to overcome their war experiences so quickly. An article in *Harper's Magazine* in late 1946 described a deeply troubled veteran who faced persistent cultural pressure to recover from the war. The vet talked about his fears, frustrations, and problems with motivation. At the end of his stirring account, he wrote, "All this doesn't sound very American, does it? The resilience and resourcefulness and the clarion call to action are all missing, aren't they? I'm not responding the way I should to the rehabilitation program, am I? I'm supposed to snap out of it, buck up, straighten out, and buckle down—and get off that twenty dollar payroll. I *know* I'm not what I'm supposed to be. That's why I'm worried, and that's why I'm trying to figure out why."[85] Though this veteran captured well the upbeat character of some postwar imagery, a close look at the news in the late 1940s might have made him feel a bit less alone in his distress.

CHAPTER 3

THE IDEA OF ME, 1945-1950

Three years after the Museum of Modern Art (MoMA) exhibit Road to Victory had toured the country in 1942, a new war-related photographic display rolled into towns across the United States. Starting at MoMA in New York City in early 1945, two versions of the exhibit Power in the Pacific traveled the country through the late spring of 1946, hitting towns such as Racine, Wisconsin; Providence, Rhode Island; Kalamazoo, Michigan; Oak Ridge, Tennessee; Waterville, Maine; and larger cities including Washington, Minneapolis, and Cleveland.[1] Viewers of the photographs, which had been put together by Edward Steichen, saw much that was familiar, much that may even have reminded them of Steichen's Road to Victory. But there was newer imagery in Power in the Pacific as well, imagery that had started to surface late in the war thanks to looser government censorship of photographs.[2]

The exhibit documented the American naval presence in the Pacific Ocean. A good deal of Power in the Pacific featured idyllic photographs of the sea, wispy clouds, sunlight on the water, and mighty warships. As tranquil as these scenes were, the MoMA press release reminded viewers that the naval vessels constituted a "tremendous convoy of powerful engines and materials of war, cargo ships, destroyers and transports."[3] These words, which were often repeated in local papers covering Power in the Pacific, celebrated American strength much like Road to Victory had in 1942. Other parts of the exhibit, however, focused on the men themselves. The first gallery featured a huge photograph of smiling sailors with text alongside: "Yesterday these men were boys; today they are seasoned warriors"—words that revived the dominant message of the war years that rendered military service a maturing experience. Nearby were dramatic pictures of waves crashing and rugged sailors at work on the high seas. Other photos could be quite frivolous, including one picture of a seaman playing the tuba.[4] Most of the sailors had an easy confidence about them, laughing in the face of the grim duty they had been asked to perform.

It was in the portrayal of that grimness that Power in the Pacific differed most markedly from Road to Victory. Pictures of wounded men, corpses, battle-fatigued soldiers, and prisoners of war balanced the other, more familiar images. One of the most enduring photographs of the war appeared in Power in the Pacific: a young soldier sipping coffee in the hull of a ship, his face grimy and marked by the strain of battle. "Yesterday," the caption read, "this boy thought only sick people died," challenging the idea of war as a redemptive experience. (See figure 7.) Another photo captured the agony of a "torn and tortured" marine, an image impossible to release in 1942. Words on a placard nearby summarized the warrior image constructed in Power in the Pacific, using the present tense to make the audience feel a part of the action: "We win the beachhead and we win the island. But not without costs. . . . Men have been wounded and killed. The living and the dead are heroes." This portion of the exhibit celebrated American victory and the heroism of American soldiers yet acknowledged the sacrifices inherent in the war effort. Reverence for the dead was particularly stark in Power in the Pacific; photographs of corpses accompanied these words: "To the dead is accorded the honors that go only to heroic men of the sea who die in battle—burial at sea with full rite and ritual while their shipmates, with all the dignity of the living, pay silent tribute."[5]

Befitting the dual nature of the images in Power in the Pacific, reviewers around the country differed widely on what they appreciated about the exhibit. In its account of the show a small paper in Maine spoke vividly of the "expressive photos of faces in the height of battle strain." Most reviews, however, downplayed the harsher sides of war shown in Power in the Pacific. A critic in Kalamazoo described the "begrimed faces of men getting a cup of coffee on ship during the interlude of battle," giving little sense of the mental fatigue written into the faces of those young soldiers. The *Providence Journal* called it an "impressive record of dramatic action and tense moments," while a writer in Memphis noted the show's documentation of "exciting moments, moments tense with danger, routine chores, [and] periods of relaxation and amusement"—with no mention of the darker moments revealed in the exhibit.[6]

Imaginative representations of the soldier in the postwar period often mixed grimness and glory this way. Like contemporary media accounts of vets, fictional depictions of GIs and veterans in the last half of the 1940s focused on the individual over the collective—sometimes making the American soldier a hero, sometimes a victim, sometimes both. As the novelist John Horne Burns put it in 1947, what now seemed important was "the idea of Me."[7]

Though the war was over, American moviegoers continued to see depictions of soldiers and veterans on the silver screen. Three of these films repre-

FIGURE 7. *Begrimed and weary marines at Eniwetok Atoll, February 1944. In Edward Steichen's photographic exhibit* Power in the Pacific *(1945) the caption said of nineteen-year-old Pfc. Faris M. Tuohy (foreground), "Yesterday this boy thought only sick people died." Courtesy of National Archives.*

sented some of Hollywood's last efforts at depicting *battle* for some time and also departed from dominant wartime conventions. As film scholar Jeanine Basinger has noted, *They Were Expendable* (1945), *The Story of G.I. Joe* (1945), and *A Walk in the Sun* (1946) all shared "a dark force, a grim sense of war as a no-win situation, in which we will hang on and endure, but not without suffering."[8] *They Were Expendable*, a John Ford film featuring John Wayne, reversed the imagined wartime transformation of raw recruits into efficient fighting units. The movie charts the deterioration of a naval squadron once it sees combat, with death a constant presence and Wayne nearly breaking down as he eulogizes a fallen buddy. Lewis Milestone's *A Walk in the Sun* was based on Harry Brown's novel of the same name, published in 1944. That book had featured a soldier incapacitated by battle fatigue, deep chasms between officers and dogfaces, cynical GIs, bungling military leadership, and a seemingly futile and aimless mission. Some of these elements appeared in the film adaptation, marking its deviation from wartime standards, though on screen the GIs successfully take a farmhouse in the final sequence (the book's ending had been more ambiguous).[9]

The Story of G.I. Joe focused on the experiences of war correspondent Ernie Pyle, and in fact quite faithfully reflected his columns from the front. Unlike almost every other war picture, *G.I. Joe* eschewed elaborate pyrotechnics, sappy love stories, grand displays of bravery or sacrifice, climactic battles, and other devices used to draw audiences to combat films. Instead, director William Wellman, in close conjunction with Pyle before his death, showed Americans the drudgery of life in the infantry. The film featured a young Burgess Meredith as Ernie Pyle; the correspondent supposedly demanded that a man as slight in frame as himself be cast in that role. Based heavily on Pyle's book of dispatches, *Here Is Your War*, the movie followed a company of foot soldiers from the battle for Italy through the D-Day invasion.

The film proved faithful to the spirit of Pyle's columns. Absent were patriotic platitudes and lofty purposes; in their place were mud, blood, and the sheer monotony of the infantryman's life. The movie showed the little things: yearnings to go home, quirks of personality, everyday gripes. As one prominent historian of film has put it, "*G.I. Joe* showed men at war, trying to survive—no more, no less."[10] Military people thought the film was uncommonly truthful. Gen. Dwight Eisenhower reportedly said *G.I. Joe* was "the greatest war picture I've ever seen."[11] One hundred and fifty combat veterans acted in the picture on their way from Italy to the South Pacific, adding to the film's realism. In between their normal training exercises, Wellman used the men extensively in *G.I. Joe*, even giving some of them speaking lines. Many of the real-life soldiers in *The Story of G.I. Joe*, in fact, later were killed in the last year of the war (as was Pyle). Wellman, an accomplished director with the films *Wings* (1927) and *Battleground* (1949) to his credit, later said, "It's the one picture of mine that I refuse to look at."[12] It was simply too painful for him to watch men doomed to die.

Soon Hollywood turned from the battlefield to the postwar home front in films about returning veterans, venues for exploring the pain and stress of postcombat life. The most widely known treatment of the subject was *The Best Years of Our Lives* (1946), an immensely popular film about vets and the readjustment process. The film won numerous Academy Awards that year, including those for best picture, best actor, best director, and best supporting actor. Harold Russell, an actual double amputee, played the character Homer Parrish and won an additional Oscar for demonstrating the capabilities of wounded veterans.[13] Other treatments of returning GIs included *I'll Be Seeing You* (1945), *Pride of the Marines* (1945), *Till the End of Time* (1946), and *Apartment for Peggy* (1948).[14]

Drawing less attention from scholars has been *The Men* (1950), a film that introduced the young Marlon Brando to American audiences. Centered on a group of paraplegic veterans in a Veterans Administration (VA) hospital a few years after the war, *The Men* combined a documentary style with the sentimentality and many of the themes of *The Best Years of Our Lives*. At the beginning a dedication explained the aim of the film: "In all Wars, since the beginning of History, there have been men who fought twice. The first time they battled with club, sword or machine gun. The second time they had none of these weapons. Yet, this by far, was the greatest battle. It was fought with abiding faith and raw courage and in the end, Victory was achieved. This is a story of such a group of men. To them this film is dedicated."[15] *The Men* delivered on its pledge to depict the wounded without sentimentality. Actual combat footage as well as the participation of forty-five paraplegics heightened the realism. Yet *The Men* also kept faith with wartime narratives of victory and recovery.

The film chronicles the trials of Lt. Ken "Bud" Wilozek (Brando) and other paralyzed vets confined to a VA hospital. Amidst the enhanced realism of postwar culture, director Fred Zinnemann confronts the exigencies of disability. Early in the film Dr. Brock (Everett Sloane) lets a group of wives and mothers know what to expect from their injured loved ones: bladder and bowel control problems, depression, self-pity, and anger. "The word 'walk' must be forgotten," the doctor tells the white, black, and even Asian women. "It no longer exists." Most of the wounded men are cynical or depressed; one of them thinks that civilians look at him as a "freak on wheels." Another veteran bets on horses all day, smokes cigars, and generally plays the class clown. Most cynical is the character masterfully played by Jack Webb shortly before his run as Joe Friday on the television series *Dragnet*. When Dr. Brock asks him whether he wants to be rehabilitated, his answer is acerbic: "No. I don't wanna be rehabilitated, readjusted, reconditioned, or re-anything. And if you don't mind, I don't wanna take my proper place in society either. Does that make my position clear?" This outburst explicitly challenges much of the hopeful language that surrounded the return of 16 million veterans after the Second World War. The last patient the audience meets, the only one in his own, private room, is Bud, whose bitterness surpasses that of the others. Dr. Brock asks him with exasperation, "You've been a paraplegic for more than a year now. Don't you think it's time you accepted it?"

Even more suggestive of his dark outlook is Bud's meeting with his fiancée, Ellie (Teresa Wright of *The Best Years of Our Lives*), whom he had shunned out of self-pity after returning from the war. He has told her never to visit him, but with the doctor's help she defies Bud's wishes. Bud reacts to her presence explosively: "Don't look at me! What do you want? What'd you come here for? I told you I didn't want you around! I told you I didn't want anything to do with you! Can't you understand English, you stupid idiot?" Slowly Ellie convinces Bud that *she* needs *him*, that she is not confusing pity and love (as he charges), that he should make an honest attempt at rehabilitating his body (which he so far has refused to do), and that he should marry her. The effect of the exchange is electric, and the next sequence shows Bud making swift progress on his mobility, strength, and attitude. Regaining one's rightful place with a woman stands as the central motivator for disabled veterans.

Bud's rehabilitation only takes him so far. Dr. Brock warns him to acknowledge his limitations: "Before you can change the world you have to accept it as it really is, without illusions. You understand that, don't you?" These words seem directed at the false hopes of so many disabled veterans who consumed—and sometimes objected to—optimistic assurances in the media, government films, newsreels, and popular advertising. [16] Civilians in *The Men*, meanwhile, are insensitive and hurtful. Bud and Ellie are driven out of a restaurant by the gawking of other patrons—just what the Office of War Information (owi) had cautioned people *not* to do in its wartime directives for the print media. Ellie's father, who likes Bud, nevertheless tells her that he does not approve of their imminent marriage. "He's not the same man," he tells her. "You've signed a contract to be his nurse." Despite her emotional rejection of her father's words, Ellie grapples with doubt. The father's final admonition—"is it so wrong to want a grandchild?"—sends

Ellie to Bud's doctor to ask if he will ever be virile. Probably not, the doctor tells her.

The couple goes forth and gets married, but with a tense soundtrack and concerned facial expressions all around. When they retreat to their new home to celebrate, giving Ellie a glimpse of life with a paraplegic, Bud senses his bride's regret. They fight and she admits, flustered, that she is sorry she married him. Of course, in good Hollywood fashion they make up and appear ready, at the end of the film, to make another go at it. In the final sequence Bud has driven his specially outfitted car a long distance to Ellie's parents' home. He wheels himself up the steep walkway to the brick steps, beyond which he cannot proceed. Ellie comes out of the house to meet him there. Bud tells her that on the way, he "had a flat tire, fixed it myself"—his *independence* intact. Then Ellie asks if Bud wants help getting up the steps. "Please," he answers, acknowledging his occasional *dependence*. If men in *The Men* still tend to favor brooding, buffoonery, or bitterness over discussing their feelings, Bud seems, at the end, on the verge of embracing a recalibrated masculinity. This updated form of manhood includes admitting weakness, accepting help, and ceding control.

Critics of *The Men* in the national press were largely appreciative of these and other elements of the veteran's postwar image. *Newsweek* lauded the "head on" handling of the damage wrought by spinal injury and "psychological mayhem" wrought by insensitive civilians.[17] *Time* called the picture "realistic, unsentimental, and emotionally powerful," approving of the novel unwillingness to end with a "slick solution" or "the easy out."[18] The *New York Times Magazine* ran a two-page spread of photos from the movie; in captions the words "crushed," "embittered," "apathy," "self-pity," and "cynical" surrounded images of the paraplegic veterans.[19] In the *New York Times* a reviewer found the wounded men "fittingly representative of all the tragic human wastage of war." In *The Men*, this critic believed, the individual suffering of soldiers was finally taking center stage: "And this in itself is a powerful, and overwhelming indictment of war—an indictment of the clash of social forces which expose the individual to horror and pain."[20] Here, again, the "idea of Me" superseded the collective endeavor.

Some reviewers, however, cringed at this new realism. A writer for the progressive *New Republic* felt like a voyeur: "Why are we being shown such pictures as 'The Men'? Is it really wise or useful to translate subtle and painful psychological problems into the vocabulary of mass entertainments?" This critic held that as a viewer you were experiencing horrors that were "none of your business." The *New Republic* granted that the soldiers' images were painted "decorously and sympathetically" but argued that they represented a sort of exhibitionism of—or worse, profiteering from—the pain of the disabled. It is unlikely that producer Stanley Kramer or Marlon Brando, who spent many weeks with paraplegic veterans, failed to care genuinely for their subjects, or that they were "pretend[ing] to be helping these men," as the *New Republic* charged. Yet this review meshed with the approach of many combat veterans who preferred to keep their emotional recovery from the war silent.[21]

Sentimentality and grimness likewise permeated the first significant combat picture to emerge in the postwar years, director Alan Dwan's *Sands of Iwo Jima* (1949).[22] After four years of waging celluloid combat during the Second World War, Hollywood producers had sensed battle fatigue among movie-going audiences. As a result, war pictures had all but disappeared from 1946 through early 1949, as filmmakers mirrored popular concerns by turning their attention to returning veterans in films such as *The Best Years of Our Lives* and *The Men*.

Now Hollywood signaled the return of the combat genre with arguably the most popular World War II picture of all time, *Sands of Iwo Jima*, starring John Wayne as Sgt. John M. Stryker. In the film Stryker leads a marine rifle squad into combat on Tarawa and Iwo Jima before dying by a sniper's bullet in the closing sequence, which replicates Joe Rosenthal's famous photograph of the marines raising the American flag atop Mount Suribachi. *Sands of Iwo Jima* enjoyed the full cooperation of the Marine Corps, which still found it valuable as a recruiting tool fifty years later.[23] Nevertheless, the movie combined familiar elements of the World War II combat picture with hints of a more ambiguous view of war—despite its reputation as the embodiment of roseate World War II mythology.[24]

The marines under Stryker's command fight amongst themselves and with Stryker almost as much as they fight against the Japanese. These conflicts range from the comic to the menacing: one new recruit's failure to master a bayonet exercise earns him a brutal clubbing in the face from Stryker. Cpl. Al Thomas (Forrest Tucker) and Pvt. Pete Conway (John Agar) have personal reasons for hating Stryker. Thomas holds a grudge dating back to some forgotten slight and feels comfortable airing his animosity before the other men: "Sometimes I don't know which I hate worse, him [Stryker] or the Nips [Japanese]."[25] Conway, whose late father had commanded Stryker a year earlier, harbors serious resentment toward both older men for their insistence on toughness. Throughout the movie Conway throws insults and even a punch or two in Stryker's direction. When Stryker refuses to leave their foxhole to retrieve a wounded marine for fear of giving away their position, Conway spits disgust and sarcasm at him: "Aren't you human at all?

Don't you realize a friend of yours may be dying? This is what my father taught you, be a *great marine*, be *tough*!?" Only by threatening to kill Conway can Stryker prevent the younger man from climbing out of the trench to save the wounded GI—hardly a ringing endorsement for the cooperation of soldier and superior. In a later tirade against the marines, Conway puts Stryker in his place: "On duty I jump when you holler. Off duty, I exercise my God-given rights under a democratic form of government, and dislike whom I please. Do we understand each other?" Stryker, who has inflicted iron discipline on his men, can only mutter, "Beat it."

The film also features some exceptionally grim battle scenes for that era—"savage realism," in the words of one reviewer.[26] Footage of the attack on Tarawa, interspersed with actual combat photography from the war in the Pacific, includes a man being shot in the face, while several others die less graphic, more familiar Hollywood deaths. One GI is bayoneted by a Japanese soldier into a bloody mess. Corpses burn after the battle for Iwo Jima. When a young soldier dies during the assault on that island, the camera closes in on his tormented facial expression, and then on the book in his breast pocket: *Our Hearts Were Young and Gay*, an account of two young women's voyage to Europe published in 1942. One soldier tells another that war amounts to "trading real estate for men."

For viewers who remembered images of soldiers from the war years, however, there was much familiar material in *Sands of Iwo Jima*. The film reaffirms the wartime notion that men become hardened or matured by battle, not broken down by it.[27] During filming in the summer of 1949, producer Edmund Grainger told reporters that *Sands of Iwo Jima* would "show the heroism of the average American *as he readjusted from civilian life to the war*."[28] Stryker's heavy drinking arises not out of trauma from battle but from regrets over his family life. Stryker does agonize over the fact that his decisions sometimes lead men to their deaths, but by and large he views his command simply as a job to be done. In *Sands of Iwo Jima*, there is little indication that postwar mental trauma awaits those exposed to heavy combat. With the technical backing of the Marine Corps, it was no surprise that the film touted combat as an opportunity for growth.

As soldiers become hardened by war they also become team players, another theme carried over from wartime culture. Despite the near-insubordination of certain characters early in the film, solidarity overcomes individuality by the end. Stryker tells the group in the beginning of the film, "You're gonna move like one man and think like one man. If you don't, you'll be dead." Indeed, throughout the movie, whenever a soldier runs off against orders he invariably gets cut down by enemy fire. In *Sands of Iwo Jima*, the two most cynical characters, in fact, are rendered *less* jaded and individualistic by their war experiences. Training and combat fashion these men into a crack marine outfit *and*, by implication, into better postwar citizens—just the message that many federal information managers had proffered during the conflict. The hatred Private Conway and Corporal Thomas feel toward Stryker melts into smiles, apologies, and a renewed sense of duty and teamwork by the end of the film. Conway even names his baby boy Sam, after his father, a choice that he had explicitly rejected in an earlier invective against the marine tradition.

Surrounded by the men who used to despise him, Stryker sits triumphantly on Mount Suribachi and declares at the end of the film, "I never felt so good in my life." Seconds later, a sniper's bullet kills him instantly. It is the grim reality of war that just when a leader has earned the trust of his men, he dies in their arms. It is also the patriotic, forward-looking American spirit that sends those men back into battle. "Saddle up!" Pete Conway cries, stepping into Stryker's shoes. If the film raised serious questions about military discipline and the relationship between sergeants and their men during the Second World War, the last sequences restored faith in military protocol. By turning its attention from Stryker's death to the raising of the American flag on Mount Suribachi, the final scene promotes wartime patriotism and sacrifice, if a bit unconvincingly. To the eminent scholar Garry Wills, the final scene "has the air of something tacked onto a story whose ethos it violates."[29]

Film critics in the national press, like some scholars years later, equated *Sands of Iwo Jima* with wartime pictures, largely missing the rising animosity between soldiers and superiors the film depicted. As an archetypal combat movie, moreover, the film left some reviewers unimpressed, belying its great success at the box office as well as its future status as a classic of the postwar period.[30] According to many critics, *Sands of Iwo Jima* contained little that was new beyond realistic battle sequences and a fine portrayal of the marine fighting spirit. A scathing review in *Time* magazine sneered, "The plot has no more freshness or emotional tug than a military manual, and it is peopled by a movie-hardened cast of characters who have served too many hitches on Hollywood's back-lot battlefields." The reviewer for *Newsweek* was kinder, praising the film's "grimly exciting footage," yet agreed with the *Time* critic that "the stories that thread the documentary record are, to put it mildly, both sentimental and hackneyed and generally unworthy of the film's obviously good intentions." Reviewers for the *New York Times* and the cinema journal *Variety* shared this annoyance with the film's abundant clichés.[31]

Stock characters and a tired plot blinded these critics to the harsh portrait of soldierly discipline shown in *Sands of Iwo Jima*. Like many audience members, however, critics may have missed this new tension because by the end of the film it had all but evaporated in a haze of victory, patriotism, and sacrifice atop Mount Suribachi. Indeed, amid other, more positive reviews John Wayne went on to earn an Oscar nomination for his performance—and to claim his position as the mythic embodiment of the Marine Corps.[32]

————

Filmmakers for federal agencies in the mid-1940s, like many Hollywood directors, were turning their attention to returning veterans. In the absence of owi or any other centralized propaganda wing, the Veterans Administration, the army, the signal corps, the Department of Agriculture, and other agencies produced films on the returning soldier to be played before public audiences, business leaders, or vets themselves. Official postwar films generally depicted three thematic situations: rehabilitation or recovery from physical wounds, rehabilitation or recovery from psychological trauma, or vocational readjustment and the search for housing. Many of the films combined these themes, portraying the job training of physically or emotionally disabled ex-GIs. The pieces varied from a straight documentary style to short skits or longer "dramatized documentaries" with actual veterans or actors playing veterans. Like many articles circulating in the postwar print media, these films set forth the disabled ex-serviceman as a worthy recipient of federal aid—needy yet deserving, vulnerable yet resourceful, eager for an opportunity but not a handout.

In 1946 the Veterans Administration released *What's My Score?* a thirteen-minute "short" for industrial executives on the physical rehabilitation and employment possibilities of disabled veterans. The film begins on a reassuring note, as a voice-over describes several wounded servicemen: "They were representing 250,000 disabled veterans—that's a lot of manpower, useful manpower, ready for all kinds of jobs." Meanwhile the veterans exit an airplane, showing off wheelchair tricks on the tarmac. The sources of their wounds are vague; one soldier "used to repair refrigerators, was really traveling in the Eighth Air Force, until, well, sometimes your luck kinda changes for a while. Now he's attending watch repair classes." Like in most of these films, the wounds themselves stay in the background.

Conforming to wartime conventions, the producers of *What's My Score?* portrayed veterans as capable, well-adjusted, eager to work, and generally not different from citizens at large. The narrator tells viewers that disabled veterans "follow a regular schedule, everyday, just like everybody else." Over images of a veteran stumbling slightly, the narrator goes on: "He's ready all the time, always keeping his balance, just like they *all* do." Gen. Omar Bradley, speaking on camera to a group of disabled veterans, calls them "self-reliant, independent, productive citizens." As in other government films, the message seems an almost defensive answer to wartime worries that disabled veterans would constitute a drain on society. Near the end of *What's My Score?* the narrator tells employers, "You see, here's the way they [disabled veterans] think of it. While they may not have the full use of their arms or legs, they can work just the same. All they're asking is a chance to prove it—prove it to you."[33]

The thirty-minute dramatized documentary *Toward Independence* (1947), an army production, shared this emphasis on productivity, resilience, and manliness. In the beginning of the picture, the paralyzed George Young is despondent, facing what the narrator calls "the grim struggle to free a personality of the crushing weight of useless limbs." But very quickly, the positive outcome of the story is foretold when Young observes the progress of another veteran, Ray Hennessey, further along in his rehabilitation, a man who "looked, well, proud, like he just pitched a no-hit ballgame." Young responds to Hennessey's example: "I, George Young, brushed off Dick Tracy and Superman, and decided to pattern myself after a real man—Ray Hennessey. . . . [I was determined to be] on my own." Hennessey even calls the hospital gymnasium "Independence Hall."[34]

Other films promoted the good prospects for *psychological* recovery from physical disability. In 1947 the Veterans Administration released *Quiet Triumph,* a seventeen-minute short focusing on the work of army chaplains in aiding the recovery of wounded veterans. Like other films it used the framing device of a discouraged ex-GI to tackle "problems of mind, problems of body, problems of soul." One amputee laments his missing leg and its effect on his love life: "I wish she would [run out on me] . . . I'm no good to her, Chaplain. . . . What does she want with a fellow like me?" Threats to one's manhood were a frequent worry of the ex-soldiers in these films. The chaplain finally convinces the veteran, "Your girlfriend needs you," and the wounded man more confidently goes forth to rehabilitate his body and mind.[35] As in Brando's *The Men,* wounded servicemen overhaul their attitudes when reminded of the romantic opportunities attached to recovery.

In *The Road to Decision* (1947), a production of the Veterans Administration, the archetypal pessimistic, disabled ex-serviceman has a barroom encounter with a fellow veteran. The depressed former GI has "dame trouble and job trouble," but the man he meets, also an amputee, is a successful architect's apprentice, repeating the "good vet-bad vet" arrangement in owı's scripts for its short film *When I Come Home*. Through the use of flashbacks, the successful veteran recounts how he recovered first from his physical wound and then from his lack of job prospects. *The Road to Decision* is essentially an advertisement for the vocational training available to disabled veterans through the vA, and thus it tells a story similar to that of *Quiet Triumph*: Veterans can recover from physical wounds and become productive members of society. At the end of the film, two attractive women join the successful ex-serviceman—once again, for government filmmakers women were first prize in the race for readjustment and restored masculinity. [36]

A thornier issue for official movie producers was the matter of neuropsychiatric veterans. The Army Signal Corps' production of *Let There Be Light* (1946) marked the limits of postwar representations of the psychologically injured veteran—not because it glossed over his problems, but because the film was not released for nearly forty years.

Let There Be Light, directed by John Huston and narrated by his father, Walter Huston, offered shocking portrayals of several neuropsychiatric patients convalescing at Mason General Hospital on Long Island. The film would have been enormously educational for Americans, given its frank treatment of an issue ignored in other movies. However, concerns over the privacy of some of the soldier-patients stalled the film's release. *Let There Be Light* was finally released to the public in 1981, when officials at the Defense Department decided it would help Americans understand the plight of Vietnam veterans suffering from post-traumatic stress disorder. [37]

World War II veterans rarely seemed as vulnerable and childlike as they did in *Let There Be Light*. Yet the film conformed to standards of the time and ended happily—too happily, according to one scholar who has questioned the patient recoveries documented in the film. Richard Dyer MacCann, an authority on films of the armed forces, has noted that the emotional troubles of some of the veterans resurfaced after Huston's cameras stopped rolling—not surprising given the psychological state of these men. [38]

"Casualties of the spirit," "the troubled in mind," "men who are damaged emotionally," "plunged into sudden and terrible situations," "the limits of human endurance," "unceasing fear and apprehension," "feeling of hopelessness and utter isolation," "death and the fear of death," "a sense of impending disaster"—these are the ominous tones of the film's opening sequences. [39] Indeed, *The Best Years of Our Lives* contained similar themes, and an actual amputee from the war, but the documentary style of *Let There Be Light* had a more disturbing, immediate quality. Upon returning from the war, one soldier "didn't feel like living," while another "just got tired of living." Two others stutter uncontrollably. When asked, "Do you feel changed?"

one veteran finally mutters, "Yeah . . . more jumpy." Several ex-GIs recount horrifying combat experiences and express guilt or regret over the loss of a buddy. Some report enormous difficulty dealing with their families. An African American soldier who had suffered from severe homesickness during the war breaks into tears during his talk with a psychiatrist. As one scholar of World War II imagery has noted, to see a GI crying was exceedingly rare in wartime iconography.[40] In fact, much of what the film revealed would have galled OWI officials just two or three years earlier.

Through group therapy, hypnosis, and drug treatments, these men recover right before the viewer's eyes. Often associated with the 1980s and Vietnam veterans, group therapy was "in vogue," according to one mental health expert, as early as 1945.[41] Huston's cameras capture a group of servicemen, black and white together, discussing their troubles with a psychiatrist. Hypnosis and drug treatments have more dramatic effects. A veteran suffering from "conversion hysteria" is physically sound, but for psychological reasons is paralyzed from the waist down. During his interview with the doctor, the boy periodically lurches forward uncontrollably. A sodium amytal injection induces a hypnotic state, and the psychiatrist "explores the submerged regions of the mind," according to the narrator. After getting the soldier to talk about some of his problems at home, the therapist goads him into walking again on camera. Woozy and a bit unsteady, the boy expresses his sheepish gratitude. Another soldier is able to remember his own name for the first time since enduring bombardment on Okinawa. And a severe stutterer recovers his ability to speak after drug therapy. He screams out in joy: "I can talk! I can talk! I can talk! Listen, I can talk! Oh god, listen, I can talk!"

As that sequence illustrates, treatment has a stirring effect on the men. The narrator tells viewers, "The shock and stress of war are starting to wear off." Veterans pursue arts and crafts, watch movies, visit with family members, engage in vocational therapy, and take classes on starting businesses. Meanwhile, some ex-soldiers express the hope that the public will accept them: "We can be just as good as anybody else," one veteran says. The film ends with the patients playing baseball. The vet who had been paralyzed by his psychiatric condition scampers around the bases. The man who could not talk now yells, "You're out!" "Are they well enough to be discharged?" the narrator asks over jaunty music. "The answer is yes." Like much else in postwar culture—particularly in the media and these government films— *Let There Be Light* reveals a more dismal picture of readjustment than seen earlier but ends on an upbeat note familiar to anyone from World War II–era America.

Alas, the army refused to release the film. The withholding of *Let There Be Light* from public viewing did an unintentional disservice to the 1.3 million veterans who suffered from debilitating psychological trauma during the war. A wide range of portraits of veterans had abounded throughout the 1940s, and some soldiers "nervous from the service" had appeared in films such as *The Best Years of Our Lives*. The images of stuttering, amnesiac, and befuddled soldiers in *Let There Be Light*, though, surpassed Hollywood's version of these men. Although the 1940s saw a great surge in the popularity of psychiatry, fuller public awareness of the damaging emotional impact of war would have to wait. [42]

———

Literature of the late 1940s offered martial imagery at odds with more upbeat configurations in the media, Hollywood, and government films. In two major postwar novels as well as some contemporary poetry about World War II, writers added intense cynicism and individuality to the warrior image.

John Horne Burns's critically acclaimed novel *The Gallery* (1947) offered a stark picture of American forces stationed in Italy. As John Diggins has remarked, the book offered a "needed corrective" to the sentimentality of works such as John Hersey's *A Bell for Adano* (1944), one of the most popular World War II novels. [43] *The Gallery* dealt frankly with soldiers' psychological trauma, resentment toward the army, concerns over their wives' fidelity, frustration with the anonymity of being a GI, sexually transmitted diseases—and even with the life of homosexual soldiers. Arranged as a series of character sketches, the novel lacked a conventional plot. A glass-domed shopping center, the Galleria Umberto Prima in Naples, served as the canvas for Burns's picture of the interaction between American servicemen and the Italians.

The book's first portrait introduces an American soldier named Michael Patrick. He has developed trenchfoot but counts himself as lucky because it has taken him away from terrifying combat near Florence: "Perhaps it was some subconscious cowardice that had broken out in his feet. He'd thought for a long time anyhow that he was going to crack, and trenchfoot was a more honorable way of doing it than becoming a psycho." Patrick suffers from more than trenchfoot and cowardice; he also laments his lowly, faceless place in the group-oriented military. This image deviated from the unquestioned commitment to teamwork of wartime iconography, particularly in government propaganda. "For his was a face pretty much like everyone else's who isn't anybody in America," wrote Burns, "and less than that in the army. . . . He was just another GI who'd been on the line and was going back to it." After emptying a bottle of cognac, Patrick's realization of his insignificance drives him to tears: "It was okay to cry because he knew with clarity and brilliance exactly why he was crying. For his own ruined life, for the lives of millions of others like him, whom no one had heard of or thought about. For all the sick wretchedness of a world that no one could, or tried to, understand. For all who passed their stupid little lives in the middle of a huge myth and delusion."[44] Gone was the celebration of belonging to something greater that wartime correspondents such as Ernie Pyle (particularly early in the war) had proffered to their readers. [45] Military voices, like those in the photo book *Soldiers' Album*, had reinforced that emphasis on teamwork in the years since war's end. Now, in its place was Michael Patrick's sinking feeling that he was an expendable pawn in a massive grudge match between the Allies and the Axis.

That sense of expendability characterized the five lines of Randall Jarrell's classic World War II poem, "The Death of the Ball Turret Gunner," published in the mid-1940s. Jarrell writes of a man killed while airborne. Once the damaged plane returns home, workers hose the gunner's shredded remains out of the turret, as if he were just a mess to be cleaned up. [46] Such unheralded sacrifice marks marine veteran Cord Meyer's popular short story "Waves of Darkness," which first appeared in *Atlantic Monthly* and then won the O. Henry Prize in 1946 for best first-published story. The protagonist, fighting like Meyer did in the Pacific, experiences a war without a cause, without patriotic motivation. It is an involuntary war of senseless brutality and anonymous death. "Most of us are not here by our own choice," the protagonist thinks. "We were taken from our peaceful lives and told to fight for reasons we cannot understand. Surely we have far more in common than that which temporarily separates us."[47] The character (like Meyer himself) pays dearly for his service, losing an eye in a Japanese grenade attack. The work of Meyer, Burns, and Jarrell did not explicitly protest the war but rather lamented the fate of individuals on both sides swept up in it.

The structure of *The Gallery*, alternating chapters on people with chapters on places, heightens this emphasis on individuality. In another vignette, an unnamed GI arrives in Italy after the usual foul journey below decks on a troop ship from America. As he acclimates himself to the prospect of dying in an overseas war, his thoughts turn to his helplessness and anonymity. Yet he also learns to value his life—and individuality—as never before. Burns's prose provides an emotional accompaniment to Jarrell's "Ball Turret Gunner":

And I remember finding myself potentially expendable according to the Rules of Land Warfare, trapped in a war which (I said) was none of my making. So I began to think of my Life with the tenderness of a great artist. I clasped myself fondly to myself. I retreated into my own private world with the scream of a spinster when she sees a mouse. And I remember that I saw the preciousness of the gift of my Life, a crystal of green lymph, fragile and ephemeral. That's all I am, but how no-accounting everything else is, in juxtaposition to *the idea of Me*! What does anything else matter? The world ceases to exist when I go out of it, and I have no one's assurance but my own for the reality of anything. [48]

The multiple uses of "my," "myself," "my Life," and "Me" underscore the irony of this GI's new situation: He celebrates his individuality just as it seems most threatened. His way of thinking dramatically reversed army protocol, reinforced in countless images of servicemen from the World War II era, for the transition from civilian to soldier. Peter Aichinger has written that in the fiction of World War II, military service almost always transformed raw, cynical recruits into committed team players. [49] And MoMA's Power in the Pacific exhibit of 1945 had indeed echoed such wartime literature in its photo caption, "Yesterday these men were boys; today they are seasoned warriors." Now, Burns's nameless, "green" soldier starts out with a gung-ho, "well-here-we-go-again-off-to-the-wars" enthusiasm, but once on foreign soil quickly becomes cynical about the collective goals of the military and grows to cherish his life more than ever before. [50]

Michael Patrick and the anonymous GI find themselves isolated and suspicious of all those around them, particularly the military brass. Other soldiers in *The Gallery* harbor similar wariness of and antipathy toward their own wives. A Red Cross nurse asks a pilot about his bride, eliciting a paranoid tirade from the flyer: "Oh, that bitch, that lovely little bitch. . . . She hasn't written for three months. And I'm over here in this arsehole of the earth eating myself out and wondering what she's doing. . . . I'll kill the slut if I ever find out anything." The nurse tries to assure him that his wife has been faithful, but he will not hear it. Burns tells readers what the nurse thinks of it all: "And Louella decided that the greatest of war crimes is the bitchery of a wife when her husband is far from her." [51] With heartless officers and unfaithful wives to contend with, it is no wonder that the GIs in Burns's novel retreat into themselves—in a way that Bill Mauldin's Willie and Joe, though they grumbled over similar things, never fully did.

Of course, the military men in *The Gallery* are no paragons of fidelity. Along with food, alcohol, and money, lust draws soldiers to the Galleria, something concealed in many wartime representations of Americans overseas. One serviceman has fallen in love with an Italian girl who stands apart from his other conquests: "With all the others, after his fever was cooled, he'd only wanted to pay them and kick them out the door."[52] In 1947, the year of *The Gallery*'s release, the renowned poet and Second World War veteran Richard Wilbur whispered of liaisons between French prostitutes and American GIs in the poem "Place Pigalle."[53] Even in Audie Murphy's popular autobiography of 1949, *To Hell and Back*, soldiers gather outside a whorehouse "patiently awaiting their turn."[54] In *The Gallery* such extramarital sex has dire consequences, as Burns shares with readers in the chapter "Queen Penicillin." Soldiers in one of the military's venereal disease clinics endure a painful and humiliating regimen of penicillin injections, along with sundry indignities of the testing, admission, treatment, and release processes. Whatever indiscretions may have led the men to the clinic, Burns's description of what they undergo there makes it seem a sorry existence indeed.

Just as Burns highlights the woes of the average serviceman, he also illuminates the shadowy world of an even more maligned subset of the military: homosexual soldiers.[55] Burns, who was gay, challenges the rock-solid heterosexism of the military and of American society more broadly. In the chapter titled "Momma," the author describes a teeming and chaotic gay bar in Naples. GIs and officers of several races and ethnicities come together at Momma's to drink, smoke, and pursue other soldiers or Italian men. Interspersed with the sexual innuendoes and bawdy language ("Done any one nice lately?") that fill the chapter are snippets of conversation subtly protesting the hypocrisy or injustice of the dominant heterosexual ethos—"[Gay] people are the embodiment of the tragic principle of life"; "[Gay] people are expressing a desire disapproved of by society"—and the narrator's voice: "Momma's boys had an awareness of having been born alone and sequestered by some deep difference from other men. . . . She believed that a minority should be let alone."[56] While Burns stops short of merely portraying the men in Momma's as helpless victims—they have developed a thriving subculture under difficult circumstances—they do share with the other soldiers in the book a forlorn, jaded outlook aggravated by their doubly embattled status in the American military. (Meanwhile, "outed" gay veterans were discovering in the mid-1940s that they were excluded from the benefits of the GI Bill.)[57] Burns's affecting prose captures the "sullen" and "dour" appearance of the men at the bar, men with "misty lonely eyes" and "some deeper inferiority sense," and depicts the "reconnoitering restlessness" and "acid tenderness" that characterize the mood at Momma's.[58] The chapter ends when a violent fight breaks out, the military police enter with night-sticks swinging, and Momma faints onto her cash register.

Critics in the United States had mostly generous things to say about Burns's work. Charles Poore of the *New York Times* called it a "rancorously vivid portfolio of portraits." The review did harp on some of the "gamier passages" in the book, evidence to the squeamish Poore that "you can say practically anything in a novel now." But Poore appreciated how Burns's characters "probe[d] desperately for a meaning behind all the brutality and chicanery and squalor" that flourished behind the lines in Naples.[59] Another reviewer applauded Burns's "fervent sensitivity" and "passionate sympathy."[60]

Causing a much greater stir the next year was Norman Mailer's best-selling first novel, *The Naked and the Dead* (1948). The book appeared to thunderous praise, though it offered a rather sinister picture of the American military. Mailer's opus, bulging at more than seven hundred pages, exposed war's psychological costs, the fate of the wounded, soldiers' worries over marital fidelity, the cruelty of some GIs, and the bitter resentment of enlisted men toward their superiors. Even more than Burns's work, it offered a steady stream of profanity and sexual content that made many contemporary readers blanch.

Mailer, himself a twenty-five-year-old veteran of the war in the Pacific, brought a refreshing candor to his account of the conflict. Inspired by wartime stories of long patrols such as John Hersey's *Into the Valley* (1943) and Harry Brown's *A Walk in the Sun* (1944), Mailer sends his fictional GIs on a terrifying mission behind the Toyaku Line to disrupt the Japanese forces from the rear.[61] Much of the action on this imaginary Pacific island, Anopopei, comes at night. Mailer paints scene after scene of almost unspeakable horror: GIs tiptoeing around a slumbering Japanese encampment; enemy soldiers screaming at the Americans in broken English as they open fire from just yards away; an American scout patrolling by himself in the dead of night, slitting the throat of a Japanese sentry. These experiences take a severe emotional toll on the Americans: "Since the day when he had lain helpless on the ground waiting for the Japanese soldier to kill him he had been feeling a recurring anxiety. Often in the night he would awaken with a start, and turn around in his blankets, trembling unreasonably." One soldier tells his buddy, "I'll tell ya, my nerves are gone. Sometimes I'm afraid I'll just go to pieces and I won't be able to do a goddam thing. You know what I mean?"[62] Other GIs respond by matching the cruelty of the Japanese step for step. The sadistic Sergeant Croft kills a Japanese prisoner in cold blood after giving him cigarettes, food, and false compassion.

Many of the GIs in Mailer's book express general disillusionment with military life and a more sharply focused resentment of superiors. Echoing some of the themes of Burns's *Gallery*, soldiers in *The Naked and the Dead* are sick of the "goddam" army and particular officers ("what a monster"). One GI after another bemoans his lowly place in the chain of command. The officers "just send you out to get your ass blown off," one grunt muses. "A man's no more important than a goddam cow." A wounded GI thinks to himself about the army brass, "They don't care if you live or die here. All they want is to get you back where you can stop a bullet." For some of the men in Mailer's novel, officers become almost as hated as the enemy. When Lieutenant Hearn dies on the patrol, one GI remarks boldly, "They're all bastards. . . . If it took him being knocked off for us to go back, then I'll settle for that."[63] Since the end of the war, such presentations of the victimized veteran had been appearing in the periodical literature. Veteran Edgar L. Jones wrote in *Atlantic Monthly* in February 1946, "Whether stationed in Washington or on a scrap of coral sand, the average GI considered himself to be the *purposeless victim* of malignant justice." Writing in the same publication a year later, cartoonist and ex-serviceman Bill Mauldin called wartime GIs "inmates" of the U.S. Army. Another vet grumbled in *Harper's* that in the military "you were wholly and absolutely in someone else's power."[64]

Back on Mailer's fictitious Pacific island, the home front, like the officer corps, draws the ire of the grunts. Few matters occupy as much of the soldiers' attention as the fidelity of their spouses. One grunt says about "green" troops arriving from the United States: "We were fightin' when they were screwin' their wives, and maybe screwin' ours too." Minetta, a GI who feigns insanity to avoid combat, lies in his bed and daydreams about his wife, until paranoia creeps into his fantasy: "He began to think of Rosie again, and he became angry. She's cheating on me; that letter where she said she wasn't dancing with anybody till I get back is a crock of . . . I know her, she likes to dance too much."[65] Readers of *The Naked and the Dead* might have remembered that right after the war, periodicals and newspapers had reported a number of real-life situations where jealous ex-GIs acted on just such impulses. A soldier from Chicago stopped receiving letters from his wife, and his sister informed him that the wife had been seen with another man. Upon his return in 1945, Pvt. Leopold Prorok confronted and killed the man, despite assurances from his wife that no intimacies had occurred.[66] Mailer's character Polack may as well have spoken for the real-life Prorok: "I wouldn't trust those bitches with a nickel."[67] While perhaps only a small minority of wives and girlfriends were unfaithful during the war, Mailer's Polack voices the insecurity and jealousy of a large number of GIs. Of course, because it is centered on soldiers, *The Naked and the Dead* says nothing of women's concerns about their husbands' infidelity, a far more plausible worry.

Some of the soldiers in *The Naked and the Dead* express a broader contempt for civilians on the home front. GIs often mention civilians not "knowing the score." By not really understanding what the war is like, these citizens are bound to underappreciate the returning GI. "What do you expect?" an angry Sergeant Brown asks. "Do you think you're going to go home a hero?" On another occasion, several soldiers discuss the homecoming they expect after the war. One man looks forward to a sweet welcome from his wife, but he is drowned out by darker forecasts. In the veiled profanity Mailer uses, Gallagher fumes, "All I know is there's a fuggin' score to be paid off, a score to be paid off. There's somebody gonna pay, knock the fuggin' civilians' heads in." Here were the frustrations of Willie and Joe, but amplified into a murderous rage that would have been unthinkable in Mauldin's cartoons (the artist himself had said in 1945 that returning GIs would be forever cleansed of a violent streak by their time at war). [68] The resentment that some of Mailer's GIs feel toward their wives, civilians, and the military hints at a profound sense of isolation, a sort of hostile individualism. "I hate everything which is not in myself," the abominable Sergeant Croft declares. [69]

Like Mauldin and Ernie Pyle, some image makers during the war had revealed the cynicism of GIs. Government films, for example, often poked fun at the good-natured and time-worn animosity of many soldiers toward their superiors. Now Mailer's work showed dissent of a deeper sort. It seemed in *The Naked and the Dead* that American soldiers questioned whether their officers—and, by extension, the whole American military—actually had their best interests at heart. Even worse, Mailer's grunts accused their own families, and the home front generally, of ignoring the sacrifices they were enduring in the hot jungles of the Pacific islands. [70] All the components of the wartime consensus on soldiers' priorities—family, country, military— came unraveled in Mailer's telling. The suffering of the individual soldier loomed larger than the collective goal.

The Naked and the Dead propelled Norman Mailer to international prominence almost overnight. The book spent eleven weeks on the *New York Times* bestseller list in the middle of 1948. [71] Critics tended either to love the book or to hate it (most loved it), but few denied its importance. Orville Prescott, a reviewer for the *New York Times*, added his name to the long list of people recommending the book, drawing an angry letter from a reader in Kentucky. "Of what earthly benefit," the man asked, "could [the book] be to society, or to an individual reading it?" He went on to ask Prescott whether he would want his own teenaged daughter to read "such filth." Prescott acknowledged that the book was raw and excessive but argued for its value. "I was revolted, too. But much human behavior, as our tragic century so plainly shows, is revolting. To be revolted may be a healthy thing."[72] Apparently many other Americans appreciated Mailer's brand of revulsion, for as 1948 ended the book was enjoying enormous popular and critical success.

The *Sunday Times* of London, for one, looked askance at the book's popularity. The paper campaigned in the spring of 1949 for Mailer's novel to be banned in England, citing its "obscenity and beastliness."[73] The attorney general there finally allowed *The Naked and the Dead* to be published in his country, stating that its release would not lead to any reaction "other than disgust at its contents."[74] No major press organ lobbied for a similar ban in the United States, but a few commentators in other circles agreed that it was a troublesome book. Writing in *Military Affairs* in 1949, a critic from the army's Historical Division, Charles B. MacDonald, called Mailer's work "bulky" and "repetitive." Even worse, it was a "depressing, fatalistic piece offering little hope." MacDonald dismissed the characters in *The Naked and the Dead* as depraved before they ever entered the army, with "combat only hastening their degeneration."[75] No doubt part of MacDonald's objection stemmed from the unflattering portrayal of GIs in Mailer's book. They were not just bad people, but bad soldiers.

These novels, despite their popularity, did not necessarily indicate widespread disillusionment with authority in the United States. After all, these were the early years of the Cold War, and the military still drew popular respect. A Gallup poll taken in the spring of 1948 showed that 77 percent of Americans believed that Congress should pass a law requiring every able-bodied young man to complete a year of military training. At the same time, however, throughout 1948, Gallup's recurring question, "What do you think is the most important problem facing this country today?" revealed an overwhelming public concern with foreign affairs, and more specifically with keeping the peace with the Soviets. If the military was popular, war was not: 25 percent of those Americans polled in September 1947 even believed it had been a "mistake" for the United States to get involved in World War II.[76]

What the popularity of *The Gallery* and *The Naked and the Dead* may have reflected was this strain of antiwar sentiment lurking beneath an abiding confidence in American military institutions. A reviewer in the *Nation* remarked that *The Naked and the Dead* helped to satisfy a public taste for less sanguine depictions of the war. It did not represent an overturning, but a departure, an extension of "knowledge." Other war books, the *Nation*'s writer added, "have not extended [the public's] knowledge, but have merely added detail or color or depth or intensity of emotion to the picture it already had."[77]

What was this new knowledge? The soldiers in Burns's and Mailer's novels displayed disillusionment with the greater cause, the military, their families, and an unsupportive home front. Indeed, such gripes foreshadowed those of a later generation of American troops in Vietnam. Just as press coverage of veterans in the late 1940s reveals the deep roots of the postwar veteran-as-victim image, the work of Burns and Mailer shows that the image of the bitter, cynical American fighting man was not born in the culture of the Vietnam War.

Around 1950 the period when veterans of World War II commanded widespread national attention came to an end. Indeed, journalists and other commentators seemed to endorse the view of social historian Dixon Wecter, who had written in 1944 that five years after war's end veterans would be fully readjusted to civilian life. "If, five years later," the former Rhodes scholar had declared, "the ex-soldier is still looking for a job or nursing injuries of body or mind, he may fairly be thought unemployable or permanently scarred."[78] A regular radio broadcast sponsored by the VA, "The Veteran Wants to Know," ended in 1950. Theodore Draper, then an up-and-coming historian, wrote in 1948, perhaps a bit prematurely, "G.I. Joe disappeared about a year ago, and nobody seems to miss him."[79] With the onset of a nasty war in Korea in June 1950, the image of the World War II vet as a social problem or a victim would drift even further from public memory.

What emerged in the late 1940s was the notion that veterans of World War II were diverse individuals with myriad problems. They often stood on the same pedestals they occupied during the war, but now they might also be victims of the housing shortage, "bums" made lazy by government benefits, frustrated job seekers, sufferers of a disability, or infantrymen hateful of their superiors. John Horne Burns and Norman Mailer went even further, reshaping the comical cynicism of Mauldin's Willie and Joe into something more bitter and violent. Many GIs, in their telling, hated war, the military, and even the home front without a sense of humor. In some cases these soldiers loathed their officers as much as they despised the Germans or Japanese. And the once-honored notions of teamwork and collective enterprise were giving way to expressions of individual frustration and isolation within an oppressive military world.

Yet postwar images of soldiers and veterans had limits. The widespread problems of social and economic readjustment, though they garnered ample attention in the press and in government materials, often seemed solvable and temporary. The films of federal agencies, for example, even those that did not sanitize the troubles that attended the readjustment process, almost invariably ended with jaunty testimonials of rapid recovery. It would take another, bleaker war, in Korea, to dampen such optimism.

THE
LONG
1950S

CHAPTER 4

KILROY IS BACK,

1950-1953

In the early, dark days of the Korean War, an anonymous American GI announced the return of a cultural hero: himself. The fictitious soldier "Kilroy," whose name had been scrawled on walls across every theater of World War II, reappeared in the deserted, war-ravaged town of Yechon, South Korea. If "Kilroy was here" during the last war, now, this weary American soldier scribbled, "Kilroy is back."[1] For a short time, the American fighting man would approach the position of cultural prominence he had attained in 1941–45. The new warrior appearing in popular magazines, photographic exhibits, and newsreels was in many ways a familiar figure. He wore the same uniform and fired the same weapons as he had in World War II. He also shared many of the attributes and miseries of the World War II citizen-soldier, particularly those publicized in imagery during the latter stages of that war. In other, subtler ways, however, the soldier in Korea that journalists and others depicted was a changed man.

The tenuous peace of the postwar world ended when North Korean troops, in the dead of night, stormed across the 38th parallel into South Korea in June 1950. Some Americans, including no small number of battle-weary veterans, had been dreading an inflammation of Cold War hostility since the end of World War II.[2] When North Korea attacked, *Time* magazine captured the worries of many observers: "Where is the Korean war leading the world? Will the fierce forest fire in the mountainous land below the 38th parallel be confined to the Korean peninsula? Will it spread around the globe, to sear the capitals of the world with atomic fire? Or is 1950 the beginning of a series of slow, limited wars that will keep the U.S. and its allies committed in battle for generations?" A map on the following page of the magazine depicted a fierce Joseph Stalin looking out from Moscow to the lands he allegedly coveted: Korea, Iran, Turkey, Indo-China, West Germany. Large lettering asked, "Next?" A similar graphic in *Newsweek* showed a vast USSR and China looming over southern and eastern Asia beneath the headline, "What We're Up Against." *Life* magazine printed its own foreboding map of the "communist sphere" in Asia the same week.[3]

Such worries were not new; the fears provoked by events in Korea culminated a twelve-month period full of menacing signals in the nascent Cold War.[4] In the early weeks of September 1949 American air-sampling technology had picked up traces of atomic fallout emanating from the Soviet Union. It was clear that after nine years of trying, Soviet scientists had exploded a nuclear weapon. A month later, on October 1, Mao Zedong had officially declared the creation of the communist People's Republic of China. To mark the occasion Mao visited Stalin for the first time, bringing the Soviet leader Chinese fruits and vegetables and staying in Moscow for an ominous two months.

What finally prompted action from unnerved policy makers in Washington, however, was Kim Il-Sung's communist invasion of South Korea six months later. American officials and much of the press strongly suspected that Stalin had sanctioned the attack, a charge later vindicated by the opening of Soviet archives in the 1990s. A week after the North Korean attack, the liberal *New Republic* asked and answered the question of Russian involvement bluntly: "*Is the Soviet Union behind the assault?* The answer is certainly, Yes."[5] Historians now know that the USSR did not *initiate* the attack, but rather gave its permission after repeated requests by Kim in 1949. Stalin assumed the United States would not intervene, but past lessons hung darkly over policy makers in Washington. Memories of the unchecked Japanese invasion of Manchuria in 1931 and the appeasement of Adolf Hitler at the Munich conference of 1938 practically ensured that the United States would get involved *this* time.[6] Nevertheless, the North Korean attack, for obvious reasons, never excited the degree of outrage in the United States that Pearl Harbor had nine years earlier—a fact that later may have contributed to the American public's fragile acceptance of the violence and bloodshed in Korea.

Whether the American military would be ready for the challenge was an open question. In June 1950, before the North Korean attack, army strength was just 592,000, half of what it had been in December 1941.[7] The great public cry to "bring the boys home" after World War II, as well as a false sense of atomic security, had severely diminished American ground forces. Already by June 1946 over 12 million servicemen and -women had returned to civilian life.[8] When Dean Acheson became secretary of state in 1949 he immediately recognized America's overreliance on nuclear weapons and convinced President Harry Truman to review the entire military arsenal. The resulting study was supposed to help replenish American ground forces, but little had changed by the time the North Koreans surged across the 38th parallel in June 1950.[9]

The "police action" in Korea and images of Americans fighting there went through four distinct stages between 1950 and 1953. From June until September of 1950, United Nations forces (mostly American troops) tried futilely to repulse the initial North Korean attack, giving up the South Korean capital, Seoul, and retreating to a perimeter around the southeastern port city of Pusan. During the second phase, from September to late November, Gen. Douglas MacArthur led a stunning amphibious landing behind enemy lines at Inchon and then chased the communists across the 38th parallel nearly to the Chinese border. Third, the introduction of Chinese forces in November led to a long, agonizing retreat during which many thousands of Americans died, until the spring of 1951, when the lines stabilized again along the 38th parallel. China's entrance into the war convinced many Americans that this would not be a short conflict, as they had hoped and assumed, leading to declining support on the home front.[10] The final phase—from the spring of 1951 through the war's end in the summer of 1953—saw a protracted stalemate in Korea and relatively stable, though limited, popular endorsement of the conflict. During these three years the United States lost 54,000 dead and suffered more than 100,000 wounded, in a war that essentially reestablished the division of Korea and was followed by decades of American military occupation of South Korea.[11]

A surprised Harry Truman responded quickly to the crisis in Korea, much to the shock of Stalin, Mao, and Kim Il-Sung. Within days of the communist attack, the administration secured a United Nations resolution to "repel the armed attack and to restore international peace" and assigned Douglas MacArthur to command the UN forces. Truman's decisive response to events in Korea belied worries over the severe underpreparedness of the American military. The tremendous weaponry and equipment that had been such an integral part of American success in World War II were outdated by the summer of 1950. "The American ground troops in Korea," wrote the *New Republic* in July, "have been fighting a World War III army with World War II weapons."[12] In the early stages of the conflict missiles from American bazookas bounced harmlessly off Soviet-made tanks.

The manpower situation was not much better. The United States had just ten understrength combat divisions around the globe, prompting the *Nation* to charge that military cutbacks had left the armed forces "so starved of men as to be virtually inoperable."[13] Existing divisions were often hardly ready for war. Eighty thousand troops in Japan who were to do much of the early fighting in Korea had been enjoying the spoils of occupation—abundant alcohol, subservient women, cheap labor to do the dirty work. Within days of the North Korean assault, many of these green troops found themselves yanked from the bosom of Japan and thrust into combat on the Korean peninsula.[14] Journalist Marguerite Higgins soon commented that most of them had never heard artillery fire before.[15]

Still, more men were needed. A one-year extension of the moribund draft brought thousands of young Americans into the military just weeks after the North Korean attack. By mid-July 18,000 Americans had been sent to Korea; by August that figure would approach 50,000.[16] Lewis Hershey's Selective Service delivered 220,000 men to the armed forces by the end of the year.[17] Scores of National Guard units and reservists were called up and sent to Korea, where American troops and matériel constituted the bulk of the UN force. The military recalled thousands of World War II officers and noncommissioned officers, soon nicknamed "retreads." Many of these men, in their thirties and forties, were plucked from civilian life and returned to war, while other men their age stood safely beyond the reach of the new draft. The World War II vets lent an air of professionalism to what was, at least in the beginning, a ragged and untested fighting force.[18] They also, however, often deeply resented finding themselves at war once again.

Joining the troops in Korea in July 1950 were scores of Western journalists. More than during World War II or the Vietnam War, the *print* media would deliver news of the conflict to the American home front. Sandwiched between the heyday of radio and movies in the 1930s and 1940s and the dominance of television in the late 1950s, glossy magazines were king during the Korean War.

In the first six months of the war there was virtually no censorship of the print media. General MacArthur believed that a free press was the hallmark of a democracy. Journalists were asked to "self-censor," or make their own choices about what sort of reporting might jeopardize American security or embarrass the administration. Late in 1950 officials imposed formal censorship, but of the late–World War II variety—images of the dead were permissible, for example. Even with no official control of the news, early in the Korean conflict reporters generally supported the military effort. Gradually, however, journalists came to distrust the official viewpoint and offer increasingly skeptical reporting, foreshadowing the all-out rivalry between press and brass during the Vietnam War.[19] While even the popular World War II had seen cracks forming in the roseate warrior image, the Korean conflict was to show that an undeclared, unpopular stalemate could evoke more ominous depictions.

Western journalists discovered dire circumstances in Korea. Manpower shortages and outdated weapons contributed to the terrible defeats suffered by UN forces in July and August. The North Koreans pushed relentlessly toward Pusan, and American military leaders planned a Dunkirk-like evacuation should the need arise. The first phase of the Korean War—from early

July to the eve of General MacArthur's landing at Inchon on September 15—was marked by retreat, desperation, and misery on the part of the American soldier.

Within the looser bounds of government censorship journalists laid bare the gloom of this early period. A prominent element of Korean War coverage was *fatigue*, one of several themes that circulated and intensified throughout the conflict. Just two weeks into the war stateside publications reported that American troops, softened by time in Japan or fresh from the United States, found the mud and heat of Korea exhausting. "American GI's, battered and dog tired," wrote *Newsweek* on July 17, "slogged south in retreat last week."[20] The same day *Life* ran Carl Mydans's large photograph of "exhausted and unshaven American infantrymen [a]sleep on ration boxes and [a] rocky roadside," according to the caption.[21] Two weeks later *Time* reported that as the reinforcement troops of Maj. Gen. Hobart Gay "moved up to the front, they met the gaunt, bone-tired G.I.'s of the 24th Division, some barefooted, some almost naked, all staggering from exhaustion."[22] Newsreel footage in the summer of 1950 frequently showed GIs sleeping.[23] (See figure 8.)

Sorrow quickly joined fatigue as a standard feature of the warrior image. With hordes of refugees, enormous civilian casualties, and ill-prepared American troops, Korea was an exceptionally sad war. One American unit at Pyongtaek, overrun by the North Koreans, tried demolition operations to stall the invaders, but failed for lack of experience with the equipment. Victims of their poor weaponry and inadequate training, many died at Pyongtaek. A lieutenant told *Time* correspondent Frank Gibney that he had to leave behind six wounded GIs, unable to walk. Gibney reported the dialogue between the hapless men and their guilt-ridden officer: "'Lieutenant, what is going to happen to us?' one asked weakly. The lieutenant said, handing them grenades, 'This is the best I can do for you.'"[24]

Robert Miller of the United Press reported the next week that only one in five wounded Americans was removed from a battle south of Chonan. "It was a slaughterhouse," said Lt. Junior Childers of California. "Nine men dropped around me and I brought out three."[25] Another soldier shared this bleakness with Marguerite Higgins, and asked if America was hearing of it: "As his lips trembled with exhaustion and anger, he said, 'Are you correspondents telling the people back home the truth? Are you telling them that out of one platoon of twenty men, we have three left? Are you telling them that we have nothing to fight with, and that it is an utterly useless war?'"[26] In fact, the popular press *was* doing so. The cover of *Newsweek* on August 7 featured the somber headline, "GI's in Korea: They Call it Hell

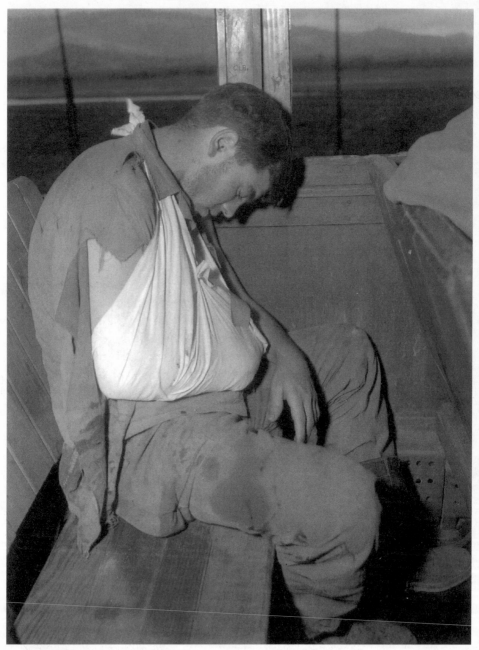

FIGURE 8. *Pfc. Orvin L. Morris rests during evacuation to Pusan, Korea, July 29, 1950. This image was typical of those from the early days of the Korean War, when journalists stressed the exhaustion of Americans fending off the North Korean onslaught. Courtesy of National Archives.*

Country"; the same month, John Osborne of *Time* called Korea "the Ugly War."[27]

Millions of American radio listeners heard a chilling firsthand account of misery in Korea in a broadcast of July 25. The Defense Department program on CBS, "Time for Defense," aired a message from an American officer to his wife. The man, returning from the fallen city of Taejon, spoke for several minutes of battle in Korea: "I don't know where to start on this. These last three weeks have been pretty rough. We're getting help here now. That's something we sure didn't have when we started. What makes it so difficult here is—[pause]—that you can't tell the damn North Koreans from the South Koreans. That caused a lot of slaughter." The future was not all gloomy, the soldier declared with confidence. "There's no question how this will come out. We'll come out on top." But this war—"more than a police action"—was not to be taken lightly: "It's something—gigantic. I know I've been through the Pacific and part of the European campaign, but I never ran into anything like this before." Surrounding the man's spoken words was triumphant music—a "rousing march" called "Liberty Land"—totally at odds with the sad tone of his account.[28] Often during the Korean War conflicting messages tugged audiences in opposite directions, as image makers grafted jaunty cultural conventions onto an ambiguous and tragic war.

As the UN forces and their South Korean allies backtracked through the summer of 1950, journalists reported that despite being outnumbered, outgunned, and bone tired, American GIs were fighting heroically. But this was not the World War II–era heroism based on commitment to a "cause," or the heroism of a triumphant power.[29] This new heroic image reflected the bleak odds facing American troops and reinforced the sense that they were somehow victims of circumstance—and a rugged, unforgiving terrain that was hot and muddy that summer. Readers of news accounts were invited to marvel at the stoicism of GIs struggling against the elements and the North Koreans, but also to sympathize with them. *Life* magazine's David Douglas Duncan described his own photographic philosophy in such terms: "I wanted to show something of the agony, the suffering, the terrible confusion, the heroism which is everyday currency among those men who actually pull the triggers of rifles aimed at other men known as 'the enemy.'"[30] During the Korean War *stoicism* would become as much a part of the GI's image as his fatigue and sorrow.

In late August a piece in *Time* magazine brought together all of these elements. Correspondent James Bell covered a marine assault on a rise known as No Name Ridge. In his article Bell repeated that designation to dramatic effect, underscoring the bravery of men willing to die for a remote chunk of earth. After hours of relentless pounding by American planes, the marines stormed the ridge but met stiff resistance. The carnage was ghastly, watched all the while by the man who had sent the boys into battle, Brig. Gen. Edward Craig.

The general's hands trembled as he held his binoculars and told Bell, "I never saw men with so much guts." For over an hour the marines advanced slowly against unyielding fire, until ten men reached the top, only to be killed there. "Finally, the assault force was ordered to withdraw," Bell wrote. "Men too exhausted to cry crawled back down the ridge with no name. For all their terrible sacrifice the ridge was still in enemy hands." Medics brought back a steady stream of the wounded during this lull in the fighting. General Craig "tried not to look at his torn kids." When a second assault wave went out, the fresh marines advanced tentatively forward past the wounded coming back. "It was a brutal way to move fresh troops into position. . . . The new wave came up unsmiling, and with not a little fear in their young faces." The second attack finally took the ridge with no name, but, wrote an emotional Bell, "It will never be good to remember those kids being carried out of that valley."[31] *Life* printed David Douglas Duncan's photographs of men crying, officers learning their ammunition had run out, and wounded men receiving frantic care in the midst of battle.[32]

Such exposure of despondency drew the ire of some American military leaders. General MacArthur criticized reporters in September 1950 for "laying too great emphasis upon the outcropping of emotional strain such as appeared at the start of the campaign." Yet he continued to believe that censorship was not the answer. Rather, such problems "in due course find their correction, as in Korea, in the maturity gained through experience as the campaign progresses."[33]

The military brass would not rely solely, however, on the presumed "maturity" of the press to counteract revelations of battle fatigue. As the war progressed, the armed forces rotated soldiers out of combat for rest and instituted a tour-of-duty system replacing the World War II policy that kept GIs in the military for the war's duration. Moreover, military officials installed formal censorship in December 1950, and the Public Information Offices (PIOs) in the field also issued their own press releases to compete with images of the exhausted American GI, especially during the dark winter of 1950–51 when Chinese troops were driving UN forces south from the Yalu River.

Meanwhile, Americans were being wounded and killed in great numbers —in the Eighth Army, which represented the bulk of the American forces, there were over 5,000 killed and 16,000 wounded by the end of the summer.[34]

Early media coverage of wounded and dead American soldiers tended toward disclosure. The first photograph from the war in *Life* magazine showed "an American Casualty," Pfc. Thomas Merante, grimacing in pain after being shot at a South Korean airport.[35] Yet a large photo on the next page featured a grinning pilot demonstrating how he had downed two North Korean planes, indicating the war's iconographic ambiguity. Darker were images the next week in *Life*, when several of Carl Mydans's photos portrayed injured and dead Americans without sentimentality. One wounded GI stands with his arm in a sling and his pants nowhere to be found. The first picture of a dead American in Korea featured several young soldiers surrounding the body of their lieutenant. In the memorable image one of the GIs lights a cigarette as he stares ahead with an expression drained of innocence.[36] Pain and death were being shown with a frankness not seen until late in World War II, a tactic that had then been part of a deliberate effort to shock Americans out of complacency and buy war bonds.[37] Now, a war that was going very badly stirred journalists to revive those tones with even greater poignancy.

The signal corps, which produced footage under the title *Combat Bulletin*, offered in the first weeks of the war images of wounded and dead American GIs that reflected the general dreariness of the period.[38] In one installment of the series not a single injured soldier offers a smile, a cheery thumbs-up, or a wink for the cameras, all fixtures of government films during World War II. Rather, several cover their faces, hiding their tears, or lie impassively as plasma is administered on-camera.[39] Late in the summer gravely wounded and dead Americans figured prominently in Universal newsreels, which were released in conjunction with the Department of Defense.[40] Yet in many of these productions, upbeat music, familiar to viewers of World War II–era newsreels, often clashed awkwardly with disturbing images on the screen.

Photographs and words during the summer of 1950 suggested that Americans in Korea were tired, miserable, and stoic. It was hard not to commiserate with the soldiers in the pictures, men with bloodshot eyes, men crying over the loss of a friend, men slumped dejectedly against each other, men pitifully wounded, men fated to die moments later.[41] At the same time, images of desperation often stood in clumsy contrast with World War II–era cultural conventions ranging from jubilant music to optimistic media accounts. It was as if producers of these images were disoriented by the way tragedy in Korea challenged what Tom Engelhardt has called the "victory culture" that emerged from World War II.[42] Somehow what was happening in Korea did not fit American expectations, and images of GIs reflected that dissonance.

This sort of ambiguity reflects the fact that news organizations may officially support a conflict even as they show images that subtly undermine the war's popularity. Ernie Pyle and Bill Mauldin gestured in that direction during the Second World War, demonstrating that journalists did not have to be "antiwar" to publicize the dreariness, pain, and monotony of martial life. In a conflict widely viewed as "just" and popular such as World War II, it is unlikely that even the direst dispatches of Mauldin or Pyle eroded public support for the war. But the case of Korea was different. Though Americans guardedly supported the war in the beginning, it was undeclared and going badly in the late summer of 1950. (And eventually, alongside mounting casualties and Chinese intervention, support for the Korean conflict eroded in a pattern "highly similar" in nature and degree to what was later seen during the Vietnam War, according to John Mueller's important study published in 1973.)[43] American editors, though they supported the containment of communism, could hardly ignore the grim news and haunting images arriving from Asia. Thus, without an overarching narrative of unanimity and success, even strongly anticommunist publications were likely to expose the ambiguity of the Korean War. The eminent oral historian Studs Terkel remarked later that despite *Life* editor Henry Luce's status as a fierce cold warrior and supporter of the war, his magazine's photographic coverage of Korea "captured the murkiness of this new conflict."[44] Media critics who later excoriated the Cold War–era press for simply reproducing official viewpoints have underestimated the complexity of meanings coursing through mainstream publications.

Some of those meanings were murky indeed in the summer of 1950, as Douglas MacArthur planned a daring attempt to come to the aid of American warriors in South Korea. The aging, egotistical general invited photographer Carl Mydans and other American newsmen to join him on the trip from Japan to Inchon. "I'm going on a little operation," MacArthur told the journalists, "and I'd like to have you boys with me if you'd like to go."[45]

By September 1950, Congress and the Selective Service had bolstered American military strength considerably. Between August and September the Americans nearly doubled their strength in Korea, to about 85,000 men; similar increases boosted Republic of Korea (ROK) forces, bringing total United Nations strength (including troops from several other UN countries) to 180,000 soldiers on September 1.[46]

After two months of almost constant retreat, the augmented UN forces were finally, in late August, holding a firm line around the southeastern city of Pusan. The North Koreans continued to pour men and material into the line at the Naktong River near the city, but as the UN forces held, North Korean losses mounted. Even worse for the communists, their forces had driven deep into South Korea, leaving themselves vulnerable to a beach landing near the 38th parallel—a move that could have devastating effects on their supply lines to North Korea. In the stifling heat of late August and early September—known to soldiers as "the days along the Naktong"—General MacArthur put the finishing touches on his "little operation," a plan he had hatched within days of the war's beginning. [47]

On September 15, 1950, UN forces swept the beaches and sea walls of Inchon to the west of Seoul, as General MacArthur watched his daring and controversial strategy unfold from the bridge of the USS *Mount McKinley*. UN troops seized Inchon, recaptured Seoul, and broke out of the Pusan Perimeter in the south, setting up a great vise around the North Korean army. By early October UN forces had driven the North Koreans all the way back to the 38th parallel. Intent on destroying North Korea's military and unifying the country, MacArthur received authorization to invade the communist state on October 9 and pushed nearly to the Chinese border—the Yalu River—by late November. For now, in October, victory seemed assured. "The war very definitely is coming to an end shortly," MacArthur declared. [48] China's imminent entrance into the conflict would make a mockery of those words. [49]

Amid the UN resurgence, the media recycled many images of the American GI in the second phase of the war. Still prominent were depictions of fatigued, wounded, or demoralized servicemen. Not surprisingly, however, the briefly triumphant American soldier now walked with a bit more swagger in his step.

One of the first images to reach American shores after the UN counteroffensive was *Newsweek*'s cover of October 9. The photograph captured the iconographic confusion of Korea, with bombast from World War II clashing sharply with a seemingly nastier war. A young American GI guards a frightened enemy soldier, whose lofted arms and dazed look signal his helplessness. The caption proclaims, somewhat defensively, "U.S. Fighting Man: Winner—and Still Champ." [50] Yet the picture inspires little confidence in the American GI. His helmet tilted sloppily to one side, his appearance generally unkempt, the youthful soldier holds his pistol out toward the prisoner with a wild, inexperienced look in his eye. That expression, familiar to any reader of popular magazines through the summer of 1950, spelled battle nerves. Viewers from a later, different time—the era of the My Lai massacre and other American atrocities in Vietnam—might have imagined the young GI killing the prisoner. Audiences of the 1950s would not necessarily have drawn such a conclusion, but the volatile nature of the scene was unmistakable. Readers would have been hard-pressed to determine which of the two men in the photo looked more scared.

Other coverage of the war's second phase produced a thicket of ambiguous meanings. The initial *Combat Bulletin* from the signal corps after Inchon featured the familiar chipper music, but the narrator did grant that fighting had reached a "peak of fury."[51] The capture of Seoul figured heavily in another signal corps film, but victory did not sanitize the images of war; still widespread was footage of prisoners, the wounded, and combat.[52] Again, upbeat music and smiling troops balanced these official versions of the war. Coverage in the popular press reflected the new optimism. "By sea, land, and air," wrote *Newsweek* on October 16, "the United Nations host this week moved in for the kill in Northern Korea." The magazine reported that 250,000 Americans and 100,000 South Koreans were smashing their way into the communist North. Pictures of cheering American GIs graced the pages of the article.[53]

That same month, *Newsweek* printed a photo of a GI crying over the loss of his friend, the "price of victory," according to the caption.[54] (See figure 9.) The picture fit into a long line of images, begun early in the war, that never shied away from the sorrow of American GIs in Korea. According to one letter to the editor, the picture should join "Marines on Iwo Jima" in the pantheon of celebrated war photos.[55] The two pictures, reprinted side by side on *Newsweek*'s letters page, offered an unmistakable illustration of the transition in popular iconography from World War II to Korea.[56]

The discovery of North Korean atrocities generated more somber imagery in the period of UN revitalization. A signal corps film in the fall reported that on October 6, 1950, the North Koreans had massacred scores of South Koreans and some American prisoners. Footage of grotesque, misshapen bodies—"evidence for a war crimes investigation," according to the narrator—drifted across the screen in nauseating close-ups.[57] Popular periodicals carried similar news of communist treachery in October. *Time* showed a picture of hundreds of South Koreans killed during the communist evacuation of Taejon and captioned it "Korea's Buchenwald" in reference to the Nazi concentration camp.[58] A *New York Times* article evoked a legacy closer to home: "Chinese Communist hordes, attacking on horse and on foot to the sound of bugle calls, cut up Americans and South Koreans at Unsan today in an Indian-style massacre that may prove to be the costliest of the Korean War."[59] The strident anticommunism engulfing American society certainly informed such coverage. *Newsweek* printed graphic shots of

FIGURE 9. *Grief-stricken American infantryman*, Newsweek, *October 9, 1950. The crying man had lost a friend to fighting in the Haktong-ni area of Korea. This photograph, which quickly became a signature image of the war, illustrated a new willingness to show the sorrow of American troops. Courtesy of National Archives.*

slaughtered South Koreans under the headline, "This is Communism: How the Reds Behaved While Winning."[60]

Though the press did not report *American* atrocities in Korea, there were visual indications of the mistreatment of prisoners. Pictures in *Newsweek* in October showed two captured communist nurses, stripped down and wrapped in white cloth, surrounded by angry-looking American soldiers; an accompanying photo depicted "Red POW's cowering in a ditch," according to the caption.[61] Quite common in the period of North Korean retreat were photographs of terrified enemy soldiers under the watch of spiteful Americans. Despite frequent, strong declarations in the media that only the communists committed atrocities, such footage invited some degree of suspicion. Indeed, a month later two letters to the editor from American women objected to the poor treatment of prisoners that *Newsweek*'s photos implied. "After all," wrote a college student, "two wrongs don't make a right." More insistent was a letter from a woman in Massachusetts: "We as Americans criticize the way the Reds treat the American prisoners of war. Some of the pictures the newspapers and magazines print concerning the Red prisoners of war at the mercy of our own soldiers are absolutely disgraceful and shameful. . . . The picture of the two Red Korean nurses partially disrobed at the mercy of four 'men' . . . makes me thoroughly ashamed of our forces in their treatment of POW's."[62] Though her view may not have been typical, this New Englander unknowingly foreshadowed a key element in the image of American soldiers fighting in Vietnam. The notion that American GIs could be war criminals was by no means part of the prevailing image in the 1950s, but the faintest hint of that idea stirred in Korea.

During the first and second phases of the Korean War, images of African American GIs joined the maelstrom of portraits flooding in through the press. Despite President Truman's executive order of 1948 calling for desegregation of the armed forces, in 1950 the army lagged far behind the air force and navy in actually integrating its units. In fact, the black GIs that would attract the most media attention belonged to the Twenty-fourth Infantry Regiment, a century-old "all-Negro" unit that violated, by its very existence, the executive order.[63] (See figure 10.) In the beginning of the Korean War the men doing the brunt of the fighting remained separated by race.[64]

Early in the war black fighting units garnered widespread praise. In late July the Twenty-fourth retook the city of Yechon after a sixteen-hour battle. *Newsweek* described the exploits of the regiment: "Its all-Negro enlisted men and its half-Negro, half-white officers outflanked the Reds, sneaked across

FIGURE 10. *General MacArthur inspects the Twenty-fourth Infantry, February 21, 1951. The segregated Twenty-fourth attracted both praise and criticism from military officials and the press during the Korean War and was eventually integrated along with many other units by the end of 1951. Courtesy of National Archives.*

paddies, infiltrated through Yechon's decrepit houses, and thus beat the enemy at its own game."[65] Whole companies died in the fight for Bloody Peak, which the black soldiers eventually held. In early August the Twenty-fourth was "brave, battered," according to *Time*.[66] An article in the *New Republic* in November quoted an American captain's letter to the Defense Department: "The 24th and the 9th Infantry Regiments are doing very well and the [Negro] service troops are slowly but surely gaining the spotlight for a job well done."[67]

Such praise of the Twenty-fourth raised the suspicions of the National Association for the Advancement of Colored People (NAACP) in 1950. Tributes to all-black units could be used to "justify continual segregation," suspected an editorialist in the organization's magazine, the *Crisis*, in October.[68] If black regiments were fighting well, why integrate them? Other observers agreed that such praise just sugarcoated segregation in the army. One man wrote a letter to the liberal *Nation* in September: "The American press is outdoing itself to praise an all-Negro unit fighting in Korea. Do we think we are fooling the American Negroes or the colored people of Asia by this? It is a segregated unit, and we are dramatically informing the whole world by our deeds that America has second-class citizens good enough to die for us but not to associate and intermingle with us."[69] Evoking a mantra of Cold War racial discourse—that discrimination and segregation undermined the American moral position against communism—this commentator believed that glorification of the Twenty-fourth was disingenuous.[70] In both cases, liberal critics were wary of positive portrayals of all-black fighting units.

Late in the fall, however, the Twenty-fourth began to attract criticism. A North Korean breakthrough at "Battle Mountain" was blamed on the unit. The army leveled large numbers of courts-martial against black troops, a development that NAACP officials thought amounted to a "smearing" of black GIs. The most celebrated case was that of Lt. Leon Gilbert, accused of cowardice under fire and sentenced to death. Thurgood Marshall soon traveled to Korea to investigate the courts-martial, some of which proved to be racially motivated.[71]

Other critiques were more measured. Military observers were beginning to maintain that African Americans who fought alongside whites displayed greater discipline and skill than those in the segregated detachments. In November Hanson Baldwin of the *New York Times* praised black *service* personnel, but reported that for black *combat* units, "it is an understatement to say they did considerably less well."[72] If NAACP officials had questioned the motives of praising African American regiments, they were even more suspicious of criticism. If the black man could not fight, why integrate the military? Why not keep him behind the lines in the service ranks? As one NAACP official put it, "Apparently the Army is out to make a catchword and a travesty of integration. How else explain the consistent pattern of Army criticism of Negro GIs in Korea? Army tradition has it that Negroes should be used in labor and personal service, since they are not good enough to fight and die for their country."[73] Another editorial in the *Crisis* asked, "Are these slurs to be forerunners of a campaign of slander against Negro fighters such as came out of the last war?"[74] The author referred to the Ninety-second Division in Italy, an all-black unit that had attracted harsh words during the Second World War.

Contrary to the worries of the NAACP, criticism of the black units actually hastened desegregation of the army. The same article in the *New York Times* that had denigrated African American combat regiments hinted at what was to come: "Many in the Army are coming around to the conclusion, despite the peacetime social problems involved, that the Negroes must be integrated with the whites in small numbers; into platoons, companies, battalions, batteries and regiments."[75] Early in 1951, reports out of Korea were to confirm that the segregated Twenty-fourth was performing poorly—but that blacks fighting alongside whites functioned just as well as anyone else. Liberals would argue that the poor performance of the segregated unit made a case for full integration of combat units.[76] Meaningful desegregation of the army came late in 1951, for reasons of military expediency rather than social justice. By that point NAACP officials, integrationists that they were, applauded the racial mixing, even if that development had arisen out of criticism of the all-black regiments.

Beyond these controversies, black GIs would increasingly appear alongside white soldiers in newsreels, media accounts, and government materials such as radio shows and films. Some African American observers had complained about the lack of publicity garnered by black troops during the Second World War; later in the Korean conflict that charge would meet a partial answer. The simple fact that blacks did a greater share of the fighting in Korea than they had during the previous war meant that they appeared more frequently in media coverage—often with guns in their hands.[77]

As early as October 3, just days before UN forces crossed the 38th parallel, Chinese premier Zhou Enlai had warned that if *American* troops crossed that frontier, his nation would intervene on behalf of the North Koreans. China followed through on its threat, and by mid-December the Chinese and North Koreans had driven UN forces back to the 38th parallel. Along the way, fierce fighting in the vicinity of the Chosin Reservoir—the "Frozen Chosin," in American parlance—claimed thousands of lives on both sides. By early 1951 the Chinese had pushed beyond the 38th parallel, and fighting around that border would persist until the lines stabilized in the spring—roughly the same time that American support of the conflict also stabilized after dropping significantly upon China's intervention.[78] Meanwhile, in early April President Truman fired Douglas MacArthur after a series of insubordinate acts by the general.[79]

With UN forces again in retreat, journalists continued to graft World War II–era cultural standards onto the Korean conflict. A Universal newsreel in mid-December painted an ambiguous picture of the UN evacuation from North Korea. Over sprightly, martial music, the narrator described the bedraggled, miserable American GIs in cheerful tones: "This is the bitter fate of the Allied armies. . . . In the subzero weather [the marines] make camp, awaiting assurance of evacuation, knowing they will not be abandoned to a relentless foe. Rations and water are scarce, but these hard-bitten troops, facing a Korean Dunkirk [the site of a major evacuation of Allied forces during World War II], never lose faith in their own ability, and that of their air and sea comrades to keep fighting when the situation is blackest. . . . This is the pack-up for the beginning of evacuation, and the hope of survival." There was no shortage of grim language in the newsreel: the narrator spoke of the "badly shattered men" who had been wounded fighting "heroically, side by side, in this grim business," and men "frost-bitten beyond belief." Yet footage of smiling troops accompanied many of these passages. The ambiguity reached a climax at the end of the report: "Facing all the terror, the misery, of evacuation and actual death, they can still laugh it off."[80]

In similar fashion a *Combat Bulletin* from the signal corps found reason for hope at the "Frozen Chosin": the resilience and bravery of the Americans fighting there, even in retreat. The short film began with the well-known quote from Gen. Oliver Smith, First Marine Division: "We're not retreating, we're just advancing in a different direction." Other language from the narrator gave indications of the misery in Korea but always with a signature, hopeful twist. American troops were "tired, cold, and weary . . . but they know they will fight their way out of the trap." Drawing on popular imagery of the military during World War II, the narrator lauded the teamwork of American forces at the Chosin Reservoir: "No matter how cold and tired they may feel on the ground, the sight of these cargo planes, dropping their parachute loads from the skies, gives the men a sense of not being forgotten, a feeling that they are still part of a vast team, fighting together."[81] Clashing

with this optimistic tone were on-screen images: wounded men being evacuated by air; Americans burning their own equipment to prevent it from
falling into Chinese hands; disheveled troops eating Thanksgiving dinner
in their foxholes. Though his tone was chipper, the narrator did say, "General winter is allied with the Chinese in this operation," and spoke of "these
desperately tired men inch[ing] their way along." Indeed, the film seemed
to emphasize the buoyancy of UN forces as a corrective to rumors that some
men *did* feel forgotten or hopeless—a mood that the footage itself confirms.
As it turned out, the notion that GIs were forgotten by the home front would
eventually dominate the Korean War narrative.

It was doubtful that many American GIs were "laughing off" their miseries in Korea, as the Universal narrator had suggested on December 14.
Indeed, the well-reported tribulations of the American GI in Korea at the
end of 1950 made him a broadly sympathetic figure as 1951 began. In mid-
January *Newsweek* put on its cover a sole American GI, his head down, carrying a heavy load through the snow. The caption read, "GI in Korea: Again
the Road Back," in reference to the second major UN retreat in six months. [82]
Meanwhile *Time* magazine named the GI in Korea "Man of the Year." On the
cover, a determined soldier in a bleak landscape appeared above the caption,
"Name: American. Occupation: Fighting-man." The accompanying article
painted a dark picture of the GI's situation in Korea—and made him seem
the victim of myriad forces outside his control. [83]

American political leaders, according to *Time*, had let down the GI—the
government "had not given him weapons as numerous or as good as he
needed and had a right to expect," while Secretary of State Dean Acheson
"and his fellow diplomats of the free world had, in 1950, notably failed to
stop the march of communism." Military leadership had also failed: "The
best commander of the year, MacArthur, had blundered and been beaten."
That left the American fighting man as the year's real hero, if something of
a tragic one. Though some of these men had fought in Europe and Asia during World War II, *Time* suggested that Korea was somehow *different*: "Most
of the men in U.S. uniform around the world had enlisted voluntarily, but
few had taken to themselves the old, proud label of 'regular,' few had thought
they would fight, and fewer still had foreseen the incredibly dirty and desperate war that waited for them." The article included close-ups of almost
twenty American soldiers, striving to argue that individuality did not mean
an abandonment of teamwork, the great achievement of World War II. The
American GI "fights as he lives, a part of a vast, complicated machine—but
a thinking, deciding part, not an inert cog." *Time* admitted that these quali-

ties "seem to be contradictory." Once again, journalists of the early 1950s reckoned with the contradiction between memories of World War II and the realities of defeat and retreat in Korea.[84]

With gloomy images swirling in the winter of 1950–51, some military leaders countered with their own versions of the war. In January Lt. Gen. Robert L. Eichelberger, former commander of the Eighth Army, complained in *Newsweek* of the media's hasty reports of "tears" and "battle fatigue" among American soldiers. "Our lads have performed miracles in Korea," read an Eichelberger quote beneath a picture of shivering, but smiling, GIs.[85] In the same period the signal corps' *Combat Bulletin* film series seemed to respond directly to suggestions in the media that American forces were plagued by fatigue, low morale, disorganization, and lack of confidence in their officers: "Throughout Korea during the first week of February [1951], observers are noticing more and more the *high morale* evidenced by the UN soldiers. With *assured faith in their leaders*, and *confidence* in their own ability as a *fighting team*, the troops of fourteen nations forge ahead with the push northward toward the Han River and Seoul." Reviving many of the dominant, positive images of the World War II years, the film sounded almost desperate to reassure viewers that teamwork and high morale were intact in Korea. Meanwhile, however, the film's images of a crying American soldier, heavy combat, casualties, and exhausted GIs clashed with the narrator's confidence. Even the fatigue of soldiers, by now a stock image of the Korean War, received perhaps its most sanguine treatment to date: "Realizing the dangers of over-fatigue, these hardened soldiers have learned to take advantage of every opportunity to rest. Now, well accustomed to the strenuous conditions of battle, the men group together in a well-earned sleep."[86] Invoking a notion of the World War II era, this signal corps production indicated that soldiers became hardened, not weakened, by combat.[87]

Other imagery, meanwhile, suggested otherwise. In the first six months of 1951 popular magazines reported war's psychological impact with a candor exceeding almost all treatments of the subject during World War II. *Newsweek*'s editors, in their issue of March 19, 1951, showed the change overtaking many GIs in Korea. An article on the war features a smiling soldier standing above the caption, "Before battle: A jaunty Marine grins." On the right, another picture shows a second leatherneck, dejected and exhausted, leaning on his rifle butt. He covers his eyes, either trying to sleep (standing up), or hiding his tears. The caption reads, "After battle: A weary Marine rests."[88] Nowhere was the downward spiral of the human spirit in battle so visually explicit as in this before-and-after feature.

In June a *Saturday Evening Post* story presented a similar version of combat's effect on its participants. Lt. Col. Melvin Russell Blair's piece, "I Send Your Son Into Battle," contained blunt images of men under the strain of combat. The first photograph showed an "exhausted" GI staggering away from a skirmish, helped through the pouring rain by two comrades, above the caption, "A short time ago he was a boy in T shirt and blue jeans." These words invited readers to grieve over war's corruption of youth, whereas World War II iconography had imagined combat as an edifying rite of passage. On the next page a soldier held his head in his hands in a posture of grief. "The reaction after the battle," read the caption. "The young soldier lived through it, and is shocked."[89] Late in World War II comparable images of battle-fatigued soldiers had crept into popular media coverage, as in the publication in *Life* magazine of Tom Lea's famous painting of a marine locked in a "2,000-yard stare." But now, such images were a mainstay of Korean War coverage. What was once the exception had become the rule.

In the meantime, NAACP officials continued to challenge the poor reputation of the black fighting man in Korea. Two weeks into 1951, Thurgood Marshall, taking time away from his efforts to desegregate American schools, traveled to Japan and Korea to investigate the numerous courts-martial against African American troops. Issued a weapon for his own protection against remaining North Korean guerrillas, Marshall discovered that most of the charges stemmed from alleged violations of the "75th Article of War," the provision against "misbehavior" in the presence of the enemy. Aimed at cowardice, the measure often ended up punishing offenses such as sleeping on duty. Marshall concluded that white soldiers were overwhelmingly acquitted of cowardice charges, while blacks, facing a predominantly white officer command, received sentences ranging from three years in prison to death. By the spring Marshall and the NAACP had succeeded in reducing the sentences of twenty black soldiers.[90]

In June 1951, however, a long feature in the *Saturday Evening Post* pictured black soldiers in a manner that seemed to justify much of the disciplinary action against them. While it characterized the African American regiment, the Twenty-fourth, as a laughable military unit, the article also made a case for integration by lauding the ability of black soldiers mixed in amongst whites. The piece attacked continuing segregation not on egalitarian grounds but on military ones. After all, "the Army is not interested in social reform." In a survey of white officers who had commanded the Twenty-fourth, "all were agreed that the only way to make efficient use of the Negro infantryman is to integrate him into the line companies without regard to his race."[91] Much of the piece acknowledged the racism that permeated the army and American society, but made the white officers seem reasonable men only interested in developing effective fighting units.

If this article made a case for integration, in doing so it perpetuated common stereotypes about the black GI. Much of the language recalled notions that blacks were lazy, incompetent, and cowardly. One officer told the *Post* that black soldiers "had a fear of darkness, of the unknown, that they just could not conquer." In a night attack, white officers could never be sure if their black charges would stand or run. Fleeing the battlefield, they said, was a rampant problem, and blacks would "abandon any equipment which was heavy or troublesome." More basic shortcomings abounded as well. "Keeping the Negro soldier awake," the article went, "is one of the most harassing problems his leaders have come to deal with." Even the black vernacular attracted criticism. White officers banned black phrases such as "the Deuce-Fo'," insisting they call their unit the "Fighting Twenty-fourth" to improve morale. One white commander found that the blacks' singing had a "rhythm to it that pleased him," but when he heard that their song was called the "Bugout Boogie" he ordered them to stop. In GI parlance, "bugout" meant retreat.[92]

Though the piece perpetuated racial stereotypes, it acknowledged that racism contributed to poor military performance. As one black captain told the *Post*, "The trouble is, you take a man who in his own country has always been treated as a second-class citizen, and you call upon him to fight as a first-class soldier. You talk to him about democracy, and liberty, and how these things are worth fighting for. But the words don't mean the same to him as they mean to a white soldier who has always been free."[93] Like much else in Korean War iconography, the article invited some degree of sympathy with the black GI, trapped as he was in a predicament with a long legacy. From the nineteenth century through the war in Vietnam, black participation in American wars was cloaked in irony. After a century of fighting wars on two fronts, African American soldiers were to see their anger boil over toward the end of the Vietnam War—albeit in a climate of increased racial activism cultivated during the 1960s. In Korea a limited version of the same anger festered among black warriors.

Consequently, observers in the military were coming around to the integrationist view in the middle of 1951, with racial mixing in the army already under way. Gen. Matthew Ridgway called for desegregation in April, and an army study, "Project Clear," found in the summer that true to the *Post*'s impression, blacks in integrated units were more effective soldiers than those in segregated ones. The survey also found that white officers had accepted integration as the necessary means to achieving military efficiency. In October 1951 the army integrated the storied Twenty-fourth almost a century after its birth in 1866. By the armistice of 1953 only eighty-eight all-black units remained of the nearly four hundred that had existed in June 1950, and the NAACP embraced the change.[94] (See figure 11.) In the last two years of the war, blacks served in combat units on a more equal footing with whites than ever before in American history—and often wartime media showed them doing so.[95] Much had changed in the short time since World War II.

––––––––––

The title of a signal corps *Combat Bulletin* film summed up the fourth and final phase of the war: "Stalemate in Korea."[96] For two years—from July 1951 to July 1953—the UN and the communists fought an agonizing war along the 38th parallel while diplomats negotiated in the tiny village of Panmunjom. By the summer of 1951, the United States had increased its ground forces in Korea to 250,000 men; the figure would grow to 300,000 by the armistice.[97] Occasional military forays kept medics on both sides busy as the two foes sought to strengthen their bargaining positions. Like before, disquieting imagery emanating from Korea stemmed in large measure from the nature of the conflict, which in 1951–53 seemed difficult to rationalize. Popular support remained relatively steady at the lower levels to which it had sunk after the Chinese attack.[98]

Meanwhile, away from the battlefields of Korea the Cold War raged on. In late 1951 President Truman established the National Security Agency; Congress pledged $7 billion for foreign aid; and Greece and Turkey joined the North Atlantic Treaty Organization (NATO). The Soviet Union exploded two more atomic weapons, officially announced its alliance with communist China, and received public thanks from Kim Il-Sung for its material aid to the North Koreans. The prospects for peace in the fall of 1951 were slim as envoys from both sides converged on the new tent city at Panmunjom.

By early 1953, however, several events shook the two sides out of the stalemate. Dwight D. Eisenhower assumed the presidency in January with promises to get the United States out of Korea, and in March Joseph Stalin died suddenly of a cerebral hemorrhage. Many observers were cheered the same month by North Korea's abrupt offer to exchange sick and wounded prisoners of war. After a brief communist military offensive, meaningful armistice talks were underway again by the summer of 1953. On the morning of July 27, with artillery fire audible in the distance, generals from both sides entered a special building constructed for the truce. Without uttering a word of greeting, the men signed several copies of the armistice agreement. It

FIGURE 11. *Integrated machine-gun unit north of the Chongchon River, November 20, 1950. Partial desegregation of the army by the end of 1950 brought together blacks and whites in fighting units, as shown here in the Second Infantry Division. Courtesy of National Archives.*

took just twelve minutes to halt the hostilities that had wreaked devastation on the small country for three years. [99]

In the spring of 1951, as the Korean War was settling into a stalemate, photographer Edward Steichen unveiled his third war-related exhibit in a decade at the Museum of Modern Art (MoMA) in New York. Joining his efforts from 1942 (Road to Victory) and 1945 (Power in the Pacific) was a new show, Faces of Korea (alternately called Korea—The Impact of War). The photographic exhibit embodied all the elements of the updated warrior image: fatigue, misery, stoicism, and physical agony. Close-ups of the faces of soldiers gave the show its name. Many of the pictures were the work of Carl Mydans, David Douglas Duncan, Hank Walker, J. R. Eyerman, and Ralph Crane of *Life* magazine; some came from Max Desfor of the Associated Press; and others represented the efforts of navy, signal corps, and air force photographers. [100] After running at MoMA from February to April, Faces of Korea toured the country in the summer. [101] Meanwhile, Duncan, a former marine, published many of the same images in his book of 1951, *This Is War!* which was released a year after the North Korean invasion. Some of the Duncan photos also had run in *Life* magazine's issue of September 18, 1950.

A large number of these pictures showed American soldiers in states of despondency. The working titles of photographs in Faces of Korea suggested the emphasis on misery: "Senselessness and Brutality; Badley [sic] wounded medic shot and left for dead; Exhausted American soldier on the Taegu front; Two wounded men with clasped hands; Army medical officer collapses at death of one of his staff wounded in action; Eyes of Marine; Crying jeep driver; Three men looking at their dead friends; The Living walk—the dead ride; Hands of corpse coming through snow." [102] Scores of other photographs captured similar scenes of death and destruction. Steichen showed little of the lighter side of war so often included in World War II iconography, including his own exhibitions of 1942 and 1945. Sadness dominated *This Is War!* and Faces of Korea, in which whole sections were devoted to close-ups of men crying. Two such sequences were especially heartbreaking.

Just after the landing at Inchon a jeep carrying several wounded American GIs had run over a land mine. "Parts of machine and men were blasted over a wide area," Duncan's caption in Faces of Korea read, "one Marine killed, and three others terribly wounded." The words continued, "The driver was among the wounded, and was crying heart-brokenly—not because of his wounds but because the dead Marine had been his buddy, and now he felt responsible for the other man's death. Of course, it wasn't his fault, yet the driver's sorrow over the tragedy reflects something of the marine's magnificent spirit—it is the interdependence of men, men who place unquestioning faith in the man in the adjoining foxhole."[103] Photos of the crying driver and another man with tears streaking his face followed a picture of the wrecked jeep and the American corpse. The sequence ended (in both the book and the photo exhibit) with a shot of the wounded men departing in another jeep. One man's face still shows his tears, and all the soldiers look pensive. "Wounded and broken," wrote Duncan in *This Is War!* "each lost in his thoughts, each still alive, that isolated group of men represented all other men, perhaps civilization itself."[104]

The second story offered a rare glimpse of how GIs in the field reacted to seeing themselves in the media. A photo of a soldier crying had appeared in *Life* back in September 1950, part of Duncan's spread depicting the battle for No Name Ridge. Cpl. Leonard Hayworth had descended from the ridge, where all but two of his squad had perished, and broke into tears of frustration and anger before Duncan's camera.[105] (See figure 12.) A few weeks after the picture ran in *Life* magazine Hayworth's buddies discovered it and showed it to him. Duncan was on hand again when Hayworth saw it for himself, and he described the scene in *This Is War!* several months later: "Corporal Leonard Hayworth had been first embarrassed, then good-naturedly shy when shown his pictures made earlier in the month down along the Naktong River. Surrounded by his buddies—it was nearly dark—he said nothing." Not everyone present kept silent. An older soldier exclaimed, "Lousy goddamned picture. Hell! We all cry sometime."[106] The man seemed to accept such shows of emotion, yet believed they should not be paraded before American audiences.

Perhaps compounding the offense (at least for that grizzled marine), Duncan snapped a picture of Hayworth looking at himself in *Life*. Now, in *Faces of Korea*, audiences saw *that* photo. If the initial shot of Hayworth crying was heartrending, this one surpassed it for a different reason. The caption told viewers Hayworth had been killed the morning after seeing his picture.[107]

Other stark imagery abounded. A picture of Ike Fenton, a marine captain at No Name Ridge, appeared in both *Faces of Korea* and *This Is War!* One of the more memorable images of the Korean War, Duncan's photo caught Fenton at the moment he realized his men were out of ammunition. (See figure 13.) His eyes convey all the frustration, misery, and stoicism of American warriors in Korea, an effect heightened by the fact that Fenton stares directly into Duncan's lens.[108] Not only did the picture appear in the MoMA exhibit and Duncan's book, it had also appeared in *Life*'s issue of September 18, 1950. Four years later, Fenton's piercing gaze would resurface in another MoMA installation, the enormously popular Family of Man exhibit.

FIGURE 12. *Cpl. Leonard Hayworth breaks into tears*, Life, *September 18, 1950. Hayworth descended from No Name Ridge, where all but two of his squad had perished, and broke into tears of frustration before David Douglas Duncan's camera. The morning after seeing this picture of himself in Life, Hayworth was killed. Courtesy of David Douglas Duncan and the Photography Collection, Harry Ransom Humanities Research Center, University of Texas at Austin.*

FIGURE 13. *Capt. Ike Fenton learns he is out of ammunition,* Life, *September 18, 1950. The eyes of this marine conveyed the frustration, fatigue, and stoicism of American warriors in Korea. Courtesy of David Douglas Duncan and the Photography Collection, Harry Ransom Humanities Research Center, University of Texas at Austin.*

Steichen's panoramic show on the human experience was viewed in its ten different editions well into the 1960s. [109]

Faces of Korea and *This Is War!* elicited strong reactions from reviewers and audiences. Charles Simmons of the *New York Times* grasped Duncan's innovations: "Duncan has done for Korea what none of the hundreds of men with cameras achieved in World War II." [110] Reviewers appreciated the stark portrayal of human suffering and the new focus on the *individual* GI in Duncan's book. Critic Orville Prescott wrote, "What it means for the individual American soldiers who are fighting and dying there for the rest of us is vividly revealed in these terrible and beautiful photographs." [111] In Charlottesville, Virginia, a university paper suggested that viewers of the exhibit "will undoubtedly renew Sherman's conviction that 'war is hell'" and praised the show's revelation that war was a "terror to soldiers and civilians alike." The *Miami Herald* hoped that if Faces of Korea would not actually stamp out war, it would at least take "the first feeble step in that direction." [112]

Yet Steichen believed that viewers of his exhibition were missing the point—or at least forgetting it. He meant for Faces of Korea to incite a hatred of war, which he called a "horrible monstrosity" and a "butcher shop." As he put it in a press release, Steichen wanted to shock people out of complacency: "Human nobility, compassion, devotion, inexhaustible endurance, senselessness and brutality are scrambled together under the impact of war. Here photography, *bridging remoteness and apathy*, dumps a place and a moment called, 'Korea' right into our laps. . . . Here are photographs with something important to say and they say it." [113] The images in the MoMA exhibit shocked audiences, but Steichen thought such revulsion was short lived. People would report to him the deep impression the photos had left, but then "go out and have some drinks," in Steichen's words. [114] A publicity report for the show hinted at this problem when it quoted a viewer in Miami, who reacted to the grim photos by exclaiming, "And we complain about the heat. I'm ashamed." [115] It seemed, at least to Steichen, that Americans were already forgetting the suffering in Korea, and there was little his pictures could do about it. "I had failed to accomplish my mission," he wrote a decade later. Visitors "left the exhibition and promptly forgot it." [116]

Whatever their reception, Steichen's three war-related photographic exhibits suggested an evolving grimness in war iconography, particularly in their portrayal of the dead and wounded. [117] Road to Victory had revealed little of the underside of war in 1942, preferring to focus on American might and purpose. Three years later, Power in the Pacific also emphasized American military strength but hinted at the human cost in a few depictions of dead, wounded, and battle-fatigued soldiers. In Faces of Korea, nearly every warrior image conveyed agony. The show's guiding antiwar impulse hinted at something that was to become much more prominent during the Vietnam War: an image maker such as Steichen could grow cynical about the war itself, or all war generally, but remain a steadfast supporter of the troops themselves. In this case "support" meant broadcasting the suffering and stoicism of the individual GI. Pyle and Mauldin had done the same for the World War II dogface. But in the context of an unpopular, stalemated war, depicting the soldier in this way suggested that he might be a victim of his leaders in the field and in Washington.

True to Steichen's impression, during 1951 the GI in Korea would begin to fade from the American imagination. Bill Mauldin articulated the victim image in 1952, writing about the fate of the American GI in Korea: "He fights a battle in which his best friends get killed and if an account of the action gets printed at all in his home town paper, it appears on page 17 under a Lux ad. There won't be a victory parade for his return because he'll come home quietly and alone, on rotation, and there's no victory in the old-fashioned sense, anyway, because this isn't that kind of war. It's a slow, grinding, lonely, bitched-up war."[118] Mauldin was right that journalists were paying less and less attention to American troops. In February 1952 *Time* magazine stopped running its weekly "War in Asia" feature, a fixture of the magazine since July 1950. Senator Harry Cain of Washington, a vigorous critic of Korean War policy, told interviewers on television late in 1951, "In the last three or four months, one has generally found it necessary to refer to the middle sections of our American press to determine our American losses."[119] On the whole, Cain charged, the media was much more diligent in reporting enemy body counts. Newsreels in particular were certainly guilty of this offense.

Some observers in late 1951 came to believe that the American public was failing to support the troops in Korea, a charge that was to resurface in the last few years of the Vietnam War. The same television interviewer asked Senator Cain in October 1951 whether the country was "keeping faith" with the American soldiers "fighting hand-to-hand battles on the heartbreak ridges." Cain answered with obvious emotion: "I must speak very personally in answer to that question, as an American. I feel that we have not begun, at home, politically, and among our people, to make contributions, and to give the kind of support which justifies the blood which young Americans are shedding so willingly in Korea. To me, it's the tragedy of my lifetime, sir."[120] Cain and other conservatives were highly critical of Truman's limited war in Korea, some (including Cain) calling for use of the atomic bomb. Senator Joseph McCarthy of Wisconsin also leveled such criticisms at the administration as part of his wider assault on alleged communists and timid foreign policy makers. On the same television program that Cain visited, McCarthy couched his disapproval of war policy in terms of its abandonment of the men fighting in Korea: "I assume that many American mothers who have lost sons will now wonder why we didn't follow Gen. Douglas MacArthur's sensible theory of hitting back. As you know, [Dean] Acheson's argument, and [George] Marshall's argument, was that if we hit back, if we tried to win that war, we might make the Chinese communists mad. Now, why we should worry about making someone mad who is blowing the heads off our boys I don't know."[121] This sort of language prefigured the charges that some conservatives leveled at Lyndon Johnson in the late 1960s, when the United States pursued another limited war in Asia. How could our fighting men win, critics of both wars claimed, with one hand tied behind their backs?

One of the most outspoken champions of the American soldier in Korea was the popular novelist James Michener. In a *Saturday Evening Post* article of May 1952, "The Forgotten Heroes of Korea," Michener touted the courage of Americans in Korea as he rebuked the public for its short memory: "We forget. Even those of us who know better forget that today, in the barren wastes of Korea, American men are dying with a heroism never surpassed in our history. Because they are so few, we forget that they contribute so much."[122] Forty years later Michener's views on Korea had not budged. He wrote in his memoirs that during the war "we assured the general public: 'Don't inconvenience yourself. Don't even pause in whatever you're doing. Make a bundle. There's no war.'" By that time Michener's uneasiness with the "immoral aspects of the Korean War"—namely the incomplete dedication of American society to the war—had already resurfaced in his opposition to the Vietnam War.[123] As a liberal Democrat who would run unsuccessfully for Congress in 1962, Michener came from a different ideological place than conservatives such as Cain and McCarthy, but the three men shared a commitment to the forgotten American serviceman.

Central to Michener's account in 1952 was a group of naval pilots whose work, he felt, was no more important than anyone else's in Korea but who merited attention for the "absolute kind of courage" their effort required.[124] In the summer of 1950 journalists often had linked the valor of Americans in Korea to their dire military situation and the miserable terrain of the country. By 1952, in Michener's telling, American fliers in Korea were heroic not just for their aerial exploits, but also because they labored and risked their lives without the support of the home front. Michener drew the comparison with World War II directly, saying of the naval pilots: "I hold their heroism to be greater than what I witnessed in 1941–45, for then the soldier on Guadalcanal could feel that his entire nation was behind him, dedicated to the job to which he was dedicated. Civilian and soldier alike bore the burden." To Michener the men in Korea "seem to fight in a vacuum, as if America didn't care a damn." Here Michener painted the American serviceman as a lone hero, wholly different from the team player of World War II mythology. Thus the sense that these warriors were isolated and forgotten joined portrayals of their fatigue, distress, and stoicism. "When the men of Marsh Beebe's squadrons go forth to hold the enemy," wrote Michener, "they are, I am ashamed to say, alone."[125] The American public, apparently, was finding it increasingly difficult to stomach the violence and death in Korea, perhaps because the stalemated war's origins lacked the threatening and grimly motivational qualities of the Japanese attack on Pearl Harbor in 1941. In fact, as John Mueller has shown, Americans were more likely to support the Korean War when pollsters reminded them of the "communist invasion" of South Korea; without such prompting, respondents were more inclined to view American intervention as a mistake.[126]

Michener also objected to the prevalent notion that Americans fought in Korea bereft of a greater purpose. It was always doubtful, even during World War II, that soldiers on the ground ever fought for anything more than the guy next to them or hopes of survival. But many image makers of World War II had endowed GIs with a sense of purpose now woefully lacking, in Michener's estimation, in comparable portraits of the soldier in Korea: "It is difficult in these cynical days to state in simple words that young men fly dangerous missions to sometimes certain death because they believe that what their country is doing is right. But that is the simple truth." A crotchety admiral echoed Michener's view: "These damned fools who are always saying modern young men are no good. . . . They ought to see the men aboard this carrier." These observers believed that the soldiers fighting in Korea were every bit as dedicated to a cause as their now-mythic forbears of World War II.[127]

Michener's portrait of that admiral, John Perry, demonstrated the author's efforts to restore a sense of respect for military leaders. His article lacked any indication that officers bungled or lacked compassion for their men. "In case I haven't made the point clear," Michener wrote, "Admiral Perry and Marsh Beebe keep a close watch on their men." Perry was the "epitome of the historic crusty, taciturn Navy man," an ornery character who was "a holy terror to inefficiency, and one of our greatest living air admirals."

Beebe, who led a squadron of fliers, was "rugged, tough and willing," could apparently fly any plane, and had, in Korea and the last war, destroyed more than his share of enemy aircraft. His men—pilots below him in the pecking order—called him the "greatest of the follow-me boys." Airmen would stick with Beebe in all sorts of perilous situations. For his part, Beebe minded his pilots like sons. It was said aboard the aircraft carrier, "He flies every inch of the way with us. He makes every landing. This guy dies in every crash."[128]

His time with naval pilots would eventually result in Michener's novella *The Bridges at Toko-Ri*, a major work of the Korean War published in 1953 both as a book and in its entirety in *Life* magazine (it also became a Hollywood film in 1954). Like the *Post* article, the novella suggested that soldiers, not war, deserved commemoration. "All wars are stupid," growled a salty admiral, perhaps modeled after John Perry. "But we'd better learn to handle the stupidity."[129] In 1952, though, Michener used the pages of the *Saturday Evening Post* to drum up support for the men slogging through the Korean War. The author surely hoped that Americans would mimic the habit of naval pilots, who greeted every returning flier with the greeting, "Welcome Home, Hero."[130]

As the warring parties signed the armistice of July 1953, little land had changed hands. To many Americans, the Korean War seemed a colossal waste of time, money, and especially lives. Through three years of fighting, more than 2 million civilians suffered death or injury as four armies churned over the landscape. The South Korean military suffered casualties (dead and wounded) numbering some 270,000, while the Chinese and North Koreans bore over 1.5 million. The United States lost 54,000 dead and more than 100,000 wounded.[131] In terms of casualties per year, the "police action" in Korea was far costlier to the United States than the Vietnam War. Like the conflicts that preceded and followed it, Korea produced a sizable population of veterans, injured men, and returning POWs. Five million Americans served on active duty during the Korean War, almost a third of the figure for World War II.[132]

Reporters covering the brief but bloody war in Korea revived—but also amplified—some of the image-making practices of World War II. Toward the end of that war journalists had begun to reveal the agonies and ambiguities of combat to audiences that had previously seen lots of smiling soldiers and little of the dead and wounded. Also in 1944–45, image makers in the press had suggested to a limited degree that warfare might psychologically damage GIs. If the media during World War II had *hinted* that soldiers might be sad, stoic, fatigued, and shocked, reporters in Korea made those themes central to their dispatches. It was likely they would do so, given the great difficulties of American troops in the beginning of the war as well as the lack of formal censorship of the media.

Although press coverage of the Second World War had hinted at the deleterious effects of warfare, the majority of images in the 1940s ascribed to the GI traditional soldierly virtues: responsibility, honor, sacrifice, and teamwork. Government propagandists as well as journalists continued to describe soldiers with unflagging toughness, bravery, and confidence, though they showed more dead and wounded after 1943. This was the stoic citizen-soldier, the masculine hero, of World War II mythology. He did not shed tears, and he did not shy away from a challenge. He was part of a vast, democratic effort and proud of it.

Journalists in Korea added complexity to the warrior image. By showing a greater degree of discouragement, sorrow, agony, and fear, these image makers widened the definition of the masculine, American fighter.[133] When reporters showed a GI in Korea crying, often alone, they did so without questioning his toughness, making sensitivity seem an acceptable and even desirable male attribute. They helped expand the terms of manliness for these visible, traditionally masculine members of American society. No longer a cultural hero just because of his contribution to a worthy collective effort, now the individual American GI was valorized in the media for his *suffering* as well.[134]

And for his suffering, the serviceman in Korea sometimes seemed the victim of American policy makers and military leaders. First he was pulled from cushy occupation duty in Japan, or civilian life in the United States, or a well-deserved rest after service in World War II. Then, as the media reported, he was thrust into battle ill equipped and ill trained. As the training and weaponry improved the weather turned arctic, and the Chinese entered the war despite public assurances from the military brass that they would not. Finally, the GI continued to fight even as the American public forgot about him. Journalists and other observers such as Steichen and Michener, who depicted the American serviceman as a victim, drew a sharp line between the war effort itself and the men fighting it. They identified with and supported the troops, even as they lost enthusiasm for the war. In fact, as their cynicism about the Korean conflict grew, they may have become *more* sympathetic toward the individuals on the front lines, since now those men seemed to be toiling in a war of questionable value and scant public endorsement. Despite widespread and enduring charges to the contrary, a similar blend of support (for the troops) and skepticism (about the war) was to characterize antiwar activists and eventually journalists and filmmakers of the Vietnam era.

The soldier in Korea, then, was heroic precisely because he struggled against long odds and miserable conditions, and later in the war, because he fought against a backdrop of apathy and forgetfulness in the United States. That updated warrior image surely both reflected and shaped the cynicism some Americans felt about the ability of their leaders to manage the armed forces and foreign policy, long before the war in Vietnam would make cynicism a household word.

CHAPTER 5

THE TRUE STORY OF THE FOOT SOLDIER, 1951-1966

To children of the 1950s, it seemed that every uncle or neighbor was a veteran of the armed forces. Almost all able-bodied young men had entered the service during World War II, and from the Korean War through the late 1950s roughly 70 percent of all draft-age males served in the military.[1] By 1954 there were more living veterans in the United States, some 20 million, than ever before in American history.[2] A collection of interviews with World War II vets would later be called *The Hero Next Door*, capturing both the ubiquity and the mythic stature of ex-servicemen in the postwar period.[3] The great outpouring of predictions, prescriptions, and concerns that met the veterans of World War II had largely subsided by 1950. When no comparable discussion greeted the smaller population of 5 million Korean War–era vets, it would be left to the purveyors of culture to craft the image of the American fighting man.[4]

Conflicting memories of war circulated in American culture of the 1950s, just as they perhaps did in the minds of these millions of veterans. Battlefield names such as Normandy, Anzio, Guadalcanal, Iwo Jima, and the Bulge still evoked a hushed reverence, as would Korea's Heartbreak Ridge and the Chosin Reservoir after 1953.[5] In the spring of 1950 the Dutch Masters cigar company called to mind America's martial history in a national magazine advertisement addressed to veterans. The sanguine tone was meant to remind readers of the two world wars: "When the boys gather around to swap yarns about the past, from Chateau Thierry to Okinawa, the heart-warming goodness of fine Dutch Masters cigars is there to enchant the memory, making the comradeships—not the hardships—easiest to remember."[6] In fact, the hardships were many in a place such as Okinawa, and it was doubtful that a good cigar could "enchant the memory" of them. In a self-proclaimed "guide book to their own memories," marine veterans recalled in 1947 a different version of warfare on that island: "Men died here not in great concentrations as on Iwo [Jima] or at Anzio [Italy]. But they died, and their deaths were very close, because you knew them personally. There was a sharp pain in your side when you heard about 'Pappy' or 'Ski' being cut to pieces by machine-gun bullets. It was even sharper and deeper when you saw them go down, their arms flopping crazily as they fell."[7] These two ways of remembering war—one nostalgic, one somber—grappled vividly within American popular culture in the 1950s. Sometimes one overwhelmed the other; sometimes they coexisted; and sometimes they vied for center stage in, say, a particular movie or novel. Such competing mythologies marked many cultural depictions of World War II and Korea produced in the 1950s and early 1960s—but they were partly just reflections of a wider series of tensions in Cold War culture.[8]

Historians have long understood that social tensions pervaded a decade popularly known for conformity and consensus. The campaign to desegregate southern schools was meeting stiff, often violent resistance from local whites, especially after the *Brown v. Board of Education* decisions of 1954–55. White people, North and South, were often hostile to the idea of blacks moving into their neighborhoods. Senator Joseph McCarthy and other anticommunists were leading smear campaigns against members of the government, Hollywood figures, and ordinary citizens. Some Americans worried about the effects of televised violence on children, and, indeed, juvenile delinquency seemed a bigger problem than ever before. And in a shameful episode, officials in the army questioned the loyalty of prisoners of war returning from Korea to the United States in the mid-1950s.[9] Looming over all these troubles, finally, was the threat of nuclear war with the Soviet Union. Despite a skyrocketing standard of living, anxieties about the military, war, and government bureaucracy roiled in American life.

Particularly during the Korean conflict Americans voiced concerns over their leaders' handling of the Cold War. In January 1951, a bad month for United Nations forces in Korea, pollsters found that 30 percent of respondents believed the Soviet Union was winning the Cold War, against just 9 percent who thought the United States ahead. Around the same time 64 percent of those surveyed supported legislation that would prevent the president from sending troops overseas without congressional approval— surely a reflection of growing displeasure with Harry Truman's failure to consult Congress before committing American soldiers to Korea. Six months later almost half of Americans polled felt their nation was unprepared to fight an "all-out war" with Russia. More disturbing was Gallup's finding late in 1951 showing that almost 60 percent of Americans believed the United States was "behind" in its production of defense materials, attributed by most respondents to "politics, poor management, [and] bad supervision" within the halls of government. Forty-three percent of Americans late in 1952 felt intervening in Korea had been a mistake; only 37 percent still supported that decision.[10]

When the former supreme commander of the Allied Expeditionary Forces secured the presidency in November 1952, it seemed that flagging faith in government and military revived almost overnight. Most Americans instinctively trusted Dwight D. Eisenhower, his approval rating reaching

70 and even 80 percent for much of his presidency. And when that figure dipped to 54 percent in 1958, a recession year, Eisenhower nonetheless continued to dominate the Gallup Poll's "most admired man" distinction, as he had since World War II.[11] The influential columnist Joseph Alsop, writing in the *Saturday Evening Post* in January 1953, hopefully explained both the anxieties of the American people and Ike's role in assuaging them: "There are many problems, many dangers, and, one fears, many sacrifices ahead of us. But there are no problems which cannot be solved, no dangers which cannot be avoided and no sacrifices which will not be willingly made by an America with leadership worthy of this great country. If anyone is such a leader, Dwight D. Eisenhower should be."[12] Partly reflecting that sort of confidence, almost three-quarters of Americans continued to support the idea of universal military training throughout the 1950s, and large majorities also tended to favor increased defense spending.[13]

If support for the military grew after 1952 as a result of confidence in the national leadership, it relied just as heavily on profound, persistent fears of another world war. Throughout the Truman and Eisenhower presidencies Americans reported to pollsters that the "most important problem" facing the country was, variably, "war and foreign policy," "the Korean War" (the overwhelming choice early in 1953 when it was allegedly a forgotten conflict), "maintaining world peace," "keeping the peace," the "threat of war," "dealing with Russia," "keeping out of war," and the "East-West fight." Only in the wake of the Little Rock crisis in the fall of 1957 did "integration" and "racial problems" briefly, and barely, supplant world peace as the most pressing issues in the eyes of Americans. In 1954 almost 60 percent of those asked believed there was "much danger" of another world war, while the next summer over 70 percent of respondents in their twenties believed there would be a new global conflict within their lifetimes.[14]

The Cold War, then, generated an uneasy mixture of confidence in the military establishment and concern over world peace. As Tom Engelhardt has written, the period featured a discordant blend of "arcadia and apocalypse." Alan Brinkley has agreed that tensions existed between the "smooth surface of postwar middle-class culture" and the "discontents festering below its surface."[15] Christian Appy has argued in an article on "sentimental militarism" that popular films of the 1950s expressed Cold War values of unity and deference, on the one hand, and a burgeoning discomfort with militarization on the other. If sentimental militarism, as Appy has defined it, celebrated the democratic value of military service, the patriotic and heroic undertones of combat, and the peace-loving nature of American soldiers, now all of those elements—once dominant during World War II—would meet challenges in American culture. "While World War II succeeded in producing some classic works of sentimental militarism," Appy has concluded, "these formulas could not be transferred to the Cold War without revealing significant strains."[16]

One of those strains—hardly new, and visible during World War II—pitted a reverence for military authority against the notion that GIs might be victims of war, their officers, or army life more broadly. In the place of sentimental militarism arose tributes to the individual American fighting man caught in the maelstrom of war, separate from—*and sometimes opposed to*—the collective military and government structures he represented. This version of the warrior image recalled Bill Mauldin's sketches of the grumbling Willie and Joe, but without the good humor, triumphalism, and emphasis on teamwork blanketing American culture during World War II.

Yet Cold War anxieties go only partway toward explaining this strain of 1950s culture. By mid-decade both the Hollywood studio system and the production codes that had governed cinematic content since the 1930s were breaking down, making room for independent films and more diverse renderings of American life.[17] The undeclared, unpopular, stalemated war in Korea, as well, invited grimmer visions of armed conflict and American soldiers. A sampling of fiction, poetry, Hollywood films, and a popular television series from the 1950s and 1960s—some, but not all, taking the Korean War as their subject—shows a grittier combat soldier vying with the more familiar sentimentalized GI of the World War II years.

The resurgence of World War II combat pictures, inaugurated by *Sands of Iwo Jima* in 1949, continued into the 1950s alongside the release of a lesser number of movies on the Korean War.[18] Television stations began airing older movies from the war years, just as producers were creating new shows about the heroes of World War II. The foot soldier—not the general or admiral or veteran—was the focal point of this burgeoning wave of war films. An article in *Time* magazine on the revival of combat pictures announced in June 1950 that fourteen new films currently in production would commit themselves to "glorifying the U.S. soldier, sailor, marine and airman."[19] The military bureaucracy, however, was to have a hand in the image-making process. To obtain technical support from the various branches of the armed forces, movie projects had to meet the approval of the Defense Department's Public Affairs Office.[20] It was up to each individual filmmaker to decide whether garnering official endorsement—"voluntary censorship," in the words of one scholar—was worth compromising one's artistic license.[21]

As United Nations forces struggled against the Chinese and North Koreans in January 1951, moviegoers halfway around the globe in the United States were buying tickets for the first Korean War film. Within just a few months of the start of the war, Hollywood producers had been scrambling to make movies about the ever-changing conflict, and now, with the release of *The Steel Helmet*, Americans got a dramatic glimpse of what all the headlines were about.[22] While other early projects were hampered by ignorance of the Korean landscape (one film, *Rookie From Korea*, was set in a jungle until the army told the producer there were no jungles in Korea), independent director Samuel Fuller sidestepped that problem by setting much of the action of *The Steel Helmet* inside a Buddhist temple.[23] Critically and commercially successful, the low-budget film sent a potent antiwar message—and established ways of picturing the foot soldier that would resurface throughout the decade.[24]

The film's opening words—"This story is dedicated to the United States Infantry"—show that *individuals*, not the larger purpose of the war or the military bureaucracy, occupy the narrative center of the movie.[25] As the film journal *Variety* put it, *The Steel Helmet* followed "the current vogue of concentrating on the personal involvement of a small group, rather than encompassing whole armies at war," thereby muting the World War II–era emphasis on collectivity. That publication, which offered advice to theater owners, called the picture "a sure money film."[26]

The Steel Helmet featured an updated version of the multiethnic platoons seen in so many World War II films. James Edwards played an African American medic, just as the real-life army was in the throes of desegregation. A Nisei, or second-generation Japanese American (Richard Loo), joins him as the second of the two steadiest characters in the film. A young Korean boy, known affectionately as Short Round, tags along with the unit. Other characters include the mandatory Brooklynite, a spineless officer, and a conscientious objector from World War II. At the center of this motley crew is the renegade Sergeant Zack (Gene Evans), an outsider who joins the other soldiers after his own unit is massacred. In a long line of cynical soldiers with hidden hearts—stretching from John Wayne's Sergeant Stryker (1949) to Tom Hanks's Capt. John Miller in *Saving Private Ryan* (1998)—Sergeant Zack surely stands as one of the most grizzled, sarcastic, tough-yet-sensitive men ever to fight on the silver screen.

This hodgepodge outfit, cut off from its command, spends most of the movie garrisoned inside a Buddhist temple, fighting off a larger contingent of North Korean troops. Throughout the film these men teeter on the edge of rationality, fight brutally amongst themselves, grapple with matters of race and ethnicity, commit atrocities against prisoners of war, and question military authority in an every-man-for-himself sort of conflict—all elements of the de-romanticized warrior image ascendant in the 1950s.[27]

If other films, novels, and media accounts about war since the late 1940s had celebrated the individual soldier for his resilience, now *The Steel Helmet* added the notion that a man's skin color compounded his individual struggles as a soldier in the American military.[28] James Edwards's performance as an African American medic culminates when he defends his participation in the war. During a quiet moment in the Buddhist temple, a captured North Korean major grills Edwards as the black man patches up the prisoner's wounds: "I just don't understand you. You can't eat with 'em [whites] unless there's a war. Even then it's difficult. Isn't that so? You pay for a ticket, but you even have to sit in the back of a public bus. Isn't that so?" Edwards hesitates, but then answers in the placid tones that make him one of the film's sturdiest characters: "That's right. A hundred years ago I couldn't even ride a bus. At least now I can sit in the back. Maybe in fifty years, I'll sit in the middle, someday even the front. There are some things you just can't rush, buster!" The communist spits his disdain at this explanation. "You're a stupid man!" he cries, then literally spits on Edwards. Edwards roughs up the Korean a bit, regaining his domination over the scene. Yet Edwards's frustration with the realities raised by the prisoner is palpable, and his faith in gradualism sounds forced—though probably more so to a viewer fifty years later than it would have in 1951. More likely, contemporary white audiences would have appreciated the black man's patience. (Many African Americans soon were to be frustrated with such gradualism from the Eisenhower administration in the wake of the *Brown* decisions.) The scene marked a significant departure from the way World War II–era productions such as the film *The Negro Soldier* had pretended that blacks operated equally with whites in society and the military.

A similar exchange between the North Korean prisoner and the Nisei sergeant, Tanaka, follows later in the film. "You've got the same kind of eyes I have," the major tells the Japanese American. "They hate us because of our eyes. . . . Doesn't it make you feel like a traitor?" Getting no rise out of the unflappable Tanaka with that tactic, he changes direction. "They threw Japanese Americans in the prison camps in the last war, didn't they? Perhaps even your parents. Perhaps even you." The prisoner, who has met only with bored disdain to this point, has struck a nerve. "You rang the bell that time," Tanaka replies quietly. "They did."[29]

Now the communist goes in for the kill: "You Nisei are incredible. You make no sense. . . . Were you one of those idiots who fought in Europe, for your country?" Tanaka finally responds angrily, "Over three thousand of us idiots got the Purple Heart!" When the prisoner persists with his charge that Americans think of the Nisei as a "dirty Jap rat," Tanaka lectures him just as Edwards had: "I've got some hot infantry news for you. I'm not a dirty Jap rat. I'm an American. And if we get pushed around back home, well, that's our business. . . . Aw, knock it off before I forget the articles of war and slap those rabbit teeth of yours out one at a time!" Just as the black medic acknowledges the poor treatment of African Americans in the United States, the Nisei cannot deny the slurs suffered by other Japanese Americans. Though both Edwards and Loo play characters whose contributions to the group effort are unimpeachable, the North Korean reveals that the road to military conformity was pitted with motivational conflicts for some individual soldiers.[30] This version of martial race relations contrasted subtly with the collective racial and ethnic harmony trumpeted in platoon films during World War II—part of a wider wartime effort to distinguish the American military's democratic and egalitarian nature from that of its totalitarian, racist enemies.[31]

If racial and ethnic differences are at least partially resolved in *The Steel Helmet*, tensions between GI and officer are more durable and menacing. Much of the film revolves around Sergeant Zack's rivalry with his superior, Lieutenant Driscoll (Steve Brodie). The men hate each other's guts from the beginning; Driscoll's attempt to make nice with Zack ignites a harsh exchange. Driscoll approaches Zack about swapping steel helmets for the final battle as a gesture of comradeship. When Zack refuses, Driscoll lets loose a tirade: "You're too dumb to be an officer so you take it out on us," the lieutenant charges. "You're a sore head and you're jealous! That's why you hate any officer!" Zack responds with a biting indictment of the officer corps in Korea: "Well, I'll tell you about an officer. And he wasn't a ninety-day act of Congress like you! He was a colonel, and he didn't have to be there. It was D-Day in Normandy, when you were wearing bars in the States and we were pinned down for three hours by Kraut fire! And this colonel, Colonel Taylor, he got up on Easy Red Beach, and he yelled, 'There are two kinds of men on this beach. Those who are dead, and those who are about to die. So let's get off the beach and die inland.' That officer I'd give my steel hat to any day!" This exhortation pitted the memory of heroic, selfless officers of World War II against the grim, survivalist approach of officers in this new war (an approach that no one more than Zack himself employs). More crucially, here was one of the first instances where fictionalized military men—in this case fighting in Korea; later the setting would be Vietnam—failed to measure up to their mythic predecessors of World War II.

Sergeant Zack frequently acts as though he is in charge or leads by example. Often his example is not an honorable one, nor, perhaps, one his mythic Colonel Taylor would have sanctioned. He agrees to lead the other men only when they promise him their cigars (he chomps on one throughout the movie). When a young soldier is blown to pieces investigating a booby-trapped American corpse, Zack immediately rummages through his pack for cigars. ("Dead man's nothin' but a corpse. No one cares who he is now," Zack had warned the curious young soldier.) While advertisers for Dutch Masters were claiming that cigars could "enchant the memory" of battles such as Okinawa, in *The Steel Helmet* cigars represent a cynical soldier's motivation, standing in for the camaraderie that supposedly drove GIs in the last war.

Tensions between Sergeant Zack and Lieutenant Driscoll become more dramatic over the matter of war crimes. When Short Round dies in an enemy attack, the North Korean prisoner mocks the prayer the child had pinned to his own shirt: "To Buddha: Please make Sergeant Zack like me." Zack, grudgingly affectionate toward Short Round by this point, goes berserk and sprays the prisoner with bullets. Driscoll lays into Zack: "It's a good thing this army isn't made up of fat-headed slobs like you that think this war's run by idiots! Just because those little rats kill our prisoners, no reason we have to do the same! No matter how sentimental or personal you get you're supposed to be in the United States Infantry! Soldier? You're no soldier! You're just a big dumb stupid selfish fat-headed sergeant! And if it takes me twenty years I'll see that you're shot for killing a prisoner of war!" Miraculously, however, the North Korean survives. In the ultimate expression of the absurdity of war, Zack threatens the wounded prisoner, "If you die I'll kill you!" Clearly the threat of court-martial or execution breaks through the thick walls of defense this individualistic soldier has erected.

More significantly, this powerful sequence suggests that American soldiers commit atrocities only when pushed to their psychological limit (in the earlier moment, the steady Tanaka remembers "the articles of war" before losing his cool with the enemy prisoner). The scene absolves Zack of guilt even as his darkest side is laid bare. As one film critic described it, "Any shocking effect—and any violation of the Geneva Convention—is negated by the fact that Sergeant Zack is temporarily deranged by the Korean boy's death."[32] Nevertheless, the whole series of events leaves unsettled the distinction between right and wrong in wartime.

This sense of suspended ethics permeated contemporary literature of the Korean conflict. "The Korean," a poem of the 1960s by the American veteran William Wantling, spoke of summary execution:

The Korean
stood stiffly pressed against
   the wall
arms folded
     staring
. . . flinched
when the bullet sang
     fell
outward into the cobblestoned
   court
one too many holes in his head
for stealing from Americans[33]

Common in Korean War literature were troubling stories about the inadvertent or sloppy killing of civilians. In the poem "Korean Litany," released during the conflict, Howard Fast wrote of a Korean child blistered by an American flamethrower and a woman screaming as a tank flattened her house with her in it.[34] While it was possible in literature to depict such scenes without repercussions, *The Steel Helmet* suffered for its prisoner-abuse segment. The Defense Department withdrew technical support from the film over the shooting of the North Korean.[35] If they could help it, military leaders wanted to shield American audiences from the reality that soldiers killed haphazardly in wartime—a fact of battle that was to become all too clear during the Vietnam War.

The final moments of *The Steel Helmet* confirm that the story of war is not a simple one. In the climactic battle Driscoll is killed. Zack places his steel helmet atop the rifle marking the lieutenant's grave, further confusing the matter of what sort of soldier makes a hero. Mirroring contemporary media coverage of Korea, the film suggests that just fighting and toiling in such a "bitched-up" war, in cartoonist Bill Mauldin's words, makes one worthy of sympathy.[36] That sense is palpable as a shell-shocked Zack marches off with the reinforcements who have arrived at the temple, blending the new emphasis on the individual with an older celebration of the collective endeavor. Over martial music and footage of the men marching reads an inscription underscoring the ambiguity percolating throughout the film: "There is No End to this Story."

If *The Steel Helmet* attributed to soldiers a level of cynicism that was relatively new to postwar culture, in 1955 the World War II film *To Hell and Back* signaled the resilience of more familiar themes. Like *Sands of Iwo Jima*, the film enjoyed the endorsement and technical backing of the military, in this case the army.[37] Starring real-life war hero Audie Murphy as himself, *To Hell and Back* shared the focus on the common GI of other contemporary films; the retired general Walter Bedell Smith introduced this "true story of the foot soldier, as seen through the eyes of one of them, Audie L. Murphy."[38] In this instance, the commemoration of the GI did *not* come at the expense of the military brass. Nevertheless, though patriotism, sacrifice, and heroism once again occupied center stage in *To Hell and Back*, a few telling moments in the movie subtly suggested that World War II films of the 1950s were absorbing elements of Korean War imagery.

To Hell and Back follows Murphy's exploits as the most decorated American GI of World War II. (The dogface-turned-actor admitted to reporters that in his first years in Hollywood, "I cashed in on my war record.")[39] The film takes audiences from Murphy's boyhood in Texas to his courageous performance in Italy during the war. In between, Murphy enlists enthusiastically after Pearl Harbor, suffers from illness on the troop transport to Europe, struggles to prove his fitness for a combat assignment, kills hundreds of Germans single-handedly (240 in real life, according to *Newsweek*), and earns numerous promotions and decorations.[40] All the while Murphy maintains a humble, unquestioning devotion to the American cause, an attitude hewn from the simple life of duty he had led on the Texas plains after the death of his mother and disappearance of his father during the Great Depression.[41]

The positive transformation of civilians into soldiers is prominent in *To Hell and Back*. Much like *Sands of Iwo Jima*—and contrary to novels by Mailer and Burns in the late 1940s and media coverage of the Korean War in the early 1950s—*To Hell and Back* emphasizes war's *beneficial* effects on soldiers, not its scarring ones. General Smith's opening remarks make the point clearly, reviving the dominant warrior image of the early 1940s: "Armies, for the most part, are made up of men drawn from simple and peaceful lives. In time of war they suddenly find themselves living under conditions of violence, requiring new rules of conduct that are in direct contrast to the conditions they lived under as civilians. They learn to accept this, and to perform their duties as fighting men." Though Germans and some Americans die early and often on screen, those deaths are generally bloodless and quick. The GI's war seems to have been one of laughter and camaraderie.

Subtle scenes, however, chip away at that picture, reflecting additions to postwar renderings of soldiers in American culture. The element of fear in combat is prominent. One salty veteran tells a jittery Murphy early in the film, "Relax. Get through the first three or four days, you'll be just like the rest of us. That's what it means to be a veteran. You're scared all the time." Later in the film Murphy gives much the same advice to a green recruit joining the outfit. As a reviewer for *Variety* put it, "The film makes plain that if Murphy was a hero he was a scared one, as were the battle veterans he served with."[42]

In the film Murphy and others also cry at the loss of friends, something almost never seen in the iconography of World War II but which was commonplace in media coverage of Korea. One GI cracks under the pressure of a battle near Anzio, losing his good sense and his life after running out of a muddy trench. Nonetheless, this poor soul stands as an exception to the generally well-adjusted, wisecracking soldiers in *To Hell and Back*, just as rare moments of desperation in *Sands of Iwo Jima* served to raise—and then marginalize—the experience of combat trauma. In this way, these films perpetuated much of the imagery surrounding World War II and its stoic soldiers during and after the war in newsreels, magazine advertisements, Hollywood productions, and films of the Veterans Administration.

Unlike in *Sands of Iwo Jima* and *The Steel Helmet*, relationships between GIs and officers are respectful and cooperative throughout *To Hell and Back*. Even when Murphy's army outfit fights with a group of pilots over women in a dance hall, men from the two branches join forces in making excuses to the intervening military police. Moments after throwing punches, the Americans are throwing back drinks and slapping hands all around—"a real joint operation," in the words of one soldier. The film also celebrates the efficiency of American teamwork whenever Murphy requests air support for his troops. With Murphy or other officers directing them on the radio, artillerymen far away tweak their coordinates and destroy one German tank after another. Such cooperation and collectivity had been enduring themes in wartime images of soldiers, the brass, and the various services.

One moment in the film raises questions about the patriotic sense of duty that underlies the entire story. A Polish immigrant fights bravely alongside the Americans throughout the movie until his death near the end. Because the Nazis had wiped out his family in Poland, some of his American comrades hold him up as the only man among them with a real reason for fighting. One GI informally eulogizes the Pole: "Maybe he didn't mind dyin'. Maybe that's what fightin' for a cause means, something none of us really understands." This dialogue confirmed what Ernie Pyle, Bill Mauldin, and others had suggested during the war, that a grand "cause," though trumpeted often in stateside propaganda, was not what motivated the individual

American soldier. He was more likely to fight to protect himself or a buddy, or because it was part of a "job" to be done. While audiences of To Hell and Back may have noticed the unresolved question, this brief episode ends as quickly as it begins. A final shot—the faces of GIs superimposed over columns of marching soldiers—blends the emphasis in 1950s culture on both individuality and collectivity, honoring the foot soldier's contribution to a communal American endeavor.

Critics in the national press found To Hell and Back a fine war picture, if a bit hackneyed. Reviewers generally commented on the traditional elements of the film; the New York Times remarked that the soldiers "are types a filmgoer has met on more than one occasion."[43] Nonetheless, a reviewer for Newsweek wrote, the film "has the added virtue of making the rugged, griping, indispensable foot soldier come to life."[44] This celebration of the dogface would have resonated with wartime fans of Bill Mauldin and Ernie Pyle. In fact, critics had used similar language in praising The Story of G.I. Joe (1945), the Hollywood version of Pyle's war columns. Murphy himself touted To Hell and Back as "true to the life of the foot soldier."[45] Others praised the sincerity and authenticity Murphy brought to a war movie. "Credibility burns in his mild face and gentle gestures," wrote a critic in Time magazine.[46]

Yet the same reviewer saw something more in the picture, something gleaned from the few moments of desperation and fear revealed in Murphy's expressions: "And just for a nervous instant, now and then, the moviegoer glimpses, in the figure of this childlike man, the soul-chilling ghost of all the menlike children of those violent years, who hovered among battles like avenging cherubs, and knew all about death before they knew very much about life."[47] These haunting words caught the sense that war terrorized American boys—a sense strong in works by Burns and Mailer in the late 1940s, even stronger in media coverage of the Korean War, and creeping into popular films of the 1950s. The New York Times agreed that the film captured "the explosive fury of combat and, occasionally, the terror and loneliness of men exposed to sudden death."[48] Both of these critics rightly pointed out that such exposure of despondency came only "now and then" or "occasionally." In general To Hell and Back glorified an American soldier whose part in the war, according to the Times, was "admirable and, on frequent occasions, exciting."[49] If the emotional devastation of combat made an occasional appearance in To Hell and Back, it may have been overwhelmed by more familiar images of "the good war."

Other war films of the 1950s lacked such sentimentality. Stanley Kubrick's Paths of Glory (1957) depicted an insensitive and occasionally murderous French military leadership during World War I, while several World War II pictures featured less-than-harmonious relations between officers and their men. These included *From Here to Eternity* (1953), *The Caine Mutiny* (1954), *Attack!* (1956), and *Run Silent, Run Deep* (1958). *Attack!* even showed a soldier killing his incompetent officer, a practice that was to shock Americans near the end of the war in Vietnam. Several such films drew criticism from the Pentagon for their antimilitary undertones, and *Attack!* lost the cooperation of the army over its controversial scene. [50]

Amongst these films, four years after the end of the Korean War, another Hollywood treatment of that conflict hit theaters. *Men in War*, directed by Anthony Mann and released in 1957, also drew condemnation from the real-life brass for depicting a breakdown in military protocol. The disapproval of the army was just one of several similarities between *Men in War* and *The Steel Helmet*.

Both of these Korean War films were based on World War II combat experiences. *The Steel Helmet* had been culled from director Sam Fuller's diaries of his service during the Second World War, and Mann's film was derived from a World War II novel published in 1949, Van van Praag's *Day without End*. Mirroring *The Steel Helmet*'s opening dedication to the infantryman, *Men in War* staked out its narrative territory: "Tell me the story of the foot soldier and I will tell you the story of all wars."[51] Both films followed the individual GI, trapped in a war not of his own making, and documented his isolation from the military establishment and the loftier causes of war. James Edwards appeared in both movies as an African American soldier, though his early death in *Men in War* meant there would be no repeat of the *Steel Helmet* scene where he defends his participation in a white man's war. Finally, each film featured passionate hatred between two soldiers whose reconciliation at the end only partially muted the viciousness of their rivalries.

Starring in *Men in War* was Robert Ryan as Lieutenant Benson, the cool officer in charge of a unit cut off from central command (mirroring reports that real American GIs often felt isolated and forgotten fighting in Korea). Benson's nemesis is Sergeant Montana (Aldo Ray), who is escorting his shell-shocked mentor, "the Colonel," out of the war zone when he comes across the platoon and has his jeep commandeered by Benson. Thus united tenuously from the beginning, the group walks slowly behind the heavily laden jeep through a countryside of snipers, land mines, and intermittent shelling. Against this terrifying backdrop, the film emphasizes the emotional toll of war, the breakdown in teamwork between officers and enlisted men, and the individual soldier's isolation from the military bureaucracy that had landed him in Korea. Amplifying these dark themes is the film noir style of *Men in War*, replete with unnerving camera angles, stark lighting, and mysterious, sinister characters. Although many of the best-known film noir productions of the 1940s and 1950s were crime stories, *Men in War* also partook of the genre's sensibilities. A film scholar later wrote that noir pictures "deploy the darkest imagery to sketch starkly disconcerting assessments of the human and social condition."[52]

With the exception of *Let There Be Light*, the unreleased army documentary on neuropsychiatric soldiers produced in 1946, *Men in War* may have sketched the era's most disconcerting assessment of shell-shocked GIs. Terrified, nervous, exhausted soldiers are the norm in *Men in War*, and even the sturdiest characters suffer from mental breakdown at one point or another. As one film critic noted, "Half of the bruised and bearded soldiers appear to be suffering from battle fatigue, which causes them, at embarrassing moments, to do weird and incautious things."[53] The young GI Zwickley experiences crippling fear throughout the film, but in a key divergence from earlier portrayals of such men, his comrades describe him as "sick" and look after him rather than disparage him. Likewise, a soldier named Ackerman expresses his terror at advancing amid enemy shelling, and instead of meeting derision, he learns his buddies feel the same way. More familiar is the fate of Lewis, also a rank-and-file GI, who panics in a minefield and runs off pell-mell until he is blown to pieces. What had driven him to irrationality was the recognition that every step could mean death, a reality hauntingly signaled by the eerie, whispered warning that goes down the line of men: "Mines! Mines! Mines! Mines!" With their senses thus assaulted, audience members are invited to feel the same mind-numbing terror that the men feel.[54]

More disturbed than all of these characters, however, is the Colonel, Sergeant Montana's speechless and vacant mentor. The Colonel does not utter a word until the very end of the film, having endured some mysterious horror that leaves him staring blankly even in the most harrowing moments of combat ("He's hurt inside his skull," Montana tells Benson). When Lieutenant Benson and his men first encounter this pair, the Colonel has been belted into their jeep in straightjacket fashion. Montana, for his part, is so jittery from combat that he shoots prisoners on sight and kills three enemy soldiers posing as American GIs before really knowing their true identity. Prefiguring aspects of the soldier's image during Vietnam, the audience is left with the unsettling thought that such a strategy, even if borne out of paranoia and cynicism, is justified against a crafty Asian enemy.

Montana's renegade approach to combat mirrors a wider sense of lawlessness that pervades the American forces in the film. Military discipline is haphazard, relations between soldier and officer contentious—hardly the democratic army of cooperation and unity shown in most films during World War II. As Lieutenant Benson's men are wandering through the countryside, weighed down with equipment, they spot Sergeant Montana and the Colonel driving at breakneck speed nearby. When Benson stops the sergeant and questions him, it becomes clear that no one is really in charge of the sector. Montana and his comatose mentor are fleeing the battlefield, and no higher authority is directing the movements of either contingent. Benson must resort to physical force to commandeer the badly needed jeep from Sergeant Montana, and the two men are at odds until the final moments of the film, when they and one other soldier are the only three to survive a last firefight.

Nothing in the film testifies to the breakdown in discipline and teamwork more than Montana's rivalry with Benson. The sergeant projects his hatred for the military establishment onto the lieutenant, and couches that enmity in individualistic terms. When Montana finally agrees to go along with Benson's unit, he reminds the lieutenant darkly, "Just don't forget I'm fighting for the Colonel." Neither democratic values nor anticommunist fervor animate Sergeant Montana, nor does he seem to possess even a basic loyalty to American institutions or his fellow soldiers. Rather, his single-minded devotion to a deranged colonel stands in for the sense of duty imbued to soldiers by cultural producers during the previous war. Later in the movie he tells Benson, removing himself verbally from the team endeavor, "I'm not in your army and you're not in mine!"

Benson cannot stomach Montana's attitude. When the sergeant objects to one of Benson's orders, the lieutenant tries to restore discipline: "Look, Montana, I'm in command here! I don't want any more of your decisions, good or bad. From now on you don't talk, you don't fire, you don't spit without my permission!" "All right, sir," Montana replies sarcastically, revealing his palpable disgust for military protocol. When Montana kills three North Korean soldiers posing as Americans, an even harsher exchange follows. As it dawns on Lieutenant Benson that Montana had shot the men without *really* knowing they were enemy, he lays into the sergeant: "Get outta here, Montana! Go back to your colonel and get him outta here! Unload the jeep and take it with you, fast!" Montana offers his palm for an ironic final handshake, but Benson snubs him. "God help us if it takes your kind to win this war!" In 1957 these words seemed the dying wish of a bygone generation of fighters.

Much like the army that Norman Mailer described in 1948's *The Naked and the Dead*, the UN forces in *Men in War* live by a chaotic, confused code of discipline—more than a decade before that disturbing image ignited widespread public concern during the Vietnam War. Combat no longer seems the tightly disciplined, team-oriented enterprise it once had seemed (but maybe never really was). [55] Rather, men in war fight for myriad reasons, bend the rules of engagement, and generally behave unpredictably. Particularly when Montana returns to help Benson defeat a North Korean contingent, it is strikingly unclear whether Benson's by-the-book approach or Montana's renegade style is the more honorable, heroic, or effective (one critic declared it a tie, calling Montana and Benson "the two best kinds of fighting men"). [56] What is clear is that life and death in war depend on countless individual decisions, personalities, and coincidences, despite military protocol. Predictably, such a message did not sit well with the real-life military brass. Just as the Defense Department withdrew technical support from *The Steel Helmet* over atrocities committed by Americans on screen, the army condemned *Men in War* and denied its producers assistance because of Montana's insubordination and the broader lack of discipline portrayed in the film. For both of these low-budget productions, the army's denial of tanks, weapons, and other equipment presented a serious obstacle to realism.

Both the emotional trauma of war and the breakdown in teamwork and discipline in *Men in War* result, in large part, from an abiding sense of isolation. In the opening scene the camera jumps from one terrified face to the next, as the radio operator, Riordan (Philip Pine), desperately calls central command. Of course he gets no response, and when one of the soldiers discovers that a comrade has been stabbed in the back right in their midst, panic ensues. Just before the climactic battle Riordan is again on the phone trying to contact someone, anyone, who might be able to send reinforcements. Benson, by now at his wit's end, loses his composure and moans to Riordan: "Battalion doesn't exist. Regiment doesn't exist. Command headquarters doesn't exist, the USA doesn't exist! They don't exist, Riordan, we'll never see 'em again!" Riordan is stunned by Benson's words, and asks him not to say that sort of thing. "It's true," Benson replies. "I know it is," says the shaken Riordan, "but it scares me when *you* say it." Viewers of the film may have been similarly disturbed that the loyal lieutenant, forsaken by the military and government structure above him, in turn abandons his faith in that structure. When Benson reads off the names of his dead men in a lonely moment at the end of the film, it seems even memorialization occurs beyond the gaze of the American home front.

The physical isolation of the men contributes to their mental instability as well as to the sense of lawlessness that hinders military discipline. Viewers are invited to sympathize with men asked to do a dirty job and then left to their own devices—a far cry from World War II–era portraits of soldiers who almost always seemed a part of something bigger, something comforting. Military life in Audie Murphy's World War II film of 1955, with its prompt air support, memories of home, and finely tuned coordination, was absent from this account of the Korean War. In contrast to soldiers in films during the Second World War, who reminisced often about home, GIs in *Men in War* seem isolated from such memories, stranded out on the bleakest reaches of American foreign policy and public consciousness.

James Michener had captured that remoteness four years earlier in his classic novella *The Bridges at Toko-Ri*. He describes a pilot shot down in hostile territory: "Harry Brubaker, a twenty-nine-year-old lawyer from Denver, Colorado, was alone in a spot he had never intended to defend in a war he had not understood. In his home town at that moment the University of Colorado was playing Denver in their traditional basketball game."[57] Stories about the literal and figurative abandonment of American GIs in Korea, in fact, were to characterize the small body of literature that emerged from the Korean War in subsequent decades. Such themes marked short stories or poems published during and after the war by Eugene Burdick ("Cold Day, Cold Fear"), William Chamberlain ("The Trapped Battalion"), Stanford Whitmore ("Lost Soldier"), and James Magner Jr. ("Repository").[58] Magner laments the unnoticed death of an American soldier in Korea:

Vanesca!
(Do I spell his name correctly?)
Vanesca!
(I say it again, so someone will remember.)
Vanesca!
(What is this repository that keeps the names,
the souls of men!)[59]

"Lost Soldier," which appeared in the literary magazine *Accent* in 1953, pictured the war as an encounter between a Chinese and an American soldier, both separated from their units. Such tales of isolation, whether of a GI from his patrol or from his society more broadly, partook of a wider trend in literature of the period, according to one scholar, toward the "deterioration of a literary and rhetorical tradition that glorified war"—a trend developed more fully during the Vietnam War but already strong after Korea.[60]

Contemporary critics noted this sense of isolation running through Anthony Mann's film *Men in War*. As a cinema reviewer for *Time* noted, "Never for an instant does he [Mann] let the moviegoer escape from the appalling situation the platoon is in. Never for an instant does the moviegoer know where he is—or where They are. He marches, hides, fights, watches every minute with the fighting men, and the watching is the worst. For as the watcher stares down his gunsights into the bright summer grasses . . . there comes a moment when any averagely sensitive person will begin to get that cold sensation along his spine, and to realize a little how a fighting man feels when he is buying a Section Eight."[61] This emphasis on the GI's isolation set *Men in War* apart from many World War II films. *Newsweek* pointed out that Mann's use of terrifying silence and skillful acting made the movie "much more persuasive than most of its whopping and colorful war-story predecessors." Though he disliked the movie, critic Bosley Crowther of the *New York Times* agreed that *Men in War* was "one long display of horror and misery"—nothing new, in his judgment, for celluloid combat.[62] It was clear that Mann's sympathies, like those of many Korean War correspondents, lay with the soldiers rather than with the government that put them into action.

Rounding out the mini-genre of Korean War films in the 1950s was *Pork Chop Hill* (1959). Despite its reflections of producer Sy Bartlett's antiwar sentiments, the film earned the approval of the Pentagon. According to Bartlett, the Defense Department supported the movie because it showed men following orders, carrying out their mission, and fighting to the bitter end, contrary to "world-wide gossip that the American soldier broke and ran"—and also contrary to moments in *The Steel Helmet* and *Men in War*.[63] *Pork Chop Hill* told the story of infantrymen under the command of Lt. Joe Clemons (Gregory Peck), fighting to retake a hill of meaningless military value to bolster the position of negotiators at nearby Panmunjom. Notwithstanding a roseate ending, the film highlighted the victimization of American troops by their superiors.

Pork Chop Hill departed in significant ways from *The Steel Helmet* and *Men in War*. Recalling movies of the World War II era, teamwork *among* officers is efficient and respectful, particularly between Clemons and a Japanese American, Lt. Suki Ohashi (George Shibata). While *The Steel Helmet* and *Men in War* showed GIs isolated from the brass and from American society, in *Pork Chop Hill* the military leadership controls the men like chess pieces. Gone is the sense of frontier justice, but in its place is a no-less-sinister manipulation of the men from above.

In other respects the film fit squarely with the other Korean War pictures. *Pork Chop Hill* depicts powerless GIs victimized by the politicians and generals above them. In this instance officers who fight alongside the men share the resentment toward the brass, just as they share in the misery of combat. Often in the film, higher-ups in the army deny reinforcements, make mistakes, or promise things they cannot deliver. And building on the brief exchange between James Edwards and the North Korean prisoner in *The Steel Helmet*, *Pork Chop Hill* hints at the struggles of African American soldiers fighting on behalf of a racist society.

Pork Chop Hill reveals, as well, the futility of warfare. The film suggests that men die only so diplomats can save face at the negotiating table. "The pain and the killing go on," *Variety* magazine said of the movie, "defying logic and reason."[64] The GI's unwillingness to die for American envoys is not lost on the brass; a colonel tells Clemons early on, "It's a cinch they won't want to die in what may be the last battle"—all the more reason, in the colonel's view, to push the men relentlessly forward up the hill.[65] Soldier after soldier gripes about being the final GI to die in Korea—foreshadowing John Kerry's famous testimony before the Senate Foreign Relations Committee in 1971, when he implored the senators to end the war in Vietnam: "How do you ask a man to be the last man to die for a mistake?"[66]

The foot soldier's distrust of the brass also rests on real and perceived errors by the higher-ups. In the middle of a nighttime assault on Pork Chop Hill, someone in the rear mistakenly illuminates the onrushing GIs in bright searchlights. Lit up that way, numerous Americans are mowed down by the enemy guns. A radio operator tells Clemons what happened: "They just apologized. They got us mixed up with some other hill." As the Americans regroup in a trench atop the hill, artillery fire whistles and crashes nearby, injuring some of them. Though Clemons claims to recognize it as Chinese shelling, some of the men are convinced that American artillery is falling in their midst. Their rage reveals that this would not be the first time friendly fire has victimized the GIs.

The officers, Clemons and Ohashi, ascribe to the military leadership heartlessness as well as incompetence. Throughout the assault on the hill Clemons receives messages from headquarters that question why he has not advanced further, why he wants reinforcements, why he asks for more ammunition and flamethrowers. Instead of receiving any of these things, Clemons gets a chipper army photographer arriving to take pictures of a so-far-elusive American victory. This slap at official, sanitized images of war ends when the lieutenant sends the photographer away, but not before ordering him bitterly to "tell division what you saw here." When the battalion sends a runner to order one company off the hill, long before the Americans have won it, Clemons loses his temper: "You take this message back. Tell 'em that I do not think that the crisis up here is appreciated either by battalion or regiment! Tell 'em I have very few men left, and they're all exhausted!" As Bill Mauldin's cartoons had shown humorously, combat officers and GIs during World War II surely railed against distant higher-ups who did not understand the situation at the front. Yet Clemons delivers his message with more venom. Even his words, though, pale in comparison to Korean War poet William Childress's later invective in "Combat Iambic," published in the 1986 collection *Burning the Years and Lobo: Poems 1962–1975*:

Once in a distant war which was no war,
mired in the unclean paddies, bleeding clean
my buddies died while tracer bullets tore
through earth and armored vests like acetylene.
Our General, in rearmost echelon,
with fancy unfired pistol near his thigh,
barked militant commands and acted out
his manly role untouched by fire. O, sir,
I pray Beelzebub, Lord of the Flies,
to rear his maggot children in your eyes,
where curled like living lashes they can give
the atmosphere that suits a General's mind. [67]

Just as *Pork Chop Hill* and some Korean War poetry critiqued the unbloodied brass, they also grieved over the disposable infantry. In the absence of better weapons, Clemons and Ohashi hatch a daring bayonet assault on the summit of the hill. "Bayonets," Ohashi mutters. "Right outta the Stone Age. Where's all this push-button warfare we been hearin' about?" Clemons's reply: "We're the push buttons." The Korean War veteran and poet Rolando Hinojosa caught this sense of individual expendability in "A Matter of Supplies," published in 1978:

It comes down to this: we're pieces of equipment
To be counted and signed for.
On occasion some of us break down,
And those parts which can't be salvaged
Are replaced with other GI parts, that's all. [68]

In other Korean War verse, according to poet and critic Robert Hedin, "The individual soldier has become nothing more than a lowly pawn on the vast, strategic chessboard of the Cold War." [69] This GI is the "push button" of modern warfare in *Pork Chop Hill*.

Once again, a Japanese American and several African Americans join the traditional white ethnic platoon of World War II–era films. Lieutenant Ohashi's heritage is scarcely mentioned in *Pork Chop Hill*, but his unwavering support of Clemons, his bravery, and his reliability reflected the wider rehabilitation of the Japanese image under Cold War exigencies of the day. [70]

James Edwards plays an African American soldier for at least the third time in the 1950s. (He was to do so again in *The Manchurian Candidate* in 1962.) Yet his character, Corporal Jurgens, is not the most prominent black GI in *Pork Chop Hill*. That distinction belongs to Franklin, played by former football star Woody Strode. His lack of enthusiasm for the assault stands out even in a company gripped by fear and reluctance. Several times Clemons has to push, prod, and cajole Franklin into advancing, at one point even assigning Jurgens to watch over him. "I've got a special interest in everything you're doing," Jurgens tells Franklin, but the relationship between the two black men is unexplored beyond that moment.

When Clemons finds Franklin hiding in a bunker near the end of the film, the simmering tension between the two men boils over. Franklin threatens to kill Clemons rather than go to jail for desertion—an image to be repeated in the early 1970s in Vietnam. The black soldier yells desperately at Clemons, "I don't wanna die for Korea! What do I care about this stinkin' hill? You oughta see where I live back home! I sure ain't sure I'd die for that!" Much had changed since 1951, when *The Steel Helmet* had briefly raised, then dismissed, the ironies of black participation in war. In the wake of both *Brown* decisions, massive resistance by southern whites, and the Little Rock fight over integration, African American impatience was more visible than it had been eight years earlier. Yet if the scene comments on the difficulties of black membership in the military, it may also have played into the stereotype that African Americans deserted in combat (an image dating back at least to the Civil War). Indeed, one critic questioned the choice of a black man for the scene: "The producers of the picture surely are aware that the tendency to generalize where a Negro is involved is far greater, and more harmful."[71] Mitigating this danger is the fact that other men of color—Jurgens and another black GI—perform dutifully and without questioning authority.

Clemons nimbly defuses Franklin's dilemma. Though the lieutenant is clearly moved by the outburst, he also needs men for the battle raging outside. He convinces Franklin to join the fight by appealing to his sense of responsibility to the men who have already died on Pork Chop Hill: "A lot of men came up here last night. They don't care any more about Korea than you do. Lot of 'em had it just as rough at home as you did. They came up and fought. About twenty-five of them left. That's a pretty exclusive club. You can still join up, if you want to." These words have the desired impact. Franklin responds to what has become Clemons's justification for the heavy losses—once men have died, the hill takes on new value. Stripping away the politicians' war, GIs on the ground must fight for each other, and for those who have died before them. If Clemons sympathizes implicitly with Franklin's reasons for withholding his services from the company, he also dismisses them by suggesting that fighting for the hill has nothing to do with society, racism, democracy, or communism. All that matters to Clemons now is the foot soldier.[72]

The GIs in *Pork Chop Hill* invite sympathy and gratitude for the colossal sacrifices American society asks of them. Men behave heroically in the face of horrific battle conditions, incomprehensible orders from above, and an awareness of their own status as cannon fodder. One wounded man asks Clemons if he can stay on the hill, rather than retreating to the rear as Clemons is ordering him to do. "Who d'ya think you are?" replies Clemons incredulously. "Audie Murphy?" If Korea was no World War II, the film suggests, the men fighting there did try to emulate the mythic stature of the men who had fought in "the good war." Perhaps reflecting a desire to imbue the soldiers of Korea with the same sort of accomplishment, the last scene shows a triumphant victory atop the hill, the long-awaited reinforcements finally arriving. Turning away from the meaninglessness of death on Pork Chop Hill, Gregory Peck's voice-over tries to redeem the effort: "Those who fought there know what they did. And the meaning of it. Millions live in freedom today, because of what they did." In the wake of hundreds of deaths that served only to guarantee a hollow diplomatic victory, these words are somehow unconvincing.[73]

Just as the small body of Korean War literature and film conveyed the grimness of that conflict, some Cold War–era novelists and poets writing about World War II captured the darkest aspects of "the good war." Without voicing an explicitly antiwar point of view, much Second World War fiction and poetry focused relentlessly on death, destruction, moral degradation, and psychological breakdown in combat.

More than ten years after the tremendous success of his novel *From Here to Eternity*, James Jones burst back onto the literary scene in 1962 with another highly acclaimed book on World War II, *The Thin Red Line*.[74] The earlier novel had depicted life in the military before and during the Pearl Harbor attack. Now, Jones turned to combat in the Pacific. (The third book in the trilogy, *Whistle*, featured returning veterans and appeared posthumously in 1978.) *The Thin Red Line* followed closely on the heels of Joseph Heller's *Catch-22* (1961), the World War II classic that also emerged from the ambivalent climate of the 1950s. In 1962 Heller commented on the potential audience for books such as his own and Jones's: "There may be a much wider current of sophisticated and discontented people than many of us believe."[75]

Such readers would have welcomed Jones's book. *The Thin Red Line* traced the activities of "C-for-Charlie" Company through its time on the Pacific island of Guadalcanal, the scene of brutal fighting against the Japanese in 1942–43. Though the setting was real, the characters, about ten of whom are described in detail, were fictional. The dedication of the book hinted ironically at what was to follow: "This book is cheerfully dedicated to those greatest and most heroic of all human endeavors, war and warfare; may they never cease to give us the pleasure, excitement and adrenal stimulation that we need, or provide us with the heroes, the presidents and leaders, the monuments and museums which we erect to them in the name of peace."[76] Such scathing irony in a *movie* dedication never would have appeared in a Pentagon-sponsored project, but novelists enjoyed considerably greater freedoms absent the need for elaborate technical assistance.[77]

The novel shared striking similarities with Norman Mailer's *The Naked and the Dead*, published in 1948. Both took place on islands in the Pacific, made liberal use of profanity, exposed the withering effects of combat on the human psyche, and received hearty praise for their supposed realism. Both authors had fought in World War II, Jones enduring a wound on Guadalcanal. Yet Jones's novel, if it picked up themes from Mailer's work, took them further than the earlier book had. It also drew, perhaps unconsciously, from images of soldiers in the Korean War and projected them onto "the good war." In *The Thin Red Line* GIs are powerless victims of a cruel military leadership; they might be cynical, cowardly, or downtrodden; and war is a gruesome affair with permanent psychological consequences for the men who bear it. All of these elements predicted the warrior image of the Vietnam era.[78] The book also featured sex between male soldiers, further revealing the gay subculture of the military introduced in the World War II novel *The Gallery* in 1947.

In the 1940s Bill Mauldin had popularized the idea that GIs harbored a good-natured resentment toward their superiors. In the work of Norman Mailer and John Horne Burns, in press coverage of the Korean War, and in films such as *Sands of Iwo Jima*, *The Steel Helmet*, *Men in War*, and *Pork Chop Hill*, that enmity became a bit more sinister. Now, in *The Thin Red Line*, Jones described GIs who hated their officers, and officers who hated the battalion commanders or generals or admirals above them—ambitious men who often played treacherously with the lives of their subordinates. In

Jones's rendering the infantryman of the Second World War was the power-less victim of his military leadership and the American government that had landed him on Guadalcanal.

As in films about the Korean War, GIs in the novel *The Thin Red Line* often focus their resentment on a vague, distant home front that, they feel, has plopped them down in dangerous terrain and abandoned them. As his unit lurches into its first combat experience, Capt. James Stein still takes a dutiful stance on the matter. "We have to do as society demands," he tells a GI named Bead, who has just killed his first Japanese. "One of these de-mands is the killing of other human beings in armed combat."[79] Stein's sanguine view is destined to change as he witnesses the haphazard lead-ership style of *his* superiors. But the foot soldier feels it already, trapped at the very bottom of the hierarchy. The soldier Fife expresses a deep resent-ment of his powerlessness: "Helplessness, that was what he felt; complete helplessness. He was as helpless as if agents of his government had bound him hand and foot and delivered him here and then gone back to wher-ever it was good agents went. Maybe a Washington cocktail bar, with lots of cunts all around."[80] Another soldier, the deeply cynical Welsh, indicts several aspects of American society in his thoughts on a platoon after bat-tle: "2d Platoon would make a great photograph to send back home . . . ex-cept that of course when the newspapers, government, army, and *Life* got ahold of it, it would be subtly changed to fit the needs of the moment and probably captioned: Tired infantrymen rest in safety after heroic capture of position. The first team at halftime. Buy bonds till it hurts your asshole."[81] Both of these soldiers, and several others in the novel, believe their lives have become mixed up in an elaborate con game. Such a view, reported dimly, if at all, during World War II itself, blamed heartless policy makers in Wash-ington for sending men to die in a remote land and then twisting their ex-periences into propaganda campaigns to shove *more* men and money into the war. As in Mailer's *The Naked and the Dead*, the wider purpose of World War II is hardly mentioned, but it matters little to the common GI—even in a "justified" war, these authors suggest, the soldier feels helpless and resentful.

If American society and government seem far removed from the battle-field, in *The Thin Red Line* individual soldiers are more immediately victim-ized by a calculating and omnipresent military bureaucracy. Captain Stein, himself the object of his men's ire at various points in the novel, resents the brass manipulating his movements, recalling Lieutenant Clemons's bitter-ness in *Pork Chop Hill*. Stein's thoughts are profound testimonials to the powerlessness of the individual:

Yes, the big brass. The observers. . . . all were up there right now, going through the identical gyrations their identical counterparts had gone through two days ago. While down below were the same blood-sweating Captains and their troops going through theirs. Only this time he himself, he Jim Stein, was one of them, one of the committed ones. . . . And tomorrow it would be someone else. It was a horrifying vision: all of them doing the same identical thing, all of them powerless to stop it, *all of them devoutly and proudly believing themselves to be free individuals*. It expanded to include the scores of nations, the millions of men, doing the same on thousands of hilltops across the world. . . . It was so horrible a picture that Stein could not support or accept it. He put it away from him, and blinked his bulging eyes. [82]

Whatever success Stein has blinking away these thoughts, he has become irrevocably cynical about his role as the intermediary between the brass and his doomed GIs. As one literary critic astutely pointed out in 1962, it is Stein's inability to "bear to see his men die uselessly" that ultimately comprises his "main failing as an officer."[83] Despite successfully completing an important flanking maneuver, Stein is relieved of his command by a Colonel Tall for being "soft."

During the same battle sequence the soldier Bell confronts his powerlessness: "Free individuals? What a fucking myth! *Numbers* of free individuals, maybe; *collectives* of free individuals."[84] If World War II culture pictured GIs who subsumed their individuality to the collective goal, they also seemed to have the leeway to perform acts of their own volition so long as they contributed to the team effort, as Audie Murphy had done. Now in place of that leeway was the obvious impotence of the soldiers, their fate as cannon fodder sealed regardless of individual volition or ability. Among the men chosen for a particular assault, "most of them, in their bodily attitudes and in their faces, resembled sheep about to be led to the slaughter pens in Chicago."[85] The culprit, the cause of their suffering, was the vast bureaucracy of military men and politicians, themselves caught up in the same strange cycle of destruction and death. As one critic wrote in 1964, "Within this hierarchy, which gets larger and larger as it moves up the chain and farther and farther from the battle lines, *the fighting soldier is a grain of sand on a beach encircling the globe*."[86]

This picture of military management would be damning enough if individual members of the brass were well-meaning, though misguided, leaders. But this is not so in *The Thin Red Line*, as scheming colonels and ambitious generals lead men to pointless deaths. In his review of the book,

Orville Prescott, who had praised *The Naked and the Dead* fourteen years earlier, recoiled at images of "officers not knowing what to do, officers doing the wrong thing, officers risking their men's lives for victory and also for their own ambition."[87] Captain Stein's message to Colonel Tall recalls the breakdown in discipline that had crept into portraits of war in the 1950s: "'Colonel, I refuse to take my men up there in a frontal attack. It's a suicide! I've lived with these men two and a half years. I won't order them all to their deaths. That's final. Over.' . . . Tall was stupid, ambitious, without imagination, and vicious as well. He was desperate to succeed before his superiors. Otherwise he could never have given such an order."[88] Equally striking is an exchange between a terrified soldier and the general who had sent him into battle:

> The division commander had been observing the day's fighting from the crest of Hill 209. Of course his career was involved in this offensive. When the groups began returning pellmell and shaken, he strode among them smiling and talking, trying to bolster them. "We're not gonna let these Japs whip us, are we, boys? Hunh? They're tough, but they're not as tough as we are, are they?" One boy, young enough to be the general's son, if not his grandson, looked up at him from where he sat with distended eyes. "General, you go out there! You go out there, general, you go out there!" The general smiled at him, pityingly, and walked on. The boy did not even look after him.[89]

Never had there seemed a greater distance between the military leadership and the troops as when this imperious general sauntered among his wrecked men. Throughout the novel ambitious military leaders, for the sake of their careers, press into combat so many sacrificial lambs—men with families, men who try to help others only to be killed themselves, men who suffer gruesome wounds before perishing, men who *know* they are about to die.

The poets of World War II navigated this same expanse between grunts and officers. Army veteran Lincoln Kirstein, in verse published in the 1960s and thereafter, sketched harsh indictments of the officer corps. "Rank" makes the point clearly in its first stanza, equating the differences between "rich and poor" and "hot and cold" with the distance between officers and enlisted men. The poem goes on to describe the exploits of a Captain Stearns, who gets drunk with some privates, starts showing off with a rifle, and inadvertently shoots and kills a French woman sleeping in the room above the bar. According to the poem he was found guilty—not of murder but of "Drinking With Enlisted Men." In "Foresight" Kirstein broadcasts the common worry that the incompetence of an officer might get a GI killed.[90]

The former pilot Howard Nemerov described the hatred such officers could arouse in "IFF," published in the 1980s:

> Hate Hitler? No, I spared him hardly a thought.
> But Corporal Irmin, first, and later on
> The O.C. (Flying), Wing Commander Briggs,
> And the station C.O. Group Captain Ormery—
> Now there were men were objects fit to hate,
> Hitler a moustache and a little curl
> In the middle of his forehead, whereas these
> Bastards were bastards in your daily life,
> With Power in their pleasure, smile or frown.

In the rest of "IFF," which stands for "Identification Friend or Foe," Nemerov details other odious "friends" of the Allied soldier.[91] Here the poet, like the novelist Jones, casts a sinister pall over the much-touted teamwork of the armed forces during World War II.

The dangers to which officers exposed their men, as this literature had it, were frightful. Rarely in the postwar period had wounds, death, and the process of dying been more graphically portrayed than in *The Thin Red Line*: "He had been hit squarely in the groin with a burst of heavy MG [machine gun] fire which had torn his whole belly open. Lying on his back, his head uphill, both hands pressed to his belly to hold his intestines in, he was inching his way back up the slope with his legs. Through the glasses Stein could see blue-veined loops of intestine bulging between the bloodstained fingers."[92] Other passages are not so much ghastly as pitiful:

> "I'm dying, Fife!" Bead told him.
>   Fife could not think of anything to say, either. "I know. Just take it easy, Eddie," he said, repeating Stein. . . .
> "Will you write my folks?" Bead said.
> "I'll write them."
> "Tell them it didn't hurt me much. Tell them the truth."
> "I'll tell them."
> "Hold my hand, Fife," Bead croaked then. "I'm scared."[93]

While it was common for soldiers to die quickly on the silver screen, in the book *The Thin Red Line* several doomed men, like Bead, have the chance to tell whoever is listening what it feels like. Some pray, some cry out desperately, some close their eyes and ask for morphine. The popular World War II poet Karl Shapiro likewise showed these tortured moments of communion between the dying and the living, stripping death of Hollywood theatrics. In

1964, two years after Jones's book appeared, Shapiro published verse known as "Fox Hole":

> Quintana lay in the shallow grave of coral. The guns boomed stupidly fifty
> yards away. The plasma trickled into his arm. Naked and filthy,
> covered with mosquitoes, he looked at me as I read his white cloth
> tag. How do you feel, Quintana? He looks away from my gaze. I
> lie: we'll get you out of here sometime today.[94]

Often in such poetry and in *The Thin Red Line*, the dead seem lucky to have left this world. Everywhere in Jones's book are spilled guts, flying chunks of flesh, bits of hurled hot metal, men who continue to fight without limbs, endless bombardments, excrement-covered enemy prisoners, rainstorms, and gruesome diseases.

As a result of such horrors, soldiers in *The Thin Red Line* experience deep psychological trauma, something rare in most World War II–era films and media coverage and barely indicated in postwar productions such as *To Hell and Back* and *Sands of Iwo Jima*. The Korean War films had always offered a franker treatment of emotional strain, but now James Jones, like Norman Mailer before him, was suggesting that a good war could crack men's spirits just as easily as a bad one. In *The Thin Red Line* dogfaces experience a dizzying range of reactions to combat: some wish death upon their cocky comrades; some vomit to escape the fighting; some take harrowing risks out of lunacy rather than bravery; and some simply begin to hate so much that killing becomes easy, or enjoyable. In all cases, combat dehumanizes the individual GI. "They were, of course," writes Jones, "undergoing the worst mental shock of their young lives."[95]

Once again, poets of World War II tenaciously explored the causes and nature of this "mental shock." Verse descriptions of combat, quite unlike many cinematic renderings of the Second World War, revealed the gruesomeness and fear of battle. Throughout this poetry ran the specter of death, one's own or that of others, along with a sampling of emotional responses to dying. In the mid-1970s the combat veteran and poet George Oppen reproduced the mood of Jones's work in "Survival: Infantry," signaling more than simple battle fatigue:

> We were ashamed of our half life and our misery: we saw
> that everything had died.
>
> And the letters came. People who addressed us thru our
> lives

They left us gasping. And in tears
In the same mud in the terrible ground[96]

Misery, guilt, shame, and death were rife as well in the new genre of aerial combat poetry. In 1969 Randall Jarrell contemplated the emotional impact of destroying civilians from above in his poem "Losses." He writes of burning cities, of killing anonymously from the air, of earning medals for this macabre work.[97] James Dickey's confessional poem of 1964, "The Firebombing," like other verse of this sort, marvels at the destructive power of flame. And it reveals the tormented imaginings of the narrator twenty years removed from dropping incendiary bombs:

. To my eye
And shown the insides of houses, the low tables
Catch fire from the floor mats,
Blaze up in gas around their heads
Like a dream of suddenly growing
Too intense for war. Ah, under one's dark arms
Something strange-scented falls—when those on earth
Die, there is not even sound;
One is cool and enthralled in the cockpit . . .[98]

Beyond the guilt and post-traumatic stress of this detached killing, fear was a constant companion of the pilots over Europe and the Pacific. Richard Hugo, who flew in thirty-five raids above Italy during the war, later conveyed the terror of a crash landing:

I was calling airspeed
christ
one-thirty-five and
pancake bam
glass going first
breaking slow
slow dream
breaking
slow
sliding
gas and bombs . . .[99]

Such vivid invocations of fear, according to literary critic and veteran Paul Fussell, had been "unmentionable" in World War I verse, but now found fuller expression in World War II poetry of the 1940s onward.[100] Poems by former bombardiers, as well as the work of infantry veterans such as James Jones, challenged the roseate versions of the war proffered in the 1940s.

Even more challenging to World War II mythology were the atrocities depicted in Jones's *The Thin Red Line*—a blot on America's martial history indicated faintly in some Korean War films. Unlike in those pictures, however, men in the novel who torture or kill enemy soldiers do not meet censure, but understanding. War, it seems in *The Thin Red Line*, strips the GI of normal ethical standards, a reality rarely admitted before but which would become a mantra among Vietnam veterans and their advocates later in the decade. A semicrazed GI named Big Un takes out his frustration and hatred on hapless, dysentery-racked Japanese prisoners: "Taking two by their scrawny necks which his big hands went almost clear around, he shook them back and forth gaggling helplessly until their helmets fell off, then grinning savagely began beating their heads together. The cracking sound their skulls made as they broke was loud in the new, palpable quiet. 'Fucking murderers,' he told them quietly."[101] Driven to rage by the Japanese torture of two GIs a few days earlier, Big Un doles out retribution in a way that no one in the company questions. Atrocities committed by the North Vietnamese and Vietcong against POWs in a later war would similarly serve as a rationale for such treatment by Americans. And just as some officers in Vietnam would look the other way, Colonel Tall feels that he must "make allowances for men in the heat of combat."[102] In a later orgy of violence against surrounded Japanese troops, Jones succinctly describes the suspension of morality in war: "A crazy sort of bloodlust, like some sort of declared school holiday from all moral ethics, had descended on them. They could kill with impunity and they were doing it."[103]

These segments of the novel seemed to critique, or more aptly mourn, the hideous violence unleashed against the Japanese in the Pacific—violence implicitly sanctioned by the American public in the wake of Pearl Harbor. Presaging a prominent theme of Vietnam-era imagery, Jones lamented the brutalizing impact of total war against another people, an impact that seemed more likely somehow when that enemy was Asian. In the passage above Jones makes a point of describing how Big Un's hands reach clear around the "scrawny" necks of these small, odd, racially different soldiers, noting how easily he kills them—actualizing, as GIs had during the war, the racial hatred carried over from home-front culture.[104] Just a few years after the publication of *The Thin Red Line*, antiwar activists and some filmmakers were to protest this sort of violence against the Vietnamese people in a conflict lacking, as they saw it, the sort of justification generated by the attack on Pearl Harbor. But James Jones and some of the prominent World War II poets were demonstrating that they did not need Vietnam to show them the dehumanizing effects of war—that even a "just" conflict, with its violence endorsed by the public, generated brutality of the worst sort.

Finally, *The Thin Red Line* illuminated the subculture of "deprivation" or "situational" homosexuality, in later parlance, as well as "overt" homosexuality. In line with the rest of Jones's novel, the matter of gay sex in the military is shot through with corruption and hypocrisy. Fife and Bead engage in repeated homosexual acts but fiercely deny being gay: "'I just dont [sic] want you to think I'm no queer, or nothing like that.' 'Well, dont [sic] you get the idea I am, either,' Fife had answered." In *The Thin Red Line* military leaders and grunts alike recognize a tacit boundary between men seeking sexual gratification in the absence of women—"guys could help each other out"—and the "fairies," "queers," and "overt homosexuals" whom everyone hated but whom might be called upon in times of need. Despite all the venomous gay-bashing in the army, moreover, there were "old-timers" who kept young male lovers in return for payment or special favors. All of this "buggering" went on, according to Jones's novel, as the authorities looked the other way, though they were ruthless when given the opportunity to purge "overt homosexuals" from their ranks via troop transfers and such. Soldiers like Fife wondered, naturally enough, about whether they were homosexual and were "terrified someone else might."[105] The military leadership, once again, comes off as self-serving, hypocritical, and corrupt. It would be bad enough, Jones suggests, if martial culture was consistently homophobic, but instead a visible homophobia persisted even as some of its enforcers engaged in gay sex themselves.[106] Images of military men were evolving to include strains of shadowy homoeroticism, indulged despite the heterosexism dominating military culture.

The same year *The Thin Red Line* appeared in bookstores, viewers tuned in for the first season of *Combat!* the longest-running World War II drama in television history. Over several seasons (1962–67) and 152 episodes airing on Tuesday nights in prime time, the army-supported *Combat!* was frequently a top-ten ratings finisher among network television programs. Vic Morrow starred as Sergeant Saunders, and Rick Jason as Lieutenant Hanley. While other shows such as *You'll Never Get Rich* (popularly known as *Sergeant Bilko*), *Gallant Men*, and *McHale's Navy* offered silly, slapstick versions of military life, *Combat!* used realism and a "good deal of violence," in the words of one television history.[107] Though often remembered for igniting a passion for war in young boys of the 1960s, *Combat!* actually sent a diverse array of messages on warfare, soldiers, and military authority—and it did so even in its early years, before the great escalation of the Vietnam War and the concurrent rise of antiwar activity.

From its inception, *Combat!* celebrated the common foot soldier. The program's creator, Robert Pirosh, was a World War II veteran and the writer of *Battleground* (1949) and *Go For Broke!* (1951), two important films that took the point of view of the individual GI. [108] During its five-year run *Combat!* perpetuated almost every disquieting aspect of the warrior image percolating in the 1950s and early 1960s. [109] There were brutal orders from officers, violent rivalries between soldiers, breakdowns in teamwork, graphic wounds and death, psychological injuries, even episodes devoted to antiwar messages. Robert Altman, an early director of the show, would go on to make the great antimilitary film *M*A*S*H* in 1970. He told *TV Guide* in 1963, "I wanted to do the war stories you couldn't do in 1946." (On the occasion of Altman's death in 2006, a television critic at the *New York Times* wrote that the show was "remarkably sorrowful and bleak. War is hell on 'Combat!' and hellishly arbitrary.") Yet like much else in the culture of pre-Vietnam America, these sorts of images mingled with more familiar holdovers from the World War II years, when camaraderie, collectivity, and patriotism had dominated war culture. Behind-the-scenes squabbles over how the war should be portrayed, in fact, marked the show's entire history, leading *TV Guide* to call the highly acclaimed program a "clash of opposites." [110] Several episodes revealed incongruous themes.

In the show's first season, "Cat and Mouse," directed by Altman, made a strong antiwar statement. Sergeant Saunders and one other GI are the only survivors of a doomed patrol into German-held territory. When Saunders returns to the battlefield, this time with the harsh Sergeant Jenkins (guest star Albert Salmi), most of the unit is again massacred. Jenkins and Saunders cannot agree on how to proceed when they find themselves trapped inside a mill house, and Jenkins eventually sacrifices his own life. The intelligence gained through the mission, for which many GIs gave their lives, proves useless to the army brass, and the Allied forces march on. [111] Portraying the futility of war, of course, was not new. Korean War films such as *The Steel Helmet, Men in War, The Bridges at Toko-Ri* (1954), and *Pork Chop Hill*, and much of the small body of Korean War literature, had lamented the absurdity of dying for temporary military objectives, and James Jones's *The Thin Red Line* had projected that theme onto the Second World War in 1962. [112] Later, many popular narratives of the Vietnam War were to revolve entirely around this notion of fleeting victories.

In the show's second season, the episode "Bridge at Chalons" considered the enmity among men leading dogfaces into battle. Much like Sergeant Montana and Lieutenant Benson in *Men in War*, Sergeant Saunders and explosives expert Sergeant Turk (guest star Lee Marvin) instinctively dislike one another yet must work together to obtain their objective, in this case the demolition of a German bridge. Turk antagonizes the squad from the beginning. When a GI accidentally kicks a stone, almost giving away the unit's position, Turk berates him: "You got loose brains! A guy with clumsy feet don't belong out here!"[113] Minutes later, Turk gets into a shoving match with another GI. "Soldier, you are going to get court-martialed, I promise you that!" Turk screams. These scenes underscore the deep antagonism between enlisted men and their immediate superiors, in this case, sergeants. Saunders finally confronts Turk with a tirade strongly reminiscent of Lieutenant Benson's in *Men in War*: "Now you listen to me—I'm going to remind you just one time! I'm in charge of this outfit until we get to the bridge. And if anything happens I'll decide what we do about it. You got it?!"

Sergeant Turk's reaction to the men arises from his profound distrust of their abilities—a far cry from the reliable soldiers presented in films of World War II. Turk blames Saunders for the death of a GI. "Where were you?" he asks with oily condescension. "Keepin' the Krauts off our necks is the escort's job. That's why you're here, Saunders. Looks like you blew it." Saunders finally asks Turk why he's so distrustful. Turk responds, "I'm only afraid of one thing, Saunders. That sometime, someplace, some jerk is gonna get me killed. . . . I'd hate to cash in now because some jerk who's not dry behind the ears yet slops off on a detail!" Soldiers who had been faithful comrades in earlier years now seem to be bunglers, perhaps more dangerous to a man than the enemy. That idea coexists precariously with more familiar carryovers from World War II culture. After Turk is wounded, Saunders must act as his hands and feet, and their ability to work together culminates in a spectacular explosion on the river. Echoing *Sands of Iwo Jima* and *Pork Chop Hill*, the show paints a dark picture of military relationships but brightens it at the end with timely cooperation.

"Hills are for Heroes," a two-part episode airing in 1966, restated an antiwar message—now in the context of the escalating Vietnam War and peace movement—and was widely hailed as the show's finest moment. Repeating the plot of countless real-life situations in the Korean War, the films *Men in War* and *Pork Chop Hill*, and the episode "Cat and Mouse," Lieutenant Hanley's mission is to take a hill that has temporary military value. With Saunders wounded and scores dead, higher-ups order Hanley again and again to assault the German machine gun bunkers. Finally, a tank and a long-awaited smokescreen help them take the position, but not before much of the unit is slaughtered on the hillside. Before Lieutenant Hanley can even claim the small consolation of climbing to the top, the men are ordered to retreat and give up the hill. An exhausted GI can hardly believe the orders, screaming at Hanley, "We ain't comin' down lieutenant! We took this hill!"[114] Slowly the dispirited dogfaces stagger down the slope, leaving their dead comrades behind.

Other episodes further reinforced warrior images of the 1950s and early 1960s. In "No Trumpets, No Drums" a squad member cracks up after accidentally killing a French civilian, just as similar actions would bring many soldiers grief in Vietnam. "Doughboy" features a shell-shocked American soldier from World War I, reliving that conflict in the 1940s. A recalcitrant GI hampers Saunders's ability to lead in "Bridgehead." A temporary officer in "Command" leads the men with brutal discipline, but only because he formerly lost an entire platoon in battle. In "Mountain Man" Saunders bribes a deserter into helping the squad. "The Linesman" features a mainstay of the show—a hostile officer forced to join the unit for a particular mission who ends up blaming Saunders for the death of one of his own men. The episode "S.I.W.," short for "self-inflicted wound," introduces a soldier to the squad who may have shot himself to escape combat. In "Nothing to Lose" one GI hides his cowardice with bravado, while another is wanted for murder; the two exchange words, punches, and even gunfire.[115]

Throughout its five seasons, *Combat!* combined such images of men in war with more familiar portraits of heroism, patriotism, and camaraderie. But it did more than that. *Combat!* made war prime time entertainment in the homes of millions of Americans, something that was to become immeasurably more real during the war in Vietnam.

––––––

According to popular mythology, when John Kennedy approached the podium for his inaugural address in January 1961, he stood at the boundary between two major twentieth-century political and cultural moods. Behind him lay a tradition of respect for the military, faith in government, and confidence in democracy. After his death came Vietnam, Watergate, and the rise of public cynicism. Behind him lay *The Best Years* and *The Years of Confidence*, after him came *The Unraveling of America*, whereby the country was *Coming Apart*, in three scholars' words.[116] Americans of the 1950s had revered war veterans, so this thinking goes, yet by the early 1970s it was common (if usually spurious) knowledge that antiwar protesters were spitting on Vietnam vets.[117] President Kennedy tapped into the earlier reverence for the institutions of government and military when he pledged that Americans would "pay any price, bear any burden, meet any hardship, support any friend, oppose any foe, in order to assure the survival and the success of liberty."[118] According to many retrospective accounts by Vietnam veterans, the spirit of those words would catapult young men headlong into the war in Southeast Asia.[119] After Lyndon Johnson and Richard Nixon had presided over a decade of war and official abuses of power, however, that heritage of respect for government and military would deteriorate rapidly.

Historians now know that this picture requires some degree of revision, and warrior images of the 1950s and early 1960s offer just such an opportunity. Several scholars have found in portraits of soldiers in the 1950s the same thing pollsters discovered at the time: discomfort with militarization, the Korean War, the Cold War, and the prospect of future hot wars.[120] Others have uncovered challenges to sanitized images of World War II that surfaced before and during Kennedy's presidency. Some of these writers, however, have minimized the strength of such challenges to nostalgia about "the good war." As Benjamin Alpers has put it, "Although revisionist accounts of World War II have surfaced regularly since 1945, they have never dominated either scholarly discourse or public opinion."[121] In fact, in various books and films of the 1950s "the good war" did not seem so good. And in the wake of an unpopular war in Korea—and due in no small part to the loose censorship of those reporting war and depicting it in film—many Americans in the 1950s confronted an individual soldier independent of, isolated from, and even opposed to the larger bureaucratic structures he represented.

A whole range of movies about war, from the flag-waving *To Hell and Back* to the gloomy *Men in War*, opened with dedications that celebrated the individual GI: "Tell me the story of the foot soldier and I will tell you the story of all wars"; "This story is dedicated to the United States Infantry"; this film is the "true story of the foot soldier." Bill Mauldin and Ernie Pyle had celebrated the foot soldier, but always for his selfless contribution to the team effort. Some writers, filmmakers, and poets in the 1950s, however, commemorated the sacrifices of individual servicemen quite apart from the broader geopolitical goals of war. In films about the Korean War, for instance, this valorization of the foot soldier carried with it a critique of the expanding federal bureaucracy that landed American boys on far-off shores, despite Cold War pressures from the military to support American foreign policy on the silver screen. Needless to say, the American experience in Vietnam would magnify such a critique immeasurably, but it did not start with the antiwar protests of 1966 and thereafter. If World War II films of the 1950s were less likely to criticize American involvement in that conflict, they still featured soldiers who were strikingly similar to those in Korean War pictures.

More than anything else, what linked these portraits of servicemen in the 1950s and early 1960s was an evolving awareness of the enormous cost of war to men engaged in it. Depictions of combat in this era suggest that memories of these earlier wars, before Vietnam, brought into postwar culture the image of soldiers as cynical, distressed victims of government policy or overbearing officers, of war as a grim, chaotic business, and of combat as a brutalizing experience. Military life may have seemed orderly and democratic during World War II, but now some writers, poets, and film producers added treacherous officers, demoralized or cruel GIs, and pointless death to the picture. Individual soldiers seemed to face all sorts of threats and obstacles besides the enemy and an occasional bout of battle nerves. Psychological trauma appeared particularly common to soldiers in Korea, though even GIs of World War II sometimes seemed more emotionally vulnerable than their mythic forebears of wartime culture, particularly in poetry. And in productions of the 1950s, soldiers in either war might succumb to their own violent impulses and commit offenses against civilians or prisoners. Belonging to a racial minority also posed special challenges, something not dealt with before in any meaningful way. If the desire for military approval of screenplays limited these sorts of images, it did not hide them completely.

Considered in hindsight, *The Steel Helmet*, *Men in War*, *Pork Chop Hill*, *The Thin Red Line*, and Korean War literature foreshadowed later disillusionment over Vietnam. Consequently, many Americans—veterans of World War II and Korea as well as younger audiences—surely entered the Vietnam era without an intact, unquestioning faith in military leaders or the federal government. Nor is it likely that most Americans harbored naive illusions about war. Later, with Vietnam in the rearview mirror, many observers would *assume* (or remember) that depictions of the military and war in the 1950s were simple, quaint, and patriotic. Vietnam veteran and author Philip Caputo remembered in 1977 that as he prepared to join the marines in 1960, he imagined himself "charging up some distant beachhead, like John Wayne in *Sands of Iwo Jima*."[122] Contrary to such memories and to the interpretations of some scholars, that film and much else in Cold War culture offered more complex warrior imagery than it would seem in retrospect after the great national nightmare in Vietnam.[123]

THE
VIETNAM
ERA

CHAPTER 6

THE PERPLEXING WAR, 1964-1968

It was not the sort of beach landing so many young men endured in Europe and the Pacific during World War II. The marines who came ashore in a drizzling rain at Danang, South Vietnam, on March 8, 1965, met neither bullets, barbed wire, nor concrete but flowers and pretty girls. And they were not the first American military personnel to arrive in the country. Others had been in Vietnam for years advising the chronically unstable South Vietnamese military in its struggle against the indigenous communist forces of the National Liberation Front (NLF), pejoratively known as the Vietcong. But now the marines were in the country to protect an American air base, soon to serve not as advisers but as a fighting force. Their appearance on the beach near Danang culminated a year-long process of escalation that dramatically raised the stakes of American involvement in Indochina.[1]

Early in 1964 South Vietnam was in turmoil, ten years after the country had been split from North Vietnam by the Geneva Convention in what was supposed to be a temporary partition. A series of coups brought Gen. Nguyen Khanh into power in January 1964. In Saigon, capital of the beleaguered nation, Buddhists and Catholics persisted in a bitter rivalry carried over from the 1950s and early 1960s, when President Ngo Dinh Diem, a Catholic, had ruled over the majority-Buddhist state. In the countryside, Khanh's new government held negligible authority. All over South Vietnam, increasingly bold NLF strikes threatened the regime's tenuous legitimacy. Meanwhile, the communist nation of North Vietnam was stepping up support for its southern revolutionary ally, the NLF. In early 1964 the north was improving the Ho Chi Minh Trail, a maze of supply routes to the south, and organizing its own troops for infiltration into South Vietnam.

President Lyndon Johnson and his advisers, cold warriors committed to the preservation of a noncommunist South Vietnam, looked with increasing concern at the infusion of northern supplies and men into the south. They wished to strike North Vietnam, but without direct provocation from the communists it would be difficult to defend an attack in the court of public opinion. That provocation came, Johnson said, in August 1964 on two dark nights in the Tonkin Gulf off of North Vietnam. On August 2, the American destroyer *Maddox* exchanged shots with North Vietnamese patrol boats. Two nights later, with a strict directive from the president to "attack any force that attacks them," the *Maddox* and the destroyer *C. Turner Joy* came under fire again—or so the sailors initially thought. [2] It is now clear that inexperienced seamen panicked in turbulent weather and repelled an assault on August 4 that never happened. Pentagon officials, however, itching for an excuse to strike the North Vietnamese, announced the second attack even as the *Maddox*'s chief officer, Capt. John Herrick, was still trying unsuccessfully to confirm it. [3]

Most Americans accepted the president's version of events and supported retaliation. The immediate reprisal came in the form of air strikes against North Vietnamese marine bases and oil storage facilities. Far more significant, however, was Johnson's use of the Tonkin Gulf incident as a pretext for widening the American military commitment in Vietnam. The president adroitly described the incidents in a statement released to the press, calling them "renewed hostile actions" that "required me to order the military forces of the United States to take action in reply." [4] Congress approved a "Tonkin Gulf resolution" almost without debate, though two Democratic senators, Wayne Morse (Oregon) and Ernest Gruening (Alaska), voted against the resolution because of its open-ended authorization to use "all necessary measures" to retaliate against future attacks. These men feared the resolution might be used to widen the war—a prophetic view—though doing so was not Johnson's intention at the time. The resolute president's approval ratings jumped from 42 to 72 percent almost overnight; convincing the American people of the value of containing communism was not a difficult task in 1964. [5] Ultimately the United States would unleash enormous destruction upon Vietnam in the long wake of the Tonkin Gulf incident, its murky nature eventually seeming an apt beginning to a murky conflict. To some portion of the American public in later years, moreover, the lack of a Pearl Harbor–type opening salvo surely helped sap enthusiasm for this violent, stalemated conflict.

After the Tonkin Gulf resolution the war escalated in irregular leaps, stirring doubts among some observers of South Vietnam. In December 1964 NBC aired the prescient documentary "Vietnam: It's a Mad War," narrated by Chet Huntley, which reported elements of the conflict soon to become familiar to television audiences: American overreliance on the body count, discord between U.S. advisers and their South Vietnamese hosts, the resolve of the communist enemy, cynicism among military officials about the conflict's chances for success. [6] *Newsweek*, the first major weekly to challenge American handling of the conflict, called it "the deadly and perplexing war" in January 1965. [7] In February the NLF assaulted the American barracks in Pleiku, killing nine. Within two days Johnson commenced Operation Rolling Thunder, a campaign of steadily increasing air strikes against

North Vietnam. As the aerial war expanded, Gen. William Westmoreland, commander of American forces in Vietnam, requested ground troops to protect American airfields. The first marines waded ashore near Danang in March. Just as the president's critics in Congress feared, it now would be difficult to stem the tide of escalation.

It was in the spring of 1965 that the war began commanding significant media attention in the United States. Vietnam had turned from a back-page news story into what the *New Yorker's* Michael Arlen later called "a central fact in American life."[8] By 1965 there were print journalists in Vietnam representing four magazines (*Life, Look, Time,* and *Newsweek*), two wire services, and several newspapers (including the *New York Times* and *Washington Post*). David Halberstam, Neil Sheehan, Bernard Fall, Stanley Karnow, and others distinguished themselves covering the war in print. Prominent photographers in Vietnam included David Douglas Duncan and Carl Mydans (both had covered the Korean War for *Life* magazine), Larry Burrows, Eddie Adams, Horst Faas, Dickey Chapelle, and military cameraman Ronald Haeberle. Photographers in Vietnam delivered striking pictures of the war: self-immolating monks, an execution on the streets of Saigon during the Tet offensive, victims of the My Lai massacre, and Vietnamese children fleeing a napalm attack.

Though such images were to remain powerful for decades, Vietnam is better remembered as the first televised war. "Most of us knew about it, felt about it, from television," wrote Arlen.[9] Each of the three main networks had correspondents in Vietnam by 1965. CBS and NBC lengthened their nightly news programs from fifteen to thirty minutes in 1963, and ABC did so in 1967, allowing more time for coverage of the war. Televised dispatches arrived in American living rooms from correspondents who would go on to distinguished careers in journalism: Ed Bradley, Garrick Utley, Ted Koppel, Morley Safer, Dan Rather, and Mike Wallace. The network studio anchors—Walter Cronkite, Chet Huntley, David Brinkley, Peter Jennings, and others—brought the stories of Vietnam to the American public. After the Tet offensive of 1968 some anchors would become increasingly critical of the war (Cronkite famously pronounced Vietnam a "stalemate"), but through 1967 these men tended to present the news with little interpretation.[10]

Indeed, as Susan Moeller has pointed out in her book on combat photography, these publications and television networks were all institutions of the "establishment media."[11] They considered themselves allies of the White House even when their correspondents in the field sent back pessimistic reports about the war. In the early period after American ground troops arrived in country—from March 1965 through 1967—even those journalists who questioned American *methods* in Vietnam seldom challenged the American *presence* there (Halberstam had leveled criticism along these lines even earlier). The media, like the public, generally subscribed to Cold War anticommunism and approved of the American intervention in Vietnam. Lest television viewers forget the threat, hanging on the wall behind Walter Cronkite's desk on the CBS nightly newscast was a map of Vietnam with "RED CHINA" looming to the north. [12]

Nevertheless, during the Vietnam War there was considerable—and unprecedented—room for dissent among the press corps. While military officials censored journalists during the Second World War and for most of the Korean War, no official control of the media occurred at any point during the Vietnam War. With all the technological advances of the 1960s, particularly television and satellites, military officials simply could not imagine censoring the news. Westmoreland himself said the logistics of censorship were "forbidding to contemplate." [13]

Some informal methods of control, however, did restrict reporters in Vietnam. Members of the media often faced official requests to withhold news of troop movements and graphic depictions of the dead and wounded. Reporters whom the military leadership in Vietnam did not favor might be denied transportation to the countryside, official accreditation, interviews with commanders, or lodging at military bases. And the brass could, as always, hold back or distort the information it released to the press. For years the military's public information officers held the much-derided "five-o'clock follies," a daily briefing that provided the official version of the war. Television networks had their own policies governing the release of footage that might disturb families of the dead and wounded. [14]

In short, there were plenty of informal ways the military and government could manage the news, but early in the war the press usually fell into line of its own volition. Eventually journalists in Vietnam would take advantage of the lack of official censorship and deliver more critical war reporting. By 1967, and even more so after the Tet offensive of early 1968, the tenor of press coverage in Vietnam would become more skeptical, and the impact of that change on administration policy and public opinion would become the subject of extensive, highly partisan debate for decades afterward. [15]

Yet if journalists generally supported American involvement in Indochina early in the war, that did not inhibit them from propagating troubling, though sympathetic, versions of the warrior image. Between 1965 and 1968 the media, particularly popular magazines and television networks, delivered sometimes disturbing reports on the condition and attitude of the foot soldier, reports that coexisted awkwardly with editorial support for the war.

The upshot was a bewildering set of portraits of soldiers and of the war effort generally—a "constant flow of words and images" bringing "obfuscation," not "clarification," according to the *New Yorker*'s noted correspondent Robert Shaplen.[16] And as the conflict lost public support, journalistic sympathy with the individual soldier remained steadfast or grew stronger—repeating the pattern established in Korea.

Reporters began by emphasizing the skill, toughness, commitment, and compassion of the American fighting man—attributes dusted off from World War II iconography. But quickly the flavor of Korean War coverage tempered those characterizations, with GIs seeming to be victims of combat, the elements, their superiors, and, gradually, the very presence of the American military in Vietnam. The heroic, selfless soldier of World War II mythology was transforming into a different sort of cultural hero, one inviting sympathy, even pity, along with respect. The terms of what made a soldier honorable—indeed, the terms of what made him a *man*—were widening and changing. So when coverage of the Tet offensive in early 1968 delivered what seemed to be startling imagery of the war and the American GI, it was more intense, but not new.

———

Between the Tonkin Gulf incident of August 1964 and the attack on Pleiku of February 1965, a number of editorialists around the country had developed serious concerns about the instability of the South Vietnamese regime and President Johnson's vague declarations of American purpose in the region.[17] The arrival of American ground troops in March 1965 did not stabilize the military situation in South Vietnam right away, nor did it quiet the administration's critics in the press, but it did seem to galvanize public support for the war. The majority of Americans, inasmuch as they thought about Vietnam at all, were guardedly supportive of the conflict. In April 1965 a Gallup poll revealed that just 17 percent of those questioned believed the United States ought to withdraw from Vietnam; 57 percent felt the administration should continue its involvement, but they endorsed proposals ranging from negotiation to a declaration of war.[18] As one authoritative account of American antiwar sentiment has put it, public opinion was "confused and contradictory" in this period. Its authors have summarized well the national mood: the public was "eager for success but reluctant to pay for it."[19]

The price of U.S. involvement in Vietnam became clearer in the summer of 1965. In July several crucial decisions boosted the American commitment to a war that was "going very badly," in the words of *Life* magazine.[20] The president doubled monthly draft calls to 35,000, granted Westmoreland

100,000 more troops by the end of the year (he announced just half that figure to the public), promised more soldiers the next year if the situation demanded it, and authorized expanded, independent ground operations against the NLF.[21] American military personnel would no longer be mere advisers, be limited to brief forays within a certain radius of the air bases, or have to rely on corrupt or inept South Vietnamese officers in the field. Said one American foot soldier later that year, "This is our war now. All that 'advisor' stuff is over."[22]

General Westmoreland's plan for these ground forces emphasized enemy casualties, not geography. The notorious "body count," or "attrition," or "search and destroy" strategy encouraged commanders in the field to kill as many Vietcong as possible, and often, to count as enemy any dead Vietnamese found in the area. This approach had dire consequences for the civilian population of South Vietnam. It also eventually frustrated military planners, the press, and the American public. Newsweek's bureau chief in Saigon, William Tuohy, described what was to become a maddening pattern in South Vietnam: "There may be a handful of Viet Cong bodies, but the next day the enemy is right back in the same dugouts in the same place again."[23]

Since 1950 various image makers had questioned the discipline and efficiency of the American military. In the early years of Vietnam, however, the media attributed a high degree of professionalism and teamwork to the armed forces—a natural image given the high proportion of professional or volunteer soldiers (compared to draftees) in the country.[24] Invoking a theme that had dominated coverage of World War II, the press once again placed individual soldiers within the framework of a well-oiled machine. Ernie Pyle and others had celebrated the individual GI of the Second World War, but for his contribution to a well-coordinated team effort. John Kennedy's inaugural address had reinvigorated this ethic of sacrifice and teamwork, and in the early years of Vietnam journalists found it in the American GI. Gone, for a time, was the sense prevalent in press coverage and Hollywood films of the Korean War that American forces operated in isolation, far from the military planners and society that had landed them on foreign shores. Though the Vietnam War is better remembered for a breakdown in military discipline after 1970, in the early period of the war reporters lauded the efficiency, teamwork, and might of the American armed forces.

In April 1965, just a few weeks after American ground forces arrived in Vietnam, Time magazine ran a cover story titled "Who's Fighting in Viet Nam: A Gallery of American Combatants." (See figure 14.) The weekly Henry Luce had founded and led until 1964 bore the imprint of his intense anticommunism, fervently supporting U.S. intervention.[25] Accordingly, the

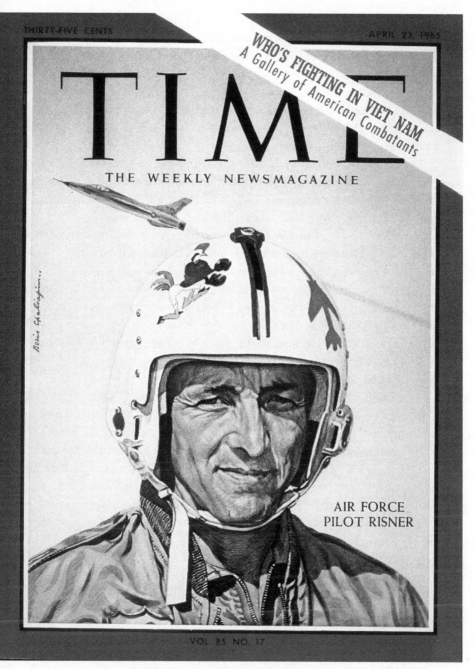

FIGURE 14. *"Who's Fighting in Vietnam,"* Time, April 23, 1965. *This cover, and the article that went with it, emphasized the professionalism, skill, and teamwork of the American armed forces in Vietnam. Courtesy of Time & Life Pictures/Getty Images.*

piece emphasized professionalism, skill, and teamwork. "The American serviceman in Viet Nam," said *Time*, "is probably the most proficient the nation has ever produced." To operate in the cockpit of a Thunderchief fighter-bomber, for example, "requires the highest degree of human ingenuity and precision." When Robbie Risner, the pilot featured on the cover of the magazine, bailed out of his Thunderchief, "his professionalism saved him." Media historian Daniel Hallin has aptly dubbed this sort of figure a "hero of technology."[26]

One demolitions expert told *Time* that unlike before the March landing, American coordination and equipment in Vietnam were awe inspiring. "Look at us now. We've got every weapon we ask for. We've got a scientifically laid-out camp with clear fields of fire and plenty of wire. When we ask for air support, we get it. We've even got a dispensary and an icebox. This time we've got what we need to do the job."[27] The press told American readers that technology, know-how, and teamwork were going to level the playing field against a shadowy enemy. And how could the Americans' lumbering military compete against guerrillas? "To this," reported *Newsweek* in July, "U.S. military men reply that today's American soldier and marine is as well prepared as any fighting man in the world for waging guerrilla warfare."[28] With equal confidence *Time* quoted Lyndon Johnson's statement that there "is no human power capable of forcing us from Viet Nam."[29]

Americans fighting in Vietnam were also brave, though reporters did not gloss over the terror and agony of combat. In November 1965 Bill Harvey of NBC interviewed several injured GIs from their beds, recalling the feel of the 1946 film *Let There Be Light*. In halting tones and obvious pain, the fallen men spoke frankly of their fears. Harvey asked Pfc. James Shaddon how he had felt during a recent ambush: "I was trying to stay cool-headed but I was a little scared anyway, [breathing heavily] tryin' to watch for snipers up in the tree but they were pretty hard to see there. A lot smarter than you think, they are, they're real camouflaged and they know a lot of good tactics." Another GI described the same ambush with terror in his voice and expression.[30] That evening ABC aired a similar report on the improbably named Toby Braveboy, hailing from the even more improbable Coward, South Carolina. Braveboy spoke from the operating table while medics tended his wounds: "They shot me about three or four times, sir. Killed my partners. [Grimaces in pain] I crawled through the bushes, see if I could help them. And I went back to see if I could find the medics. . . . I went back then and all three of them was dead. One of them was cut, cut in two."[31] These dispatches made heroes of men flat on their backs, with no attempts to shield viewers from their pain, fear, or lingering emotional trauma. Such accounts of GIs were not "antiwar," but they renewed the Korean War–era practice of showing individual suffering without sentimentality.

Alongside consistent praise of the GIs, however, a few whispers of doubt circulated in 1965 about the ability of the American military to handle guerrilla warfare. *Newsweek* reported as early as July that officials in Washington were "embarrassed" by the performance of marines guarding the Danang air base. Responding to questions about a damaging Vietcong raid on the position, a testy Pentagon official responded, "I wish we'd quit blaming the South Vietnamese for these incidents."[32]

Life, also a Henry Luce publication, sent a similar message in more measured tones when it wrote ten days later, "U.S. combat units are finding that they still have a lot to learn about guerrilla warfare." The article went on to charge that American troops were making the same "mistakes" advisers had rebuked the South Vietnamese for in previous years; namely, they were relying too heavily on logistically complicated and time-consuming air strikes.[33] *Newsweek* worried in August 1965 that if the Americans kept up their deadly air war against the Vietcong and North Vietnamese, they would soon find themselves in the position of the French colonizers of an earlier era—"alien intruders feared and hated by the general population."[34] ABC correspondent Malcolm Browne, when asked in November whether American GIs were prepared to fight and win in Vietnam, replied, "Frankly, I don't think they are. I think these boys are magnificently trained to fight World War II and fight Korea, but I think this is a different kind of conflict. In this kind of war, politics and economics and a lot of other factors are important."[35] Such depictions did not question the professionalism of GIs, but their ability to get the job done amid the particular challenges of Vietnam.

————

One of the war's most enduring and controversial images arrived in American living rooms in August 1965, just weeks after Lyndon Johnson boosted the U.S. military commitment in South Vietnam. In an early execution of the "search and destroy" strategy, marines entered the hamlet of Cam Ne on August 3. CBS correspondent Morley Safer reported that Vietcong troops were "long gone" from the alleged enemy stronghold by the time the GIs arrived. Nevertheless, the Americans had orders to destroy the village, and the CBS camera crew recorded infamous footage of American soldiers setting thatched huts on fire with Zippo lighters. Safer commented, "There is little doubt that American fire power can win a military victory here. But to a Vietnamese peasant whose home means a lifetime of backbreaking labor, it will take more than presidential promises to convince him that we are on his side."[36] Not surprisingly, the president and military leaders were furious about the story. In an oft-quoted telephone call, Johnson asked CBS president Frank Stanton, "Are you trying to fuck me?"[37] Angry enough that Safer was Canadian, administration officials also wondered if he might be a communist. The Pentagon began recording nightly television coverage of Vietnam to keep an eye on the networks. Scholars rightly have pointed out that Safer's dispatch was unusual in 1965—otherwise why the irate reaction?—and the furor it caused surely inflated its impact. As Tom Engelhardt has put it, Safer's images "were perhaps the most disturbing of the war for those who saw them that August night," precisely because they broke the mold of prior television coverage.[38]

Yet if such images were still uncommon on the small screen, popular magazines offered coverage that made Cam Ne seem less surprising. Some reports in the print media in the second half of 1965 suggested that American forces could harm the people they were trying to help. *Newsweek* spoke in August of the "unhappy consequences" of American operations: "During a sweep south of the Da Nang base, U.S. Marines poured artillery shells into the village of Chau Son, which was suspected of harboring Viet Cong. And, indeed, the Marines did succeed in killing 25 guerrillas. But they also inadvertently killed a woman and four children." In the same period *Life* magazine reported on the difficult decision of marines at Ky Hoa "whether to kill presumably innocent peasants in order to reach an enemy who have taken on protective coloration among them." The marine commander eventually did bomb two villages, killing between fifty and a hundred South Vietnamese peasants. A *Look* magazine article on naval pilots described sympathetically the outlook of the fliers on civilian casualties: "And often tighter than fear are the knots in your chest, because you know there may be women and kids down there."[39]

A related matter, though one that would emerge more fully later in the war, involved deliberate atrocities committed against civilians or Vietcong prisoners. *Look* magazine captured the cycle of vengeance afflicting troops in Vietnam: "So there is mutual terrorism, as there is in every war. Both sides have been guilty of abuse, torture and mutilation of prisoners. A kind of nameless rage builds up in most men at the dirt and heat and terrifying suspense of this struggle in which there is no front line, no real way of knowing who is with you and who is against you. Rage ebbs into hunger for revenge, then more rage piles upon it, and men begin devising ingenious, hideous ways of giving their enemies the jitters."[40] Everyone in South Vietnam knew that the Vietcong were guilty of atrocities themselves, but the communists were good at covering their tracks. America's allies in the South

Vietnamese military, on the contrary, often made their crimes "distressingly available" to the press, in the words of historian William O'Neill.[41] "Meanwhile," wrote *Newsweek* in September 1965, "scores of photographs showing South Vietnamese troops brutally mistreating Viet Cong prisoners have appeared in the Western press." An accompanying picture showed a South Vietnamese soldier stomping on a bound communist guerrilla. (*Newsweek* placed the shot alongside two others: one showed a captured American pilot, the other a Vietnamese peasant tortured by the Vietcong. The magazine labeled the trio of images "victims all," signaling the increasing tendency to depict all the sufferers of war equally—even an enemy prisoner.) The article went on to report that American GIs often felt "obliged to stand by" as the South Vietnamese abused captives by throwing them out of airplanes.[42] For now, American soldiers appeared to be accessories to but not perpetrators of war crimes.

Even more prevalent in 1965, however, were reports on the model behavior of American GIs in Vietnamese villages.[43] Just after the Cam Ne incident, Morley Safer issued another dispatch from Vietnam on "how civilians *should* be treated." The correspondent spoke of how U.S. marines warned villagers of an impending American raid and evacuated them from their hamlet. As the CBS camera rolled, a steady rain fell on the displaced Vietnamese. The voice of a compassionate American leatherneck rang out, "Tell the women and children to come in here, and get in out of the rain! This is better shelter." Safer concluded, "The marines played the whole operation very cool indeed. Few guns in evidence, in fact, few marines. The impression given was one of teamwork, of American marines helping Vietnamese marines, and together there, to help the villagers themselves. . . . This isn't a surefire way of winning the hearts and minds of the people—there isn't one. But, it is an effective beginning."[44] As scholar Chester Pach has argued, after the furor over Cam Ne Safer's dispatches tended to blame warfare itself, not the GIs, for the death of civilians (Safer spoke in late August of "the inevitable civilian suffering" in war). In this case he went even further, indicating that American soldiers were protecting South Vietnamese villagers from the Vietcong and from American firepower itself. Such was "censorship" in the Vietnam context; consciously or otherwise, Safer issued more encouraging reports after LBJ's intimidating outburst.[45] Other correspondents did so as well; in the same period NBC's Garrick Utley issued a dispatch with footage of American GIs aiding women who had been tortured by the Vietcong.[46]

The ambiguities of American treatment of civilians infused an NBC report by Dean Brelis airing on August 30. He began his dispatch with grim words accompanying footage of bedraggled Vietnamese refugees. These people had been displaced partly because of "Vietcong terrorism," but also because "Americans have turned their villages and farms into a battleground." Yet that did not mean, as Brelis said and images showed, that the civilians were worse off for their contact with the Americans. On the contrary: "More than marine guns, marine heart has helped [the refugees]. . . . In the same volunteer spirit, the marines donate medical supplies to the village dispensary." Meanwhile, navy doctors entered the area to provide medical services to the villagers, "not as part of orders, but because they want to help the living."[47]

Some of the doubts circulating in the media earlier in 1965 subsided when the American presence—some 185,000 strong by the end of the year—seemed to stabilize South Vietnam. In October the ardently supportive *Time* wrote with no shortage of drama of the "remarkable turnabout" in the country, a place that now "throbs with a pride and power, above all an *esprit*, scarcely credible against the summer's somber vista."[48] That fall a Louis Harris poll indicated that approval of Lyndon Johnson's handling of the war had risen sharply, to 67 percent, since the Americans had taken over more of the fighting.[49] Of course, not all was rosy. *Time* reported in January 1966 that 1,241 Americans had died in Vietnam in 1965, and 5,687 were wounded.[50] But as Walter Cronkite announced, quoting Secretary of Defense Robert McNamara on the evening of November 29, "We have stopped losing the war."[51] It was a fitting expression of progress in a perplexing conflict.

———

The year 1966 began with a pause. After heated debate among his advisers Lyndon Johnson decided to mount a "peace offensive," a bombing halt from Christmas 1965 through the end of January 1966. As American diplomats traveled abroad, trying to convince world leaders of America's commitment to peace, U.S. ground forces actually intensified attacks against the Vietcong. By late January the diplomatic drive was over, and the bombing resumed.[52] In Saigon the flamboyant Air Marshal Nguyen Cao Ky served throughout 1966 as prime minister of South Vietnam, as he had since May 1965. He was leading the most durable government of the country since the assassination of President Diem in November 1963. Meanwhile, amid continuing search and destroy missions, a World War I–style front was developing along the demilitarized zone (DMZ) separating North and South Vietnam.[53]

Although the press reported that the Americans had staved off the collapse of South Vietnam, the war became increasingly disturbing to many people in the United States in 1966. Though most Americans still supported military intervention in Vietnam, displeasure with Lyndon Johnson's handling of the war was rising. From March to September, Gallup pollsters recorded a decline in the percentage of Americans who approved of LBJ's management of the war from 50 to 43 percent; those disapproving rose from 33 to 40 percent.[54] Peace protests turned violent in Berkeley and New York City as "the emotional tug of war over Vietnam began taking on an ugly cast," according to the increasingly skeptical *Newsweek* in April. Antiwar sentiment also surfaced in the televised Senate Foreign Relations Committee hearings of February 1966. The committee's chairman, Democrat J. William Fulbright of Arkansas, invited both hawks and doves to testify before a daily TV audience that *Time* magazine estimated at 30 million. Whether the hearings changed any minds was open to debate, but they did lend an air of legitimacy to opposition growing among academics, members of Congress, and intellectuals such as Sovietologist George Kennan and columnist Walter Lippmann.[55] Millions of young men continued to dread Selective Service, which in July 1965 had doubled monthly draft calls to 35,000. "Not since Korea's bleakest days," *Time* magazine wrote in June 1966, "has the draft loomed quite so doomful in the eyes of high school and college graduates."[56]

Popular magazines continued in 1966 to illustrate the professionalism, efficiency, and compassion of American GIs. *Newsweek* pointed out in the summer that less than 25 percent of soldiers in Vietnam were draftees, though it presciently predicted an increase in that figure.[57] As in 1965, in 1966 journalists underscored the positive impact of the Americans on ordinary Vietnamese. *Time* took the occasion of naming Westmoreland "Man of the Year" for 1965 to write a long, sanguine piece on the war in January. "As it has done everywhere else," the article went, "the G.I.'s heart inevitably goes out to the war's forlorn victims." An accompanying photo showed American soldiers serving food to orphans on Christmas.[58]

In April *Life* ran a cover story on Capt. Pete Dawkins, an American adviser to a South Vietnamese battalion. The article included photographs of Dawkins playing cards, laughing, and strumming a guitar with his Vietnamese counterparts, as well as shots of "Saigon schoolgirls" surrounding him upon receipt of his first Gallantry Cross. The former All-American football star and Heisman Trophy winner from Army seemed the epitome of manliness in an article peppered with sports references in captions: "Captain Pete Dawkins Keeps on Winning"; "Pete Dawkins Takes the Field." Under another photo Dawkins was quoted: "This is the big stadium. This is the varsity. I want to be on it."[59] Another Heisman winner, Navy's All-American quarterback Roger Staubach, arrived in Vietnam in 1966 before his storied career in the National Football League. A broadcast from CBS's Ike Pappas in October used sports metaphors to describe Staubach's role in Vietnam: "Roger Staubach is still calling signals for the Navy, but they're of a different sort. It is Ensign Roger Staubach now, and he's quarterbacking a team of local workers at a Navy supply depot in Danang." Accompanying footage showed a dashing Staubach working with the South Vietnamese, throwing a football around, and heading off on a boat patrol of a river near Danang.[60]

Upholding the image of the paternalistic American GI were CBS and ABC dispatches in November, with reports of happy villagers, free medical attention, and benign questioning of Vietcong suspects.[61] A marine returning home from Vietnam told *Look* magazine about the kind treatment of enemy prisoners: "Regardless of how much we hated those bastards, they were men. They'd already been through hell. We didn't rough 'em up." The marine's experiences in Vietnam, in turn, helped him return to the United States "a man," according to his mother.[62]

In a rather novel turn, the press included African American soldiers in this pantheon of able, dedicated warriors. Often pictured in the past as either inept soldiers or as embittered, "uppity" veterans returning from war to a land of discrimination, black GIs in the fully integrated military of the 1960s seemed just as brave, committed, and skilled as their white comrades. Though African American activists as ideologically diverse as Dick Gregory, Malcolm X, John Lewis, and Martin Luther King Jr. protested the high proportion of black combat deaths early in Vietnam, much coverage of the black GI between 1965 and 1967 emphasized his value as a soldier and the egalitarianism he found in the U.S. military.[63]

"The Negro soldier's come into his own," General Westmoreland told *Look* magazine in October. "This is one of the most dramatic stories of the war. He has the self-respect he didn't have before. You can't tell the difference between Negro and white soldiers." Indeed, countless television reports and photographs in popular magazines showed blacks and whites fighting side by side without comment. A group of white soldiers from Texas wrote a remarkable letter (printed in *Time* magazine) to their commanding general about their black drill instructor, once again tying military service to manhood: "He has instilled in us a pride in the Army that I'm ashamed to say we didn't have when we first entered. He first taught each of us to be men. Next, he taught us to accept responsibilities. Then he gave us a gift of priceless value, to be 'men among men.'"[64] In May the press had widely reported the story of Pfc. Milton L. Olive III, an African American GI from Chicago. In order to save four of his comrades, Olive had fallen on a grenade the previous autumn, killing himself. At the presentation of Olive's posthumous Medal of Honor, President Johnson declared, "Men like Milton Olive die for honor," and said he believed Olive's decision to sacrifice himself to be "the hardest but the highest decision that any man is called upon to make."[65] Invoking a traditional association, the president used valor in combat as a defining measure of manhood.

As much press coverage had it, the black GI found unusual opportunity in the military. In articles in *Newsweek* ("The Great Society—In Uniform") and *Time* ("The Integrated Society"), African American GIs linked the terms of manliness directly to soldiering. "In the service," said an air force veteran, "I have been recognized as a man in every sense of the word." Others talked about how the military, particularly in Vietnam, was relatively free of racial discrimination. When *Newsweek* asked one navy man about prejudice, he replied, "I never thought about it . . . until you came aboard." Many of the soldiers said they felt merit, not skin color, determined promotions. Thus the military offered attractive job prospects for African Americans at a time when discrimination persisted on the home front, and they reenlisted at a rate (45.7 percent) three times higher than whites (17.1 percent) in 1965. Though the troops self-segregated on leave in Saigon, in foxholes there were apparently as few racists as atheists. "When you sleep in the same foxhole," a black GI from Detroit told *Time*, "you're just like brothers." According to these magazines most of the African American men admired Martin Luther King Jr. but rejected more radical activism. "Black power is a bunch of nuts," said one seaman to *Newsweek*. Another black GI said more generally, "Civil rights can wait, as far as soldiers are concerned."[66]

But such patience might fade after the war, it seemed. Black troops in past conflicts expected better treatment at home after serving their country; in the context of the civil rights movement such hopes were even stronger. "When I get back," said a black GI in the Mekong Delta, "I am as good as any son of a bitch in the States."[67]

Not all coverage of American GIs in 1966 touted their professionalism, compassion, and competence. Nor did popular news agencies ignore death and injury in wartime. The American military occasionally made dangerous mistakes, and the press reported these in a frank manner. In January a televised dispatch from CBS correspondent Dan Rather unconsciously repeated a scene from 1959's Korean War film *Pork Chop Hill*. Footage showed panicky GIs running for cover under fire, while the company commander frantically tried to call off what he assumed to be his own artillery.[68] In both the movie and this report the barrage in fact came from the enemy, but the quick assumption that it was American ordnance signaled the frequency of error. Indeed, later estimates suggested that as much as 20 percent of all American casualties came from friendly fire.[69]

In November a CBS camera crew caught just such a moment of error on film. As poorly aimed air strikes rained down on the GIs, one screamed into his radio: "Get the damn thing away from me! That's landing right in us!" Though correspondent Bruce Morton noted that most air support was devastatingly effective, the image of the shouting GI may have overwhelmed that fact.[70] A similar phenomenon marked an article in *Time* that fall. The text reported that American pilots had accidentally napalmed their own GIs, though the division commander of the unit "held no grudges" and said he would call in the air strikes again if necessary. The two sides were fighting in close quarters and that such an error could occur was just the reality of combat in Vietnam, he felt. More striking, however, was the adjoining photograph of two badly burned U.S. servicemen, their faces and arms completely bandaged, leaning against each other for support.[71] In March *Look* magazine described the fatal consequences of an American mortar round falling short into a marine platoon, using language that recalled Norman Mailer's *The Naked and the Dead* (1948) and James Jones's *The Thin Red Line* (1962): "The marines had just been pulled back for a rest. Their lieutenant, due to be married, woke to find his legs sheared off at the hips. He died of shock. [Lance Corporal] Beauchemin struggled to plug the hole in the sergeant's chest. The sergeant vomited all over him, stiffened and died in his arms. Eleven marines were casualties in the accident. Beauchemin, helping sort the bodies, cried."[72] Of course, the Second World War and the Korean War generated scores of similar accidents, but in the 1960s, without official censorship, reporters held them up for public scrutiny.[73]

Adding to the valorization of suffering in Vietnam, some publications now put images of the wounded on their covers. Starting with an issue in July 1965, *Life* magazine placed injured GIs in this prominent position several times.[74] In February and October of 1966 *Life* covers showed helpless soldiers with bandaged faces and ragged, torn clothing. In the interior of the February 11 issue, a series of photographs showed a medic, himself "so completely bandaged that he could barely peer out of one eye," feeding C-rations to another soldier with a head wound. Another victim of the war, a marine south of the DMZ, appeared unconscious, his head swathed in bandages, on *Life*'s cover of October 28.[75] (See figure 15.) In April a *Newsweek* article on the military situation included a large picture of Lt. Richard Lindsey, hit by shrapnel and crying in pain—an image strongly reminiscent of David Douglas Duncan's photographs during the Korean War.[76] Though they were by no means daily fare on television, nightly news stories in 1966 occasionally showed interviews with wounded American soldiers, footage of grimacing GIs, and on-screen medical procedures.[77]

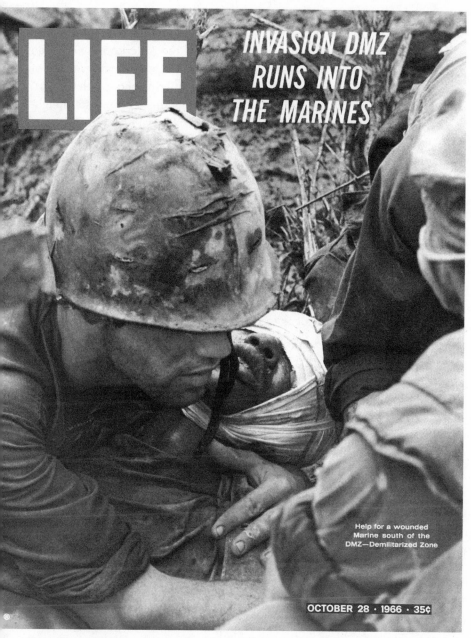

LIFE

**INVASION DMZ
RUNS INTO
THE MARINES**

Help for a wounded
Marine south of the
DMZ—Demilitarized Zone

OCTOBER 28 · 1966 · 35¢

FIGURE 15. *"Invasion* DMZ *Runs into the Marines,"* Life, October 28, 1966. *In 1966 popular magazines began featuring such helpless, bandaged soldiers on their covers or in articles. Courtesy of Time & Life Pictures/Getty Images.*

Such images were not necessarily "antiwar"; journalists surely understood that wounds and death were a part of any conflict. And most correspondents and editors in 1966 still supported the American intervention in Vietnam. But these images, like ones from Korea, reminded viewers of war's costs. In this way reporters valorized the suffering of the individual GI, made him seem pitiable, but without questioning his manliness or toughness, and without explicitly condemning the wider war effort in Southeast Asia. As Susan Moeller has written, combat photographers in Vietnam "took portraits of the troops to champion the fortitude of the individual soldiers in their sad triumph over the hardship of warfare."[78] In these portraits war was a messy, tragic business. As the conflict later stalemated, such exposure of suffering overtook support for the war in stories from Vietnam.

Deliberate or inadvertent abuse of civilians, Vietcong prisoners, and enemy suspects continued to command significant attention. Sometimes such damage seemed justified. Dan Rather reported from Vietnam in January 1966: "In this village along the Saigon riverbanks, residents admit a Vietcong battalion, with Chinese advisers, spent the night, moving out just a few hours before U.S. troops came in. Our troops continue burning every hut they find, and all crops, convinced that practically every man, woman, and child in this section belongs to the Vietcong."[79] Laura Bergquist of *Look* magazine, on the other hand, suggested just how tragic this thinking could be for the people of South Vietnam: "A visit to the jungle that is the Da Nang Surgical Hospital brings on nausea. There, two to a bed, lie hideously wounded Vietnamese civilians, children and adults. Eighty percent are war victims (mostly mortar and mine wounds, ours and Vietcong Charlie's). I couldn't look at one child, perhaps seven, who was one huge, blistered napalm wound."[80]

With different moral issues at stake the press reported the abuse of communist captives. In the spring, newspapers around the country ran a picture by photographer Sean Flynn depicting a Vietcong sniper strung up in a tree by his heels. *Time* magazine, still supportive of the war, lamented the widespread attention Flynn's photo garnered, particularly since most publications ran it without his accompanying dispatch about how the prisoner had killed a baby and was cut down unharmed after only fifteen minutes. "Such pictures," groaned *Time*, "are hardly ever balanced out by coverage of the Viet Cong's far more common tactics of terror and brutality." Evidence of American or South Vietnamese harshness "so often" received undue coverage with "indignant captions." Trying to right the wrong, perhaps, *Time* had recently reported on the killing and mutilation of two American pilots by the

Vietcong.[81] Dispatches on the brutality of the enemy often appeared in this context, as if to help justify American retribution.

Possibly feeding *Time*'s aggravation, Kenneth Gale of NBC reported from Vietnam in November about the interrogation of several Vietcong prisoners. With American GIs looking on approvingly, a South Vietnamese soldier beat one prisoner savagely. In Gale's words, "The first prisoner of the day . . . led to the other captives, but not without force. It took about an hour of this kind of treatment, karate chops and kicks administered by a Vietnamese interrogator on loan to the marines." More footage showed young boys captured by the Americans, who were "interrogated, to use the term that would go on the official report."[82] These prisoners were also struck on camera. Statistically speaking, such reports were far from common in 1966. Yet they hinted at what was to come when news of the My Lai massacre and similar incidents shocked Americans just three years later.

During the course of 1966 more than 5,000 Americans died in Vietnam, as the total force reached 385,000 troops.[83] The war continued to offer perplexing imagery. "Daily," read an article in *Look* magazine in December, "you are assaulted by the good, the bad and the wildly absurd of this peculiar war."[84] Speaking of the television networks, an editor at *Life* wrote, "Their footage *in toto* runs together as an appalling record of surprise and death, its only coherence being the Kilroyesque figure of the groggy GI slogging through the unfriendly terrain of any war, calmly convinced that he is getting a job done, the sooner the better."[85] The reference to Kilroy connected the soldier of Vietnam to his World War II–era predecessor, yet he more closely resembled the man sent to Korea in the early 1950s. As the warrior image had it, soldiers fighting in these Asian conflicts were dutiful and brave, yet also tired, cynical, and destructive.

The Vietnam War bogged down into a stalemate in 1967. Eighteen months of heavy bombing in the north had brought "dismal results," in Stanley Karnow's words; every dollar of damage done to the enemy cost ten dollars to the United States. North Vietnamese workers rebuilt bridges as fast as American bombers could destroy them. Along the DMZ the two sides remained locked in an exchange of artillery fire. In South Vietnam several major "search and destroy" operations killed huge numbers of enemy soldiers but brought few tangible gains. In fact, by the fall the communist military planners were preparing for a massive attack on sites across the south. To compensate for the somber mood in Washington and Saigon, President

Johnson and General Westmoreland made encouraging public statements on the war's progress. Particularly notorious was Westmoreland's claim in November that the United States had reached "an important point when the end begins to come into view." As journalists issued ever-darkening reports from Vietnam, such positive declarations seemed ludicrous. [86]

Accordingly, public support for the Johnson administration's policies continued to drop in 1967. In July 52 percent of those questioned by Gallup disapproved of the president's management of Vietnam, compared to 33 percent who approved. Yet nearly half of those surveyed—48 percent—did not believe that sending troops to Vietnam had been a mistake, against 40 percent who thought it had been. By October, however, those believing American involvement in Vietnam had been an error formed a majority, one that would expand in 1968. [87] Meanwhile, the draft continued to worry many families around the country. Despite widespread criticism of the inequities of Selective Service, in 1967 Congress pushed through a new draft law similar to the old one, leaving the undergraduate deferments intact. As one Vietnam veteran said years later, "The war was hanging there like a sword over everybody." [88]

In this climate of uncertainty and frustration, the press in 1967 intensified its use of imagery that had circulated since 1965 and would be popularly associated with the looming Tet offensive. Even the erstwhile supporter *Time* magazine slowly changed from hawk to dove, beginning in 1967. [89] More and more, American GIs were shown to be bitter about their situation in Vietnam, resentful of the brass, and even emotionally scarred by combat—the hallmarks of Vietnam imagery in subsequent popular mythology. Meanwhile, though, war coverage continued to ascribe traditional soldierly virtues to African American troops, overturning a long history of exclusion from such accolades.

In 1967 Martin Luther King Jr. was rapidly becoming one of the most vocal antiwar activists in the United States, at great cost to his popularity. Particularly controversial was King's speech at Riverside Church in New York City in April 1967. He called for blacks and others to refuse to fight: "As we counsel young men concerning military service, we must clarify for them our nation's role in Vietnam and challenge them with the alternative of conscientious objection. . . . Every man of humane convictions must decide on the protest that best suits his convictions, but we all must protest." [90] Mike Wallace of CBS took the occasion of the speech to question black GIs in Vietnam about King's views (which had appeared in the military newspaper *Stars and Stripes*). Wallace asked an African American officer what he thought of King's call for protest: "Well, I don't react favorably to that statement, because as a career officer, United States Army, I certainly am here because I want to be here. I believe in what the Army stands for, and I'm solidly behind what they're doing here." Wallace then asked if the man disagreed with King's view that the war was holding back progress on civil rights back home. "I do," replied the officer steadfastly. "I disagree with that portion of his philosophy."[91]

Given his high position, this officer's views might be dismissed as an anomaly; just 2 percent of officers in Vietnam were black.[92] But other GIs gave Wallace almost identical responses. The day before returning home to Hattiesburg, Mississippi, one soldier stopped to answer Wallace's question about whether he agreed with King: "No . . . I think this war is worthwhile and I think we should stay over here and see this thing out. . . . These people got to have their freedom, because every man wants his freedom, and I think it's very important." For this soldier, the limited freedom of blacks in America was all the *more* reason to fight in Vietnam, since he shared a desire for liberty with the peoples of South Vietnam. Another GI likewise saw himself as a liberator: "I feel that the war in Vietnam is a very serious thing. I feel that you have to be in Vietnam and you have to see for yourself the seriousness of this war, and to see some of the terrorism and the intimidation that the communists have placed upon these people in order to truthfully evaluate how much money we should spend in Vietnam and how much money we should spend back home." Wallace carefully granted that these men might be "out of touch with conditions back home"—each summer in the mid-1960s urban ghettos around the nation had erupted in race riots. And, reiterating media accounts of 1965 and 1966, Wallace allowed that "the army has offered the best opportunity [blacks] have ever had." Racial integration on the battlefields of Vietnam was a "fact," he said, "not just some liberal dream." Yet with all those disclaimers, Wallace ended his report with the somewhat bemused observation that the black soldiers at First Division Headquarters "come down mainly in opposition to Dr. King's views."[93]

Underscoring such sentiments was a *Time* cover story in May on African American soldiers in Vietnam by Wallace Terry. All of the black GIs he interviewed supported the war, believed in the essential goodness of the United States, and said they found racial tolerance and opportunity in the military. Though many admired King for his civil rights efforts of the early 1960s, most of the soldiers broke sharply with him on Vietnam, particularly his call for blacks to avoid military service in the Riverside Church speech. "I don't think any leader," said Lt. Col. Warren P. Kynard, "black or white, can assist the cause of freedom by preaching the cause of sedition." The boxer Muhammad Ali, who had evaded the draft for religious and political reasons, drew similar rebukes from black GIs in Vietnam. Invoking the ubiquitous link between military service and manliness, one African American soldier said of Ali, "He gave up being a man when he decided against getting inducted, and I don't want him as no Negro either." Radical activists such as Stokely Carmichael and Elijah Muhammad raised the ire of many black servicemen in Vietnam, according to the article, for their "separatist" philosophies. As for the fighting and looting in American cities, a black GI told *Newsweek* in November, "I don't believe in this rioting shit personally." Many of those interviewed would have agreed with Capt. Clifford Alexander, who tied his participation in Vietnam to more moderate civil rights activism in the United States. He told a *Time* reporter, "We are fighting over here against the Viet Cong and at home against discrimination; together we can win in both places."[94]

Motivated in this way, black soldiers were performing heroically in Vietnam. According to interviews with GIs, in fact, the much-protested death rate of African Americans arose out of their desire for dangerous (and well-paying) duties. "I get my jollies jumping out of airplanes," one black paratrooper told *Time*, and he was just one of many blacks who were "can-do, must-win competitors" hungry for hazardous assignments. The black man was proving to be a tough but humane fighter: "Often inchoate and inconsistent, instinctively self-serving yet naturally altruistic, the Negro fighting man is both savage in combat and gentle in his regard for the Vietnamese. He can clean out a bunker load of Viet Cong with a knife and two hand grenades, or offer smokes to a captured V.C. and then squat beside him trying to communicate in bastard Vietnamese."[95] Although it employed exotic imagery to describe African Americans, this characterization did incorporate black soldiers into the universe of rugged, professional fighting men established during World War II. In December NBC aired an hour-long documentary, "Same Mud Same Blood," that upheld this version of black masculinity in Vietnam. "I'm given every opportunity," Sgt. Lewis Larry told correspondent Frank McGee, "to prove beyond a doubt in anybody's mind that I'm a man."[96]

While black masculinity flourished in the military, the press occasionally used deeply controversial terms to describe it. The African American GI "may fight to prove his manhood," Terry reported in *Time*, "perhaps as a corrective to the matriarchal dominance of the Negro ghetto back home."[97] This notion—that the female-headed black family was pathological or in need of a "corrective"—had been advanced just two years earlier in Daniel Patrick Moynihan's report, *The Negro Family: The Case for National Action*. Although Moynihan, Johnson's assistant secretary of labor, had written a wide-ranging assessment of the problems plaguing the black community, critics zeroed in on the connections he drew between slavery and the allegedly weakened condition of the modern black family.

Scholars E. Franklin Frazier and Stanley Elkins had drawn similar conclusions in the past, and Kenneth Clark's book *Dark Ghetto* did so in 1965, the same year Moynihan's report became public.[98] In a climate of increasing black militancy and pride in the mid-1960s, however, Moynihan's report sparked a firestorm, becoming what the writer Nicholas Lemann has called "probably the most refuted document in American history."[99] Commentators trying to discredit Moynihan praised the female-dominated household and asserted the strength of the postslavery black family. Yet *Time* magazine's coverage of the African American GI in 1967 showed that some image makers continued to forge connections between the allegedly irrelevant black male and the allegedly pathological, matriarchal black family.[100] Although the article in *Time*, as well as Mike Wallace's dispatch from Vietnam, included the black GI within the fold of tough fighters, these reports also hinted that the young African American male could best find his manhood in the white-dominated military, far from the damaged, female-headed black community.

Just as in 1966, there were signs of trouble to come when black GIs returned home. The *Time* cover story quoted an uncharacteristically combative warning from the Urban League's Whitney Young Jr. that skills of "guerrilla warfare, of killing, of subversion" might serve blacks well should the home front not welcome them properly. An embittered African American veteran told *Newsweek* more forcefully, "Y'know, if I was back in Vietnam, I'd shoot every white guy I could find. They didn't tell me that I was going to be just another nigger when I got back here."[101] Such acrimony would deepen as the war stretched into the 1970s. Yet overall, in 1967 journalists made black GIs exemplars of patriotism, masculinity, and professionalism, even if, on occasion, they employed controversial stereotypes in doing so.

Images of combat were going through subtle changes in 1967. Some battle coverage continued to emphasize American military successes. Typical was a report from CBS's Igor Ogenessov on a major U.S. victory in the Delta. Yet his words indicated that even victory could be tragic, a reality of battle captured in Korean War coverage and the early 1960s television show *Combat!* Ogenessov spoke over footage of the American wounded: "The toll of American dead and wounded began rising this afternoon. It may be one of the most dramatic military victories in recent months; it's hard to say at this moment from here. But some American soldiers will never know how well they did."[102] Elsewhere in Vietnam, the war was beginning to take on the feel of a stalemate. Nowhere were depictions of futility and disillusionment among GIs more evident than in coverage of fighting near the DMZ.

Interviews with GIs at places near the border such as Con Thien and Dong Ha preserved the media's emphasis on individuals, a practice that dated back to World War II. But now, as in much Korean War imagery, the press valorized the suffering of the individual, rather than lauding his participation in a wider military campaign of unquestioned value. More and more, the American GI seemed the victim of foreign policy that had landed him in a war that brought mounting devastation without gains on either side. CBS's Robert Schakne reported from Con Thien in September on the inadequacy of the American position there: "Most of the wounded here are victims of shell fire. The bunkers in Con Thien are not deep enough, the trenches in the muddy ground are too shallow. They don't protect everybody when the heavy barrages come in. Simply surviving, day after day, is no easy matter on this hillside." When asked whether he was frightened by the shelling ("You don't look happy, but you don't look scared stiff."), Cpl. Ron Hensley told Schakne: "Well, I can't say that I'm scared stiff but I'm scared. I mean, after a while, you know it's gonna come, you can't do nothin' about it. And you just look to God. It's about the only thing you can do."[103] If other accounts of GIs in Vietnam valorized their professionalism, skill, and teamwork, reports such as Schakne's appreciated the simple endurance of what Burt Quint of CBS called the "violent and bloody normalcy" of combat near the DMZ.[104]

John Laurence of CBS pressed that message through interviews airing in September 1967. Stan Ottenbacher, a good-natured GI from Montana, told Laurence all about living with artillery shelling. His easy smile recalled something of the World War II–era brand of stoicism, showing that such a spirit was far from dead. But his words suggested that war was alternately terrifying, boring, dirty, and pointless. He spoke of "wallowing around in the mud," a hardship that got "pretty depressing at times," just as it had been for the GI of Korea: "Since we got up here it's been raining pretty bad and the mud gets thick, and you jump in it, you roll in it, you gotta dive in it to get out of the rounds and it's . . . you just learn to live with it." He talked wistfully about his hometown in Montana, a quiet place with "no incoming, no rockets, no artillery, no mortars, no nothin'." But most of all, he spoke of the terror of the shelling. Asked whether he had learned to live with *that*, he replied: "No. That's a new thrill every time it comes in. Stuff landing all over, bouncing off you, and, uh, you're just so scared every time. And it gets worse. Closer they get the more they throw, the more you get scared, then you get up. It's a wonderful feeling just to be alive, to be able to walk around after one of those." Young men like Stan Ottenbacher were becoming rattled and disillusioned by the artillery barrages, focusing the entirety of their efforts on survival. Ottenbacher appealed to the American people to recognize the soldiers' suffering: "Sit up and take notice of what you've got, appreciate it. Because we don't have it, wish we did."[105]

None of the emotions revealed in these interviews would have likely surprised combat veterans of World War II or Korea. Tension, depression, misery, and terror were simply a part of combat, yet in the 1950s and during the Vietnam War, especially after 1966, these experiences were more closely and vividly attributed to the American soldier than before. Journalists were widening the universe of acceptable male reactions to battle, just as image makers of the Korean War had helped remove the stigma attached to men crying. Also intensifying during Vietnam was the sense that the GI might be a victim of overly sanguine or even deceitful leadership. Widely associated with the Tet offensive, critiques of military officials had deeper roots. As Daniel Hallin has rightly pointed out, the year 1967 saw stirrings of doubt in the press corps, but they appeared in small doses earlier as well.[106]

In his report from Con Thien, Robert Schakne interviewed Maj. Gordon Cook, commander of the marines stationed there. Major Cook admitted that the GIs "don't have too much flexibility as far as moving out of here," but he brusquely dismissed comparisons to the doomed French garrison at Dien Bien Phu in 1954: "I don't feel in any way, shape, or form that this is anything like Dien Bien Phu. This is a complete connotation that is erroneous, and I don't want anybody to think we're in this position. We're in a good position here. I feel pretty confident, frankly." Another officer cheerfully declared that he would be able to get his men all the supplies they needed by helicopter, despite widespread reports on the difficulties of flying aircraft into the DMZ. If the gap between these assurances and the interviews with GIs was not obvious enough, Schakne concluded his report with words and footage that clashed with official optimism: "On this day, forty-three wounded marines were brought out of Con Thien. Some of them had to lie on stretchers for over two hours before the helicopters could come in and get them and take them out. They had to wait through one ten-minute barrage of over one hundred shells. This is the way it is, this is the way it's been, and this is the way it's going to be for quite a while at Con Thien." When the network cut back to Walter Cronkite, the esteemed anchor said journalists returning from the DMZ were reporting marine losses much heavier than the military was admitting. "And today," Cronkite intoned, "the U.S. command ordered sharp restrictions on information that is given out about the communist shellings." Though Cronkite famously lost faith in the American war only after the Tet offensive of early 1968, on the evening of September 25, 1967, he described a widening gap between image and reality in Vietnam.[107] *Time* echoed those misgivings about a week later with a cover story on Con Thien, showing a marine under fire in fetal position beneath the headline, "Rising Doubt About the War."[108] (See figure 16.)

Meanwhile CBS broadcast an even more disturbing report. Correspondent John Laurence traveled to Con Thien in September, telling the soldiers he wanted to "take pictures of you winning the war up here" and "tell the people back home how well you're doing"—an unintentional yet precise reenactment of a scene from 1959's *Pork Chop Hill*.[109] Laurence found a war different from what he expected: "The constant problem of cleanliness, the periodic shortages of food and water, the boredom, and the loneliness, and the fear, have created a kind of mass depression on Con Thien." To soldiers near the DMZ war itself was not the only culprit in their suffering. Quite critical were the words of Lt. John Theisen: "I think we're just occupying ground, and losing too many men. I'm losing too many men. [If] we were to stay here too much longer, we wouldn't have much left of this platoon, let alone the company. I see about three, four people get it a day. Not real bad, but enough to be medevac'd [medical evacuation by helicopter], cut my platoon down." But is that not part of war, Laurence asked, "as the generals say?" Theisen granted that it was, but he had his own ideas as well: "For seven months up here one battalion ain't gonna have much left, if that's part of war. Gotta rotate a little more, I think. Send us back where we can get new men and train 'em. See, we're getting new men out here, they're coming out, well, what you might call green, and they don't know really how to act out here." Theisen went on to say that these green troops caused other men to die by their own lack of experience.[110] Like Lieutenant Clemons in *Pork Chop Hill* and Captain Stein in *The Thin Red Line*, Lieutenant Theisen showed that officers, not just infantrymen, might resent or feel isolated from the leadership above them. In turn, CBS's grim portrayal of the situation at Con Thien irritated the military brass. Col. Roger Bankson, director of defense information, told *Newsweek*, "The enemy firing 200 rounds of artillery at Con Thien doesn't mean a rat's ass tactically."[111]

Despite official protests, reporters at the DMZ painted a bleak picture. Americans there were demoralized, dirty, tired, scared, hungry, thirsty, and, often, wounded or killed. Occasionally they seemed skeptical of their superiors, though other doubts of that sort surely remained concealed.[112] Official accounts of the fighting often contradicted impressions given by interviews with individual GIs. In short, the American soldier seemed a stoic victim

FIFTY CENTS

OCTOBER 6, 1967

Rising Doubt About the War

TIME
THE WEEKLY NEWSMAGAZINE

Under Fire at Con Thien

DANA STONE—UPI

VOL. 90 NO. 14
(REG. U.S. PAT. OFF.)

FIGURE 16. *"Rising Doubt About the War,"* Time, *October 6, 1967. Images such as this one visually linked "rising doubt" about the war to the suffering and vulnerability of individual men on the front lines. Courtesy of* Time & Life Pictures/Getty Images.

of forces far beyond his control, an image strongly reminiscent of Korean War coverage and some cultural productions of the 1950s. The power of the armed forces seemed particularly ominous during a CBS broadcast in April 1967. A military official interviewed by Mike Wallace, when asked whether the American people would accept projected losses of 25,000 dead, replied, "Do they have any choice?"[113]

By the end of 1967, with 486,000 American troops in Vietnam, the war was at an impasse. Despite crushing losses for the enemy, there were no signs his will was breaking. Neither the North Vietnamese nor the Americans were willing to de-escalate unless the other side did so first. Lyndon Johnson vowed, at Christmas, no longer to expect the enemy to honor overtures of peace. "A burned child dreads the fire," the president said, in what was surely one of the most ill-chosen metaphors of a napalm-laced war.[114]

In September CBS broadcast more measured words from the president. Grieving for the casualties of war—the year saw 9,378 Americans die in Vietnam, almost double the number of deaths in 1966—Johnson said, "No one hates war and killing more than I do. No sane American can greet the news from Vietnam with enthusiasm."[115] Given the grimness of imagery in 1967, few Americans, even the tenuous majority still supportive of the war, could muster enthusiasm for the news. "We want to tell people what this war is like," CBS's Robert Schakne told *Newsweek* in a year-end article on television coverage of Vietnam. "It's nothing like a John Wayne movie."[116]

On January 30, 1968, more than 70,000 communist troops launched coordinated attacks on at least one hundred cities and towns in South Vietnam, including Saigon, Khe Sanh, and the ancient city of Hué. The seemingly desperate NLF and North Vietnamese forces achieved almost total surprise, violating a temporary truce in observance of Tet, the Lunar New Year. After the initial shock wore off, the Americans and South Vietnamese inflicted enormous and often irrevocable losses on the enemy.[117] Although the communists paid dearly for the Tet offensive, they did succeed in further shrinking Lyndon Johnson's credibility at home. Those Americans disapproving of the president's war policies rose from 47 to 63 percent during the month of February.[118] Official pronouncements of optimism seemed hollow in the face of a widespread assault that looked new and unexpected, even if it was repelled with devastating force. As Stanley Karnow has put it, surprised American television viewers suddenly saw "a drastically different kind of war"—or in Tom Engelhardt's phrase, Tet sparked a "home front televisual disaster."[119]

It was true that urban combat and coordinated enemy attacks were novel elements in a war that had seemed, to American audiences, an endless string of jungle patrols. Yet much war news during Tet and thereafter reiterated, if more intensely, elements of media coverage between 1965 and 1968.[120]

Abuse of civilians and Vietcong suspects continued, as before, to attract media attention, though coverage intensified in the weeks of the offensive. One of the most horrific and widely reproduced images of the war appeared on NBC the evening of February 2, 1968. Correspondent Howard Tuckner introduced it: "Government troops had captured the commander of the Vietcong commando unit. He was roughed up badly, but refused to talk. A South Vietnamese officer held the pistol taken from the enemy officer. The chief of South Vietnam's national police force, Brigadier General Nguyen Ngoc Loan, was waiting for him." Tuckner then went silent as Loan casually waved his comrades away from the prisoner and shot him in the head, hardly pausing to look at him. Footage before the execution showed allied forces rounding up other Vietcong suspects and terrified civilians, recalling televised scenes in hamlets around South Vietnam throughout the war.[121]

There is little doubt that General Loan's act—publicized in Eddie Adams's photograph in almost every major newspaper the next day—shocked American audiences, but it was more or less business as usual in Vietnam. Popular magazines showed many bloodied, battered, or hooded enemy prisoners in the hands of allied forces, including one on the cover of *Life* magazine on February 9—though of course, the on-screen death of Loan's victim exceeded these images in sheer violence.[122] For his part, the Brigadier General seemed quite unperturbed by the worldwide furor raised over his act. In the following days television crews followed Loan wherever he went, showing him brandishing his infamous bone-handled pistol in prisoners' faces (as viewers surely held their breath), but also joking and smoking cigarettes with American GIs and fighting fires on the streets of Saigon.[123]

Often, as well, the media showed evidence of Vietcong atrocities, which were rife in Saigon and elsewhere. Some observers continued to hope that people would remember the enemy's crimes before casting aspersions on American or South Vietnamese retaliators. A doctor wrote to *Time* magazine, "I only hope that alongside [the photo of Loan killing the Vietcong] in the history books is placed the picture of the South Vietnamese officer carrying the body of his child murdered by these same Viet Cong."[124] Just before Tet, when CBS broadcast footage of dead Vietcong with their ears severed by American GIs, correspondent Don Webster explained, "You must understand the emotional state of these men, and their anger and sorrow at the loss of their buddies."[125] This would become a familiar refrain in the coming years as more systematic atrocities came to light in the American media.

Journalists focused heavily during Tet on the suffering of civilians at the hands of both the communists *and* the Americans. *Newsweek* correspondent Merton Perry reported from a hospital in Can Tho near the end of February: "According to the doctors at the hospital, when the fighting started about 50 per cent of the civilian casualties were caused by the Viet Cong and about 50 per cent by the U.S. and South Vietnamese. But as the U.S. began counterattacking with its immense fire power, it also began accounting for almost all of the casualties." An accompanying photograph showed twenty or so frightened children "surrendering" to American marines in Hué, while a picture in *Life* presented a large group of terrified civilians approaching GIs under a white flag. In this period *Look* magazine ran a "Vietnam Diary" of a GI describing the killing by Americans of a South Vietnamese father in front of his children. "I can't stop thinking about those kids. They'll hate us for the rest of their lives. And who can blame them?"[126]

For the most part these dispatches suggested the allies were friendlier to civilians than were the communists. Yet it was clear that many South Vietnamese considered the Americans the greater evil. In the midst of Tet a reporter for *Newsweek* wrote, "Not a single Vietnamese I have met either in Saigon or in the Delta blames the Viet Cong for the events of the past two weeks."[127] As if to reassure viewers of continuing American compassion, an NBC report of February 15 showed GIs setting up medical facilities in Saigon and announcing their creation over loudspeakers.[128] Media coverage of the war before Tet, though, was shot through with similar ambiguities.

Standards that had governed the exposure of corpses and injured GIs more or less held up during Tet, though the proliferation of a large number of bloody images in a three-week period lent an air of catastrophe to press coverage of the offensive. (See figure 17.) Just before Tet, *Newsweek* had placed a staggering, wounded GI on its cover, and many similar images evoking sympathy would follow.[129] Soldiers with bandaged faces, in particular, reappeared with striking regularity (*Life* had run such pictures earlier in the war, including on its cover). Perhaps magazine editors used images of bandaged faces and heads to protect the identity of the wounded, but whatever the reason, these haunting, masked GIs seemed more helpless, more *violated*, than other wounded men.[130] Similarly, a long interview with the wounded and captured pilot John McCain, later a Republican senator and presidential candidate from Arizona, appeared on CBS on February 13. A French journalist had gained entry into the North Vietnamese camp to question McCain in his bedclothes. Lying on his back, McCain repeatedly broke into tears as he spoke of his injuries and his family back home.[131] Like

FIGURE 17. *American marines at Hué City during the Tet offensive, February 6, 1968.*
Such photographs of wounded men were particularly intense if not novel reminders of the
Vietnam War's violence and unpredictability. Courtesy of National Archives.

other features since 1965, the interview valorized the suffering of individual American soldiers, and signaled the difficulty they would have overcoming that suffering.

The American dead also seemed ubiquitous during Tet. In some cases they were shown in particularly inglorious positions, heightening the abiding sense of chaos in some coverage of the offensive. *Time* magazine ran a photograph of two dead GIs lying nearby their seemingly oblivious comrades. In another color image dead American GIs were piled onto an armored vehicle, intertwined haphazardly in a manner reminiscent of pictures from the Holocaust. An additional photograph showed two soldiers under fire, dragging a fallen GI face-down by his ankles through the muck. Ten days later *Newsweek* ran a picture capturing the moment a GI was hit by gunfire as he tried to cross a street in Hué, recalling Robert Capa's famous photograph published during the Spanish Civil War. And *Life* magazine, in late February, showed a series of pictures by David Douglas Duncan, the great chronicler of the Korean War, including an image of Americans pulling charred bodies out of a smoldering plane at the besieged airstrip of Khe Sanh. Duncan, who had helped make crying an acceptable aspect of martial masculinity in the early 1950s, also snapped a photo of the base's rescue team chief, his face streaked with "helpless tears."[132]

Vivid imagery like this was too much for some American readers. A woman from Great River, New York, reacted especially strongly to *Time's* color photographs: "What earthly purpose do you serve by showing our wounded or dead in such heartbreaking pictures? What consolation is this for the families who have lost men in battle?" Another reader seemed more saddened by the image of the American dead heaped in the armored vehicle than upset at its publication: "I look at your pictures of our boys' bodies dumped on a truck in a country that no longer matters, and I weep. I am tired, tired, tired of this war. Why can't we get it over with or get out?" A man from San Pablo, California, felt no one could "applaud" the publication of such pictures, but believed they might serve to remind viewers, inured by the nightly television coverage of Vietnam, of the grimness of war. He believed most Americans had become "steeled" to the televised dispatches.[133]

Whether that was true or not, people still listened to Walter Cronkite. After traveling to Vietnam the CBS anchor delivered his own interpretation of the war on the evening of February 27, 1968. The program, "Who, What, When, Why," offered further evidence that Tet, if it sharpened American skepticism about the war, did not initiate it: "We have been too often disappointed by the optimism of the American leaders, both in Vietnam and

Washington, to have faith any longer in the silver linings they find in the darkest clouds. . . . To say that we are mired in a stalemate seems the only realistic, yet unsatisfactory, conclusion."[134] These words crushed Lyndon Johnson, who apparently said, "If I've lost Cronkite, I've lost Middle America."[135] Frustrated by the stalemated war, and bitter over the diversion of resources from his beloved Great Society programs, the president announced a month later he would not run for reelection. More than 14,000 Americans were to die in Vietnam in 1968, bringing the total number of dead under Johnson's watch to over 30,000.[136]

Lyndon Johnson's remark about Cronkite reflected his persistent fretting about the influence of the national news media. The ribald president once said of the press, "I feel like a hound bitch in heat in the country. If you run, they chew your tail off, if you stand still, they slip it to you." On the matter of the Vietnam War in particular, LBJ believed the news organizations opposed his actions and delivered biased, negative coverage, showing "bad things" from the war zone designed to make readers and viewers "hate us."[137] After the war a wide variety of commentators—from scholars to politicians to former military and diplomatic officials—echoed and elaborated upon Johnson's view, accusing the media of sensationalizing the war with bloody, misleading, or "oppositional" dispatches.[138] The political scientist Guenter Lewy wrote in 1978 that television had offered "one-dimensional" portraits of "devastation and suffering": "War has always been beastly, but the Vietnam war was the first war exposed to television cameras and seen in practically every home, often in living color."[139]

An equally diverse set of observers has provided a vital corrective to such critics of the Vietnam-era press corps. Where others saw excessive pessimism and gore, these writers have seen excessive loyalty to government aims and sanitized depictions of combat. In his oral history of Vietnam veterans published in 1981, Mark Baker articulated this view: "We didn't see it all on television. The Technicolor blotch of napalm flickering on the screen while Walter [Cronkite] recited the day's body count like a grim blessing over our suppers had little to do with gagging on the stench of a burning man. *We sanitize war with romantic adventure and paranoid propaganda to make it tasteful enough for us to live with it.*"[140] Other writers have agreed that the press offered fairly bloodless and uncritical reporting—especially in the years between the commitment of American ground troops in March 1965 and the Tet offensive of January–February 1968.[141] These scholars of the media have stressed that before Tet, most television and magazine reports reproduced the viewpoint of the Johnson administration, while editors withheld particularly gruesome realities of combat. As Daniel Hallin has put it, before 1968 "most news coverage was highly supportive of American intervention in Vietnam." In terms of violence, William Hammond has suggested, "what the public saw . . . was hardly the carnage that critics of the press have tended to allege."[142] Noam Chomsky, among others, has taken this view further and argued that the media during the Vietnam War, as at other times, acted as a mouthpiece for the American government.

Despite the usefulness of such interpretations, the common implication that Tet was a turning point in news coverage—and the emphasis on journalists' commitment to the war effort before it—may obscure the fact that troubling images of American GIs did circulate in the media early in the Vietnam War. News from Vietnam between 1965 and 1968 presented the war as anything but a "romantic adventure." Supporting the war did not prevent journalists from airing the grievances and setbacks of Americans fighting in Vietnam. Although the mainstream press was not explicitly "antiwar" before Tet, it did lay bare the confusion, misery, difficulty, and tragedy of the conflict. At the same time, though, the media did not merely sensationalize the war through constant blood and gore. Early coverage of the Vietnam War on television and in popular periodicals was enormously complex, at times foreshadowing the grim and critical reporting of the post-Tet years.

During the Vietnam War journalists began by chronicling the professionalism, skill, and compassion of the American GI. Fully committed to Cold War anticommunism, many figures in the media portrayed the soldier as part of a well-oiled machine like his forebears of the Second World War. At the same time, reporters hinted that the particulars of the situation in Vietnam—the resemblance of civilians to enemy soldiers, the dense terrain, the insurgent aid of the North Vietnamese—posed difficulties for this professional army. Journalists usually made this point not by showing violence but by showing its *aftermath*, often through interviews with wounded or shaken GIs.

Conflicting reports soon emerged about whether the GI on the ground was loved or hated by the South Vietnamese villager. In 1965 most dispatches suggested the Americans were helping a grateful civilian population, but in the ensuing years doubts crept into coverage of those interactions. Close observers of the news, meanwhile, could not help but notice that America's ally and its enemy were both guilty of war crimes. Increasingly, the American GI's complicity in the abuse of prisoners and villagers came into view, but significantly, such behavior often seemed unavoidable amid the special brutality of Vietnam. William Calley's public status as a victim after the My Lai trials was to uphold this pattern in subsequent years.

Meanwhile, American journalists participated in an ongoing revision of what it meant to be a manly fighter. World War II coverage had emphasized selflessness and toughness, and these elements remained prominent in portraits of the Vietnam-era GI. Particularly for African American soldiers, masculinity seemed linked directly to valor in combat. Surely aware of the older stereotype that African American soldiers were cowardly in battle, journalists stressed black soldiers' courage during the Vietnam War, and in doing so updated the notion of martial masculinity just by including black GIs under the umbrella of tough male fighters.[143] But journalists also occasionally invoked controversial assumptions about race, namely that black boys could only become men away from the stultifying, female-dominated ghetto household.

Yet public images of soldiers in Vietnam (and in Korea, for that matter) indicated that the very *terms* of manliness may have been changing. Author Susan Faludi, the poet Robert Bly, oral historian Mark Baker, and other commentators have found that events of the Vietnam era drove boys to hate or disappoint or distrust their fathers, thus muddying what it meant to be a man—part of an ongoing masculinity "crisis" that has preoccupied scholars of postwar America.[144] Baker has expressed what he saw as the terms of manliness before Vietnam: "What does a man do? A man stands alone against impossible odds, meets the Apache chief in single combat to protect the manifest destiny of the wagon train, plays guitar and gets the girl, leaps tall buildings in a single bound, plants the flag on Iwo Jima, falls on a grenade to save his foxhole buddies and then takes a bow to thundering applause."[145] The GIs portrayed sympathetically in the context of Vietnam possessed an ever-widening series of characteristics: sensitivity, compassion, loneliness, depression, fear, trepidation, victimhood. Heroic manliness, in the older sense, was not dead; witness the frequent celebrations during Vietnam of classic war heroes, some of whom even fell onto grenades to save their foxhole buddies. Such an act was now, perhaps, just one route to honor in the male world of the military.

Journalists covering the Vietnam War, then, proffered a dynamic and intricate warrior image. Such complexity had arrived very quickly after World War II, appearing and reappearing in Korean War coverage and some films and novels of the 1950s and early 1960s. Almost from the moment U.S. soldiers started humping through the jungles of South Vietnam, journalists continued publicizing soldiers' acts of bravery and cruelty, feelings of loneliness and comradeship and bitterness, and expressions of patriotism and manliness. Though they have drawn widespread criticism from two opposite poles—one arguing the media showed too much, the other claiming they did not show nearly enough—journalists, in fact, produced a body of work that faithfully reflected the intricacies of the American fighting man.

CHAPTER 7
I GAVE THEM A GOOD BOY, 1969-1973

Just three years after American ground troops had come ashore at Danang, Lyndon Johnson made the stunning announcement that he would not run for reelection in 1968. In those thirty-six intervening months, between March 1965 and March 1968, Vietnam ruined the president. Funds for the social programs of his Great Society were stretched thin as the government spent billions on the war. Thirty thousand American dead in Vietnam, sanguine official statements of progress about the war effort, and finally the communist Tet offensive had turned public opinion against the conflict. When, late in 1967, a narrow plurality of Americans first agreed that the war had been a mistake, it was a sign of things to come.[1]

As the election of 1968 approached, Lyndon Johnson began scaling back the war that had cost him his political life. Plans for withdrawing American ground forces passed across LBJ's desk in 1968, though his successor would ultimately put those movements into action. Johnson announced a bombing pause when he withdrew from the presidential race, and another one that fall, boosting the electoral chances of his vice president, Hubert Humphrey. The Minnesotan had won the nomination at the Democratic National Convention in Chicago, where antiwar activists clashed violently with police. The searing, televised images of protesters and cops slugging it out confirmed either that the police were fascists or that young activists were violent revolutionaries, depending on one's viewpoint. Many Americans probably fell in between these poles but were fed up with scenes of unrest, and many such voters cast their ballots for Richard Nixon or Alabama governor George Wallace. Whatever lift LBJ's bombing halt provided, Humphrey lost narrowly to Nixon in the general election.

The Republican from California assumed the presidency in January 1969 vowing to end the war in Vietnam. In fact, it would take four more years and an additional 20,000 American dead—and more than half a million Vietnamese—before a cease-fire in January 1973 ended direct U.S. military involvement. Nixon sought "peace with honor" in Vietnam, yet he would have hated nothing more than looking weak before the North Vietnamese, or worse, his enemies at home. So he walked a tightrope throughout his presidency, withdrawing American troops to appease (or, more aptly, divide and weaken) the growing antiwar movement in the United States, while escalating the war in other ways. Nixon aggressively bombed North Vietnam and mined the northern port of Haiphong Harbor, steps that Johnson had avoided out of fear of drawing the Chinese into the war. Nixon also secretly bombed Cambodia early in his presidency and ordered invasions of that nation as well as Laos.

This new strategy, known as "Vietnamization" because it handed most of the fighting to America's South Vietnamese ally, at first failed to head off antiwar sentiment. Although hundreds of thousands of American troops returned from Vietnam between 1969 and 1972, Nixon's other escalations—the unannounced bombing of Cambodia in 1969 and especially the invasion of that country in April 1970—ignited the greatest peace demonstrations in American history. Hundreds of thousands of protesters gathered routinely in this period, including at Kent State and Jackson State, where student-activists died in clashes with national guardsmen and police. Millions participated in a national moratorium against the war on October 15, 1969, while a similar event in Washington, D.C., a month later drew hundreds of thousands of marchers. The peaceful demonstrators listened to speeches by Senator George McGovern of South Dakota and music by John Denver and Arlo Guthrie. In the wake of the deaths at Kent State and Jackson State in 1970, 100,000 protesters came to the nation's capital under the direction of the New Mobilization Committee to End the War in Vietnam, or the "New Mobe." And in April 1971, when the media was giving less attention to the peace movement than earlier, half a million protesters gathered in Washington, D.C.—the largest single demonstration of any kind in American history.[2] With Students for a Democratic Society (SDS) hobbled by internecine warfare by 1969, the great antiwar rallies of the early 1970s included a growing population of moderates and liberals who felt the country had made a wrong turn in Vietnam. One man at the April demonstration said, "I am a member of the Silent Majority who isn't that silent anymore."[3] These rallies also included *veterans* in numbers unprecedented in American history.

One of the widely noted ironies of the Vietnam era was that the only thing less popular than the war was the antiwar movement. Although the protests of the Nixon years (and earlier) incorporated a wide array of activists, many of them neither students nor revolutionaries, the movement as a whole still carried a reputation for being elitist, radical, and unpatriotic—due in large part to the Nixon administration's massive efforts to color it as such.[4] Reaction to protesters could be ugly and even violent. When National Guardsmen shot four students at Kent State in May 1970, hundreds of letters poured into the local *York Gazette and Daily* defending the killings and castigating the students. "How dare they!" wrote a housewife from Ravenna, Ohio: "I stand behind the action of the National Guard! I want my property defended. And if dissenters refuse to obey the final warning before the punishment, hurling taunts, rocks (stones, they say), sticks, brandishing clubs with razor blades imbedded, then the first slap is a mighty sting."[5] Just days after the tragedy at Kent State, construction workers in the liberal bastion of New York City beat up scores of antiwar demonstrators in the Wall Street area, as police officers sympathetic to the "hard hats" looked on with approval.[6] The Nixon administration harbored equal disdain for the peace movement. When the president's people lashed out against perceived enemies in the antiwar ranks, they set in motion a series of abuses that would culminate in the Watergate scandal.

Many Americans who found peace activists obnoxious nonetheless lost their enthusiasm for the war. By the summer of 1971 the proportion of Americans who thought the Vietnam War had been a mistake reached 61 percent, against 28 percent who still favored the intervention. Approval of Nixon's war policies also dropped during his tenure. Early in his administration the law-and-order president earned high marks from a public tired of riots, lawlessness, drugs, and other perceived excesses of the vanishing 1960s. Many Americans, early on, also supported Nixon's handling of the war. In April 1969, 44 percent of those polled by Gallup approved of Nixon's actions in Vietnam, against 26 percent who disapproved. By the spring of 1971, however, the proportion of those *disapproving* had risen to 46 percent, against a minority of 41 percent who supported the administration's handling of the war.[7] These numbers would continue to shift according to the ebb and flow of the war, but overall they indicated a deepening public exhaustion with the war in Vietnam, now almost ten years old.

Into this tumultuous atmosphere poured hundreds of thousands of American veterans, leaving fewer and fewer troops in Vietnam. From a peak of over a half-million soldiers in South Vietnam at the end of 1968, American troop levels fell to 475,200 at the end of 1969; 334,600 in 1970; 156,800 in 1971; and 24,200 in 1972 (the last ground troops left in August 1972, with airmen and support personnel staying through the cease fire of January 27, 1973).[8] The withdrawal of so many troops had a devastating impact on the morale of those Americans left in the war zone, particularly since a larger proportion than before were draftees (in 1970, 43 percent of those killed in Vietnam had been drafted, up from 16 percent in 1965).[9] Americans continued to go on patrols, to inflict damage on the enemy, and to sustain casualties. But more than these things, which had figured heavily in portraits of soldiers before Tet, by the 1970s symptoms of low morale and lax discipline began dominating popular representations of GIs in Vietnam.

On first glance the warrior image of the Nixon years seemed scarcely recognizable. Some indeterminate number of GIs, according to media coverage by the 1970s, was using drugs, killing officers, committing atrocities, refusing orders, and clashing with other GIs, often along racial lines. Much of this behavior developed out of the sinking morale of soldiers, a story journalists covered assiduously. Now, though, veterans were taking a prominent role in shaping these distressing images of themselves. Most vocal in this regard was Vietnam Veterans Against the War (VVAW), formed in 1967. In three major demonstrations in 1970–71, VVAW explicitly used the image of the troubled American GI to protest the war in Southeast Asia.

Yet even painted in dark colors, soldiers often appeared as *victims*—as they had in one way or another since the late 1940s. Now, however, they were the victims of their own excesses, vices, crimes, and prejudices. According to some imagery in the media and in VVAW rallies, these pathologies evolved out of the larger military and societal structures that kept American soldiers in Vietnam. Thus even when a soldier was killing civilians, or using heroin, or refusing to fight, he might still be portrayed in the media as a victim, since it was the war or the military itself that drove him to such acts.

Ironically, the GI's status as a victim was never clearer than after the revelation of the My Lai massacre, which had taken place in March 1968 but did not come to light until the fall of 1969. One of the few matters of widespread agreement in the Vietnam era, in fact, was that those who pulled the triggers at My Lai should not be held responsible. The prosecution of one man for those crimes convinced activists in VVAW of what they already suspected: American soldiers were becoming the scapegoats for an official policy that encouraged brutality. Serving as a reliable cog in the military machine, a notion exalted during World War II, now might make one a war criminal. As much imagery of the early 1970s indicated, the My Lai massacre was yet another example of how the American military victimized the individual GI in Vietnam.

The bleary-eyed soldiers of Company C, First Battalion, Twentieth Infantry awoke early on the morning of March 16, 1968, just a few weeks after the Tet offensive. With the sun barely up, the American GIs climbed aboard helicopters bound for an area with many names. Military maps called it My Lai 4; the GIs called it Pinkville for its rose color on those maps; others called it Song My village; the Vietnamese who lived there called it Tu Cung; but to history it would be known simply as My Lai ("mee-LYE"). The company commander, Capt. Ernest Medina, was a tough disciplinarian nicknamed "Mad Dog" who nonetheless enjoyed the respect of his men. The same could not be said of the officer leading the first platoon from "Charlie Company" to enter the hamlet, Lt. William Calley. The diminutive lieutenant, known as "Rusty," was an ineffectual leader and a menace to the Vietnamese. Recently he had thrown an old man down a well, then shot him dead as the man clung to the sides. Michael Bernhardt, one of Calley's men, remembered wanting to kill Calley after watching the lieutenant sexually assault a young Vietnamese woman, but there were "just too many guys around." He would later see it as a missed opportunity.[10]

The night before the GIs boarded the choppers headed for My Lai, Captain Medina had briefed his junior officers on the situation there. Intelligence reports suggested that soldiers of the Forty-Eighth Vietcong Battalion and their families were encamped in the hamlet, and the recent experiences of Charlie Company in the area seemed to confirm those accounts. In the preceding weeks the GIs had encountered a maddening, though not unusual, number of snipers, land mines, and booby traps. The popular Sgt. George Cox had been killed just days earlier, and the company held an emotional memorial service for him just before Medina's briefing. Unable to see the enemy that bedeviled them, the soldiers of Charlie Company were simmering with a pent-up rage. Though accounts vary widely as to how explicit he was, it seems the company commander gave permission to his men to lay waste to My Lai 4. According to one account, "Medina let slip the dogs of war."[11]

The men of Charlie Company, then, walked into My Lai that bright, warm morning in a bloodthirsty mood borne of shared miseries and reinforced by the decree of their officers. As the Vietnamese villagers finished breakfast, the Americans spread out from the helicopters into the hamlet. They first shot a woman and her child, then cut down at least a dozen more unarmed civilians scurrying for cover. It was not unusual to fire upon any Vietnamese running away from the scene of a skirmish, but this was no skirmish. By every account of the events of March 16, the GIs did not take a single round of hostile fire that day.

Over the next several hours, the Americans of Charlie Company fanned out over the hamlet in small groups, none quite aware of the enormity of what was happening. Spurred on by a chaotic din of gunfire, screams, and choppers circling overhead, the GIs murdered the Vietnamese villagers singly and in clusters. They killed with bullets, with grenades, with bayonets. They raped females ranging in age from ten to forty-five.[12] They destroyed homes and slaughtered livestock, stopping only to break for lunch. Varnado Simpson testified in 1969 about what he did at My Lai:

I continued into the village and found a place where a boy had been shot by a well near a hut. A woman, carrying a baby, came out of the hut crying and carrying on. . . . Brooks told me to kill the woman, and, acting on his orders, I shot her and her baby. I have been shown a group of photographs and I identify the photograph of the woman and the baby as being the ones I shot as related here. I remember shooting the baby in the face.

We were on the left, moving ahead and burning huts and killing people. I killed about 8 people that day. I shot a couple of old men who were running away. I also shot some women and children. I would shoot them as they ran out of huts or tried to hide. [13]

A few soldiers in Charlie Company refused to take part in the massacre, and one man outside the unit tried to stop it. Hugh Thompson, a helicopter pilot circling overhead, saved a handful of Vietnamese villagers when he landed his aircraft amid the carnage and told his gunner to shoot any Americans who tried to intercede. But most of the GIs followed orders, as they saw them, and some of them even seemed to enjoy the killing. It was "just like a Nazi-type thing," one participant told a reporter the next year. [14]

All told, the American GIs executed at least five hundred men, women, and children in four hours on March 16. As evening fell, the GIs of Charlie Company camping out near My Lai performed the day's final act of absurdity by sharing their supper with the Vietnamese who had survived the massacre.

Almost immediately the army brass covered up the killings at My Lai, beginning with a press statement from Sgt. Jay Roberts. An official with the Public Information Department of the Eleventh Brigade, Roberts had gone into My Lai with the GIs on March 16 and had seen the slaughter with his own eyes. His press release, picked up by major newspapers including the *New York Times*, badly distorted what had happened: "For the third time in recent weeks, the Americal Division's 11th Brigade infantrymen from Task Force Barker raided a Viet Cong stronghold known as 'Pinkville' six miles northeast of Quang Ngai, killing 128 enemy in a running battle." [15] Already the massacre had become a "battle." A large number of officers throughout the chain of command knew about the killings, but in their official reports they erected a series of distortions. These included the spurious claim that artillery fire was responsible for most of the Vietnamese deaths. It would not be until March 1969, a full year after the massacre, that a former serviceman named Ronald Ridenhour (who was not at My Lai) would blow the whistle on the men of Charlie Company. After hearing repeated rumors about something "rather dark and bloody" occurring in the hamlet, Ridenhour wrote a letter to military leaders, administration officials, and members of Congress, outlining what he knew.[16] The letter set in motion an investigation that culminated with charges brought against William Calley and several other soldiers of Charlie Company in late 1969 and 1970. A second investigation examined the subsequent cover-up by military officials.

Meanwhile, in the fall of 1969 news of the My Lai massacre broke into public view. The army formally charged Calley with murder on September 5, the day before he was to be honorably discharged. A small paper near Fort Benning, Georgia, where Calley was stationed, published the story with little detail or fanfare, and the *New York Times* ran a similar, two-paragraph story from the Associated Press several weeks later. Neither of these articles attracted national attention. Then the freelance reporter Seymour Hersh got wind of the story and knew it would cause a sensation. After tracking down and interviewing Calley, Hersh shopped around his piece to *Life* and *Look* magazines, but neither was interested. He finally found a buyer at the Dispatch News Service, a small company devoted to disseminating radical articles among widely circulating publications. That service pitched the story to papers around the country, and thirty-five of them ran it on November 13.[17]

A week or so later stories about My Lai were dominating news coverage of the war.[18] On November 20 the *Cleveland Plain Dealer* ran eight black-and-white photographs taken during the massacre by army photographer Ronald Haeberle, and four days later Mike Wallace interviewed My Lai participant Pvt. Paul Meadlo on CBS. According to researchers Michael Bilton and Kevin Sim, Meadlo appeared "as much a victim of the war as the people he had murdered." A piece in the *New York Times* by J. Anthony Lukas, "Meadlo's Home Town Regards Him as Blameless," carried a similar tone.[19] Meanwhile President Nixon publicly vowed that those responsible for the massacre would be brought to justice, but privately he ordered secret investigations of Seymour Hersh and Ronald Ridenhour.[20]

The most sensational coverage appeared in *Life* magazine on December 5, 1969, featuring Haeberle's photographs, now in color, as well as a long article and interviews with Vietnamese survivors of the massacre. The images were appalling—mounds of dead women and children, young boys and old men in the throes of death, a group of women, some holding babies, pleading for their lives moments before being gunned down. The text of the piece recreated the moral confusion of Vietnam. At one moment the GIs were crying at the memorial service of Sgt. George Cox, as if to help explain the ensuing massacre. Yet it was repeated often in the piece that Charlie Company received no enemy fire, and several grisly or heartbreaking scenes appeared in detail. Michael Bernhardt refused to shoot the villagers of My

Lai and called it "point-blank murder," but Varnado Simpson, who admitted to killing civilians and would live out his life in a haze of depression and guilt, nevertheless told *Life*, "To us they were no civilians. They were vc sympathizers." While Sgt. Charles West called Charlie Company "the best company to ever serve in Vietnam," Private Meadlo recounted the systematic slaughter of Vietnamese children and babies. [21]

One week after publishing this story, *Life* magazine ran a long feature on public reaction to the massacre. Most of the responses, gleaned from interviews with Americans and letters written to the magazine, either absolved the GIs of blame or went further and made *them* seem victims of the massacre. Senator Mark Hatfield, an antiwar Republican from Oregon, spoke of the war's impact on American GIs: "If the Mylai massacre proves to be true, it will be further evidence of what this war is doing to all of us, not just the soldiers." A housewife from Oklahoma City said, "I don't blame the soldiers. They've been brainwashed or they wouldn't be able to shoot anybody over there. They're guilty, but no more than every person in the United States who allows our government to carry out the war." A Chicago policeman wrote, "If you give guns to 500,000 men, things like this are going to happen." Foreshadowing the defense William Calley's attorneys would use later, another Chicagoan said, "What happened was a part of the American military policy." Others were devastated by the pictures of My Lai, but sympathized equally with the GIs and the Vietnamese. "I feel as sorry for our men in it [the massacre] as for those who are dead," wrote a woman from Miami. [22]

Several people quoted in *Life* accurately predicted (and lamented) that culpability for the atrocities at My Lai eventually would rest with one man. Of all the GIs and officers implicated in both the execution and the suppression of the massacre, only William Calley was convicted of any wrongdoing. Despite a mountain of evidence, every man but Calley either was acquitted or had his case dismissed by army judges and juries. And in Calley's trial, the jury of military peers *wanted* to find him innocent, searching in vain for "some flaw in the testimony," in the words of one juror. [23] Try as they might to avoid it, the jury delivered a guilty verdict on March 29, 1971, holding Calley responsible for the murder of twenty-two villagers and sentencing him to life in prison. At the posttrial press conference, Calley's attorney George Latimer became irritated when asked why Calley killed the Vietnamese. His comments, rife with the language of victimhood, aired on the NBC nightly news. "This was a product of a system," the former judge said, "a system that dug [Calley] up by the roots, took him out of his home community, put him into the Army, taught him to kill, sent him overseas to kill, gave him mechanical weapons to kill, sent him over there and ordered him to kill. . . . Society and the country itself has to take a large measure of blame for My Lai."[24]

If the *Life* interviews of December 1969 are any indication, a large number and wide range of Americans essentially agreed with Latimer's contention —that Calley was a typical American boy who had been victimized by the brutality of the military and then singled out by his superiors in the army. Accordingly, sympathy for Calley arrived from many quarters. President Nixon, who had earlier stated publicly that the My Lai killers would be brought to justice, immediately declared that Calley would be freed from prison and returned to house arrest (Nixon fully pardoned him in 1974). From the other end of the political spectrum, the antiwar senator George McGovern was outraged by the verdict, declaring that he and the American people were "disturbed about any implication that one young junior officer should bear the burden for the tragedy of this war."[25] The former GIs in Vietnam Veterans Against the War issued a press release condemning the verdict: "Those of us who have served in Vietnam know that the real guilty party is the United States of America."[26] Television broadcasts reported that troops interviewed in Vietnam also believed Calley to be a scapegoat, while in Georgia a clergyman compared the lieutenant to Jesus Christ, saying, "We don't need any more crucifixions."[27]

Other voices chimed in on Calley's behalf as well, making him something of a folk hero in America for a brief time. A hastily assembled singing group, "C Company," released "The Battle Hymn of Lt. Calley," a record that sold 200,000 copies in three days and enjoyed extensive air time in the United States and South Vietnam. Georgia governor Jimmy Carter declared an "American Fighting Men's Day" to "honor the flag as 'Rusty' had done."[28] A series of newspaper articles by journalist Martin Gershen on the "true story of My Lai" became a book in 1971, one that fully exonerated the "innocent infantrymen": "These kids were pawns in a global game of chess played by brighter minds. . . . I realized the members of Charlie Company were victims of the worst type of exploitation. The society they served had used and abused their bodies, confused their minds, and now was grasping for their souls." Seymour Hersh's own book on My Lai, though Gershen criticized it for being too critical of the GIs, also suggested that the military was to blame for programming the soldiers. It ended with the widely quoted words of Pvt. Paul Meadlo's mother: "I gave them a good boy, and they made him a murderer."[29] Opinion polls showed that 80 percent of Americans disagreed with Calley's conviction, and that almost half, 49 percent, thought the evidence against him was a fraud.[30]

Not all observers endorsed Calley's apotheosis. When Nixon released Rusty from the stockade, *Time* magazine ran a cartoon on April 19 depicting the lieutenant standing atop a pedestal with a medallion reading "hero" hanging on his chest. Above him were ghostly versions of Willie and Joe, the cartoonist Bill Mauldin's famous grumblers of World War II. Joe looks down sadly at Calley, and says, "You sure we were fighting for the same country, Willie?" A letter to the editor in the same issue urged Americans to "shed not a tear" for Calley but instead "for his victims." The following week another letter writer asked with exasperation, "Has this nation gone mad? Can a convicted murderer of women and children really become a folk hero?"[31]

According to some alarmed mental health experts, what happened at My Lai—and Calley's status as a "folk hero"—exposed a disturbing trend toward violence in American culture. At a time when members of the media and psychiatrists were debating the effects of televised brutality on children, one such expert wrote in *Look* magazine, "Our whole culture has fostered a climate of fear and hate that has driven many people to violence."[32] Two scholars who studied public reaction to the verdict went further, concluding in 1972 that much of the public condoned the suspension of morality in the military. As these academics put it in *Psychology Today*, "There is a *readiness* for violent actions of the type committed by Calley and his men in large segments of the American population."[33]

Despite the concerns of social scientists and other Americans, William Calley indeed became a cultural hero in the spring of 1971. As Tom Engelhardt, Susan Faludi, Michael Bilton and Kevin Sim, and others have pointed out, many Americans considered *Calley* the victim—of his military indoctrination, of his superiors in Vietnam, of the brutality of war, of the legal branch of the army.[34] Though atrocities committed by Americans were a fairly new addition to the warrior image, the portrayal of Calley as a victim did recall depictions of the soldier that had circulated since the late 1940s. Particularly in Korean War films and media coverage, officers and GIs sometimes seemed the victims of inept or insensitive leadership above them. Now a soldier who carried out an immoral order seemed a victim (and even a hero) for receiving that order, carrying it out, and suffering the legal consequences. Years earlier journalists like Ernie Pyle and Bill Mauldin had celebrated the GI of World War II for his selfless subordination to the wider war effort. Some of those who defended Calley argued that he, too, was a faithful participant in the military system—but that the system was now corrupt and immoral. In either case, reporters and other observers continued to identify with and defend the individual soldier.

Public support for the lieutenant, then, suggested that dissent and cynicism were not the sole property of young radicals on college campuses. A wide cross-section of Americans, people of all political persuasions, apparently harbored not just a lack of confidence in the military, but a deep *distrust* of it. Popular magazine articles showed that some Americans in the South and West, traditionally conservative regions, believed that Calley had been trained to kill by the government and then prosecuted for doing a good job of it. Those who participated in "rallies for Calley" expressed not only their support for the troops, but also leveled a passionate critique against the structures of military justice in the United States. And antiwar Americans thought Calley represented everything that was wrong with the conflict and should not be held responsible for the illegal policies of his superiors. Thus the lieutenant became a martyr for the left, the right, and many Americans in between.

As their press release indicated, members of Vietnam Veterans Against the War took a particular interest in the ongoing story of Lieutenant Calley. Many of these antiwar veterans claimed to have perpetrated or witnessed just the sort of atrocities that had taken place at My Lai, if on a smaller scale. They believed, as many Americans did, that Calley had been made a scapegoat. "What he did is what was done on an everyday basis all over Vietnam by every unit," remembered vvaw organizer Joe Urgo years later.[35] vvaw activists would set out to prove that Calley's crimes—and their own—were simply part of U.S. military strategies in Vietnam: search and destroy, free fire zones, the body count, and attrition. If Calley seemed a victim for his legal troubles and tarnished name, though, vvaw would stress the mental anguish of men asked to execute those strategies.

The organization eventually known as vvaw had humble beginnings. On June 1, 1967, six antiwar veterans gathered in an apartment in New York City and formed a peace organization they hoped would have a unique influence on the American people as well as policy makers in Washington. Led by Jan Crumb (later Jan Barry), the men decided to allow only *Vietnam* veterans into the new organization, feeling it was crucial to rely on firsthand experience of this particular war to convince people of its immorality. Many members of vvaw had gone to Vietnam as committed soldiers but had become disillusioned by what they saw there—heavy-handed American tactics, atrocities against civilians, a series of corrupt and brutal South Vietnamese regimes, a war they felt could not be won. Though vvaw's initial purpose was to end American involvement in Vietnam, the organization was to develop an ever-widening agenda as it grew in numbers: improving

Veterans Administration (VA) hospitals, providing counseling services for veterans, studying drug addiction among soldiers in Vietnam, and aiding homeless vets.[36]

Members of the fledgling VVAW participated in several large antiwar demonstrations in 1967–68, including the clash with Chicago police at the Democratic Convention in August 1968. Demoralized by the defeat of antiwar presidential candidate Eugene McCarthy that fall and lacking funds, VVAW all but folded late in 1968. The next year the moribund organization attracted hundreds of new members by associating itself with the Vietnam Moratorium Committee and the New Mobilization Committee, large antiwar groups in Washington, D.C. After My Lai emerged from the shadows of military cover-up in 1969, VVAW activists set out to show what they had believed even before the massacre became public: the policies of the government and military in Vietnam forced individual American soldiers to commit war crimes.[37]

But why would anyone listen? VVAW leaders never were able to claim they represented the 8 million Vietnam-era servicemen, nor even the 3 million or so who went to Indochina. The organization numbered just 1,500 in 1970, though it did increase to 8,500 in 1971 and then more than doubled to at least 20,000 by 1972.[38] These numbers did not approach those of a New Left organization such as Students for a Democratic Society, which boasted 100,000 members by the end of the 1960s.[39]

Yet VVAW members were surely the most visible antiwar veterans, if not the most visible Vietnam vets of any stripe, organized in the early 1970s. Their service in the military, moreover, earned them a grudging respect from Middle America that SDS could never attract (though the Nixon administration, which claimed to represent the "silent majority," feared VVAW and tried often to subvert it). And by the 1970s, a significant current of antiwar sentiment was coursing through the military and the veteran population, feeding men into VVAW. Historian Richard Moser has estimated that 20 percent of Vietnam-era soldiers and vets "actively resisted the conflict" in Vietnam.[40] These were the people on behalf of whom VVAW protested the war. In doing so, they painted a bleak picture of the American GI in Vietnam. In the eight months between September 1970 and April 1971, these antiwar vets put themselves on display in three dramatic demonstrations.

Throughout the summer of 1970 VVAW planners arranged a new sort of antiwar protest, one that would recreate the conditions of combat in Vietnam on the streets of small-town America. Activists planned to march over Labor Day weekend from Morristown, New Jersey, to Valley Forge, Pennsylvania, two important sites of the Revolutionary War, reenacting American combat tactics in towns along the way to show the American public what was being done in its name. Dubbed Operation Rapid American Withdrawal (RAW), the march would end with an antiwar rally in Valley Forge. VVAW planners secured the endorsements of several prominent antiwar figures, including Democratic senators Edmund Muskie and George McGovern, actress Jane Fonda, and retired general Hugh B. Hester, a longtime opponent of the Vietnam War.[41]

Expressions of victimhood were to dominate Operation RAW. VVAW members understood the emotional tug of a uniformed man sitting in a wheelchair, missing a limb, or walking on crutches and actively sought out such veterans for Operation RAW. (See figure 18.) Before they let them join the march, VVAW lawyers asked wounded vets to sign a statement that made clear the organization's intentions:

(a) The purpose of the March is to attract as much public attention as possible. My *physical condition* and that of the wounded Vietnam veterans who will participate in the March is intended to be a *primary factor in attracting such attention.*

(b) You are interested in my participation primarily because of the physical condition resulting from wounds suffered in Vietnam. You expect to *publicize and feature that condition* together with the physical condition of other persons wounded in Vietnam as a means of *attracting attention to our cause.*[42]

Distinguishable by their red armbands, many wounded vets later marched, rolled in wheelchairs, or were carried on stretchers in Operation RAW. One of the aims of the march was to bring attention to the state of VA hospitals where these men received treatment. An early memo explained the seven official objectives of Operation RAW—one of them was to demand funds to improve "the deplorable inhumane conditions that prevail in V.A. hospitals."[43]

Beyond the physical condition of veterans, VVAW planners intended to expose the subtler ways American policy victimized the GI in Vietnam. Two of the official goals of Operation RAW drew attention to how military training turned peaceful boys into bloodthirsty men, just as Lieutenant Calley's many defenders had claimed. VVAW sought "to demonstrate that our military tactics dehumanize soldiers and civilians and to make clear the underlying governmental policies of the U.S. military and the Nixon administration in prosecuting an unjust and immoral war in Indochina." The final objective of the march drew more specifically on the allegations against Calley. "Most Americans," read the memo, "are shocked by the isolated reports of atrocities

FIGURE 18. *Bill Henshaw, disabled Vietnam veteran, 1973. Vietnam Veterans Against the War (VVAW) often deployed disabled veterans to protest the war, believing that they showed vividly what Vietnam was doing to American soldiers. Some of these men considered themselves "agent-victims" of the conflict, perpetrators of criminal violence against the Vietnamese people but also sufferers of great personal trauma in the aftermath of such violence. Courtesy of Wisconsin Historical Society, Image 49679.*

and blame only the individual soldiers involved. We believe, however, that true blame lies at this time with President Nixon, the Joint Chiefs, [defense secretary] Melvin Laird, [and] high ranking military officers."[44] Although VVAW activists overstated the degree to which Americans blamed Calley or other individual GIs for war crimes, they nonetheless sought to convince those Americans to grasp the brutality of official policy in Vietnam.

Once Operation RAW was under way over Labor Day weekend, the veterans illuminated the nature of war policy by staging performances of "guerrilla theater." In small towns along the route from Morristown to Valley Forge, VVAW members and actors from the Philadelphia Guerrilla Theater troupe reenacted American military tactics used in Vietnam. Former soldiers, dressed in combat fatigues, some with long hair, some with peace symbols embroidered on their uniforms, dragged the actors roughly across the ground, screamed at them, and waved plastic M-16s in their faces. As local people looked on in astonishment, the VVAW members simulated executions, interrogations, and torture. Printed instructions for the marchers gave them a sense of what VVAW expected throughout the weekend. One example read, "The action will take place in a church (New Britain Baptist Church). Squad will enter church and capture young man. Will drag him down the aisle and out the front where he is searched, beaten and taken prisoner."[45] In isolated instances veterans became overzealous as they relived experiences from the war, treating the actors from Philadelphia far too roughly. Some of them pressed knives against throats, slammed people into brick walls, and even strung victims up by their wrists over tree branches. No serious injuries resulted, but such spectacles left the impression that the horrors of Vietnam were hard to suppress.[46]

Before leaving each town VVAW members distributed fliers intended to explain the performances people had just witnessed: "A U.S. infantry company just came through here! If you had been Vietnamese, we might have burned your house . . . shot your dog . . . shot you . . . raped your wife and daughter . . . turned you over to your government for torture . . . If it doesn't bother you that American soldiers do these things every day to the Vietnamese simply because they are 'Gooks,' *then* picture yourself as one of the silent victims. Help us to end the war before they turn *your* son into a butcher or a corpse."[47] "They" required no identification. It was the same "they" mentioned by the mother of Paul Meadlo, participant in the My Lai massacre, who said, "I gave them a good boy, and they made him a murderer." VVAW implicated the entire American government and military leadership in the turning of young boys into seasoned killers. In that vein, another flier handed out during Operation RAW described Vietnam as a "trap, an ambush for American G.I.s, and you have said nothing to prevent our buddies (your sons) from going into it."[48]

By drawing attention to American atrocities committed against the Vietnamese, these performances may have unwittingly reinforced the infamous "baby killer" image. As President Nixon gradually withdrew American ground troops between 1969 and 1973, a large number of returning veterans reported that antiwar people spat on them and called them "baby killers."[49] Far from disputing that image, activists in VVAW embraced it to protest the war, admitting to killing children and other civilians but blaming those acts on officials higher up the chain of command. One of the leaflets distributed in towns during Operation RAW told readers, "As members of the United States armed forces, we were required to kill innocent noncombatants (children, women, old men)" and to "forsake our moral principles."[50] VVAW activists admitted to murdering children, but saw little choice in the matter.

The vets closed Operation RAW in Valley Forge, where several prominent antiwar figures spoke. Jane Fonda spoke of her belief that "My Lai was not an isolated incident," while her fellow Hollywood celebrity Donald Sutherland (recent star of the antimilitary film M*A*S*H) read from Dalton Trumbo's great antiwar novel, *Johnny Got His Gun*. Congressman Allard Lowenstein and the Rev. James Bevel of the Southern Christian Leadership Conference rounded out the diverse set of speakers. But none was as engaging as John Kerry, a rising star in VVAW and the future U.S. senator and 2004 Democratic presidential nominee. While working on the congressional campaign of Father Robert Drinan, dean of the Boston College Law School and a prominent antiwar critic, Kerry had appeared on the *Dick Cavett Show*, speaking eloquently against the war. At Valley Forge in the fall of 1970, Kerry emerged as the voice of VVAW. Kerry summarized the victimhood of American GIs when he told the cheering throngs, "It is not patriotic to allow a president to talk about not being the first president to lose a war, and using us as pawns in that game." One impressed member of VVAW told Kerry's sister Peggy that the future senator "looks like Lincoln and sounds like a Kennedy."[51]

The march was big news in small towns previously untouched by the antiwar activity sweeping across many college campuses, and local papers covered it extensively. The *New York Times* and the television networks offered brief daily coverage as well, but there were few other national feature stories. More widespread renown for the organization, though, was not far off.[52]

vvaw was not alone in 1971 in its campaign to expose American war crimes. Attorney Mark Lane, author of a controversial critique of the Warren Commission, *Rush to Judgment* (1966), had just published *Conversations with Americans*, a series of interviews with Vietnam veterans that included shocking accounts of atrocities committed by GIs. The Citizens' Commission of Inquiry into War Crimes in Indochina (CCI) had been holding small war crimes tribunals across the United States and Canada, and in December 1970 the organization staged a major one in Washington, D.C. During Operation RAW, vvaw planners announced their intention of holding a similar event, the group's second major demonstration of this period.[53]

Teaming up with Mark Lane and his close friend Jane Fonda, as well as CCI, vvaw began even before Operation RAW to plan what would become the Winter Soldier Investigation (WSI), a public hearing on war crimes in Vietnam to be held in January 1971 in Detroit. Lane's suggestion for the name derived from language in Thomas Paine's Revolution-era pamphlet *The American Crisis*: "These are the times that try men's souls. The summer soldier and the sunshine patriot will, in this crisis, shrink from the service of his country; but he that stands it *now*, deserves the love and thanks of man and woman."[54] For the veterans, the "summer" had been spent fighting the war in Vietnam, and the "winter" would be spent protesting it in the United States. In Detroit the "winter soldiers" were to come forward and testify to their own atrocities committed against the Vietnamese people. vvaw activists often invoked the language of the American Revolution this way, drawing connections between themselves, as antiwar veterans, and the colonists of the late eighteenth century. Deceitful, undemocratic American policy makers of the 1960s now stood in for the oppressive British authorities of two centuries earlier, and the vets joined the American revolutionaries as latter-day guardians of democracy and liberty.

An early call for participation in WSI affirmed that GIs were not to blame for atrocities committed in Vietnam: "Individual soldiers should *not* be made scapegoats for policies designed at the highest levels of government. Instead, responsibility for War Crimes should be placed where it truly belongs—upon the U.S. government."[55] vvaw vice president Craig Scott Moore wrote in a letter at Christmas 1970, "We know that 'my lai' is the inevitable outgrowth of official and de-facto United States military policy in Indochina. We have personally witnessed and participated in the daily flagrant violations of the Geneva Accords [governing the treatment of prisoners]."[56] Equally grave was vvaw's claim that the brutal policies of the U.S. military in Vietnam psychologically traumatized the American foot soldier. As an internal memo put it in the period just before WSI, "It will become apparent during the course of the testimony that the toll of the war (aside from the known damage to the Vietnamese, their culture and their land) has exacted *a terrible price, both physically and psychologically, on the American youths who as soldiers have perpetrated these atrocities.*"[57] A letter updating members on preparations for the hearings reiterated VVAW's commitment to "point out as well the severe psychological problems caused many Vietnam vets by having had to carry out this insane policy."[58]

In a note to potential WSI supporters including folk singer Pete Seeger, historian Howard Zinn, and pediatrician Benjamin Spock, Jan Crumb explicitly linked the commitment of atrocities with psychological disorders: "Thousands of our young men are returning from that war with serious mental problems arising in most part from misplaced guilt feelings."[59] These statements reflected VVAW's close work with psychiatrist Robert Jay Lifton, who was invited to speak at WSI. Together, therapists and VVAW subjects were already engaging in "rap groups," counseling sessions that revealed what Lifton initially termed "post-Vietnam syndrome," but which by 1980 would be called "post-traumatic stress disorder," or PTSD.[60]

After months of planning, more than a hundred veterans gathered in Detroit on January 31, 1971, to reveal their darkest secrets of the war. There had been bumps in the road—Neil Sheehan of the *New York Times* had discredited some of the witnesses in Lane's book, and the union with CCI had dissolved bitterly—but now hundreds of spectators jammed two ballrooms at the Howard Johnson's New Center Motor Lodge. VVAW member Bill Crandell's opening statement proclaimed the patriotism of WSI witnesses by continuing to forge a link with the American Revolution: "Like the winter soldiers of 1776 who stayed after they had served their time, we veterans of Vietnam know that America is in grave danger. What threatens our country is not Redcoats or even Reds; it is our crimes that are destroying our national unity by separating those of our countrymen who deplore these acts from those of our countrymen who refuse to examine what is being done in America's name." Crandell went on to describe broadly a host of war crimes being committed in Vietnam by American soldiers. But he made clear where responsibility lay: "We intend to tell who it was that gave us those orders; that created that policy; that set that standard of war bordering on full and final genocide. We intend to demonstrate that My Lai was no unusual occurrence, other than, perhaps, the number of victims killed all in one place, all at one time, all by one platoon of us. We intend to show that the policies of Americal Division which inevitably resulted in My Lai were the policies of other Army and Marine divisions as well."[61] After Crandell's introduction came a three-day parade of veterans testifying to war crimes in Vietnam. For observers who believed in the mythic, heroic past of the American armed forces, it must have been a depressing spectacle.

Audience members heard gruesome accounts of atrocities, including mutilation of corpses, torture, rape, and all varieties of killing—pushing prisoners out of helicopters, gunning down civilians willy-nilly in "free fire" zones, shooting for sport at farmers, fishermen, and animals. The veterans reported the rampant destruction of homes, crops, and livestock without justification. Close followers of the news since 1965 would not have been shocked at much of this evidence, but others surely were astonished at the litany of American misdeeds in Vietnam. Widely reported in midwestern newspapers, read into the *Congressional Record* by Senator Mark Hatfield, and published as a book in 1972, the testimony painted a horrifying picture of military discipline run amok in Vietnam. More crucially, in a war that administration officials were having trouble selling as necessary or just—a war conspicuously devoid of a Pearl Harbor–like moment—the "war is hell" excuse rang hollow. Antiwar activists, vvaw members, and some portion of the American public found it enormously difficult to sanction the violence visited upon the Vietnamese in the service of foggy goals.

Like the guerrilla theater participants of Operation raw, wsi witnesses often testified to the killing of children, again perhaps reinforcing the "baby killer" image so resented by many Vietnam veterans during and after the war. Sgt. Michael McCusker recounted the story of a marine who clubbed a baby to death after covering its face with straw to depersonalize the killing. Later, when McCusker's unit received sniper fire from a village, the commanding officer called in napalm. Inspection of the village revealed thirty incinerated children, laid out by survivors in the center of the hamlet. An officer reported the deaths as Vietcong atrocities. S/Sgt. Jack Smith echoed other witnesses when he testified to throwing full cans of C-rations at begging children alongside truck convoys, occasionally splitting their heads open or drawing them beneath the treads of other vehicles. Pvt. Jack Bronaugh spoke of how his unit was ordered to open fire on women and children fleeing toward them, away from their own village that was under attack by American ground troops. [62]

Just as the planners of wsi had hoped, many witnesses attested to the fact that they had been *programmed* by the military to commit atrocities. "They brainwash you," said James Duffy. "They, they take all the humanness out of you and you develop this crust which enables you to survive in Vietnam." Maj. Jon Bjornson agreed: "When you become an automaton, you begin to follow orders—the idea of killing and sticking bayonets into the model soldiers, the whole business of the gooks, the Vietnamese are inferior, which is constantly drummed into your heads. It's a kind of programming." He went on to absolve the soldiers of responsibility for crimes like those committed at My Lai: "The American GI has a great deal of difficulty disobeying an order after the kind of training he goes through." Sgt. Ed Murphy remembered his platoon leader, a Mormon minister who was a "high-character" man when he got to Vietnam. But quickly the brutality there swept up this clergyman as well. "This hell changed him around. And he would condone rapes. Not that he would do them, but he would just turn his head to them because who was he in a mass military policy[?]" When the moderator asked Sgt. Scott Camil how he could justify killing and raping the Vietnamese, he replied, "We were conditioned to believe that this was for the good of the nation, the good of our country, and anything we did was okay."[63]

Programmed to kill this way, the veterans laid bare their own suffering over acts they had perpetrated. "This is me, holding a dead body, smiling," one ex-GI told the audience as he showed a slide of himself. "Don't ever let your government *do this to you*."[64] Pfc. Charles Stephens reported, "When I came back from Vietnam, I went to a psychiatrist again *because of the things I did*, cutting off ears, castration." Speaking of his own acts against the Vietnamese, Lt. Larry Rottmann nonetheless phrased it this way for the audience: "I have nightmares about things that *happened to me* and my friends." Other veterans also used the language of victimhood to describe how they had been programmed. The drill instructors at boot camp "*make you* want to kill"; at officer candidate school, "I started realizing some of the things that *were being done to me*"; in the military my "moral worth *was completely destroyed*."[65] This testimony recalled the novels of Norman Mailer and John Horne Burns in the late 1940s, in which individual soldiers mourned the subordination of their own desires, impulses, and morals to the brutalizing enterprise of war. Now actual veterans were grieving the death of their innocence on a public stage.

A few of the ex-soldiers challenged traditional measures of masculinity. Pfc. William Light criticized the racist and macho atmosphere in Vietnam that forced Latinos and African Americans to walk point on patrols "to more or less prove their manhood." S/Sgt. Franklin Shepard remembered with horror how his unit handed out "Kill Cong" badges to GIs who could prove they had killed a Vietnamese (enemy or otherwise): "This was considered quite an honor, in fact, to have one of these badges. It was, it now seems rather sick, but over there it was the accepted thing that you were a real man if you had one."[66] In all of its protests VVAW rejected the notion that manliness in war meant selfless devotion to the group effort—the ethic of many imagined GIs of World War II. In its advocacy of counseling, as well, the organization encouraged men to share their feelings, to seek the emotional support of other men, and to shed the thick skin demanded by their military superiors. No VVAW demonstration or gathering was complete without a large quota of tears and hugs.

In his closing remarks, Don Duncan restated the notion of the veteran as victim in a sweeping indictment of the military, of the education system, and of American society as a whole:

> For those of you who have never been in the service and have listened to this testimony, you might well be amazed at how our people—our men, our boys, our sons—could do some of these things that they described in this room. Otherwise normal individuals, creating terror, torture, destruction. . . . How could they have done this? How could they *have been changed* that dramatically in eight short weeks of basic training? I think the fact that *so much can be done to so many men* by so few people is the greatest testament to the fact that our colleges, our high schools, our everyday life is nothing but pre-basic training.[67]

With these words, the hearings closed on February 2, 1971. It had been an emotional, difficult three days for both audience and participants, many of whom were discussing their tours in Vietnam for the first time. For these men WSI was enormously helpful on a personal level, as they purged years' worth of demons. The hearings also motivated antiwar members of Congress to call for investigations into war crimes.[68]

As a public relations ploy, however, the Winter Soldier Investigation was less successful. Organizers were disappointed by the sparse national media coverage. Only one television network, CBS, did a piece on the hearings.[69] CCI's National Veterans' Inquiry, held the previous December in Washington, D.C., had garnered more substantial national attention; WSI's location in Detroit meant the story drew little interest outside of the Midwest.[70]

Still, coverage in that region was extensive, and the occasional story appeared elsewhere as well. The *New York Times* emphasized the crushing guilt veterans experienced after their tours had ended but left little doubt as to where the GIs thought the blame belonged. A subheadline in that paper read, "100 Who Served in Vietnam Hold Leaders at Fault." A similar headline appeared days before the hearings in the *New York Daily World*: "'They trained us for war crimes,' vets charge." As a writer for the *New Republic* said of the witnesses a month after the hearings ended, "They were only slightly less conscious of themselves as victims than as victimizers."[71] Submission to authority, once venerated as a prerequisite for martial manhood and honor, now seemed conformist, destructive, and harmful to the GI.

Though relatively few Americans were aware of the Winter Soldier Investigation, it did attract many new antiwar veterans to VVAW, as did a concurrent recruiting advertisement in *Playboy* magazine. With membership rolls now approaching 10,000, VVAW organizers began planning a more elaborate demonstration, at least their third major event since September 1970. Set for April 1971, the impending assembly was called Operation Dewey Canyon III; Dewey Canyon I and II had been military incursions into Vietnam's neighbor, Laos. Organizers expected thousands of Vietnam vets to come to Washington, D.C., to partake in marches to Arlington National Cemetery, lobbying efforts in Congress, memorial services, and guerrilla theater. To take advantage of the prime media attention in the nation's capital, the antiwar veterans also planned a couple of more dramatic moments for the five-day demonstration.

Dewey Canyon III was to echo Operation RAW and WSI in its exposure of illegal violence in Vietnam, the victimhood of GIs asked to commit that violence, and the suffering of veterans back from the war. A VVAW newsletter summarized the agenda of Dewey Canyon III, urging members to talk to their congressmen and local press: "Tell them the national unemployment for Vn-era vets is 500,000 (Time magazine) or 15 percent–11 percent for white vets, 21 percent for black vets (New Republic); that the March issue of Reader's Digest has condemned the VA hospital system as so bad it should either be fixed immediately or closed down; that My Lai was only the tip of the iceburg [sic] where U.S. war crimes policy is concerned (refer them to the Winter Soldier Investigation); and that we will be making demands to end all these atrocious situations—both in 'Nam and here."[72] As this account suggested, the press was diligently reporting GI victimization in these years. *Life* magazine ran a cover story in June 1969 entitled "The Faces of the American Dead in Vietnam: One Week's Toll," showing prewar photographs of more than 200 Americans who had died that week; in May 1970 the same publication's cover story on "our forgotten wounded" included shocking images of decrepit VA facilities; *Newsweek* in early 1971 joined the chorus on soldier woes with its feature, "The Troubled Army in Vietnam."[73] In turn, racism, unemployment, and the condition of VA hospitals were attracting more and more of VVAW's attention.

With these and other matters on their minds, 400 Vietnam veterans arrived in Washington on the morning of April 18, 1971, and camped out in Potomac Park. The unkempt but uniformed vets reminded more than one observer of the Bonus Army of 1932, an assemblage of unemployed World War I veterans demanding their war bonuses. That group had been expelled from the capital at the points of bayonets; this one, though it had to overcome various legal injunctions against sleeping in the park, would complete its mission without violence or eviction. In the ensuing days the number of veterans at the demonstration swelled to more than 2,000. Many of them marched to Arlington National Cemetery, where security officials turned them away in a disgraceful moment, though they were admitted the next day. Others performed guerrilla theater with the same troupe from Philadelphia that had participated in Operation RAW. Still other vets made vain attempts to turn congressional hawks against the war. As cathartic as these exercises may have been, none of them attracted much media attention, the primary goal of the organizers.[74]

Far more successful in that regard were the two crowning moments of Dewey Canyon III. In the early afternoon of April 22, John Kerry settled into a chair before the Senate Foreign Relations Committee. Kerry lent an air of clean-cut legitimacy to the scruffy VVAW, appearing in combat fatigues decorated with his Silver Star and three Purple Hearts. He stirred millions of television viewers with a speech on American atrocities, VA hospitals, the accountability of the Nixon administration, and the legacies of the war in Indochina. Kerry eloquently hoped that one day, thirty years in the future, Vietnam would "not mean a desert, not a filthy obscene memory, but mean instead the place where America finally turned and where soldiers like us helped it in the turning."

Beyond those words, the most widely quoted part of the speech, Kerry articulated the victimhood of Vietnam veterans. For those who had missed the Winter Soldier Investigation, Kerry summarized the findings of that tribunal and then issued VVAW's standard explanation for the crimes it revealed: "Yet we, the actual executioners of this policy, *are also among its victims*. As with Calley, Mitchell, Torres, Hutto, Medina and the others at My Lai, we are its present scapegoats. Yet we did not send ourselves to Vietnam. We did not make the orders. We did not give the commands. We did not write the policy. Most of us were not even old enough to vote when we were inducted in this role of military executioners for United States foreign policy."[75] Many Americans would thereafter recognize Kerry as the standard bearer of VVAW. He became something of a media darling at Dewey Canyon III, though many in VVAW resented his upper-class roots, Ivy League education, and aversion to radicalism. If Kerry's speech drew jealousy from some members of the organization, it also earned VVAW much-needed media attention and legitimacy in the eyes of many legislators and ordinary Americans.[76]

The next day, Dewey Canyon III concluded with one of the most disquieting scenes of the era. Between 600 and 3,000 Vietnam veterans (accounts varied) filed to the steps of the Capitol, spoke a few words into a microphone, and hurled their combat medals onto the steps of the building (the moderate Kerry had argued for delivering the medals in body bags). Several veterans broke down in tears as they returned their unwanted decorations, acting out confessional displays before about 2,000 onlookers. "I'm turning back all this crap," said one bearded, bespectacled vet. "The bronze star, here, they gave it to me for killing fourteen people, man. It's not worth shit."[77] These anguished words protested and mourned the officially sanctioned violence GIs had been ordered to carry out. Though many Americans opposed such confrontational tactics, VVAW's message surely resonated with the increasing number of people wondering why their own sons and brothers and husbands—to say nothing of the Vietnamese people—had to suffer such hardships for an unclear purpose.

Dewey Canyon III finally attracted the national attention that VVAW organizers had been craving for eight months.[78] Kerry's speech and the medal-throwing ceremony, in particular, earned extensive media coverage. "Etched vividly in the consciousness of millions of Americans," wrote an editor in the *Akron Beacon Journal,* "will always be the pictures of scores of these heroes throwing away their medals." From an opposing perspective the *Christian Science Monitor* sneered at the veterans' self-proclaimed victimhood: "They get credit for any pain they may suffer among their contemporaries and this could even become the first step to success in a political career."[79] Falling variably along this spectrum was press coverage in Milwaukee; San Diego; Louisville; Cincinnati; Chicago; Minneapolis; Cleveland; Augusta, Georgia; and Greeley, Colorado, and in national weeklies such as *Time.*[80]

Through on-screen interviews television reporters gave the vets a platform for broadcasting their victimization. Kerry spoke of how important it was for participants in the war to protest, given that they "know what they've *been made to do.*" The next evening, after Walter Cronkite introduced Dewey Canyon as evidence of a "new dimension" in the peace movement, correspondent Bruce Morton quoted a vet who said, "They *made me fight* the war, and that's got to be more illegal than sleeping in a park." CBS cameras caught another veteran speaking with tourists about how his actions in Vietnam had affected him. "We don't feel really at home with you people any more," the ex-GI told his rapt audience, "because we've done something really awful."[81] Former soldiers in the organization never shied away from admitting that they had done monstrous things in Vietnam, but ultimately the vets blamed their military superiors or American society for creating the monsters they had become.

Antiwar activism of returning vets was just one manifestation of the plummeting morale afflicting GIs in Vietnam. A far higher proportion of servicemen there by the 1970s were draftees, perhaps less motivated than the career men who had comprised much of the armed forces early in the war. Antiwar sentiment, rising in the United States between 1969 and 1971, was gradually finding its way to Vietnam; a *Newsweek* cover in January 1971 showed a soldier with a peace sign hanging from his neck. For many soldiers, the sense that the war was unpopular and winding down sapped whatever motivation they initially possessed. As John Kerry had said in his speech during Dewey Canyon III, "How do you ask a man to be the last man to die for a mistake?"[82]

The disillusionment coursing through the armed forces in Vietnam manifested itself in a host of serious problems. Drug use, interracial conflict, and the refusal to fight (or even the killing of one's officers) were the three most discouraging signals of declining morale in Vietnam. Journalists and VVAW activists alike were stressing the pathologies of GIs in the early 1970s. Although such behaviors—some of them criminal—often invited disciplinary action, members of VVAW as well as other observers in the press often presented them as further evidence of the ways military service and the war in Vietnam victimized the individual American soldier.

On January 11, 1971, *Newsweek's* cover story on "The Troubled Army in Vietnam" vividly described the triple crises of drug use, racial tension, and indiscipline. First Sgt. Ernest R. Davis conveyed the extent of the drug problem: "The drug situation is horrible, really horrible. The farther north you go in Vietnam, the more drugs there are. Some of the forward fire bases are among the worst. The men are using marijuana, heroin and sometimes opium. In my unit, some of the medics were on heroin, using needles from our own stores. You could see the punctures right up and down their arms." Accompanying photographs showed two GIs smoking pot from the barrel of a gun. The author noted that during one two-month stretch in 1970, almost a soldier a day had died of a heroin overdose. So extensive was the use of addictive drugs that the army had even arranged an amnesty program for GIs to get help without fear of disciplinary action.[83] In March Walter Cronkite reported to his huge American audience that the Pentagon had "released figures confirming the obvious: the armed forces have a rapidly growing drug problem"; in April he grimly described how 10 to 15 percent of U.S. servicemen were using high-grade heroin. Psychedelic drugs, popular in the counterculture of the 1960s, were also prevalent in the Southeast Asian drug scene. In January 1971 Howard Tuckner of ABC visited a naval base in Vietnam and interviewed a sailor, on camera, tripping on acid. As if that image was not alarming enough, Tuckner told his audience that the man had been a police officer before the war. Apparently even proponents of law and order might be corrupted by Vietnam. [84]

In the same period a story in *Time*, "As Common as Chewing Gum," told of a respected colonel in the air force who was convicted for using marijuana and distributing it to his men. Military surveys suggested that around 40 percent of American GIs in Vietnam used illegal substances, mostly marijuana. The crackdown on that drug, according to *Time*, led directly to the rise of heroin, an odorless narcotic that could be eaten, injected, or snorted. Responsibility for the epidemic of drug addiction lay not with the soldiers themselves, the article suggested, but with the stultifying rhythms of military life in Vietnam: "There appears to be no real antidote for drugs in an expeditionary force whose members are lonely, bored, at times frightened, and always under tremendous pressure from their peers to go along. . . . It is one sorry byproduct of the war that cannot be eliminated by Vietnamization: as the U.S. soldiers come home, all too often they bring their new habits with them."[85] VVAW members agreed that drug addiction in Vietnam was further evidence of the soldier's victimization. When Jimi Hendrix overdosed on barbiturates in September 1970, VVAW issued a press release on the famed guitarist, "a brother veteran." Hendrix had served in the army early in the war, and activists in VVAW believed his time in the armed forces had led to his drug use. "Jimi is also typical of the degradation that came from serving in a racist military. He turned to junk [drugs] in order to escape from a reality so oppressive it finally killed him."[86]

VVAW's language about a "racist military" echoed an increasingly prominent militancy among black soldiers serving in Vietnam. While earlier in the war journalists had described African Americans as dependable and talented GIs, now they were finding a greater number of blacks fed up with persistent racism in the military. Wallace Terry, a reporter for *Time* magazine who had written a glowing article on martial race relations in 1967, recalled later that by 1969 "the spirit of foxhole brotherhood I found in 1967 had evaporated." Terry largely attributed this change to the higher number of draftees in Vietnam after the Tet offensive: "Replacing the careerists were black draftees, many just steps removed from marching in the Civil Rights

Movement or rioting in the rebellions that swept the urban ghettos from Harlem to Watts. All were filled with a new sense of black pride and purpose."[87] In 1966 a black sailor had told *Newsweek*, "Black Power is a bunch of nuts." Now, in January 1971, the same magazine published a picture of several smiling African American soldiers, fists clenched, holding up a sign reading, "Black Power is Number One." The adjoining article reported that white soldiers found symbols of black unity menacing and exclusionary. The "dap," a series of handshakes that became the standard greeting among African American GIs in Vietnam, frightened or irritated many white soldiers. As one black GI put it, "In the beginning, you know, we used to dap sort of quietly on the side. But then, wow, it looked like it annoyed some of the white guys. So the idea got around to dap a little louder, do it a little more."[88] An NBC report in January 1971 showed viewers what the dap, or "liberation handshake," looked like and featured blacks explaining that most white soldiers thought it was a belligerent signal.[89] These rituals, and the reactions they elicited, contributed to self-segregation of the races in Vietnam, something that had always been an issue away from the front lines but now appeared even in combat units, where there were often separate black and white bunkers.

Indeed, a small minority of black GIs in Vietnam *did* intend whites harm. A particularly troubled African American soldier's feelings appeared in an anthology of "protest and resistance" published in 1973: "We were all fed up with the racist bullshit not only in our detachment but all through the Army. . . . At times we would go out and wait for white cats to open their mouths. Some nights, just to break the tension, we'd start a fight in a bar that catered to white soldiers. We would just walk in and smack the first devil that jumped up, and when his partners came to his aid, the whole bar broke out into a brawl. That was just the way we felt."[90] While most altercations probably did not start with such one-sided aggression, other racial fights did erupt on bases all over Vietnam. In one incident, according to *Newsweek*, four hundred blacks and whites exchanged gunfire, leaving one white GI dead. In a reversal of the way justice often had been conducted in the American South, several whites faced charges of conspiracy to murder blacks.[91]

Even more common than physical altercations, however, were more mundane complaints about white racism in the military. Jim Giggans of ABC interviewed a black GI who had deserted to the streets of Soul Alley in Saigon, a popular spot for African American soldiers on leave. Racism, the deserter said, had driven him from the service—apparently not uncommon since the U.S. command in Vietnam was finding that a far greater percentage of blacks than whites deserted. "Here, in Vietnam," the renegade GI told Giggans, "if you just spit on the street, you know, the white man [will] just take you in, if you're black." Nonetheless, he preferred Vietnam to "the world," as many servicemen called the United States. "You have more of a chance livin' over here than you would back in the world. I'll stay here."[92]

Other soldiers of color had similar complaints. At VVAW's Winter Soldier Investigation in January 1971, an African American GI named Orville Carey told the audience in Detroit, "There was no chance for a promotion. You were handed out all the vile details, and in general we got a lot of practical jokes and pranks pulled on us." Pfc. William Light of the Americal Division said, "Whitey would play this game. He'd have us ready to go into the field before we even got over there. We were trained to go to the field back in the States—so Whitey gets the typewriter, you get the rifle." Asian Americans also testified at WSI about the racism of the military. Two soldiers of Japanese descent spoke of how they had been associated with the "gooks" of Vietnam. L/Cpl. Scott Shimabukaro explained: "You go to a class, and they say you'll be fighting the VC or the NVA. But then the person who is giving the class will see me and he'll say, 'He looks just like that, right there.' Which goes to show that the service draws no lines, you know, in their racism." Mike Nakayamo remembered being called a gook by his American comrades.[93]

Thus blacks and other minorities faced special challenges fighting for the U.S. military—a fact well-known for generations but only hinted at in prominent imagery since the 1950s. Korean War films such as *The Steel Helmet* (1951) and *Pork Chop Hill* (1959) had dealt tentatively with matters of race. Now, the national media found open hostility and violence between the races, even at a time when the military was more integrated and egalitarian than ever before. Such were the expectations raised by the civil rights movement of the 1950s and 1960s.

Racial divisions and drug use were not the only problems plaguing the military in Vietnam during the Nixon years. Enmity between the new generation of draftees and the "lifers," or career military men, occasionally erupted into ugly words, defiance, and even violence. *Newsweek's* cover story on "the troubled army in Vietnam" described grunts who cheered the deaths of their officers. The lifers, in turn, sometimes scorned the draftees. One sergeant told the magazine, echoing contemporary generational conflict, "These young GI's make me sick. They're soft. They have no guts. They're afraid of being shot at. They've been spoiled because their parents made it too easy for them."[94] It was true that more and more GIs in Vietnam were refusing orders, or deserting the military altogether (one account has suggested that desertion rates increased 500 percent between

1965 and 1971).[95] Such disobedience was not fully measurable by statistics but rather by rumor and experience. Everyone in Vietnam by the 1970s seemed to have participated in or witnessed or heard about desertions and mutiny.

In April 1971 *Time* reported that near the Laotian border, an entire armored cavalry unit refused an order to retrieve some military equipment from enemy territory. Recalling coverage of the Korean War, *Time* described the mutineers in a way that tacitly justified their rebellion: "Fatigued, red-eyed and black with dirt and dust, the troopers had the comatose look of men *pushed beyond their limit.*" When Lt. Col. Gene Breeding arrived on the scene to repeat the order, according to *Time*'s sanitized version, one of these bleary troopers shot back, "You must be out of your f—— mind." Breeding then lined up the troopers and asked who was willing to go on the mission. Fifty-three of the fifty-five men declined. The brigade commander did not discipline them—perhaps due to the embarrassingly large number of soldiers involved—but he did replace their unit commander. As *Time* put it just a week after William Calley's conviction, in the army "there always is a scapegoat."[96]

In some cases, mutiny could turn murderous. Officers who jeopardized the lives of their men occasionally found their own safety threatened. The preferred method for killing or wounding an officer was lobbing a fragmentation grenade at him or into his tent—hence the practice became known as "fragging." *Newsweek*'s cover story on the problems of the military in Vietnam included these words from a captain in the army:

> One night I went out to check on our perimeter and I found everybody—I mean everybody—asleep in five bunkers in a row. I just decided enough was enough, and at the last bunker, I woke the men up and took their names. I was walking away when I heard one of the guys yell, "I'm gonna kill you, you mother-f——." I heard him pull the pin, and I went down fast into a ditch. The frag sailed right past me and went off a few feet away. As soon as the dust cleared, I was right back on top of that bunker, and I really whaled on that guy. I think I would have killed him, but people pulled me off.[97]

In one three-year period, 1969–71, the army alone reported over six hundred incidents of attempted fragging. A retired officer touring Vietnam in 1971 summarized the epidemic of murder, desertion, and other crises plaguing American operations there in a widely quoted issue of *Armed Forces Journal*: "By every conceivable indicator, our army that now remains in Vietnam is in a state approaching collapse, with individual units avoiding or having refused combat, murdering their officers and noncommissioned officers, drug-ridden and dispirited where not near-mutinous."[98]

Even the scourge of fragging, however, sometimes attested to the victimization of American GIs. In a CBS report of April 1971 Walter Cronkite recounted the alarming rate of fragging incidents, quoting Senate Majority Leader Mike Mansfield, a Democrat from Montana and an opponent of the war. Mansfield believed the appalling statistic was "just an outgrowth of this mistaken, this tragic conflict." Mansfield lamented "this atmosphere that drives an American GI to kill his fellow GI."[99] The senator did not exactly absolve murderous soldiers of blame, but he did suggest that the war's particular ambiguity sullied traditional military ethics.

In January 1971 an ABC report on these deadly breaches of discipline likewise claimed the innocence of the individual soldier. When correspondent Steve Bell asked a GI what he thought of the fact that officers were afraid to move around at night, the soldier replied, "Well, it's their own fault, because they treat their men kinda bad in the field, treat 'em like a bunch of pigs." An officer, who himself felt threatened on a daily basis, ascribed the rash of fraggings to "the fact that people resent authority." Bell wrapped up the report by suggesting that some people blamed the problem on a "military generation gap, others on the war itself. Whatever the truth, there are commanders here who are saying privately that unless American troops are out of Vietnam soon, the entire military structure is seriously threatened."[100] The mutual resentment between officers and their foot soldiers, treated humorously during World War II and then more darkly in some novels and films of the postwar period, was now more visceral and violent than ever. Yet it also appeared to be a product of the Vietnam War itself, not necessarily a matter of individual deviance or wrongdoing.

In short, commentators usually linked racial conflict, drug abuse, and indiscipline as inevitable consequences of low morale among the troops. A long NBC report in January 1971 explored the prevalence of drug use and fighting among members of the First Battalion, Twenty-Second Infantry. Interviews with black and white troops showed that segregation and mutual misunderstanding plagued the compound. Whites blamed the blacks for drunkenness and aggressiveness; blacks charged the whites with racism and paranoia. A drug search carried out while the NBC crew was visiting yielded several "marijuana cigarettes." The narrator of the piece, however, painted the troops as victims of their assignment, stuck in a stultifying role in a hated war: "They *were* a combat unit, but now find themselves relegated to the role of security forces. They feel that the war has gone away, that withdrawal is the order of the day, and they want to go home now." Brief quotations followed from two soldiers, one white, one black. The African American GI said, "We don't seem to be accomplishing anything, really." The other grunt put it more forcefully: "The war's over so why the hell don't they get us home?"[101] The soldiers appeared as the helpless victims of a network of military and political leaders above them, a notion hinted at in Korean War coverage and renewed by 1967 in Vietnam War coverage. Any sense that the GIs were contributing to an important endeavor was waning. And that futility, that aura of hopelessness that hovered over the troops, seemed to be responsible for the pervasive racial conflict, drug use, and indiscipline plaguing the American armed forces in Vietnam.

––––––––

The warrior image became murky and troubling between 1969 and 1973. In his heyday during World War II, the imagined foot soldier was a selfless, manly participant in a wider war effort of unquestioned value. He did not kill civilians (even as fliers did so from the air), he followed orders (even if he did not like them), and he became a man in the military (even if he grumbled along the way). By the early 1970s, in the midst of a divisive and unpopular war, the armed forces seemed beset by breakdown—of discipline, of race relations, of military effectiveness, of personal health and morale, even of the macho ethic that had coursed through the military for generations. According to the dominant imagery of the 1970s, the GI in Vietnam might kill civilians, use illegal drugs, oppose the war, commit or report atrocities, desert the battlefield, or kill his officers, even if it was widely known that only statistical minorities did any of these things. Or more broadly, the soldier might simply be human like anyone else. In his 1977 memoir *A Rumor of War*, Vietnam veteran Philip Caputo wrote that as a leader of marines he came "to recognize them as fairly ordinary men who sometimes performed extraordinary acts in the stress of combat, acts of bravery as well as cruelty"—an observation strikingly similar to Walt Whitman's impression of Union and Confederate soldiers in the Civil War, who were all "addicted to the same vices, ennobled by the same virtues."[102]

Yet the imperfect GI of popular imagery during Vietnam was also the *victimized* GI. Since the late 1940s some filmmakers, journalists, and other commentators had been valorizing the suffering of American soldiers. Whether it was a postwar housing shortage, a brutal officer, or the horrors of war, something often seemed to be oppressing the individual serviceman. If he was black, there were special struggles for him in the military. If he was fighting in the last days of the Korean War, or under a sadistic sergeant, or in a miserable climate far from home, he seemed a victim.

Almost as soon as American ground troops arrived in South Vietnam in March 1965, these images found amplification in the uncensored media of the new war. As the conflict in Indochina began losing public and press approval in 1967, early doubts gave way to the most disturbing warrior imagery of the Cold War era. The agony of combat for the American foot soldier, increasingly apparent throughout the 1950s and 1960s, burst into full view when large numbers of people began questioning the value of this *particular* war. Few groups did so as loudly or passionately as VVAW, and those veterans' ardent portrayal of their own suffering—and their attempts to overcome it through cathartic confession—reinforced in a new and powerful way the image of the GI as victim.[103] Now, in VVAW demonstrations as well as more widely consumed depictions of soldiers in the national media, almost all of the problems plaguing GIs in Vietnam could be traced to the fact that national leaders were keeping American boys in harm's way longer than necessary. For VVAW as well as countless other Americans, even a character as odious as William Calley might become a hero and victim in this climate. And when they returned home, according to much media coverage, veterans of the war found inadequate VA hospitals, a bad economy, poor GI benefits, and an indifferent or even hostile public.[104] If novelists such as John Horne Burns, Norman Mailer, and James Jones as well as various filmmakers had described individual servicemen in distress in the setting of World War II, it was only to be expected that an unpopular war would generate even more disquieting imagery. Despite persistent charges that antiwar Americans failed to "support" the troops, it was precisely when journalists were turning against the conflict that they most identified and sympathized with the plight of the individual soldier—just as Ernie Pyle remained a steadfast supporter of the troops in World War II even as he grew more hateful of war in general.

In terms of public imagery, then, the adversarial relationship between GIs and their leaders (officers, the higher brass, and civilian leaders in Washington) originated earlier but became widely visible during the Vietnam era. What changed by the 1970s was that the institutions of authority in the United States—namely the military and government—now seemed increasingly deceitful rather than merely inept or overly cautious or overly aggressive. In the 1950s depictions of soldiers had suggested they might be victims of poor decision making or the occasional rogue lieutenant. By the early 1970s, dishonesty seemed to be coursing through the veins of authority in America. Amid Johnson's credibility gap, the public relations disaster of Tet in 1968, the My Lai cover-up, and the revelation of the Pentagon Papers in 1971, images of soldiers dying and suffering in war became much harder to stomach. Depictions of death were unsettling enough in a "good" war, let alone in a war of uncertain purpose like Korea, *let alone* in a war that appeared to be wrapped in deception and false optimism.

Indeed, this grim warrior image surely contributed to the deep distrust of the armed forces that was a chief legacy of the Vietnam War. There is little question that the stalemate in Vietnam sapped public confidence in the much-maligned military of the 1970s.[105] But if many Americans lost faith in the armed services over their alleged failures in Vietnam, many also surely objected to the way *soldiers appeared to be victimized by their leaders.* American television viewers unfamiliar with military tactics and terminology could still easily sympathize with GIs who told reporters they wanted to come home, or disagreed with their officers, or were hooked on drugs, or had deserted their units. Many Americans would not necessarily have condoned such behaviors, but a large number certainly saw them as reasons to sympathize with the American soldier.

Sure enough, a major study of American attitudes toward Vietnam veterans published in 1980 suggested that the public held overwhelmingly positive views of soldiers who had fought in Indochina. While many Americans distrusted the military, the pollsters from Louis Harris wrote, "The public rates its feeling toward Vietnam Era Veterans as very warm and overwhelmingly believes [83 percent] that these veterans deserve respect for their service. The public's feelings toward the veterans who actually served in Vietnam are especially warm and on a par with their feelings toward veterans of World War II and Korea."[106] (The survey noted that these findings replicated similar polls taken in 1971.) While many vets have felt the public held them accountable for the war's ignominious outcome, the survey found that most Americans neither blamed nor resented individual GIs for Vietnam. This view mirrored press coverage during the war, when contemporary journalists and other observers consistently *separated* soldiers from the brass above them or the war effort generally. In fact, although the media have drawn criticism from many quarters for portraying soldiers in Vietnam negatively, a "very substantial majority" of Americans believed that press coverage of the war made them *more* favorably disposed toward the GIs and *more* likely to support government programs to help them. This compassion persisted even when soldiers were shown using drugs, killing officers, and committing atrocities toward the end of the war.

Finally, the pollsters asked respondents to name the most significant effects of the Vietnam War on American society. Two answers came forth the most: 34 percent mentioned the erosion of public confidence in the institutions of government and military, and 33 percent cited "the harm done to the veterans who served in Vietnam, especially the 60,000 in-country hostile fatalities." The combination of these two responses attests to the impact of wartime coverage that pictured the American GI as the victim of a suspect foreign policy. It was the superstructure of military and government, not the soldier on the ground, that most Americans blamed for the tragedy of Vietnam. And surely playing a crucial role in the shaping of that opinion—in stimulating the very notion that Vietnam was "tragic"—was popular imagery of the individual GI in Southeast Asia.

CHAPTER 8
A DARK SIDE TO MAN'S SOUL, 1967-1978

When the television network FX premiered the short-lived Iraq War drama *Over There* in 2005, cultural critics noted that it was an unprecedented attempt to depict an ongoing American conflict on TV.[1] A similar reluctance to tackle current wars had prevailed in Hollywood since the 1960s. Yet it was not always so. During World War II more than 450 films about that conflict ran in American theaters, tied as the movie industry was to the national crusade against the Axis powers. The Korean War inspired nine commercial pictures while it lasted. In the years of heavy American military involvement in Vietnam, however, just one major film about the war appeared in cinemas—*The Green Berets* (1968), a commercially successful yet critically panned apologia for the war starring John Wayne.[2] Most filmmakers believed that the combination of television coverage of the war and its unpopularity by 1968 destined any movie about Vietnam to fail (just as public overexposure to Iraq War news contributed to the cancellation of *Over There* in 2005). The same assumption persisted through the mid-1970s, until a trickle of pictures on the war in Indochina became a flood in the 1980s.

Yet audiences often confronted the Vietnam War in film whether they realized it or not. Indeed, as one scholar has pointed out, "Some would say that a Vietnam allegory underlies virtually every significant American film released from the mid sixties to the mid seventies."[3] Vietnam-related or -inspired themes coursed through movies about World War II (*Beach Red*, 1967; *The Dirty Dozen*, 1967; *Kelly's Heroes*, 1970; *Patton*, 1970), the Korean War (*M*A*S*H*, 1970), and the American West (*The Wild Bunch*, 1969; *Little Big Man*, 1970; *Soldier Blue*, 1970; *Chato's Land*, 1971; *Ulzana's Raid*, 1972). It was only after the fall of Saigon in 1975, though, that Hollywood pictures interpreted the war directly. Film producers initially addressed veterans' post-traumatic stress, in *Taxi Driver* (1976), *Black Sunday* (1976), and *Heroes* (1977).[4] The first post–Vietnam War combat picture hit theaters in 1978 (*The Boys in Company C*), followed quickly that year by *Coming Home*, *The Deer Hunter*, and *Go Tell the Spartans*. In 1979 Francis Ford Coppola's long-awaited surreal epic, *Apocalypse Now*, premiered in American movie houses.

Literature on the war followed a similar pattern. Arriving in bookstores in 1965 was the best-selling novel by Robin Moore, *The Green Berets*, which provided the inspiration for Wayne's movie.[5] A couple of other books appeared as well—Victor Kolpacoff's *The Prisoners of Quai Dong* (1967) and William Eastlake's *The Bamboo Bed* (1969)—but most of the recognized canon of Vietnam War literature was published after the war ended. These memoirs and novels included Tim O'Brien's *If I Die in a Combat Zone* (1973), *Going After Cacciato* (1978), and *The Things They Carried* (1990); Ron Kovic's *Born on the Fourth of July* (1976); Philip Caputo's *A Rumor of War* (1977); Michael Herr's *Dispatches* (1977); W. D. Ehrhart's *Vietnam-Perkasie: A Combat Marine Memoir* (1983); and *Free Fire Zones* (1973), a collection of short stories by Vietnam vets.[6]

A smattering of American poetry about the Vietnam War emerged during the conflict, particularly from stateside antiwar activists such as Robert Bly and Denise Levertov. Yet by the early 1970s it became clear that the war had inspired an enormous body of poetry from soldiers and veterans. An early collection of wartime verse by GIs, *Winning Hearts and Minds*, appeared as the conflict was winding down in 1972. Major edited collections of poetry came in the 1970s and thereafter, including *Demilitarized Zones* (1976), *Carrying the Darkness* (1985), and *Unaccustomed Mercy* (1989), as well as works by individuals, including John Balaban's *After Our War* (1974); W. D. Ehrhart's *To Those Who Have Gone Home Tired* (1984), a collection of his published poetry from the 1970s and early 1980s; Yusef Komunyakaa's *Dien Cai Dau* (1988); and Kevin Bowen's *Playing Basketball with the Viet Cong* (1994).[7] Ehrhart, the most prolific chronicler and producer of such verse, has estimated that the Vietnam War generated a greater poetic outburst than any other conflict in American history, except, perhaps, the Civil War.[8]

Cultural critics often suggest that these imaginative representations of the Vietnam War broke sharply from past works in terms of theme, tone, and style. In the cinematic realm, for instance, one prominent film historian has written, "Not until the growing disenchantment with the Vietnam conflict did Americans begin to explore their long-standing love of the martial spirit and their previously unquestioned respect for the military establishment." The preface to an anthology of Vietnam War poetry published in the 1980s said much the same thing about verse, describing as "new" the themes therein of soldiers' guilt, "extreme bitterness," and resentment toward ignorant American civilians, as well as the "causelessness" of the war: "Overall, a reader senses that each of these [Vietnam War] poets feels used, hardly a cog in a mighty machine but rather a misfit, one who understands what no other American can."[9] In one case, an imaginative treatment of the Vietnam War contained in its very title the sense that the war in Indochina killed off the spirit of World War II: McAvoy Layne's long poem, *How Audie Murphy Died in Vietnam* (1973).

There is much truth to these characterizations. Vietnam War movies and literature did present American audiences with more disturbing imagery about their culture, soldiers, and institutions of authority than ever before. The suggestion in Vietnam War fiction and film, for example, that the adventure in Southeast Asia fed a voracious, imperialist appetite emerged from the new radicalism of the 1960s. A heavy emphasis on American atrocities against civilians and the landscape, too, belonged largely to literature about the war in Indochina, as did accounts of attacking one's own superior officers and using drugs in the field. Yet imaginative representations of the Vietnam War also *reinforced* and *amplified* many ideas about war ascendant since the late 1940s, suggesting that perhaps the difference between Vietnam-era imagery and what came before was a matter of degree more than essence.

In much Vietnam War literature as well as the films *Beach Red, M*A*S*H, Soldier Blue, Ulzana's Raid, The Boys in Company C, Coming Home,* and *The Deer Hunter,* what had been simmering distrust of federal and military authority finally boiled over in the late 1960s and 1970s. Soldiers and vets, in turn, appeared more than ever as the victims of combat trauma, postwar government neglect, and also, in media coverage of the My Lai massacre, victims of their own officially encouraged violence on the battlefield. Some of these elements were new, but others had deeper roots, particularly dating to the Korean War. The shapers of warrior imagery in the Vietnam era delivered them only with greater fervor and immediacy.

In 1967 the steady current of World War II pictures, which had begun anew with *Sands of Iwo Jima* in 1949, continued with the release of *Beach Red,* based on Peter Bowman's verse novel of the same name published in 1945. Directed and produced by Cornel Wilde, who also starred in the film as Captain MacDonald, *Beach Red* was an independent production that recalled the low-budget feel of Korean War films *The Steel Helmet* (1951) and *Men in War* (1957).[10] Along with relatively small audiences, it also shared with those pictures a potent antiwar message, now set against the tragedy unfolding in Vietnam. *Beach Red* appeared in theaters during the summer of 1967 amid the steady erosion of public support for Lyndon Johnson's handling of the war. As one scholar put it years later, in all likelihood "Vietnam was more on Cornel Wilde's mind than World War II."[11]

Captain MacDonald, a thoughtful and well-liked officer, leads his men into an assault on a nameless Japanese-held island during the Second World War. Using flashbacks and the inner thoughts of various marines under

MacDonald's command, Wilde provides a frightful and intimate account of war's impact on the individual. The filmmaker also laments the violent nature of the human race—a prominent theme of Korean War pictures that was to intensify as the Vietnam War ground on.

Whatever the moral justification for war, as *Beach Red* has it, the infantryman suffers crippling fear in combat—also a prominent component of World War II poetry of the 1960s and 1970s.[12] In an opening sequence that presages the beginning of the Second World War film *Saving Private Ryan* (1998), the marines head toward the Japanese-held island in a landing craft. The first words of the film are the private thoughts of Captain MacDonald: "Some of us put up a better front than others, but underneath, all of us, we're god-awful scared."[13] Cliff (Patrick Wolfe) thinks, "I could get killed today!" as another marine vomits over the side of the boat. The camera flashes from one terrified face to the next, much like the opening scene in *Men in War*. Some soldiers pray, others try to lighten the mood, but the abiding atmosphere is one of fearful anticipation.

When they finally hit the beach, the marines must wade through murderous machine-gun fire. One frightened soldier cowers on the beach, muttering, "Oh please! Oh please!" Eventually his arm is blown off as he lies there, and the film again prefigures a scene from *Saving Private Ryan* as the other soldiers stare in horror at the armless man staggering about. The specter of emotional devastation is a constant presence in *Beach Red*, as soldiers experience flashbacks to disturbing scenes from earlier in the movie. The fear and hatred of combat is so great that some soldiers wish for an injury; Colombo (Jaime Sanchez) thinks, "The best thing to do is to get yourself a wound, a good one, that doesn't hurt that much, and then you're on your way home, out of this muck!" He later rejoices when his thumb is shot off, even thanking the dead Japanese soldier whose last act had inflicted the damage.

As this macabre sequence suggests, *Beach Red* mourns the depravity of mankind. Captain MacDonald thinks regretfully in the opening sequence, "Only man among living things says prayers, or needs to." In the lobbies of theaters audiences saw similar language on film posters: "Of all the creatures on earth—only man hunts his own kind. 'Beach Red' is not just a war movie."[14] William Eastlake's Vietnam-based novel *The Bamboo Bed*, which appeared two years after *Beach Red*, contained a strikingly similar, though ironic, passage about the degradation of human beings in combat. "Oliver and Elgar no longer believed in war," Eastlake wrote. "They had become completely uncivilized. They no longer wanted to kill their own kind."[15] In the same period the Vietnam veteran and poet Stan Platke gestured at humanity's irrepressible hunger for violence in his poem "Nation against Nation":

> God, man is at it with the sword again
> Nation has gone against nation
> The land and the soil erodes away
> Still, barren and lifeless
> . . . like the many sons who left it[16]

Beach Red likewise avoids discussion of the wider goals of the war, leaving only the inherent violence of mankind as an explanation for why men are slaughtering each other on a remote island in the Pacific. In fact, one of the lobby posters for the film explicitly rejected the patriotic undertones replete in other World War II pictures: "It waves no flags and beats no drums. It just pulls the pin on a grenade and throws it—Catch!"[17]

Such language reflected the popularity of violent action pictures in the late 1960s and 1970s. Blood and guts splashed across the screen in a diverse array of films: *Bonnie and Clyde* (1967), *The Wild Bunch* (1969), *A Clockwork Orange* (1971), *Dirty Harry* (1971), *The Texas Chainsaw Massacre* (1974), and *Jaws* (1975).[18] Most significantly, though, *Beach Red* tapped into the wider antiwar view developing in the mid-1960s, pushed by Vietnam Veterans Against the War (VVAW) activists and others, that violence against the Vietnamese brutalized *the Americans* perpetrating it. Cornel Wilde applied that thinking in looking back toward World War II, at which time people in the United States had sanctioned the great violence unleashed against the Japanese. Like James Jones in *The Thin Red Line*, Wilde suggested that although the American people had accepted the destruction of Japan and Japanese soldiers, those acts of retaliatory violence were still tragic and dehumanizing.

Yet if *Beach Red* laments the violent nature of humanity, most of the individuals in the movie, including the enemy, are gentle souls. Wilde makes ample use of flashbacks to the civilian lives of the Japanese as well as of the Americans, and the audience is invited to mourn the deaths of soldiers on both sides. Cliff is particularly averse to the enterprise of war, thinking to himself, "There's gotta be some other way, there's just gotta be. Or what's the point?" He does, at the appropriate moments, kill the enemy, though it shakes him each time and he cries after his first experience taking the life of another man.

Less gentle is Sergeant Honeywell, played by Rip Torn. Calling to mind the rivalry between Benson and Montana in *Men in War*, MacDonald and Honeywell feud over the treatment of an enemy prisoner. When the captain discovers that Honeywell has fractured the captive's arms, he is outraged: "What was the point? Was it necessary to break both his arms?" Honeywell replies with equal rancor, widening the discussion to include his general philosophy on the war: "That's what we're here for, to kill! That's what they're doing to us, any way they can! Everything else is just a lotta crap!" MacDonald is not convinced: "I want this company to fight hard, as hard as they can! But I don't want these boys to be professional killers!" This exchange recalled the discussion among social scientists and journalists during the Second World War over whether 16 million "trained killers" would later rampage through American society. And predicting questions raised by the My Lai massacre, director Wilde felt compelled to comment on how easily some individuals might become swept up in the hatred and brutality of war.

The film does not, however, admonish Honeywell personally for his cruelty—just as in *Men in War*, the tension between brutality and compassion is unresolved. Viewers are left with the thought that combat simply dehumanizes soldiers to the point that otherwise sane young men are able to treat the enemy like animals. As one film critic put it, "The point is that war is hell for everybody"—for the enemy, the sensitive draftee Cliff, the thoughtful MacDonald, and the merciless Honeywell. [19]

Three years after the appearance of *Beach Red*, filmmaker Robert Altman made his own comment on war and the military with the release of *M*A*S*H* (1970). Much had changed in those three years. The Tet offensive of January 1968 deepened antiwar sentiment among the public, with peace demonstrations drawing hundreds of thousands by 1969. In the fall of that year Seymour Hersh broke the story of the My Lai massacre. After the appearance of *M*A*S*H* early in 1970, even greater antiwar convulsions erupted at Kent State and elsewhere. If the independent film *Beach Red* had sent an antiwar message to small audiences in 1967, by early 1970 domestic support for the war had slipped enough for an irreverent, antimilitary picture to command a large and appreciative following. Altman already had established his pacifist leanings early in the 1960s, directing several antiwar episodes of *Combat!* before leaving that TV show amid disputes over its content and tone. *M*A*S*H*, set during the Korean War, was Altman's first major Hollywood picture. Critically acclaimed and the top-grossing movie of 1970, the film soon inspired one of the most popular and enduring television shows in the history of that medium.

Based on the novel *M*A*S*H* (1968), by Korean War surgeon Richard Hooker, the film follows the exploits of three impudent army surgeons in the 4077th Mobile Army Surgical Hospital in Korea: Hawkeye Pierce (Donald Sutherland), Trapper John McIntyre (Elliott Gould), and Duke Forrest (Tom Skerritt). Under the relaxed watch of Colonel Henry Blake (Roger Bowen), the three doctors drink heavily, chase nurses, hit golf balls, and work long hours in the operating theater. The cynical surgeons also harass the career military people, particularly Maj. Margaret Houlihan (Sally Kellerman). Drawing equal derision is the hypocritically pious Maj. Frank Burns (Robert Duvall), whose sexual escapades with Houlihan are broadcast over the camp loudspeaker by the prankster surgeons (her cries give her the unwelcome nickname "Hot Lips"). These and other indignities cause Burns to snap, and he is led away in a straightjacket. The film, which essentially lacks a plot, ends with a football game between the 4077th and the 325th Evacuation Team, coached by a drinking and gambling general. After their victory (aided by drugging key players among the opposition), Hawkeye and Duke receive orders to go home.

Although not a combat picture in the classic sense—the only foot soldiers are lying anonymously on operating tables—M*A*S*H reinforces themes developing in war movies and war reporting for two decades. Depictions of casualties were increasingly explicit in American culture, and now audience members saw more of what happened once the wounded left the front lines. Like other directors of his era, Altman is not shy about showing blood and gore, often heightening the sense of shock by having his surgeons joke and flirt with nurses in the operating room (at one point Hawkeye asks an attendant to scratch his nose for him while he is sawing through a soldier's bone).[20] Though combat *deaths* do not play a prominent role in the film, in one scene several doctors and nurses stare somberly at a corpse passing by on the hood of a jeep. As one appreciative reviewer described the sequence, "We have a momentary view of the ironic complexities of life that 'M*A*S*H' means to contain."[21]

M*A*S*H is most clearly a product of its time in its antiauthoritarian message. Military leaders are inflexible, incompetent, or both. Colonel Blake is a lovable but inept commander; Major Houlihan is dogmatic and stern; Major Burns is pious and cruel. Houlihan and Burns prove hypocritical when they pursue a wild sexual tryst, scoffing at military discipline, Burns's religiosity, and his wedding vows. The surgeons drink throughout the film, dress how they please, sport beards and mustaches, and laugh at the military police, all under the nose of Colonel Blake, whose central preoccupation is making lures for fly fishing. When Houlihan discovers that the nurses call Hawkeye by his first name, she drips with sanctimony: "Well, that kind of informality is inconsistent with maximum efficiency in a military organization."[22] Hawkeye responds angrily, calling her a "regular army clown" and storming off. Houlihan asks out loud how such a "degenerated person" could have reached a position of some authority in the army. Chaplain Dago Red (René Auberjonois) responds wryly, "He was drafted."

Altman's antimilitary classic also challenged the traditional terms of masculinity. Just as some members of vvAw were then protesting the macho ethic in the military, *M*A*S*H* lampooned the homophobia coursing through the armed forces. When the unit's dentist, nicknamed "Painless Pole" (John Shuck) discovers he is suffering from impotence, he concludes that he must be gay. The distraught Painless tells Hawkeye, "I'm a fairy. A victim of latent homosexuality. I've turned into a fairy." He opts for death over homosexuality; hence the film's theme song, "Suicide Is Painless." In one of *M*A*S*H*'s more absurd moments, the other doctors give Painless a fake suicide pill and treat him to a mock Last Supper (not Altman's only stab at religion—Hawkeye and Duke sing "Onward Christian Soldiers" while watching Frank Burns pray).[23] Of course, Painless does not die, and Hawkeye convinces Lieutenant Dish (Jo Ann Pflug) to sleep with the knocked-out and well-endowed dentist on her last night in Korea. Her sexual wares have the desired effect, and he happily awakens the next morning, homosexuality narrowly averted. Just as this absurd sequence mocks military homophobia, Altman also satirizes the sexism of military people by showing them as womanizing jerks.[24] The film's oft-alleged misogyny was, according to the director, a deliberate attempt to *criticize* male chauvinism. "The precise point of that character [Hot Lips Houlihan]," Altman said later, "was that women *were* and *are* treated as sex objects. They can't blame me for the condition because I report it."[25]

*M*A*S*H*, in fact, was just the most prominent example of a darkening satire about the military circulating in American culture by the final years of the Vietnam War. In the 1940s Bill Mauldin and others had poked fun at the military brass, and there were comedic films and musicals set in World War II during and after that conflict. The Korean War, with its long, bloody retreats and stalemated outcome, did not lend itself well to humor; Mauldin's own book on Korea, cartoons included, lacked the comedy of his earlier work.[26] By 1970, when wide swaths of the country were questioning military discipline amid reports of My Lai, drug use among GIs, and race riots on bases, the armed forces were ripe for antiauthoritarian satire. Altman, who did not dare release a commercially risky picture on the Vietnam War in 1970, projected such irreverence back onto the Korean War. Others, including the producers of *The Dirty Dozen* (1967) and *Kelly's Heroes* (1970), used the setting of World War II to lampoon the military hierarchy. The heroes of *The Dirty Dozen* were violent criminals rounded up to fight the Nazis. An advertisement for the film signaled the transformation of valor: "Their violence brought them together for a mission that would set them apart from all war heroes!"[27] *Kelly's Heroes* featured a set of oddballs and scoundrels trying to steal German gold against the wishes of their commanders. As a lobby poster for the film put it, "Kelly's Heroes: They had a message for the Army: 'Up the brass!'"[28]

Others broadcast their irreverence in cartoon books aimed at the GIs in Vietnam. A series of these collections emerged from the Wayward Press in Tokyo: Ken Melvin's *Sorry 'Bout That* and *"Be Nice"* (phrases from GI parlance in Vietnam) and *How to Live in Vietnam for Less than 10 Cents a Day*, by Ken Abood and Tony Ranfone.[29] Beneath a veneer of humor, these books far outstripped Bill Mauldin's World War II cartoons in their cynicism. In doing so they evoked most of the particular difficulties of fighting in Vietnam. One of the limericks in *Sorry 'Bout That* satirized the threat of seemingly innocent Vietnamese civilians:

> Just a cute little tyke in her braids,
> Selling snowcones and pink lemonades.
>> She hung out by the gate
>> And they found out too late
> She was expert at throwing grenades.[30]

Both Ken Melvin books had drawings of Vietnamese prostitutes on their covers, revealing a component of GI life long obscured. *"Be Nice"* featured a busty hooker, her dress riding high up her leg, with the racy caption, "Be nice, Cuthburt! Where could I be hiding grenades?"[31] Other drawings in the Melvin and Abood/Ranfone collections drew humor from Vietcong tunnels, sexually transmitted diseases, "Dear John" letters, alcohol abuse, booby traps, readjustment problems, and other hazards of life in the military.

Cynical configurations of the war experience met something of an official answer in the work of Sgt. Mike Hodgson. Touted by military officials as the new Bill Mauldin, Hodgson syndicated his drawings in 1966. A collection of these cartoons, *With Sgt. Mike in Vietnam*, appeared under the auspices of the army in 1970, the year of *M*A*S*H*'s release. On the back cover, the book's editors praised Hodgson in terms that captured the appeal of Mauldin: "Fighting men of his company are Mike's strongest fans. They tell him their gripes—enlisted men always have plenty—and he depicts them. They love what he does." None other than Lady Bird Johnson extolled Hodgson's ability to "convey humor in the midst of a situation which is not conducive to lightness."[32] The drawings were essentially updated copies of Mauldin's World War II cartoons, with lighthearted jabs at the military brass, antiwar protesters, and the media. Like Willie and Joe, Hodgson's characters were perpetually filthy, unshaven, and haggard. While it is difficult to say for certain how GIs reacted to Hodgson's work, by 1970 a greater portion of foot soldiers probably would have been partial to the satirical antiauthoritarianism of cartoonist Ken Melvin and the film M*A*S*H.

As popular as Altman's movie was in 1970, most Americans would come to know its characters through the television adaptation that ran from 1972 through 1983. More people watched the final episode, which clocked in at over two hours, than any single program in the history of television.[33] That M*A*S*H delivered an irreverent and cynical view of the military throughout its run testified to the shape of that institution's reputation in post-Vietnam America.[34]

———

While *Beach Red*, *The Dirty Dozen*, *M*A*S*H*, and *Kelly's Heroes* used other twentieth-century conflicts as stand-ins for the Vietnam War, several filmmakers of the same period set their allegories in the American West. The cultures of the West and of American wars overlapped even before the spate of "Vietnam westerns" appeared around 1970. GIs routinely called Vietcong-held territory "Indian country." In William Eastlake's novel *The Bamboo Bed* (1969), a soldier dying in Vietnam imagines himself somewhere else: "All I remember is that I was with Custer's Seventh Cavalry riding toward the Little Big Horn and we were struck by the Indians. After we crossed the Rosebud we made it to Ridge Red Boy and then we were hit. No. I must have my wars confused."[35] In film, too, war and the American West blended. The Hollywood hero of both the nineteenth-century frontier and twentieth-century warfare was the same John Wayne—and more than a few Vietnam veterans later cited Wayne's dramatic personae as inspiration for their own martial dreams. Thus it was not surprising that movie producers chose to comment on the Vietnam War through stories of cowboys, Indians, and Indian-hunting federal troops. After the revelation of the My Lai massacre in the fall of 1969, such films became natural venues for remarking on the killing of women and children by American soldiers.

Typical of this genre were *Soldier Blue* (1970) and *Ulzana's Raid* (1972). In these movies the nineteenth-century army regular, fighting Indians on the Great Plains, strongly resembled the American GI in Vietnam—before and during the uproar over My Lai. Like some of their counterparts in the media and in VVAW, producers of Vietnam westerns emphasized the powerlessness and victimhood of soldiers ordered to kill civilians, the depravity and corruption of officers, and humankind's violent and degenerate nature.

According to one film scholar *Soldier Blue* was an "intentional evocation" of the My Lai tragedy, and contemporary reviewers could hardly fail to notice the same.[36] The opening words scrolling on the screen suggest immediately where the movie is heading: "Mankind's noblest achievements reveal a divine spark. But there is a dark side to man's soul that has festered since Cain slew his brother. The climax of 'Soldier Blue' shows specifically and graphically the horrors of battle as bloodlust overcomes reason. Brutal atrocities affect not only the warriors, but the innocent as well . . . the women and children. The greatest horror of all is that it is true."[37]

The movie begins with an army unit traveling through Colorado territory during the Civil War, transporting a large cache of money as well as the beautiful Cresta Marybelle Lee (Candice Bergen), who had been abducted by the Cheyenne. Of patrician roots and engaged to an officer in the army, Cresta nonetheless harbors sympathy for the Indians, whose devastation at the hands of American soldiers she has witnessed. When the detachment is attacked by the Cheyenne, only Cresta and Pvt. Honus Gant (Peter Strauss) survive. Gant recoils at the slaughter of his fellow soldiers by the Indians ("Murdering savages!"), while Cresta defends the right of the Cheyenne to the territory.

The pair repeats this argument as they wander through hostile territory until reuniting with the army. Their exchanges roughly mimicked debates of the 1960s over the right of American troops to be in Vietnam and over the savagery committed by both sides. Cresta's stunning looks and fiery defense of the Cheyenne surely reminded contemporary theatergoers of Jane Fonda (at one point Gant calls Cresta a traitor to her country, a charge Fonda was to endure for decades), or more generally of the archetypal female antiwar protester of the 1960s. One film critic scoffed at how Cresta's words often "ring like notes from an SDS meeting."[38] Gant stands in for the wide-eyed, naive inductee of the Vietnam era, at first patriotic and hateful of the enemy but soon to become radicalized by the violence he is ordered to perpetrate against women and children. Gant's conversion from hawk to dove, so to speak, is completed when he and Cresta witness the Sand Creek Massacre at the end of the film, an event that took place on November 29, 1864, in Colorado territory. In shocking footage, the producers of *Soldier Blue* recreate the slaughter of hundreds of Cheyenne and Arapaho innocents. American soldiers take Gant away in chains after he tries to thwart the massacre.

The ongoing debate between Cresta and Gant over the comparative savagery of the army and the Indians parallels contemporary discussion of the My Lai massacre. One exchange in particular evoked not only that atrocity but larger questions of whether the Americans had any right to be in Vietnam (or, in the film, the West):

> Cresta: Puttin' up their [army] forts in a country they've got no claim to. So what the hell do you expect the Indians to do, sit back on their butts while the army takes over their land?
> Gant: You saw for yourself what they did, taking off scalps . . .
> Cresta: Yeah, and who taught 'em that little trick? The white man!
> Gant: And cutting off hands, and cutting off feet, and cutting off . . .
> Cresta: I know what they cut off. But at least they don't make tobacco pouches out of 'em. That's something else you soldier-boys made up.
> Gant: You're lying!
> Cresta: You ever see an Indian camp after the army's been there? Huh? You ever see the women and what was done to them before they were killed? You ever see the little boys and girls stuck on the long knives, hmm? Stuck and dying?! Well I have.

This argument evoked several specific forms of violence in Vietnam—the severing of body parts, rape, torture—that journalists and filmmakers were ascribing by 1970 to the Americans, their South Vietnamese allies, and the Vietcong. *Soldier Blue* portrays both the Cheyenne warriors and the army as savage, stripping each side in the conflict of any particular moral superiority, leaving warfare and human nature as the true enemies.

The climactic scene in *Soldier Blue* shows the Sand Creek Massacre in its full, bloody detail. (Critics roundly panned the film for its visual excesses, though even more graphic footage was left out of the final version.)[39] Almost every element of atrocity narratives from Vietnam, by then familiar to Americans who read *Life* magazine or watched the news on television, figured prominently in the long sequence. The commanding officer reminds his men before they head into the Cheyenne settlement of the Indian's penchant for "murder," "rape," and "torture," paralleling the real-life buildup to My Lai in March 1968, when the men of Charlie Company held a funeral service for a favorite comrade and listened to the anguished cries of a tortured American somewhere off in the night.[40] Images of soldiers torching teepees recall Morley Safer's televised dispatch from Cam Ne in 1965. Other soldiers laugh as they rape and torture Indian women, a reality in every war, including Vietnam, but an abiding feature of the American warrior image only in the wake of My Lai. An old Cheyenne woman holds a child tightly moments before they are both gunned down, replaying one of Ronald

Haeberle's most disturbing photographs from My Lai. Other such pictures reappear as well, particularly in footage of slaughtered women and children piled haphazardly. One officer kills a young girl to put her "out of [her] misery," just as some American GIs testified to doing at My Lai. [41]

Newspaper advertisements and posters for *Soldier Blue*, as well, equated the soldiers in the film with William Calley, Paul Meadlo, and the other GIs facing murder charges over My Lai. "The order was massacre, and good soldiers follow orders," the large caption read. "These soldiers were the best."[42] Like coverage of the My Lai massacre in the press and in VVAW protests, this language suggested that military superiors, not the troops, were responsible for the deaths of civilians. Ironic praise for their efficiency and obedience grimly revived the World War II–era notion that a good soldier contributed unquestioningly to the team effort.

In a prosaic imitation of the St. Crispin's Day speech in Shakespeare's *Henry V*, the proud commanding officer in *Soldier Blue* addresses the men after the massacre of the Cheyenne is complete: "For the rest of your lives, you men will hold your heads proud when this day is mentioned." In ironic fashion these words may have reminded viewers that such atrocities weighed heavily on the minds of their perpetrators, something well covered in the case of My Lai in *Life* magazine, on television, and in VVAW demonstrations. Likewise, in the introduction to *Winning Hearts and Minds*, a collection of Vietnam War poetry published by VVAW members in 1972, the editors characterized themselves and the other contributors as "agent-victims" of their own criminal actions in Vietnam. The poet-GIs both induced pain in others and suffered pain themselves for doing so. "We were, and are," the vets wrote, "a part of the evil."[43]

Accordingly, Vietnam War poetry and fiction released in the 1970s contained tales of American atrocity and guilt. [44] The poet-veteran Stan Platke, in 1972's "And Then There Were None," confronted the soldier's nature:

Yea as I walk through the valley of death
I shall fear no evil
For the valleys are gone
And only death awaits

And I am the evil[45]

In the same period W. D. Ehrhart wondered whether Vietnamese civilians imagined Americans as the embodiment of wickedness, in the poem "Making the Children Behave":

Do they think of me now
in those strange Asian villages
where nothing ever seemed
quite human
but myself
and my few grim friends
moving through them
hunched
in lines?

When they tell stories to their children
of the evil
that awaits misbehavior,
is it me they conjure?[46]

In his 1988 collection *Dien Cai Dau* Yusef Komunyakaa described the rape of a Vietnamese mother by American GIs in "Re-creating the Scene," while in "'You and I Are Disappearing'" he recalled the elements of fire and regret in World War II bombardier poetry:

The cry I bring down from the hills
belongs to a girl still burning
inside my head. At daybreak
    she burns like a piece of paper.
She burns like foxfire
in a thigh-shaped valley.[47]

The notions of culpability, suffering, and guilt in their verse rendered these vets the "agent-victims" of whom VVAW activists spoke.

Occupying the same thematic territory as *Soldier Blue* was *Ulzana's Raid*, a western directed by Robert Aldrich (*The Dirty Dozen*) and featuring Burt Lancaster as McIntosh, a crusty Indian fighter. The film hit movie theaters in 1972, just as tens of thousands of American ground troops were returning home from Vietnam under President Richard Nixon's Vietnamization plan.[48] *Ulzana's Raid* takes place in Arizona territory during the 1880s, as McIntosh and a naive West Point graduate, Lt. Garnett DeBuin (Bruce Davison), set out to pursue a group of Apache raiders under the command of the fierce warrior Ulzana. In something of a parallel to Cresta in *Soldier Blue*, McIntosh understands the Apaches (he lives with an Indian woman), while DeBuin sees them only as murderous savages (as Gant initially does in *Soldier Blue*). The detachment of soldiers discovers gruesome atrocities at several homesteads before engaging Ulzana in a climactic battle. McIntosh and Ulzana both die in the skirmish.

For much of the film DeBuin and McIntosh grapple over the savagery of the Apaches. The audience sees the aftermath of unspeakable atrocities, some of which resembled contemporary stories circulating about the Vietcong. One settler has been tied to a tree and tortured, his dog's tail stuffed in his mouth—mimicking, in faintly sanitized fashion, the reputed Vietcong act of packing detached genitalia into victims' mouths. When DeBuin is horrified to find some of his *own* men mutilating a dead Apache, his exchange with McIntosh recalls debates between Gant and Cresta in *Soldier Blue*:

> DeBuin: Killing I expect, Mr. McIntosh, but mutilation and torture, I
>   cannot accept that as readily as you seem to be able to.
> McIntosh: What bothers you, Lieutenant, is you don't like to think of
>   white men behaving like Indians. Kind of confuses the issue, don't
>   it?[49]

Indeed, what bothers Lieutenant DeBuin in this instance is precisely what bothered many Americans after the revelation of the My Lai massacre in the fall of 1969—and is precisely what "confused the issue" for many opponents of the Vietnam War. McIntosh has come to accept the essential depravity of human beings, while DeBuin clings to an idealized belief in American exceptionalism and moral superiority. He appears foolish in the film for doing so, just as Gant seemed naive in *Soldier Blue*. As McIntosh says to him at one point, hating the Apaches is like "hating the desert because there ain't no water in it." Here the film does not glorify the Indians, just as most antiwar protesters of the Vietnam era did not glorify the Vietcong (contrary to popular belief). Instead, it puts the Americans and their enemies on the same moral plane. A promotional poster for the film incorporated both the Apache and the white man into this cynical view of human nature: "One man alone understood the savagery of the early American west from both sides."[50] Likewise, Eastlake's novel *The Bamboo Bed* described dead Americans with severed penises stuffed into their mouths by their Vietnamese enemies, but also spoke of American atrocities going back to the nineteenth century: "Clancy [an officer in Vietnam] is dead but the crimes that Clancy did live after him. Custer too. Custer liked to destroy the villages and shoot up the natives too. . . . Collecting ears is not new."[51]

It is this climate of violence that is the enemy in *Ulzana's Raid*, not any particular player in the conflict. In fact, the individuals engaging in war's brutality are its primary victims. As one appreciative reviewer of *Ulzana's Raid* said of the West inhabited by McIntosh, "It's a wasteland where people find themselves living out lives that have long since been *beyond their control*, where cruelty is a matter of form and a method for power, and where the only hope for salvation lies in something as nebulous as seeing things through."[52] It would be difficult to describe more aptly the life of an individual soldier in modern warfare. Indeed, the phrase "seeing things through" vividly recalled the stoicism journalists and filmmakers had found in American GIs fighting in World War II and the Korean War, and which contemporary correspondents were finding in the jungles and rice paddies of Vietnam.

Accordingly, McIntosh resembles Sergeant Zack of *The Steel Helmet* and Sergeant Montana of *Men in War*, both of whom operated in ethically murky worlds. As the film's director, Robert Aldrich, said of McIntosh, viewers "don't know whether he's the good guy or the bad guy. They're sorry to see him die but they don't really understand whether he represents good or evil."[53] Some magazine readers had felt similar ambiguity in 1970 and 1971 about the American GIs who killed five hundred civilians at My Lai. The letters section of *Life* magazine, for instance, showed that Americans who recoiled in horror at what the soldiers had done simultaneously sympathized with them, particularly with Lieutenant Calley. A line in Eastlake's novel *The Bamboo Bed* expressed this muddier vision of wartime ethics: "There are no villains, there are only wars."[54]

More broadly, *Ulzana's Raid* challenged notions of American moral superiority so pivotal to many war films of World War II vintage. Comparable postwar cynicism had appeared in novels by Norman Mailer, John Horne Burns, and James Jones, as well as in some films of the 1950s. But now in the wake of My Lai, filmmakers and writers were reshaping such critiques into sweeping indictments of the American military, the federal government, and the once-glorified history of westward expansion. In 1969 *The Bamboo Bed* pictured the Vietnam War as a brutal and insane enterprise. Poets of the Vietnam era often privileged personal experience over big-picture political commentary, but their work nonetheless revealed a war fraught with illegality, irrationality, and immorality. Without a sense of elevated moral purpose—a sense that this was a "just" war—American fighting men seemed, in news coverage, allegorical films, and contemporary literature, to be degraded and damaged by their experiences in Vietnam.

Such cynicism about institutions and authority, in the offing since the 1940s, deepened in the early 1970s. The Watergate scandal of 1972–74 further eroded whatever faith in government remained after the Vietnam War. The reputation of the military had never been lower. National economic leaders seemed incapable of overcoming rising gas prices, unemployment, and inflation. When Jimmy Carter assumed the presidency in early 1977, he declared that the recent past had left the American people "sick at heart"; he later would use the expression "crisis of confidence" to describe public attitudes. [55] Hollywood films that featured cynical soldiers were just one expression of this contemporary malaise.

When Saigon fell in 1975, America's thirty-year diplomatic and military effort to preserve a noncommunist South Vietnam was finally, and unsuccessfully, concluded. Yet the public dialogue about the *meaning* of the Vietnam War—particularly in the form of direct representations of the conflict in American culture—was just gathering steam. Important novels, memoirs, and poetry emerged relatively quickly from the pens of Ron Kovic, Philip Caputo, Michael Herr, Tim O'Brien, John Balaban, W. D. Ehrhart, and many others. An unorganized army of scholars, mental health experts, veterans, and journalists began studying Vietnam vets, producing a torrent of literature on that subject in the 1980s. [56] And in 1978, just three years after television networks showed American civilians scrambling to escape into helicopters from the roof of the Saigon embassy, several films hit theaters with Vietnam as their subject. As disturbing as some of the characters in these movies seemed in 1978, in fact they were the cultural descendants of many soldiers and veterans depicted since the 1940s.

The first combat picture about Vietnam since *The Green Berets* featured a motley crew of individuals. *The Boys in Company C* (1978), produced by the Hong Kong–based Golden Harvest studios and directed by Sidney Furie, tells the story of a group of raw enlistees and draftees who undergo marine training at Fort Bragg, North Carolina, before shipping off to Vietnam. In an updated, formulaic replay of the World War II platoon film, the men come from myriad backgrounds. There is Tyrone Washington (Stan Shaw), an African American drug dealer from Chicago; Vinnie Fazio (Michael Lembeck), the requisite Brooklynite, now with a hyperactive sex drive; Billy Ray Pike (Andrew Stevens) from Galveston, Texas; Dave Bisbee (Craig Wasson), a pacifistic hippie; and Alvin Foster (James Canning) from Kansas, an aspiring writer whose journal entries form the basis for his narration throughout the film.

When they are not in combat, company members fight among themselves along racial lines, use drugs, contemplate the murder of their officers, and contract sexually transmitted diseases. The film ends with an absurd sequence reminiscent of the football scene in *M*A*S*H*, as the company plays a soccer game against a team of South Vietnamese soldiers. Told to throw the game to improve public confidence in the Saigon regime (and also to win a reprieve from combat), the Americans refuse to bow to what is now the firmly established corruption of their military superiors. They win the game, but all in attendance quickly fall under attack by the North Vietnamese. The poor discipline of the American soldiers, the incompetence and cruelty of officers, and the excessive violence visited upon the Vietnamese people make up the core of the film's potent antiauthoritarian message. Indeed, *The Boys in Company C* gathers almost every cynical comment on federal and military authority from the previous thirty years into a single two-hour production.

Most troubling are the junior officers and those above them at the battalion level. If earlier works had suggested the individual foot soldier was a victim of incompetent or vicious leadership, in *The Boys in Company C* official ineptitude and cruelty reach new heights. From the moment the recruits arrive at Fort Bragg, they are subjected to the harshest brand of indoctrination and training. "When you left home you were under your mother's care," barks a drill instructor (DI). "You are now under mine. From now on you will not eat, sleep, blow your nose or scratch your ass until someone tells you to do so. . . . Your ass is mine!"[57] Moments later the recruits meet a Latino DI who makes this first man seem gentle. He also far outstrips in nastiness John Wayne's Sergeant Stryker from *Sands of Iwo Jima*, who may have clubbed one of his marines in the face but ultimately seemed to care for them. Now, the DI screams at the newcomers, calling them "faggots," "turds," "maggots," and "varmints." He later punches one of the men in the testicles. Boot camp seems to have little purpose except to abuse soldiers and train them to "Kill! Kill! Kill!" as one DI shouts during an exercise. A contemporary critic wrote approvingly of the "savage authenticity" of these boot camp scenes.[58]

The use of the word "faggot" signaled the homophobia coursing through the military, the acknowledgment of which was rare in most prior depictions of the service. In the novels *The Gallery* (1947) and *The Thin Red Line* (1962) soldiers engage in homosexual activity at great peril; occasionally books and movies featured references to "fairies" and "ladies" from acid-tongued officers. In that vein *The Boys in Company C* lampoons the heavy machismo of the military—but faintly hints as well that some of the abusive comments by officers serve to hide their own homoerotic desires. When the recruits are forced to go under the barber's shears, DIs snicker at how "cute" this one or that one looks. They frequently call the men "sweethearts"—a trope appearing five years earlier in McAvoy Layne's long poem *How Audie Murphy Died in Vietnam* (1973). In that work a hateful DI threatens the central character with a menacingly sexualized fate:

"You're going to jail, boy.
But first,
You're going with me & Feiring
Into
The
Rodeo
Room."[59]

The Boys in Company C contains a remarkably similar sequence. When Fazio tries to run off from Fort Bragg with the colonel's daughter, the military police beat him severely, and the MP in charge of the jail (or "brig") tells him, "We'll take care of your over-active sex drive, *in here!*" He goes on to call him a "faggot" and "the cute one." After punching the one recruit in the genitals, the Latino DI goes around poking others in the same area, exhorting them to work together to protect their manhood. Among many other meanings, these scenes hint that all the shouting about "faggots" and "sweethearts" may mask a latent homoeroticism in the military.

In another segment the obnoxious Latino DI finally exudes some sense of what the recruits are supposed to be learning from all this abuse: "Look around you. You like the man next to you? You think he's a nigger, or that one['s] a Jew? Or that one's a spic? I don't care! That motherfucker's gonna save your life one day! And you better depend on your buddy!" These words are a stripped-down, vulgar version of what reporters found in Vietnam early in the war, that racism had no place in combat. Indeed, racial matters in the first half of *The Boys in Company C* mirrored media coverage of such issues during the Vietnam War. Though black soldiers in Southeast Asia found a degree of equality unprecedented in the annals of American military history, toward the end of the war racial tensions heightened and surged into public view.

The film documents racial strife and racial progress in equal measure. Despite his drug-peddling past (and aborted attempts to ship drugs home from Southeast Asia), Tyrone Washington becomes the moral hero of the movie, earning the respect first of his drill instructors and then of the men put under his command. Yet racism is prevalent as well. When he arrives at the recruiting station at the beginning of the movie, Tyrone's black friend rants before dropping him off: "Them . . . honky motherfuckers is draftin' my main man away! They sendin' you off to kill chinks!" Once again, in vulgar fashion these words capture the dilemma facing African American troops since the nineteenth century—a dilemma particularly stark for blacks in Vietnam who came to view the war and their own oppression at home as twin extensions of American racism. Later in the film, before leaving for Vietnam, several southern whites call Tyrone "sambo," "nigger," "boy," and a "cannibal." More than films about the Korean War or World War II, *The Boys in Company C* simultaneously depicts the advancement of blacks in the military along with persistent, virulent racism.

In *The Boys in Company C*, what starts as official cruelty at Fort Bragg becomes, in Vietnam, treacherous and reckless treatment of the soldiers. Just as "good" and "bad" lieutenants feuded in films about the Korean War, the evenhanded Lieutenant Archer (James Whitmore Jr.) faces off against the wicked Captain Collins (Scott Hylands). Collins is obsessed with the enemy body count and seems willing to sacrifice his own troops in foolhardy maneuvers in order to inflate his statistics. Over the objection of Archer, Collins sends the men of Company C across a bridge in hasty, bunched-up fashion, and the troops become easy targets for an enemy ambush. Collins orders an artillery strike on a village that he assumes to be unfriendly, and when the pacifistic Bisbee refuses to call in the order Collins has him reassigned to a dangerous mine-clearing outfit. Billy Ray Pike suffers the same fate after he tries to intervene in the murder of a young Vietcong suspect, getting into a physical scrape with Collins over the matter. In his book *If I Die in a Combat Zone* (1973), the famed novelist Tim O'Brien had condemned this sort of heartless careerism through the odious character Captain Smith, who says after a bloody operation, "What's my commander to think? He's gonna see a damn casualty list a mile long, and it's only my first operation. My career is in real jeopardy now."[60]

At times in *The Boys in Company C* the generals and colonels above Collins and Archer are the real villains, just as Gregory Peck's fictional Lieutenant Clemons had discovered two decades before in *Pork Chop Hill*. Early in the film the marines are ordered to escort a convoy of covered "vital equipment" to an army base. Two marines are killed when the procession comes under Vietcong attack, and the soldiers become enraged when they discover the cargo is liquor, cigarettes, expensive furniture, and meat for a general. A "Happy Birthday" banner for the feted official confirms the frivolous nature of the shipment and the pointlessness of the marines' deaths. Later a distant "battalion" sends Company C into an area purely to draw Vietcong fire— which was essentially the basis for countless patrols during the Vietnam War. Nevertheless, Lieutenant Archer is livid. Recalling the words of Captain Stein in the novel *The Thin Red Line*, the lieutenant indicts his commanders: "We're bait! We're goddamn, motherfuckin' live bait! That's all we are! We're gonna draw 'em out of the bush, and those bastards on that hill [battalion command] are gonna let loose with their big, fancy-ass, million-dollar hardware! And they're gonna get a nice, big, juicy body count!" To spite battalion, Archer calls an enormous artillery strike into a meaningless location, as the foot soldiers enjoy the fireworks. The whole enterprise of war rarely had seemed so absurd.

Though some contemporary critics found in *The Boys in Company C* a rehashing of World War II–era themes, some of its warrior images were distinctively of the Vietnam era.[61] The treachery of Captain Collins, itself a departure from films made during the Second World War, draws the murderous enmity of Tyrone Washington. After Collins shows little compassion for Americans enduring friendly artillery fire, Washington vows to "frag" the officer. Later he tries to do so, only to be stopped by Lieutenant Archer, who also despises Collins but puts a halt to this greatest of disciplinary breaches. Tyrone Washington spends much of the movie trying to engineer a massive shipment of drugs back to the United States in body bags, and Billy Ray Pike, a clean-cut kid at the beginning of the film, becomes addicted to and overdoses on heroin. Vinny Fazio catches "the clap" from Vietnamese hookers.

Vietnam War poets of the 1970s and 1980s corroborated such evidence of indiscipline. Yusef Komunyakaa's "Fragging," published in 1988, has men planning to kill an officer by the standard method:

"We won't be wasting a real man.
That lieutenant's too gung ho . . ."
. . . Yes, just a flick
of a wrist & the whole night
comes apart. "Didn't we warn him?
That bastard.". . .[62]

In the same volume Komunyakaa wrote of the world's oldest profession, via dialogue common to the streets of Vietnamese cities: "You want a girl, GI?" / "You buy me Saigon tea?"[63] Narcotics likewise pervaded imaginative representations of the Vietnam War. "I'm sick and tired of smoking grass," wrote Illinois native and Vietnam veteran Lenny Olejarz in the poetry collection *Demilitarized Zones* (1976). "I get sad when I take a puff / If only I had peace of mind instead."[64] In postwar writings by Tim O'Brien and Michael Herr, among many others, drug use figured prominently, just as it had in televised dispatches from Southeast Asia in the early 1970s.[65] And in *Apocalypse Now* (1979), a GI tripping on acid was just the most overt drug reference in Coppola's broader treatment of the Vietnam War as a hallucinatory experience.

Surpassing *The Boys in Company C* artistically and commercially in 1978 were *Coming Home* and *The Deer Hunter*, which swept the Academy Awards that year. Through memorable performances by some of Hollywood's biggest stars, these Vietnam War classics underscored the conflict's emotional impact on vets and their loved ones.

The readjustment of disabled veterans had been the subject of prior Hollywood pictures, including *The Best Years of Our Lives* (1946) and *The Men* (1950). *Best Years* featured one real-life amputee, and *The Men* was devoted entirely to the wounded, many of them actual veterans. In 1978 audiences once again confronted these men—the "detritus" of war, in the words of one critic—in *Coming Home*.[66] Director Hal Ashby's film featured Bruce Dern along with former antiwar activists Jane Fonda and Jon Voight, both of whom had been involved in financing and organizing a VVAW chapter in California during the war. Despite earning Academy Awards for best actor (Voight) and best actress (Fonda), *Coming Home* drew criticism from some contemporary reviewers (and scholars later) for its cluttered plot, overwrought antiwar sentiments, and liberal use of Hollywood clichés.[67]

Voight plays Luke Martin, a paraplegic Vietnam veteran recuperating in a VA hospital where Sally Hyde (Fonda) volunteers her time. She is inspired to do so when her gung-ho marine husband Bob Hyde (Dern) ships off for Vietnam, just after the Tet offensive of 1968, leaving Sally with free time and an unfulfilled desire to do something on her own. Also instrumental in motivating Sally is her friend Vi (Penelope Milford), whose brother Billy (Robert Carradine) has come home after just two weeks in Vietnam with grave emotional problems and now resides in the VA hospital. Sally, a loyal and conservative military wife, gradually becomes politicized while working with the victims of war. She tries in vain to publicize the needs of the VA hospital, while slowly falling in love with her old high school classmate Luke. Like Marlon Brando in *The Men* (and to a lesser extent, Harold Russell in *Best Years*), Luke is bitter and hostile in the beginning of the film but gradually brightens as he learns to love a woman again. With Sally and Luke in the throes of a passionate affair, Bob returns from Vietnam with a leg wound (accidentally self-inflicted), but worse, he is also emotionally unhinged from what he has seen in combat. In a final sequence, Bob learns of the affair, confronts Sally and Luke (both of whom agree that Sally should try to patch things up with Bob), and, in utter despair, swims out into the ocean to die.

Coming Home in many ways represented a culmination of trends in the development and proliferation of the warrior image after 1945. It paints the ex-serviceman as a victim in ways reminiscent of, but exceeding, those appearing in popular culture and media coverage since World War II. Early in the film Sally listens to a litany of gripes from a paraplegic African American veteran: "You can get paralyzed in a war that doesn't make sense. . . . They don't tell you anything about how to manage your finances, they don't tell you anything about going back into society. Half the people today still can't go back into society. What about your sex life? They don't tell you anything about that. I went out the first time and didn't know what to do. What happens if my gizmo busts? What happens if I have a bowel movement?"[68] This passage hints at something well covered later in the film—the virility problems of paralyzed veterans. But it also recalls imagery from after World War II, the halcyon days of the GI Bill, when some veterans nonetheless complained bitterly about being used for war and then left helpless afterward. Indeed, in the novel *Whistle* (1978), the posthumously released finale of his World War II trilogy, James Jones wrote of a more polite but equally patronizing form of treatment greeting wounded veterans returning from that war: "We were like a family of orphaned children, split by an epidemic and sent to different care centers. That feeling of an epidemic disease persisted. The people treated us nicely, and cared for us tenderly, and then hurried to wash their hands after touching us. We were somehow unclean. We were tainted." He went on to describe the feeling many paralyzed veterans of the Vietnam era certainly shared, the sense of being "a group of useless unmanned eunuchs."[69]

As these passages from the film and from Jones's novel indicate, war inflicts great trauma on the individual. Like *The Men* had in 1950, *Coming Home* starkly portrays the helplessness and pain of wounded vets, but it goes beyond earlier treatments of the subject in conveying the emotional aftershocks of combat. Vi's brother Billy eventually commits suicide by injecting air into his veins, and indeed, Bob's fate will be similar. Bob tells Sally while she visits him on "R-and-R" in Hong Kong, "It's all this bullshit about Nam, it's in my head, I can't get it out." He gazes vacantly into space in a revived 2,000-yard stare, and later tells her about watching his men cut the heads off of dead Vietcong. During the climactic scene Bob threatens Sally, flashing back to the war and calling her a "slope cunt." The segment evokes tamer flashback scenes from films such as *Best Years*, but the overall picture of emotional breakdown is closer to what was shown in *Let There Be Light*, the unreleased documentary film of 1946 about neuropsychiatric veterans.

Coming Home also continued to rewrite the terms of masculinity. Since World War II, what made a manly hero had undergone significant revision—and *Best Years* and *The Men* represented key moments in this transformation. Movie audiences gradually saw men in uniform crying, comforting other men, refusing to fight, and speaking more freely about their feelings. During the Vietnam War, media coverage persisted in portraying these traits approvingly, yet *Coming Home* far surpassed anything that had come before it in recasting the masculine hero.[70] Indeed, Fonda's friend and collaborator on the initial planning for the film, Bruce Gilbert, told a reporter about the original idea: "It would be a home-front story, [and] we would attempt to re-define what manhood and patriotism meant."[71]

In the beginning of the film Luke resists help, but like Marlon Brando in *The Men*, he eventually learns to accept his dependence. The first time Luke goes to Sally's house for dinner, she must help lift him over the threshold, a favor he accepts graciously—something Brando's character was unable to do until the final scene of *The Men*. As in other films about paraplegic veterans, accepting help from women, and foregoing some of the dominant roles of the traditional male, are key elements in coming to grips with disability.

Luke's humility and willingness to accept help from Sally draw her to him, but so do other aspects of this changing male hero. Sally's attraction to Luke takes noticeable leaps whenever he shows sensitivity, vulnerability, or compassion. When Billy suffers an emotional breakdown, it is not his sister Vi or Sally who comforts him, but Luke. The two men cry together in an emotional embrace, as the women look on in sad, dry-eyed bewilderment. (In his classic novel of 1990, *The Things They Carried*, Tim O'Brien envisioned a combat version of this sensitive male relationship. With the protagonist racked by guilt over killing a young Vietnamese soldier, a buddy asks him, "Why not talk about it? . . . Come on, man, talk.")[72] These sequences signal the importance of male empathy and communion in the veteran's attempts at overcoming his suffering, whereas World War II–era vets might have endured in silence. And the display, though obviously sincere, earns Luke a possible sexual payoff as well. "I think you were wonderful with him, I really do," a smitten Sally tells Luke afterward. It is moments later that Luke asks for help getting into Sally's house, once again endearing himself to her without traditional displays of machismo. Sally's fateful decision to go to bed with Luke—the moment when an innocent crush turns into an extramarital affair—comes after she sees Luke on television grieving over Billy's suicide. In a move VVAW members would have appreciated, Luke protests the war by chaining himself to the gates of a marine recruiting station. During his arrest Luke rants against the war in front of television cameras. When Sally picks up the emotionally drained Luke from the police station, she tells him she wants to go home with him. His sensitivity, conviction, and passionate opposition to the war have finally drawn Sally out of her staid marriage.

The ensuing scene in Luke's bedroom pushes *Coming Home* beyond films such as *Best Years* and *The Men* (*Best Years* features subtle sexual tensions when the amputee Homer shows Wilma his bedtime routine; in *The Men*, Brando's movie fiancée asks a doctor about virility, but that is as far as the subject goes).[73] Drawing upon informal talks with scores of paraplegics about their sex lives, Voight and Fonda act out a tender, honest love scene. Sally experiences the first orgasm of her life.[74] One scholar of military films has criticized the scene because, he argues, it wrongly suggests that Luke is able to have sex normally.[75] Yet Luke's frank words about his lack of sensation confirm that he must be pleasuring Sally in some other manner, so in fact the sequence realistically attests to the sexual capabilities of otherwise disabled veterans. Indeed, in an interview with *Newsweek* Voight said of the paraplegics he met, "If you want to become a better lover you should hang around with them."[76] As part of the film's recalibration of masculinity, then, the scene indicates that impotent men can still satisfy women sexually and retain a sense of physical attractiveness. If many of them did feel like "useless unmanned eunuchs" at first, they might redefine the traditional measures of masculinity and sexuality, and thus "re-man" themselves.

The concluding scenes of *Coming Home* persistently stress victimhood and modified masculinity. When the three sides of the love triangle finally end up in the same room, Bob confronts Luke and Sally with a bayoneted rifle. With an inglorious wound, a discharge from Vietnam, and a wife who has cheated on him, Bob essentially goes mad. Luke is able to calm him only by invoking the sense of victimhood shared by the two veterans: "I'm not the enemy. Maybe the enemy is the fucking war. But you don't want to kill anybody here. You have enough ghosts to carry around." Bob settles miserably into a chair as Sally tries to comfort him. He is inconsolable: "I'm fucked. I just want to be a hero, that's all. I just want to be a fucking hero! One day in my life, one moment. I want to go out a hero! That way I would have done something that was mine, that *I've* done!" Bob feels deprived of heroism, the one thing he had grown up believing war could offer. Without that, he is a helpless victim of his experiences in Vietnam.[77] During the war novelist Tim O'Brien wrote of the same problem: "It's sad when you learn you're not much of a hero."[78]

In the final segment, the camera shifts between Luke, who addresses a group of high school students, and Bob, who heads for the ocean. Luke begins by reciting a common story: "You know, you want to be a part of it, and patriotic, and go out and get your licks in for the U.S. of A. . . . When you get over there, it's a totally different situation. I mean, you grow up real quick, because all you're seeing is a lot of death." At the same time, Bob is shown beginning to remove his carefully pressed marine uniform, hanging the various accessories on a lifeguard stand. Luke continues, "And I'm telling you, it ain't like it is in the movies!" Bob finishes undressing, and removes the wedding ring Sally gave him on the eve of his departure for Vietnam. The scene shifts back to Luke, who is becoming more heated: "I wanted to be a war hero, man. I wanted to go out and kill for my country!" Bob, naked, is running into the surf. Luke goes on: "And now I'm here to tell you, that I *have* killed for my country, or whatever. And I don't feel good about it. Because there's not enough reason, man. To feel a person die in your arms or to see your best buddy get blown away. I'm here to tell you, it's a lousy thing, man. I don't see any reason for it." Luke breaks down in front of his rapt audience, testifying visually and verbally to the brutalizing impact of war on perpetrators of violence. His confessional words epitomize VVAW's idea of the "agent-victim" as Luke broadcasts his guilt and suffering as part of a cathartic attempt to overcome them, implicitly rejecting World War II–era expectations of stoic male anguish: "And there's a lot of shit that I did over there [sobbing], that I find *fucking hard to live with!* And I don't want to see people like you, man, coming back, and having to face the rest of your lives with that kind of shit. It's as simple as that. I don't feel sorry for myself, I'm a lot fucking smarter now than when I went. And I'm just telling you, that there's a choice to be made here." Bob is now far out to sea, swimming vigorously against the waves.

Bob's unraveling recalls the words of the critic of *Ulzana's Raid* who described the western frontier: "It's a wasteland where people find themselves living out lives that have long since been beyond their control, where cruelty is a matter of form and a method for power, and where the only hope for salvation lies in something as nebulous as seeing things through."[79] Unable to see things through, Bob presumably chooses suicide as "something that was mine." Luke, meanwhile, represents a composite of many soldiers and veterans, real and imagined, that had appeared in American culture since the late 1940s. This male hero endears himself to the audience through his sensitivity, vulnerability, and willingness to admit weakness or mistakes. Such traits had been building in figures from Homer Parrish in *Best Years*, Sergeant Stryker in *Sands of Iwo Jima*, Bud Wilozek in *The Men*, and Sergeant Saunders in the TV show *Combat!* to the American GIs of David Douglas Duncan's combat photography, John Kerry and others in VVAW, and the perpetrators of the My Lai massacre.

Combining with *Coming Home* to dominate the Oscars in 1978 was *The Deer Hunter*, directed by Michael Cimino.[80] Winning five Academy Awards, including best picture, best supporting actor (Christopher Walken), and best director, the movie centered on three blue-collar friends from the Russian American steel towns of Pennsylvania: Michael (Robert De Niro), Nick (Walken), and Steven (John Savage). Meryl Streep earned a nomination for best supporting actress for her performance as Nick's fiancée. The three-hour film follows the trio from their days working in the steel mills of Clairton, Pennsylvania, and hunting in the Allegheny Mountains, to their terrifying tours of duty in Vietnam, and back to their postwar experiences in Saigon and Clairton. Like *Coming Home* before it, *The Deer Hunter* depicts military service in Vietnam as a shattering experience for soldiers and their families alike.

In the days before heading off to war, the friends attend Steven's lavish wedding, embark on one last hunting trip, drink heavily, laugh wildly, chase women, and say emotional good-byes to their close-knit community. This is conservative Middle America—though it is 1968 there are no protests, hippies, or drugs, nor so much as a whisper of fleeing to Canada. The immigrant town is patriotic and proud of its young men heading off to war. One friend, in fact, is embarrassed that his bad knees are keeping him from joining Michael, Nick, and Steven in the service.

After the revelry of the first hour, the scene shifts abruptly to the jungles of Vietnam, where combat is petrifying and gruesome. The Vietcong are portrayed as savage beasts, as if to help justify American involvement in the war. Enemy troops force the Americans, now prisoners, to face each other in a horrifying game of Russian roulette while the captors wager on the results. Though there is little evidence the Vietcong ever engaged in such a practice, the scene conveys the horrors of war as powerfully and memorably as any other cinematic moment of the twentieth century.[81] As the enemy troops look on, each prisoner must press a gun to his skull, pull the trigger, and either collapse in tortured relief at the empty click or blow his brains across the squalid room. After Michael and Nick get lucky and survive the game, all three friends flee as Michael turns the pistol on their captors. In their escape Steven loses his legs, and Nick suffers a complete emotional breakdown and deserts the military.

Back in the United States after the war, Michael meets a hero's welcome but finds it difficult to readjust to civilian life. Steven is slowly learning to live without his legs, and Nick is still missing somewhere in Vietnam. When Michael returns to Saigon in 1975, just before the fall of the South Vietnamese regime, he finds Nick embroiled in the seedy underworld of the war-torn city—earning money playing Russian roulette, of all things. A hollow-eyed, suicidal shell of his former self, Nick kills himself in a final match against Michael, who once again draws a blank chamber during his turn. Michael had hoped to shock Nick out of his catatonic state, but Nick only smiles as he pumps the bullet into his brain. Fulfilling a promise made early in the film, Michael brings Nick's body back to Clairton for burial. The film ends with the shattered group of friends and loved ones singing "God Bless America" in the bleak bar where they had once played pool, drunk, and laughed innocently years earlier. As if the audience needs a reminder, the closing credits roll over scenes from the beginning of the film, when each of the characters showed an exuberance now utterly destroyed by the war.

In *The Deer Hunter*, war and the military victimize the individual soldier, wreaking havoc on his emotional state, his physical well-being, and his family. Like *Soldier Blue* and *Ulzana's Raid*, the film lays bare the capacity of human beings to inflict suffering on one another.[82] When Nick is briefly hospitalized in Saigon before deserting, he sees the detritus of war, and indeed, becomes a psychological casualty himself as he breaks down in the hospital. A reviewer in *Newsweek* called Nick "the ultimate war victim—a man stunned into a horror of life itself."[83] Steven, whose legs are the cost of his own time in the service, returns to American society utterly unable to cope. He shouts at Michael, who is trying to convince him to leave the VA hospital and go home: "Come on, I don't fit! I don't fit!"[84] Though he is the most stable member of the group, even Michael snaps. On a hunting trip after the war, he becomes angry with a friend who has brought a pistol, inserts a single bullet into the gun, spins the cylinder, and "shoots" the man in the face. Luckily for both of them, the chamber is empty.

Underscoring these tales of tormented homecomings were poems by Vietnam vets published in the anthology *Demilitarized Zones* (1976). Charles Purcell, echoing much other verse of the era, initiates the journey back:

> A tightness worse than hunger
> Grips my gut like a vise
> Jungle tan
> Unemployed killer
> Where in hell am I?
>
> I'm coming home[85]

In the same volume Peter Mahoney writes of the next step homeward, the reunion with now-distant family members. Michael and Nick of *The Deer Hunter* come to mind as Mahoney reminds audiences that some injuries "do not pierce the skin" in his poem "The Airport."[86] And how to sleep in such a condition? Earl E. Martin invites readers into his tortured nocturnal mindscape. Here he wakes up from a nightmare, just like other veterans sleeping fitfully in poems of the postwar years:

> and I threw up on the quilt
> rushed to the bathroom
> banging my head
> and the day was colored grey
> by the night
>
> Do you suppose
> Being a vet
> has anything to do with it?[87]

These and other such configurations of the returning serviceman fore-shadowed a stock figure in many films and television programs of the 1980s: the Vietnam veteran as "psycho" (a characterization that has irked more than a few Vietnam vets). In *The Deer Hunter* Nick and Steven are completely wrecked by their tours of duty, and even Michael, the most levelheaded of the trio, nearly murders his own friend after the war. All of the men suffer from post-traumatic stress disorder (PTSD), which psychologists named and diagnosed in Vietnam veterans in the 1970s. Though they are portrayed sympathetically, the vets in *The Deer Hunter, Coming Home,* and much Vietnam War literature seem *damaged* by their experiences. For decades some architects of the warrior image had suggested that combat injured the human spirit, but now filmmakers and poets left out the happy endings altogether. A slow, thirty-year process had transformed soldiers who seemed *better* for their time in the military into ones who seemed *devastated.*

If *The Deer Hunter* did not end with a reassuring coda, it did suggest that the war altered the terms of the masculine hero, potentially for the better. In fact, the film essentially charted the changing nature of admirable male qualities that had been ongoing in American war-related culture since the end of World War II. At the beginning of *The Deer Hunter,* the friends are classic macho guys, hard drinking and skirt chasing. Men in the town beat their daughters, hit on each others' wives and girlfriends, and kill animals for sport. Michael and his friends are like brothers, but they ruthlessly mock one another, often using terms such as "faggot" to question someone's manliness.

The war, ironically, softens some of this aggressive, macho attitude. On the postwar hunting trip, Michael purposely fires above an elegant deer, choosing to spare rather than take another life. Like Luke Martin in *Coming*

Home, he cements his place as the film's central male hero through sensitivity, not belligerence. The most touching scenes in *The Deer Hunter* show Michael desperately trying to save his two buddies, first from the enemy in Vietnam, then from postwar depression, and finally, in the case of Nick, from emotional devastation. When Nick dies, Michael sobs and cradles him like a baby. Now, rather than the World War II–era soldier finding in the military a collective, edifying experience, the serviceman in Vietnam is frightfully isolated and damaged by his service in war and must connect with a supportive group *after* combat to overcome his trauma. Veterans exalted in film overcome their machismo, too, as they learn to support their suffering comrades this way. Robert De Niro's Michael, once the cocky hunter of Clairton, has grown into an older, more mature, less carefree, but perhaps wiser and more sensitive version of his younger self.

One scholar of military films has articulated a common piece of the mythology surrounding the Vietnam War: "When America went off to fight communism in the jungles of Vietnam, twenty years of glorious World War II imagery from films accompanied the troops and policy makers. But something went awry in Southeast Asia."[88] He and other writers have pointed to a sharp break between abiding confidence in American institutions before the Vietnam War and deepening cynicism afterward, whether manifested in popular films, literature, or public opinion polls.

Yet the evolving warrior image of Cold War culture suggests a more gradual, though no less dramatic, shift. What had been whispers of doubt about the competence and honesty of the American military in the early 1950s became anguished shouts by the Vietnam era. Before 1965 Americans met characters such as Sergeant Stryker, Sergeant Zack, Lieutenant Benson, Sergeant Montana, Lieutenant Clemons, and Captain Stein, who gradually revealed the chaotic and ethically murky environment of war, the depravity of the military brass, and the damage combat could inflict on the individual. In the Vietnam era Captain MacDonald, Hawkeye Pierce, Private Gant, McIntosh, Tyrone Washington, Bob Hyde, and Luke Martin promoted an even more unflattering vision of the U.S. military. The creators of these characters suggested that Americans might commit atrocities, refuse to fight, threaten their officers, abuse drugs, fight along cleavages of race, and defy military authority. The inclusion of some of these actions within the purview of the male hero, meanwhile, abetted an ongoing revision of the terms of masculinity within American culture. With combat leaving fighters damaged or disillusioned—alongside the obvious cost to civilians, the land, and families awaiting the return of loved ones—warfare seemed a fruitless and wasteful enterprise.

Two American officers proved somewhat unlikely custodians of this idea that war was a futile endeavor. The first was Capt. Jim George, who had not yet reached Vietnam in the summer of 1967. On board the ship that took George and thousands of marines and army troops to Southeast Asia, the captain brooded over the war awaiting him. "I've had a lot of time to engage in deep thinking," he wrote to his wife, Jackie, "and it's really sickening how the world is so full of conflict and what's more how we're so much a part of it. . . . I've already started to dream of killing and am already tired of the smell of death." Going further was the future VVAW leader, senator, and Democratic presidential nominee John Kerry, whose best friend Dick Pershing was killed in combat in February 1968. The loss prompted Kerry to write to his girlfriend, "Judy, if I do nothing else in my life I will never stop trying to bring to people the conviction of how wasteful and asinine is a human expenditure of this kind."[89] His was an ambition that a growing number of war correspondents, filmmakers, and writers shared throughout the decades following the Second World War.

Between 1982 and 2004, public and private interest groups funded and built three major memorials to the soldiers of World War II, the Korean War, and the Vietnam War in Washington, D.C. With a measure of incongruity they went up in reverse chronological order. Yet if advocates erect memorials partly to honor people they feel are insufficiently venerated in the culture at large, perhaps the sequence of these three commemorations made sense.[1] Vietnam veterans, believing other Americans had failed to welcome them home properly in the 1970s, applauded the appearance in 1982 of the Vietnam Veterans Memorial ("the Wall"). In 1995 nineteen larger-than-life statues of soldiers in the Korean War went up near the Wall, forty-two years after the end of "the forgotten war." And nearly six decades after the end of World War II, in the spring of 2004, organizers unveiled a magisterial monument to "the good war." On the face of things, these memorials honored soldiers in strikingly different ways.

The Vietnam Veterans Memorial emerged from the efforts of Jan Scruggs, a wounded Vietnam veteran who organized a private fund-raising campaign for a memorial in the late 1970s. After raising millions of dollars and successfully lobbying Congress for use of land on the national mall, Scruggs and his fellow veterans held a competition to determine the memorial's design. Yale student Maya Lin's winning proposal—a broad, V-shaped granite wall inscribed with the names of all those killed or missing in Vietnam—aroused sharp controversy from the beginning. Conservatives and some veterans assailed it as an overly negative "black gash of shame" in the national consciousness. Other groups, including the normally conservative American Legion and Veterans of Foreign Wars (VFW), supported Lin's proposal. The controversy persisted until Secretary of the Interior James Watt and financial contributor Ross Perot, irate over the gloomy nature of the design, spearheaded a successful campaign to have three statues added to the plaza. The result, sculptor Frederick Hart's *The Three Fightingmen*, featured one black, one white, and one possibly Latino GI, all of them gazing in the direction of the Wall. In time most visitors, whatever their views on the war, came to appreciate the simple commemoration of those who had perished—and to pay far more attention to the Wall itself than to the bronze figures.[2]

The creators of the Korean War Veterans Memorial, on the other hand, put the soldier's likeness front and center. From its inception as Public Law 99–572 in 1986, the memorial was to honor the *individuals* who had served in Korea—not just soldiers but clerks, nurses, supply staff, chaplains, mechanics, and surgeons. Visitors to the memorial after its dedication day (July 27, 1995) encountered a large stone mural with more than two thousand etched images of such personnel beneath the inscription, "Freedom is Not Free." But the emotional centerpiece of the monument was a procession of nineteen stainless steel figures trudging through low shrubbery, many looking fearful and tired, some looking sorrowful.[3] Like GIs in Korean War films of the 1950s, the statues were diverse—African American, white, Asian, Latino, and Native American. At 7'3", the figures were cast at "heroic scale," according to the website of the Army Corps of Engineers. But this was heroism in the context of the harsh and stalemated Korean War. Like their real-life counterparts four decades earlier, the metal soldiers inspired wonder and appreciation not for their contribution to a glorious military victory, but for their fortitude under dreadful conditions. As the army corps website says of the landscape around the statues, "The juniper bushes are meant to be symbolic of the rough terrain encountered in Korea, and the granite stripes of the *obstacles overcome in war*."[4]

Quite different still was the National World War II Memorial, dedicated in May 2004. Authorized by Congress in 1993, the monument to "the good war" emerged in the thick of a national groundswell of appreciation for the "greatest generation."[5] With the ranks of World War II veterans dwindling—and amid ceremonies marking the fiftieth anniversaries of Pearl Harbor, D-Day, and the end of the war in 1991, 1994, and 1995, respectively—advocates believed it was high time to pay homage to those vets' service in America's grandest and most successful war mobilization. Yet the memorial itself, like much wartime imagery of the early 1940s, stressed the collective effort over the individual participant; it is the only memorial of the three without the word "veterans" in its title. As the official memorial website described it before its dedication,

> Symbolic of the defining event of the 20th Century, the memorial will be a monument to the spirit, sacrifice, and commitment of the American people to the *common defense* of the nation and to the broader causes of peace and freedom from tyranny throughout the world. It will inspire future generations of Americans, deepening their appreciation of what the World War II generation accomplished in securing freedom and democracy. Above all, the memorial will stand as an important symbol of *American national unity*, a timeless reminder of the moral strength and awesome power that can flow when a free people are at once *united* and *bonded together* in a *common* and just cause.[6]

On the memorial itself were few prominent renderings of soldiers. Two large arches, inscribed with "Atlantic" and "Pacific" to indicate the two major theaters of the war, dominated the memorial plaza. Linking these in two semicircles were fifty-six columns, each inscribed with the name of a state or territory that contributed to the war effort. A field of four thousand gold stars commemorated the four *hundred* thousand Americans who died.[7]

These monuments, like all forms of public memory, surely speak volumes about the political climates in which they emerged—stories too complex and contentious to tell here. But they also, perhaps without the deliberate intent of their creators, revive and amplify the cultural character of each war. Purveyors of the warrior image in the early 1940s tended to downplay individual suffering and play up collective purpose—just as the World War II memorial stresses teamwork and grandeur over the role of the foot soldier. In American culture the Korean War often seemed bleak, stalemated, and unpopular—and that memorial features stoic, grim-faced American GIs (individualized up close but not when viewed from a distance) trudging along under a terrific burden. During the Vietnam War the attitude and condition of the individual soldier came into sharper relief than ever before—and now on the Wall those killed in Southeast Asia, each and every one of them, are *named*.[8] A young visitor to this outdoor exhibit of conflict might guess that the three wars were very different—and they were—in their popularity, purpose, and, sure enough, in the ways they are memorialized.

Yet these differences should not obscure the great continuities of war imagery proliferated between 1941 and 1978. Of course, there *were* changes in the depiction of soldiers and veterans in these years, but they came more gradually—and earlier—than is generally assumed. Although scholarly and popular accounts often locate a great upheaval in the 1960s (in the portrayal of war as in other aspects of American life), in fact such imagery showed signs of changing long before the American intervention in Vietnam foundered.

———

During the first two years of World War II the soldier or veteran seemed a specimen of American manhood, a good citizen in the postwar economy of the future, a selfless team player, and a beneficiary of his time in the military. Journalists Ernie Pyle and Bill Mauldin joined newsreel producers, Hollywood filmmakers, and government propagandists at the Office of War Information in celebrating the tough, dependable, honorable GI—standard features of soldierly virtue for decades in the United States. Mauldin's scruffy cartoon characters, Willie and Joe, were famous for their grumbling, but like the soldiers Pyle described, they were sturdy cogs in the democratic war machine. In the wake of Japan's unprovoked attack on Pearl Harbor, most image makers (and ostensibly the public at large) implicitly sanctioned the devastating retaliatory violence aimed at the Japanese, in part by avoiding the issue of whether perpetrating that violence would permanently brutalize the reluctant American warriors. Blacks and ethnic minorities, when they appeared at all in wartime culture, often were unflinching patriots in that mass effort. Purveyors of early wartime culture exalted the collective over the individual, anticipating the national memorial of 2004.

Yet by the end of the Second World War some commentators were challenging its allegedly redemptive character. Before Pyle was killed in combat in April 1945, he became cynical about the war yet steadfastly sympathized with the GI, writing dispatches that portrayed the impact of battle without sentimentality. That journalists remained broadly committed to the war effort did not prevent some of them from showing combat's ambiguous, confusing, and tragic nature. A vocal cadre of psychological experts, sociologists, and reporters worried that soldiers might carry home the violent tendencies encouraged in the military, even if almost everyone accepted that the violence was necessary. These notions surfaced in postwar fiction and poetry, as well as in some media coverage of World War II vets adjusting to life after the war. By the late 1940s it appeared the soldier or veteran might be a *victim* of his military superiors, of the horrors of war, or even, amid the abundant benefits of the GI Bill, of government neglect. Some observers, including John Horne Burns and Norman Mailer, went beyond Mauldin by lamenting the powerlessness of the individual GI and the totalitarian nature of the military. Portraits of the collective endeavor as a damaging rather than edifying experience crept into view after the war ended, when films and novels increasingly took the suffering of the individual (and often, the *overcoming* of that suffering, as in *The Best Years of Our Lives* and *The Men*) as their primary narrative focus.

The Korean War pushed such imagery even further. This early Cold War conflict, situated in the midst of Joseph McCarthy's anticommunist witch hunt, drew early popular support in spite of distressing news from the battlefield. Journalists covering the "police action" showed individual American GIs who were dog-tired, battered, and suffering from the emotional strain of battle—something dimly indicated during the Second World War. The media revived the approach and tone of some of Ernie Pyle's late war coverage, questioning the conflict more than Pyle had yet, like him, sympathetically reporting the condition and attitude of the American GI. Although many mainstream publications maintained editorial support for the war, their pages regularly showed the desperate state of soldiers and the war effort in Korea. Powerful photographs by David Douglas Duncan, running in *Life* magazine and in MoMA exhibits, revealed traumatized yet resilient soldiers, at times in tears—a rarity in the iconography of World War II. Celebrations of the collective endeavor, held over from World War II, lingered in some war coverage, but paeans to teamwork often receded behind the exposure of individual suffering. Some observers publicly addressed the contradictions and conflicts inherent in African American participation in the war, even as federal officials began the process of desegregating the armed forces.

Throughout the 1950s and early 1960s—bland times, by many accounts— bleak images of soldiers appeared and reappeared in popular films, novels, and television programs. While many reverent accounts of World War II continued to materialize, even some of these (such as the film *To Hell and Back* and the television show *Combat!*) challenged the sentimental portraits of GIs circulated during the war. Movies about the Korean War in the 1950s showed individual soldiers who were frightfully isolated from the military leadership and American society, reflecting and perpetuating that conflict's reputation as "the forgotten war." The ennobling experience of collective effort, publicized during World War II and then challenged afterward, now seemed weakened or irrelevant in the context of the Korean War, a conflict generating themes of isolation and abandonment in its imaginative representations. Films and literature about Korea and World War II before 1965 also expressed tentative concerns over the violence perpetrated against foreign populations and enemy prisoners, violence endorsed by the American public during those conflicts. African American and Asian American soldiers, some Korean War films suggested, had labored under a special burden. Though the racial tensions of the Vietnam years were still distant, producers of the warrior image insinuated that ethnic and racial minorities faced contradictions fighting for a segregated and discriminatory society.

When American ground troops arrived in Vietnam in 1965, a supportive press nonetheless quickly portrayed GIs victimized by the difficult terrain, a shadowy enemy, and an increasingly brutal and stalemated war. When such views of American soldiers appeared on television in the wake of the Tet offensive in January 1968—as the press, along with the public, was turning against the war—they were only stronger echoes of meanings that had multiplied in American culture since late in World War II. Whether reporters or news organizations supported the war effort or not, they were increasingly likely to identify with and expose the trials of the individual GI, as were many filmmakers and writers of the Vietnam era.

African American soldiers in Vietnam likewise joined the ranks of victimhood—even as they enjoyed opportunities often sorely lacking for blacks in civilian life. Before 1968 reporters frequently publicized the relative equality of opportunity in the armed forces, racial harmony in the field, and black troops' unwavering commitment to the war. Empowered by the civil rights movement, however, African American GIs eventually spoke out as never before against the persisting inequities of the service. Particularly after 1970 the media widely covered racial conflict and even rioting as military discipline broke down throughout Vietnam.

Late in the war soldiers appeared in media accounts and Hollywood films as victims of something newer—their own violent training in the U.S. military. William Calley and other American soldiers who killed civilians at My Lai, for instance, became folk heroes to much of the public for their alleged scapegoating at the hands of the military that had taught them to destroy life. While many defenders of Calley did not sanction the violence being unleashed against the Vietnamese people, they believed one lieutenant should not shoulder the burden of America's broader crimes in Southeast Asia. Vietnam Veterans Against the War (VVAW), at demonstrations in 1970–71 and in poetry collections it sponsored, shared this view of the American vet as both victim of his military superiors and perpetrator of unacceptable violence against the people of Vietnam. According to VVAW members and some reporters and filmmakers, subsuming one's own interests to the collective military effort—an honored notion during World War II—in fact led to atrocities and postwar stress. So some soldiers rebelled—by using illegal drugs, refusing to fight, or even turning their own violent training on hated officers. Available evidence suggests that the public steadfastly supported and sympathized with the grunts of Vietnam, even when—or especially when—they were shown running afoul of military justice and as the war lost support in the early 1970s. The victim image, ascendant since the late 1940s, had been updated for the Vietnam War.

This evolving imagery of soldiers and veterans has had wider implications for American society and culture in at least three general areas. First of all, it suggests that the origins of postwar cynicism about military and governmental institutions appeared late in World War II, long before American involvement in Vietnam further magnified doubts about federal authority. During and just after World War II martial life often appeared to benefit the soldier, to grow a boy into a man or turn a dependent kid into a productive citizen. As the years passed after the war, however, images of soldiers increasingly suggested that fighting in foreign adventures did far more harm than good to the grunts on the front lines. Journalists and filmmakers in these years, moreover, challenged the competence, wisdom, and even honesty of officials in the government and military.

Films such as *Sands of Iwo Jima* (1949), *Men in War* (1957), and *Pork Chop Hill* (1959) and the novel *The Thin Red Line* (1962) progressively exposed the chaos of war, the corruption of the military brass, and the shattering impact of combat. Such themes became more prominent in cultural representations of the Vietnam era, through figures ranging from real-life officers and enlisted men in television news coverage to the characters Captain MacDonald in *Beach Red* (1967) and Tyrone Washington in *The Boys in Company C* (1978). Without the Vietnam War it is difficult to imagine the decay of the military's reputation in the 1970s, but Vietnam alone did not precipitate that decline. Through portraits of real and imagined warriors, Americans between the 1950s and the 1970s encountered persistent criticism of and cynicism about the stewards of their country's militarization during the Cold War—the government and the armed forces.

Second, architects of martial culture took part in a dynamic recasting of the masculine hero between the 1940s and 1970s—a period usually associated with a masculinity "crisis" in the thriving field of gender studies.[9] If image makers of the Second World War had emphasized loyalty and toughness in the American soldier, later ones valorized his sensitivity and suffering. This shift began in the late 1940s and 1950s, when moviegoers met characters such as *The Men*'s Bud Wilozek and Homer Parrish of *The Best Years of Our Lives*; received fuller expression in the tear-filled Korean War photographs of David Douglas Duncan; and culminated in the deeply sensitive male heroes Luke Martin (*Coming Home*) and Michael Vronsky (*The Deer Hunter*). As white middle-class men navigated suburban life—and their memories of war, if they were veterans—they had a range of models beyond John Wayne to emulate. And even Wayne's classic *Sands of Iwo Jima* authorized male sensitivity more than is generally assumed.

This cultural turn from stoicism to sensitivity has not gone unnoticed. The historian Peter Novick, among others, has been rather critical of that shift, holding it at least partly responsible for the increasing willingness of Jews to embrace their status as victims of the Holocaust. In contemporary American culture, Novick wrote in 1999, "Stoicism is replaced as a prime value by sensitivity. Instead of enduring in silence, one lets it all hang out. The voicing of pain and outrage is alleged to be 'empowering' as well as therapeutic."[10] In his popular account of the World War II era, *The Greatest Generation* (1998), Tom Brokaw wrote approvingly of the silence of most Second World War veterans about their combat experiences, leveling explicit and implicit criticisms at the contemporary victim culture.[11] More broadly, since the late 1960s conservative critics have lamented the culture of victimhood and its allegedly evil bedfellows: rights consciousness, interest groups, cultural permissiveness, and the decay of individual responsibility.[12]

To me, this sort of thinking paints too dark a picture. The rising prominence of sensitive soldiers in American culture may have helped inspire a widening range of acceptable male public (and perhaps private) behavior, in my view a positive development for the collective psyche of the country. By the end of the twentieth century, crying—unseen in depictions of GIs during World War II—had become common for powerful, tough men in public moments. In 2003 tears of troops in the Iraq War flowed freely on the front pages of major news publications.[13] In July of that year a sportswriter for the *New York Times* authored a long piece on the frequent public crying of professional athletes, and in 1999 Tom Lutz discussed the same phenomenon among political figures such as Bill Clinton and Bob Dole in his book *Crying: The Natural and Cultural History of Tears*.[14] These writings charted the distance covered since 1972, when Edmund Muskie wept publicly and severely damaged his chances for the Democratic presidential nomination. If reporters of the Korean War and others in the postwar era did not directly encourage men of later decades to show their emotions, they surely helped widen the universe of permissible male conduct by favorably portraying men in moments of vulnerability, fear, sorrow, and agony. While Clinton's emotionalism drew derisive jeers from his critics, it is hard to imagine that many Americans would begrudge soldiers in Iraq their tearful reactions to combat. And though World War II veterans receive proper admiration for their stoicism—people with a veteran grandfather often marvel at how "he never talks about the war"—perhaps those still languishing in the psychiatric wards of Veterans Administration hospitals in the late twentieth century would have benefited from a fuller public, or even private, understanding of their emotional struggles. As the scholar Patrick Hagopian wrote in 2006, soldiers of World War II "were silent veterans who never achieved recognition of the emotional and psychological burdens they suffered after service."[15]

Third, martial imagery between the 1940s and the 1970s should impact the study of historical memory. In an argument still influential many decades later, Maurice Halbwachs declared in the 1930s that cultural memory is socially constructed, serving contemporary needs and often simplifying or distorting the history of an event to suit those needs (as in the case of war memorials). Generally speaking, scholars have thought this model applied quite readily to memory of American wars, particularly in the case of

World War II. Image makers and opinion shapers, this thinking goes, have painted a sanitized and sentimentalized picture of World War II, which has been eagerly gobbled up by a public hungry for unambiguous heroes and causes in the murky environment of the Cold War, and since then, of the war on terror—witness George W. Bush's widely noted appeals to 1940s-era imagery during the Iraq War. (The two conflicts were murky in different ways; the Cold War because most of it was waged surreptitiously or in proxy battles, the war on terror because America's enemies were difficult to locate and "defeat.") Scholars have acknowledged cultural challenges to roseate imagery of World War II but have more or less argued that those challenges have not stuck. "Whatever the logic of history or memory," literary critic Philip Beidler has written, "somehow World War II has shaken off all the challenges along the way and really has proven itself to have been what we have been calling it all along, 'The Good War.'"[16] But if World War II in fact has shaken off the challenges, what has happened to them? When Americans in 2007 think of the Second World War, do they think of *Sands of Iwo Jima* or *Slaughterhouse-Five*? Perhaps they think of *Saving Private Ryan*, a film difficult to categorize since it contained the most graphic and gruesome combat depiction to date as well as traditional "good war" ethics of duty, teamwork, and sacrifice.

In teaching courses on American cultural memory of World War II, I have periodically asked students to interview relatives and friends about their perceptions of the conflict. From that admittedly small sample, we have concluded the following: Everyone (students, interviewees, myself) has agreed that "good war" mythology is "out there" in the culture, visible in the success of Brokaw's book and the fact that most of his readers imbibed and probably agreed with his laudatory picture of that generation. Yet we also have found that people often see World War II for what it was: a tragic, dirty, violent, terrifying, necessary conflict. We have seen that some textbooks and readings commonly assigned to students put forth a similar picture. Unfortunately the answer to how Americans "remember" World War II in 2007 is a messy one. The many competing narratives about the war coursing through American culture since the 1940s—the *architecture* of World War II memory, established in countless films, television programs, novels, poems, and memorials and in the personal recollections of vets—just add to the messiness.

The "greatest generation" version of World War II mythology is certainly alive and well in 2007, and perhaps with the passing of that generation will only grow stronger.[17] But all the challenges to that picture leveled since the war ended must reside somewhere, must stick in the minds of a good number of Americans, whether from a snippet of conversation with a vet, from reading *Catch-22* or *Slaughterhouse-Five*, from the constant stream of World War II films replayed on television, or from gritty and violent video games such as *Call of Duty* and *Brothers in Arms*. In other words, the good war myth *itself* may be something of a myth, considering some of the murky and disturbing depictions of World War II peppering American culture since that conflict ended. Certainly when one considers the representations generated by the Korean and Vietnam Wars—especially those produced after the endpoint of my study in the late 1970s—the warrior image hardly seems romanticized. Once again, configurations of the three wars often have shared more themes, meanings, and messages than is usually assumed—or remembered.

How much of an impact, finally, have representations of war and soldiers had on American society since the end of World War II? It is difficult to characterize the relationship between culture and other aspects of American life. Culture, values, and behavior are surely mixed up in a complex web of cause and effect, each component both reflecting and shaping the others. But it does not seem too much to say this: From the late 1940s onward, the portrayal of cynical, skeptical, disillusioned, and, above all, victimized soldiers in American culture has broadened public understanding of war's terrors. A *New York Times* critic praised Clint Eastwood's film of 2006, *Flags of Our Fathers*, for just this sort of revelation: "Mr. Eastwood insists, with a moral certitude that is all too rare in our movies, that we extract an unspeakable cost when we ask men to kill other men."[18] Though that reviewer thought *Flags* unusual in its revelatory spirit, in fact filmmakers, journalists, poets, authors, and photographers have often put the steep costs of combat at the center of the warrior image.

NOTES

INTRODUCTION

1. Gellhorn, *Face of War*, 2–3.
2. The esteemed journalist Walter Cronkite wrote in 2004 that poets, not correspondents, were best able to capture the nature of war; see Cronkite foreword in Hedin, *Old Glory*, xiii. Academics and even soldiers, as well, have trouble conveying the realities of combat. On soldiers see Linderman, *World within War*, 2; on scholars see Russell Weigley's introduction in Kindsvatter, *American Soldiers*, vii–ix. John Keegan attempted to overcome military history's traditional inability to capture the feeling of war in his classic work, *The Face of Battle*.
3. See notes throughout my introduction for some of this scholarship, and its limitations. In 1997 Daniel Hallin wrote of the small but growing body of work "which connects media representations of war to larger structures of meaning in society"—precisely my aim in this book. See Hallin, "Media and War," 222.
4. On the state of military history at the turn of the twenty-first century, see Lynn, "Embattled Future of Academic Military History"; Bruscino, "Bringing Together Social Histories"; on the advent of cultural history, see Lee, "Mind and Matter"; Organization of American Historians roundtable, "Interchange: The Practice of History." John Lynn writes, "The only guise in which the *AHR* [*American Historical Review*] seems to tolerate anything with military overtones is as new cultural history" (787).
5. A useful survey of European representations of war, stressing the persistence of glorified martial imagery until World War II, is Mosse, *Fallen Soldiers*.
6. For pictures of the *Dying Gaul*, the Chinese soldier statues, and the Mayan temple mural, see Tansey and Kleiner, *Gardner's Art Through the Ages*, 176, 497, 564.
7. Ibid., 407–8.
8. See Varley, *Japanese Culture*, 89–90.
9. *Life of King Henry V*, act IV, scene 3. See Wells and Taylor, *William Shakespeare*, 588; Harari, "Martial Illusions," 70.
10. For *The Third of May, 1808* and *Liberty Leading the People* see Tansey and Kleiner, *Gardner's Art Through the Ages*, 938–40, 946.
11. See Molotsky, *Flag, the Poet, and the Song*.
12. See Harris, *Blue & Gray*, 1–2.
13. For this assertion see Sandweiss, *Photography in Nineteenth-Century America*, 101.
14. See Hannavy, *Camera Goes to War*.

15. On the wartime press see Sachsman, Rushing, and van Tuyll, *Civil War and the Press*; Harris, *Blue & Gray*.

16. See *Civil War: A Centennial Exhibition*.

17. Blight points out that some writers did expose the horrors of the Civil War. Walt Whitman, for instance, "did not sanitize the 'hell-scenes'" in his retrospective work *Specimen Days* (1882), nor did Union veteran John W. De Forest in *Miss Ravenal's Conversion from Secession to Loyalty* (1867), nor did Ambrose Bierce in his various writings. But amid a national trend toward reconciliation—and with a reading public unwilling to relive the tragedies of the war—most veterans' accounts by the 1880s were nostalgic and sentimental. See Blight, *Race and Reunion*, 4, 21, 152, 179–85; Cullen, *Civil War in Popular Culture*; Wilson, *Patriotic Gore*.

18. See Moeller, *Shooting War*, xiii.

19. Musicant, *Empire by Default*, 144–45.

20. On Davis, see Seelye, *War Games*; Lubow, *Reporter Who Would Be King*. For Hearst quote see O'Toole, *Spanish War*, 82.

21. On photographers and journalists during the Spanish-American War, see Moeller, *Shooting War*, 29–83; Hoganson, *Fighting for American Manhood*, 184.

22. David Kennedy, *Over Here*, 177–80. Robertson, *Dream of Civilized Warfare*, argues that the image of the World War I flying ace also deflected attention from the horrors of trench combat.

23. See Stallworthy, *Wilfred Owen*, 99.

24. Fussell's work remains the classic one on cultural memory of World War I. See Fussell, *Great War and Modern Memory*, 336. Yuval Noah Harari and others have criticized Fussell's work, arguing that he overprivileged the writings of elite French and English soldiers in making his case for the proliferation of "disillusionment" narratives after World War I. See Harari, "Martial Illusions," 45–46.

25. See Kennedy, *Over Here*, 214–24.

26. For accounts of the Bonus Army, see Keene, *Doughboys*, 179–204; Barber, *Marching on Washington*, 75–107. Keene's work suggests that the notion of the veteran-as-victim—a key component to the story I have to tell—has a long history.

27. For *Guernica* see Russell Martin, *Picasso's War*.

28. Kershaw, *Blood and Champagne*, 42.

29. See Aldgate, *Cinema and History*.

30. On the literature and poetry of the Spanish Civil War, see Thomas, *Novel of the Spanish Civil War*; Rosenthal, *Poetry of the Spanish Civil War*.

31. On Hemingway, Gellhorn, and Orwell, see Sanderson, *Blowing the Bridge*; Gellhorn, *Face of War*, 9–41; D. J. Taylor, *Orwell*, 200–234; and introduction by Lionel Trilling in Orwell, *Homage to Catalonia*, v–xxiii.

32. See Valleau, *Spanish Civil War*, 1–7.

33. The phrase is from Roeder, *Censored War*.

34. According to historian Mark D. Van Ells, *disabled* women vets enjoyed some vocational and educational benefits, but uninjured ones were excluded from the wider educational offerings of the GI Bill. On discrimination against women —as well as gay soldiers—in the doling out of veterans' benefits, see Van Ells, *To Hear Only Thunder Again*, 137; Loss, "'Most Wonderful Thing'"; Canaday, "Building a Straight State." Quite valuable would be a close study of the ways women *did* appear in depictions of war in the decades after World War II, particularly in the early twenty-first century as their roles in the military expanded.

35. See Torgovnick, *War Complex*; Adams, *Best War Ever*; Alpers, "This Is the Army"; Basinger, *World War II Combat Film*; Beidler, *Good War's Greatest Hits*; Doherty, *Projections of War*; Fussell, *Wartime*; Gerber, "Heroes and Misfits"; Hale, "Representation of the Veteran"; Koppes and Black, *Hollywood Goes to War*; Roeder, *Censored War*; Tobin, *Ernie Pyle's War*; Winkler, *Politics of Propaganda*; Kimble, *Mobilizing the Home Front*.

36. A few works cover imagery over multiple wars, including Korea, but generally focus on a singular medium (film, photography, literature, and so on). These include Aichinger, *American Soldier in Fiction*; Harari, "Martial Illusions"; Lundberg, "American Literature of War"; Moeller, *Shooting War*; Suid, *Guts and Glory*; Kindsvatter, *American Soldiers*. Among the few works that cover several decades and multiple cultural forms are Engelhardt, *End of Victory Culture*; Faludi, *Stiffed*.

37. See Arlen, *Living-Room War*; Bates, *Wars We Took to Vietnam*; Beattie, *Scar that Binds*; Braestrup, *Big Story*; Franklin, *Vietnam and Other American Fantasies*; Hallin, *"Uncensored War"*; Lembcke, *Spitting Image*; Neilson, *Warring Fictions*; Pach, "And That's the Way It Was"; Rollins, "Vietnam War"; Landers, *Weekly War*.

38. Hallin and Gitlin, "Gulf War as Popular Culture," 161–62.

39. For a view similar to my own see Bodnar, *"Saving Private Ryan."* Other works that likewise challenge the notion of uninterrupted consensus before the Vietnam War include Alan Brinkley, "Illusion of Unity"; Engelhardt, *End of Victory Culture*.

40. The numerous American veterans' organizations are peripheral to my study except when they garnered widespread attention. Nevertheless, there is an important story to tell about how these groups—notably the American Legion and Veterans of Foreign Wars—opposed, reinforced, or reacted to war imagery.

41. A diverse literature posits Vietnam's shattering effect on American innocence. See Margolis, *Last Innocent Year*; O'Neill, *Coming Apart*, 319–54; Baritz, *Back-*

fire, 19–52; Herring, *America's Longest War*, 304–5; Isaacs, *Vietnam Shadows*, 20–21; Suid, *Guts and Glory*, 2; Hallin and Gitlin, "Gulf War as Popular Culture," 161–62; Harari, "Martial Illusions," 46–47.

42. Elegant, "How to Lose a War," 73; see also Lewy, *America in Vietnam*; on critics of the press among former military and diplomatic officials, see Hammond, "Press in Vietnam," 312–13; Carruthers, *Media at War*, 108–20; on scholars of American politics who find an "oppositional" tone in media of the 1960s and 1970s, see Hallin, "Media, the War in Vietnam, and Political Support."

43. For a brief discussion of this position see Carruthers, *Media at War*, 112.

44. Kaplan, "American Journalism Goes to War," 209.

45. Quotes from Thussu and Freedman, *War and the Media*, 8; Magder, "Watching What We Say," 36. For other such critiques of the media's alliance with official sources in the post-9/11 era—and this is only a small sampling of that sizable and growing literature—see Boggs and Pollard, *Hollywood War Machine*; Torgovnick, *War Complex*, 16; Miller, "Information Dominance"; Schecter, *Media Wars*; Williams, "New Media Environment," 177.

46. See Herman and Chomsky, *Manufacturing Consent*; Philip M. Taylor, *War and the Media*; Carruthers, *Media at War*; Hallin and Gitlin, "Gulf War as Popular Culture"; Kellner, *Persian Gulf TV War*; Clarence R. Wyatt, *Paper Soldiers*; Hallin, "*Uncensored War*"; Arlen, *Living-Room War*; Lichty, "Comments on the Influence of Television"; Hammond, "Press in Vietnam"; Kaplan, "American Journalism Goes to War." Similarly, Mermin, *Debating War and Peace*, suggests that after Vietnam official sources in Washington were able to "set the news agenda" in times of conflict (quote on 145).

47. See Linderman, *World within War*, 311–15; Fussell, *Wartime*, 188–92; Kindsvatter, *American Soldiers*, 289.

48. Hallin and Gitlin, "Gulf War as Popular Culture," 161.

49. Carruthers, *Media at War*, 8.

50. For discussion of militarization and American anxieties about war, see Sherry, *In the Shadow of War*; Bacevich, *New American Militarism*. Yuval Noah Harari also finds a turn toward victim narratives in twentieth-century war memoirs but attributes it to broader changes in what soldiers expected from life and combat. "For soldiers who entered war expecting life to be the continuous development of a self, and who then strove to somehow integrate the war into such a life, the idea of 'disillusionment' provided the key." Harari, "Martial Illusions," 68.

CHAPTER 1

1. Publicity pamphlet for Road to Victory, p. 12; MoMA Exhibit #182; Record II.1/98 (1); Museum of Modern Art Archives, Department of Circulating Exhibitions, New York, N.Y. (hereafter MoMA Archives).

2. Itineraries for Road to Victory, MoMA Exhibit #182, Record II.1/98 (1), MoMA Archives. On Steichen see Heller, *War and Conflict*, 8–15.

3. *New York Times*, June 7, 1942; *Cleveland Plain Dealer*, February 2, 1943; *Cleveland Press*, February 18, 1943; *Chicago Sun*, March 31, 1943; *Madison (Wis.) Capital Times*, March 28, 1943; *St. Louis Globe-Democrat*, May 16, 1943.

4. "Comments upon the Exhibition" for Road to Victory, MoMA Exhibit #182, Record II.1/98 (1), MoMA Archives.

5. *Chicago Tribune*, April 4, 1943; *Chicago Tribune*, March 30, 1943; *Chicago Herald-American*, March 31, 1943; *Monterey (Calif.) Herald*, July 3, 1943.

6. Roeder, *Censored War*, 2.

7. Around 800,000 blacks served in the army, 167,000 in the navy, and 19,000 in the marines during World War II—somewhat below their proportion of the American population (10 percent or so), particularly in the navy. On those numbers and the Tuskegee Airmen, see Astor, *Right to Fight*, 188–89; Nalty and MacGregor, *Blacks in the Military*, 103, 133–34; MacGregor, *Integration of the Armed Forces*, 56, 98. The exploits of the 442nd were captured in the film *Go for Broke!* (1951).

8. For casualty figures see Ellis, *World War II*, 254; for psychological casualty rates, see Wanke, "American Military Psychiatry," 127. Ellen Herman has used slightly different numbers, writing that neuropsychiatric admissions reached 1 million, incorporating about 850,000 individual soldiers. See Herman, *Romance of American Psychology*, 96.

9. Van Ells, *To Hear Only Thunder Again*, v.

10. See Adams, *Best War Ever*, 97.

11. Bowker, *Out of Uniform*, 88–102.

12. Perhaps the best-known invocation of the phrase "the good war" is Studs Terkel's use of it as the title of his sweeping oral history of World War II. In that work he notes that Herbert Mitgang suggested the title: "It is a phrase that has been frequently voiced by men of his and my generation, to distinguish that war from other wars, declared and undeclared. Quotation marks have been added, not as a matter of caprice or editorial comment, but simply because the adjective 'good' mated to the noun 'war' is so incongruous." See Terkel, *"The Good War,"* front matter.

13. Nemerov, *War Stories*, 31.

14. See Adams, *Best War Ever*, 98–113 (from which the previous paragraph is drawn); Linderman, *World within War*; Fussell, *Boys' Crusade*; Kindsvatter, *American Soldiers*; Hastings, *Armageddon*; on the particular ferocity and racism of the Pacific war, see Dower, *War without Mercy*.

15. On radio propaganda, see Horten, "'Propaganda Must Be Painless,'" 374; Savage, *Broadcasting Freedom*, 118–19; MacDonald, *Don't Touch That Dial!* 264–71; Winkler, *Politics of Propaganda*, 60–63; Winkler, *Home Front U.S.A.*, 29. On films

and other elements of American culture inundated with government propaganda or roseate imagery, see Alpers, "This Is the Army"; Fussell, *Wartime*; Linderman, *World within War*, 311–15; Kindsvatter, *American Soldiers*, 289; Suid, *Guts and Glory*; Doherty, *Projections of War*; Basinger, *World War II Combat Film*; Dick, *Star-Spangled Screen*; Adams, *Best War Ever*, 1–19; Roeder, *Censored War*.

16. For critiques of sanitized World War II reportage, see Steinbeck, *Once There Was a War*, ix–xxi; Knightley, *First Casualty*, 364; Tobin, *Ernie Pyle's War*, 138; Adams, *Best War Ever*, 9–12; Fussell, *Boys' Crusade*, 49–50.

17. One prominent example from radio was the popular series, *This Is War!* by the famed Norman Corwin.

18. See Roeder, *Censored War*, 1–2.

19. Letter inserted in OWI Media Program Book, *Veterans' Information Program*, February 20, 1945 (hereafter *Veterans' Information Program*); Project File, *When I Come Home* (hereafter *When I Come Home* File); Correspondence Regarding Film Production, September 1943–October 1945; Records of the Bureau of Motion Pictures; Records of the Office of War Information, Record Group 208 (hereafter OWI Records); National Archives at College Park, College Park, Md. (hereafter NACP).

20. See Winkler, *Politics of Propaganda*, 1–4; Leuchtenburg, *Perils of Prosperity*, 43–48.

21. For a lively account of life at OWI, see Schlesinger, *Life in the Twentieth Century*, 277–94.

22. On the contentious and confused nature of wartime information management see Sweeney, *Secrets of Victory*, 91–99; Doherty, *Projections of War*, 43; Heller, *War and Conflict*, 11.

23. See Koppes and Black, "What to Show the World," 88.

24. See Winkler, *Politics of Propaganda*, 5–7.

25. *Veterans' Information Program*, 1, OWI Records, NACP. The other departments involved were the Selective Service System, War Production Board, War Manpower Commission, Federal Security Agency, Department of Commerce, and Civil Service Commission.

26. See Giangreco, "'Spinning' the Casualties."

27. *Veterans' Information Program*, 11, 18, OWI Records, NACP.

28. Roeder, *Censored War*, 16.

29. Arthur Waldman, Brecksville, Ohio, to Dr. Ira Scott, Vocational Adjustment Division, VA, August 12, 1944; Correspondence Regarding Readjustment of Veterans to Civilian Life, 1944; Office of Assistant Administrator for Administration, General Policy Files, 1917–59; Records of the Veterans Administration, Record Group 15 (hereafter VA Records); National Archives Building, Washington, D.C. (hereafter NADC).

30. OWI Domestic Radio Bureau, *Background Material on Veterans' Readjustment*, March 1945, p. 2, *When I Come Home* File, OWI Records, NACP.

31. Roeder, *Censored War*, 16.

32. OWI Domestic Radio Bureau, "Fact Sheet No. 305: The Veteran's Assets," March 1, 1945, p. 4, *When I Come Home* File, OWI Records, NACP. Emphasis in original.

33. *Veterans' Information Program*, 13, 18, OWI Records, NACP.

34. At the same time, military psychiatrists were coming to believe that *breakdown* in combat was a normal response. In her book on twentieth-century American psychology, Ellen Herman has written, "The sheer numbers of cases seen by clinicians . . . finally led them to view the typical psychiatric casualty not as an intrinsically predisposed or mentally disordered individual but as a perfectly ordinary person under incredible strain—an 'Everyman.'" See Herman, *Romance of American Psychology*, 96. For a look at how the military used in-service educational programs to fight the effects of battle fatigue, see Loss, "'Most Wonderful Thing.'"

35. *Veterans' Information Program*, 7, OWI Records, NACP.

36. Radio commanded the largest audiences in wartime America of any media—110 million souls who listened to an average of four hours of radio a day. See Winkler, *Politics of Propaganda*, 60; Horten, "'Propaganda Must Be Painless,'" 374.

37. *Background Material on Veterans' Readjustment*, March 1945, p. 6, OWI Records, NACP. Emphasis in original.

38. "Fact Sheet No. 305," March 1, 1945, pp. 4, OWI Records, NACP.

39. *Background Material on Veterans' Readjustment*, March 1945, pp. 6–7, OWI Records, NACP. Emphasis in original.

40. Allen M. Whitlock, War Department, to James R. Brackett, OWI, December 23, 1944, *When I Come Home* File, OWI Records, NACP.

41. OWI sought to capitalize on the booming movie industry. Untold thousands watched government films on 16mm projectors in churches, schools, clubs, civic organizations, and other public places. But the largest numbers attended movies in the nation's sixteen thousand public theaters. Every week during the war and after, attendance at these numbered approximately 80 million Americans. See Correspondence with Distributors of Non-theatrical Films, 1939–45, Records of the Bureau of Motion Pictures, OWI Records, NACP; MacCann, *People's Films*, 118–19.

42. Paul Trivers, "When I Came Home," September 5, 1944, pp. 1–14, *When I Come Home* File, OWI Records, NACP.

43. Taylor M. Mills, "Comments on *When I Come Home*," September 12, 1944, p. 3, *When I Come Home* File, OWI Records, NACP.

44. Dore Schary, "Synopsis for Short on Wounded Veteran," March 26, 1945, pp. 1–5, *When I Come Home* File, OWI Records, NACP.

45. Robert L. Hutton Jr., Program Manager, OWI, to Allen M. Whitlock, War Department, April 4, 1945; Whitlock to Hutton, April 11, 1945, *When I Come Home* File, OWI Records, NACP.

46. Howard H. Montgomery, U.S. Navy, to Comdr. Ralph A. Sentman, U.S. Navy, April 9, 1945, *When I Come Home* File, OWI Records, NACP.

47. See *Welcome Home* (1945), Motion Picture 111-M-1226, Records of the Office of the Chief Signal Officer, Record Group 111; *Peace Comes to America* (1945), Motion Picture 56.43, Records of the Department of the Treasury, Record Group 56; *The Returning Veteran* (1945), Motion Picture MT-MT-11.9, "March of Time" Productions, Collection MT, NACP.

48. Roeder, *Censored War*, 124.

49. For discussion of this literature, see Cole, "Home from the War."

50. *American Mercury*, January 1944, 75–81.

51. *Ladies' Home Journal*, July 1944, 122; *Life*, May 15, 1944, 28; *Rotarian*, June 1945, 26–27. On *Life*'s mainly middle-class appeal see Baughman, "Who Read *Life*?"

52. *Newsweek*, September 4, 1944, 76; *Time*, August 6, 1945, 58; *Life*, September 3, 1945, 29. On such instances of "remasculinized" wounded men in World War II–era media, see Jarvis, *Male Body at War*, 86–118.

53. *Newsweek*, March 20, 1944, inside cover (emphasis in original); *Saturday Evening Post*, July 7, 1945, 53.

54. *Life*, June 11, 1945, 64; *Life*, August 20, 1945, 38B; *Life*, July 2, 1945, 4.

55. See Roeder, *Censored War*, 1, 7–25; Kimble, *Mobilizing the Home Front*; Jarvis, *Male Body at War*, 88. The first picture of American dead in *Life* magazine appeared in September 1943, almost two years after Pearl Harbor.

56. *Saturday Evening Post*, April 14, 1945, 112; *American Mercury*, September 1945, 326–27; *Nation's Business*, September 1945, 21.

57. *Time*, June 5, 1944, 63–64; *Newsweek*, March 13, 1944, 56; *Life*, June 12, 1944, 21.

58. *Ladies' Home Journal*, July 1944, 122; *New York Times*, February 4, 1945; Grinker and Spiegel, *Men under Stress*, 185.

59. See Dean, *Shook over Hell*, 30–35.

60. *Time*, February 7, 1944, 44–48.

61. *Life*, June 11, 1945, 65; *Newsweek*, March 6, 1944, 103; *Life*, August 20, 1945, 3.

62. Waller, *Veteran Comes Back*, 13 (emphasis in original); *Time*, April 3, 1944, 24; *Nation's Business*, April 1944, 84; *Time*, September 11, 1944, 65–66.

63. See, for example, *Newsweek*, December 25, 1944, 74; *Atlantic Monthly*, December 1944, 66; *American Mercury*, August 1945, 147; *Atlantic Monthly*, June 1945, 71; *Harper's Magazine*, April 1945, 385.

64. *Nation's Business*, August 1944, 28; *Ladies' Home Journal*, January 1945, 10; *Rotarian*, June 1945, 26 (emphasis in original).

65. *Saturday Evening Post*, July 14, 1945, 1; *Newsweek*, March 6, 1944, 16. For a further look at wartime advertising, see Hart, "Madison Avenue Goes to War"; on American manhood during the war, see Jarvis, *Male Body at War*.

66. See Stephen Ambrose's introduction in Mauldin, *Up Front*, v–x; Tobin, *Ernie Pyle's War*, 88, 203.

67. See Mauldin, *Up Front*, v–x; Tobin, *Ernie Pyle's War*, 5–74.

68. Pyle, *Here Is Your War*, 73–74, 84; Pyle, *Brave Men*, 270. Paul Fussell has emphasized Pyle's "wartime journalistic habit" of seeking out the good news in even the most disastrous situations. See Fussell, *Boys' Crusade*, 49.

69. Tobin, *Ernie Pyle's War*, 112, 132, 199; Pyle, *Brave Men*, 451.

70. Mauldin, *Up Front*, 21, 41, 47.

71. This information and the quotations from Mauldin, *Up Front*, vi, 178; Tobin, *Ernie Pyle's War*, 110–11; Pyle, *Brave Men*, 465.

72. Mauldin, *Up Front*, 13, 32, 83, 123, 163.

73. Meanwhile, military psychiatrists were routinely showing soldiers in World War II graphic illustrations of how to handle the very loss of individual agency that Mauldin bemoaned. Ellen Herman has written of drawings that taught GIs it was "normal" to resent the scarcity of privacy, privileges, and free thinking within the military and that "letting off steam" would shrink that resentment. Perhaps Mauldin's cartoons fulfilled such a role. See Herman, *Romance of American Psychology*, 101–7.

74. Mauldin, *Up Front*, 5.

75. Indeed, as Benjamin Alpers has argued, much wartime imagery and government propaganda sought to portray the military as democratic, despite plain evidence to the contrary. See Alpers, "This Is the Army," 129–63.

76. Mauldin, *Up Front*, 21, 24, 57, 128, 130–32. In a broader scope Russell Weigley has written of the inherent clashes between civilians and soldiers, dating back to the founding of the United States. See Weigley, "American Civil-Military Cultural Gap," 218.

77. Mauldin, *Up Front*, 9–10; Pyle, *Brave Men*, 466.

78. Mauldin, *Up Front*, 15; Pyle, *Brave Men*, 465.

79. Terkel, *"The Good War,"* 11.

80. *Congressional Record*, 79th Cong., 1st sess., vol. 91, 6995. Eastland's comments reflected the long-standing refusal of white men to view blacks as good soldiers. See Hoganson, *Fighting for American Manhood*, 131.

81. *Crisis*, March 1945, 85.

82. See Rampersad, *Collected Poems of Langston Hughes*, 299.

83. Quoted in *New Republic*, March 13, 1944, 339.

84. *Crisis*, January 1945, 8.

85. Much of the information in this paragraph relies on Sitkoff, "African American Militancy"; Sitkoff, *Struggle for Black Equality*, 12–13.

86. *Crisis*, February 1944, 39.

87. Reverend C. L. Evans, President, Petersburg, Virginia, Branch of the NAACP, to OWI Bureau of Motion Pictures, February 17, 1944; Project File, *The Negro Soldier* (hereafter *Negro Soldier* File); Correspondence Regarding Film Production, September 1943–October 1945; Records of the Bureau of Motion Pictures; OWI Records, NACP.

88. *The Negro Soldier* (1944), Motion Picture III-OF-51, Records of the Office of the Chief Signal Officer, Record Group III, NACP.

89. Taylor Mills, OWI Bureau of Motion Pictures, to Reverend C. L. Evans, NAACP, March 2, 1944, *Negro Soldier* File, OWI Records, NACP.

90. *Crisis*, March 1944, 72.

91. Clayton Koppes and Gregory Black have argued, more generally, that the agendas of black activists and government propagandists were "incompatible." See Koppes and Black, "Blacks, Loyalty, and Motion-Picture Propaganda."

92. Stanton Griffis, OWI Bureau of Motion Pictures, to Maj. Gen. A. D. Surles, Director, Bureau of Public Relations, War Department, February 11, 1944, *Negro Soldier* File, OWI Records, NACP.

93. Taylor Mills, Chief, OWI Bureau of Motion Pictures, to Truman K. Gibson Jr., Civilian Aide to the Secretary of War, War Department, February 22, 1945, *Negro Soldier* File, OWI Records, NACP.

94. See Cripps and Culbert, "Negro Soldier"; Holsinger, *War and American Popular Culture*, 287–88.

95. According to two film scholars, however, the movie had a major impact on the postwar civil rights movement, demonstrating the power of film to promote racial tolerance. See Cripps and Culbert, "Negro Soldier."

96. Blum, *V Was for Victory*, 63.

97. Mays, "Veterans," 209.

98. *Life*, August 20, 1945, 38–38A.

99. *Time*, September 17, 1945, 19.

100. Goulden, *Best Years*, 40–41.

101. Corwin, *Untitled, and Other Radio Dramas*, 439, 441–42, 449.

102. Blum, *V Was for Victory*, 55, 64; *Time*, September 11, 1944, 66; John F. Kennedy to his parents, September 12, 1943; File, "1943-Family"; Personal File, 1943–9; Correspondence, 1943–1952; John F. Kennedy Personal Papers; John F. Kennedy Library, Boston, Mass.; Leinbaugh and Campbell, *Men of Company K*, 276.

CHAPTER 2

1. See *Time*, September 10, 1945, 25–27.

2. *Newsweek*, October 8, 1945, 33.

3. Susman, "Did Success Spoil the United States?" 19; Stoler, "Second World War," 25. For coverage of these postwar crises, see Patterson, *Grand Expectations,* 20–60; O'Neill, *American High,* 10–11; Goulden, *Best Years,* 19–65, 91–142.

4. Gerber, "Heroes and Misfits." See also Goulden, *Best Years,* 37–51; Adams, *Best War Ever,* 1–13. These authors are well aware that a great ambivalence greeted World War II veterans, one blending fear and gratitude. In fact, Gerber has placed this treatment within a long history of similar feelings toward war veterans going back to classic antiquity.

5. *Harper's Magazine,* February 1946, 156.

6. Ibid., October 1946, 295.

7. Ibid., November 1945, 454; *Atlantic Monthly,* February 1946, 49.

8. Administrator for Veterans Affairs, *Annual Report, 1946,* 1.

9. Bolté, *New Veteran,* 1. In 1946, a men's magazine would name Bolté one of the "ten outstanding young men" of 1946, along with Joe Louis, Arthur Schlesinger Jr., Bill Mauldin, John F. Kennedy, and others. See *Future: The Magazine for Young Men,* February 1947, cover.

10. Crespi and Shapleigh, "'The' Veteran—A Myth," 361; Bowker, *Out of Uniform,* xi.

11. *Nation,* August 10, 1946, 147.

12. *New York Times,* August 2, September 7, September 30, 1946.

13. *Time,* September 19, 1949, 28–29.

14. *Collier's,* October 12, 1946, 17.

15. See, for example, Mays, "Veterans," 209.

16. See Dittmer, *Local People,* 1–18.

17. *Crisis,* September 1946, 276–77; *Time,* August 26, 1946, 21.

18. *Crisis,* October 1946, 298–301.

19. Egerton, *Speak Now Against the Day,* 366. According to *Historical Statistics of the United States,* one African American was lynched in 1945, six in 1946, and one in 1947 and 1948. Five lynchings occurred over the next five years, until 1955, when eight blacks were lynched, presumably in the backlash against the *Brown* decision. See U.S. Bureau of the Census, *Historical Statistics,* 422.

20. Zangrando, *NAACP Crusade Against Lynching,* 174.

21. *Time,* April 1, 1946, 21.

22. Rogers and Wallen, *Counseling with Returned Servicemen,* 1–3.

23. A sampling of the wealth of literature on education and the GI Bill includes Olson, *GI Bill;* Frydl, "GI Bill"; Nam, "Impact of the 'GI Bills'"; Loss, "'Most Wonderful Thing.'"

24. The information in these paragraphs derives from Van Ells, *To Hear Only Thunder Again,* 135–70.

25. *New Republic,* January 7, 1946, 12; *Time,* March 18, 1946, 75; *Newsweek,* March 11, 1946, 88; *Life,* April 21, 1947, 107.

26. *Life*, April 21, 1947, 105, 113; *Time*, August 26, 1946, 77.

27. *Time*, June 16, 1947, 30.

28. See Van Ells, *To Hear Only Thunder Again*, 135.

29. Quoted in *Newsweek*, March 11, 1946, 87.

30. *Atlantic Monthly*, May 1947, 28.

31. U.S. Bureau of the Census, *Historical Statistics*, 135.

32. See "History of H.R. #5363," undated; "Veterans Affairs" File; Campaign Files, '46 and '52 Campaigns; Pre-Presidential Papers; John F. Kennedy Library, Boston, Mass. (hereafter JFKL). See also *Boston Globe*, April 15, 1946.

33. *Boston Globe*, April 16, 1946.

34. *Boston American*, April 10, 1946. Emphasis added.

35. *New York Times*, May 28, 1946.

36. U.S. Senate Committee on Military Affairs, *Superseniority Rights of Veterans*.

37. U.S. House Committee on Veterans' Affairs, *Laws Relating to Veterans*.

38. *Time*, February 16, 1948, 8.

39. Universal Newsreel, "Airmen Seek Peacetime Pilot Jobs," January 10, 1946; Vol. 19, Reel 468; Universal Newsreels, Record Group 200; National Archives at College Park, College Park, Md. (hereafter NACP).

40. Paramount News, March 2, 1946, Vol. 5, Number 53, Paramount News, Former Record Group 200, NACP.

41. *New York Times*, January 17, 1946.

42. *Collier's*, October 12, 1946, 17; *New Republic*, April 28, 1947, 20.

43. *Time*, August 26, 1946, 17.

44. *New Republic*, March 3, 1947, 28–29; *Time*, August 1, 1949, 10.

45. For a ground-level view of postwar housing woes see McEnaney, "Nightmares on Elm Street."

46. See Van Ells, *To Hear Only Thunder Again*, 216–21.

47. *Nation*, February 9, 1946, 161.

48. Kenneth T. Jackson, *Crabgrass Frontier*, 232.

49. Goulden, *Best Years*, 132; Jackson, *Crabgrass Frontier*, 232.

50. Giangreco, *Dear Harry*, 108.

51. O'Neill, *American High*, 10–11.

52. *Time*, November 18, 1946, 30.

53. See Wilson Wyatt, *Whistle Stops*, 58–86.

54. Universal Newsreel, "More Homes Promised," January 5, 1946, Vol. 19, Reel 466, Universal Newsreels, Record Group 200, NACP.

55. *Congressional Record*, 79th Cong., 2nd sess., vol. 92, 4762–64.

56. *Nation*, January 5, 1946, 8.

57. See *Congressional Quarterly*, vol. 2, no. 2, 1946, 255–59; see also Van Ells, *To Hear Only Thunder Again*, 216–21.

58. See *Congressional Quarterly*, vol. 2, no. 2, 1946, 260.

59. *Nation*, February 9, 1946, 161.

60. *Time*, August 26, 1946, 81.

61. *Collier's*, October 12, 1946, 17.

62. See Goulden, *Best Years*, 135–36; Jackson, *Crabgrass Frontier*, 236; O'Neill, *American High*, 15–19; Patterson, *Grand Expectations*, 71–73.

63. O'Neill, *American High*, 15. Using similar language, another scholar has written that after the decline of VEHP, "housing programs for veterans disappeared from the national debate over housing." See Van Ells, *To Hear Only Thunder Again*, 221.

64. *Commonweal*, March 28, 1947, 582.

65. U.S. House Committee on Veterans' Affairs, *Legislative Programs of Veterans' Organizations*, 5, 46.

66. *Springfield (Mass.) Daily News*, February 17, 1948. On the AVC's reputation in 1946, see *New Republic*, January 28, 1946, 118; *Nation*, June 22, 1946, 740–41.

67. See *Washington Post*, February 15, 1948; *Bronx (N.Y.) Home News*, March 1, 1948; *Chicago Sun*, February 23, 1948.

68. Unmarked newspaper clippings, [March 1948?], Publicity II: Newspaper Clippings, House Files, National Veterans Housing Conference, 1948, JFKL.

69. *Time*, May 17, 1948, 26; Paramount News, April 20, 1949, Vol. 8, Number 68, Paramount News, Former Record Group 200, NACP.

70. "Bulletin: National Veterans Housing Conference," February 1948, Press Releases, House Files, National Veterans Housing Conference, 1948, JFKL. Emphasis added.

71. *New Republic*, March 11, 1946, 333.

72. *Congressional Quarterly Almanac*, vol. 5, 1949, 273–86.

73. U.S. Bureau of the Census, *Historical Statistics*, 1140.

74. Wanke, "American Military Psychiatry," 127.

75. *Harper's Magazine*, November 1945, 454.

76. *Atlantic Monthly*, February 1946, 50.

77. See Dupuy and Bregstein, *Soldiers' Album*. Unlike some works by military officials, the book had a commercial publisher.

78. *New Republic*, March 3, 1947, 36.

79. Dupuy and Bregstein, *Soldiers' Album*, 168–69.

80. *Atlantic Monthly*, December 1946, 84–90.

81. *New Republic*, January 7, 1946, 12. Emphasis added.

82. *Saturday Evening Post*, April 13, 1946, 18–19.

83. *Time*, August 19, 1946, 68.

84. *New Republic*, January 6, 1947, 26–27.

85. *Harper's Magazine*, October 1946, 297. On wartime narratives of masculinity and capability, see Jarvis, *Male Body at War*.

1. Itineraries for Power in the Pacific, MoMA Exhibit #275; Record II.1/95 (1); Museum of Modern Art Archives, Department of Circulating Exhibitions, New York, N.Y. (hereafter MoMA Archives).

2. See Roeder, *Censored War*, 1–25. For a brief discussion of Power in the Pacific, see Staniszewski, *Power of Display*, 224–27.

3. Press release for Power in the Pacific, MoMA Exhibit #275, Record II.1/95 (1), MoMA Archives.

4. Captions for Power in the Pacific, MoMA Exhibit #275, Record II.1/95 (1), MoMA Archives.

5. Ibid.

6. *Kalamazoo (Mich.) Gazette*, November 11, 1945; *Bangor (Maine) News*, May 3, 1946; *Providence (R.I.) Journal*, March 24, 1946; *Memphis Press-Scimitar*, June 20, 1946.

7. Burns, *Gallery*, 21.

8. Basinger, *World War II Combat Film*, 121.

9. For coverage of these films see ibid., 120–39. In these years the authoritarian studio system and production codes established in the 1930s still governed cinematic content, perhaps accounting for *A Walk in the Sun*'s happier celluloid ending. See Hall, *Crossroads*, 2–8.

10. Suid, *Guts and Glory*, 94.

11. Ibid., 95.

12. Ibid.

13. For discussion of *The Best Years of Our Lives*, see Jackson, "Uncertain Peace"; Gerber, "Heroes and Misfits"; Goulden, *Best Years*, 3–6; Holsinger, *War and American Popular Culture*, 238–39.

14. Two dissertations from the 1990s addressed the veteran in postwar American film. See Hale, "Representation of the Veteran"; Deutsch, "Coming Home." A short survey of veterans in film appears in Langman and Borg, *Encyclopedia of American War Films*, 614–17.

15. All quotations are from *The Men*, dir. Fred Zinnemann (United Artists, 1950). For an extended discussion of *The Men*, see Jarvis, *Male Body at War*, 107–12. I largely agree with Jarvis's interpretation of the film, though I see Marlon Brando's character giving up more of the traditional elements of manliness than she does.

16. It was just this world of illusion that had angered some disabled veterans early in 1946, when they told reporters from the *New Republic* that they resented upbeat accounts of the wounded in the media. See *New Republic*, January 7, 1946, 12.

17. *Newsweek*, July 17, 1950, 80–81.

18. *Time,* July 24, 1950, 78.

19. *New York Times Magazine,* May 28, 1950, 44–45.

20. *New York Times,* July 30, 1950, II, 1.

21. *New Republic,* July 31, 1950, 22–23.

22. Two other films of 1949, *Home of the Brave* and *Battleground,* also offered stark looks at military life. For brief analysis of them see Bodnar, *"Saving Private Ryan."*

23. The marines sought the public relations benefits and federal funding that a blockbuster picture would bring. See Roberts and Olson, *John Wayne,* 319.

24. Much analysis of *Sands of Iwo Jima* has identified a replay of World War II themes (such as the multiethnic platoon) in the service of chest-thumping Cold War patriotism; see Doherty, *Projections of War,* 274; Suid, *Guts and Glory,* 118–19; Boggs and Pollard, *Hollywood War Machine,* 59, 69, 72; Jarvis, *Male Body at War,* 188–89. Philip Beidler, though, has also pointed out that "the preponderance of the movie is really devoted to the decidedly non-guts-and-glory shaping up of the unit; and it is thereby heavily oriented as well toward Stryker's own drunkenness, anger, abuse of trainees, abandonment of a spouse, estrangement from a son, and mastiff professionalism." My reading of the film stresses these elements, also noted by John Bodnar, Randy Roberts and James Olson, and Garry Wills. See Beidler, *Good War's Greatest Hits,* 63–64; Bodnar, *"Saving Private Ryan";* Roberts and Olson, *John Wayne,* 319; Wills, *John Wayne's America,* 155.

25. All quotations are from *Sands of Iwo Jima,* dir. Alan Dwan (Republic, 1949).

26. *New York Times,* December 31, 1949, 9.

27. As Michael C. C. Adams has put it, soldiers in the film "became seasoned veterans and mature adults" through combat. See Adams, *Best War Ever,* 14.

28. *New York Times,* August 7, 1949, II, 3. Emphasis added.

29. Wills, *John Wayne's America,* 155.

30. *Sands of Iwo Jima* was the top-grossing movie of 1949. See Holsinger, *War and American Popular Culture,* 301.

31. *Time,* January 16, 1950, 86; *Newsweek,* January 16, 1950, 78; *New York Times,* December 31, 1949, 9; *Variety,* December 14, 1949, 8.

32. For these positive reviews in the press, and Wayne's embodiment of the marines, see Suid, *Guts and Glory,* 129; Roberts and Olson, *John Wayne,* 321; Wills, *John Wayne's America,* 149–56.

33. *What's My Score?* (1946); Motion Picture 15.18; Records of the Veterans Administration, Record Group 15; National Archives at College Park, College Park, Md. (hereafter NACP).

34. *Toward Independence* (1947); Motion Picture 306.212; Records of the Department of the Army, Record Group 306; NACP.

35. *Quiet Triumph* (1947); Motion Picture 15.14; Records of the Veterans Administration, Record Group 15; NACP.

36. *The Road to Decision* (1947); Motion Picture 15.19; Records of the Veterans Administration, Record Group 15; NACP.

37. For discussion of *Let There Be Light*, see MacCann, *People's Films*, 170–71; Holsinger, *War and American Popular Culture*, 277–78; Hale, "Representation of the Veteran," 144–85.

38. MacCann, *People's Films*, 170.

39. *Let There Be Light* (1946); Motion Picture 111-M-1241; Records of the Office of the Chief Signal Officer, Record Group 111; NACP.

40. See Roeder, *Censored War*, 124–25.

41. Braceland, *Retraining and Re-Education of Veterans*, 20.

42. See Herman, *Romance of American Psychology*.

43. Diggins, "American Writer," 612. Paul Fussell, who has continually offered correctives to roseate World War II imagery, wrote in his introduction to the 2004 release of *The Gallery* that the book "revealed . . . intense moral feelings about the worst war in history and its power to corrupt soldiers and civilians alike." See Burns, *Gallery*, xi.

44. Burns, *Gallery*, 4, 6, 16–17.

45. David Lundberg has written that in American fiction during the war, "on the battlefield as on the home front, individualism was an obstacle to victory: the key to success was group effort." See Lundberg, "American Literature of War," 385.

46. See Pritchard, *Randall Jarrell*, 12.

47. Meyer, "Waves of Darkness," 21.

48. Burns, *Gallery*, 21. Emphasis added.

49. See Aichinger, *American Soldier in Fiction*, 41–42. According to Aichinger, novels that featured this transformation from raw recruit to seasoned team player included *A Walk in the Sun* (1944), *That Winter* (1948), and *The Caine Mutiny* (1951), though *A Walk in the Sun* did also depict the cumulative trauma of combat.

50. Burns, *Gallery*, 18.

51. Ibid., 43.

52. Ibid., 285.

53. See Wilbur, *Beautiful Changes*, 12.

54. Murphy, *To Hell and Back*, 13.

55. Michael Sherry and Allan Bérubé have shown how the World War II experience both encouraged same-sex encounters and fueled and reflected rampant homophobia within American society and the armed forces. See Sherry, *In the Shadow of War*, 104–5; Bérubé, *Coming Out under Fire*. On *Life* magazine's

wartime embrace of male-male friendship and even homoeroticism, see Ibson, "Masculinity under Fire."

56. Burns, *Gallery*, 133, 146, 149–51.

57. On the GI Bill's heterosexual favoritism, see Canaday, "Building a Straight State."

58. Burns, *Gallery*, 144–45, 147, 150.

59. *New York Times*, June 7, 1947, 11.

60. *New York Times Book Review*, June 6, 1947, 7, 25.

61. See Rollyson, *Lives of Norman Mailer*, 38.

62. Mailer, *Naked and the Dead*, 445, 461.

63. Ibid., 85, 144, 199, 202, 354, 605.

64. *Atlantic Monthly*, February 1946, 49; April 1947, 29; *Harper's Magazine*, October 1946, 296. Emphasis added.

65. Mailer, *Naked and the Dead*, 120, 360.

66. *Time*, October 1, 1945, 32.

67. Mailer, *Naked and the Dead*, 184.

68. See Mauldin, *Up Front*, 14.

69. Quotes in this paragraph from Mailer, *Naked and the Dead*, 16, 164, 710–11.

70. Scholars writing decades later have also explored the gripes of the American infantryman, though they tend to maintain that these and other gritty realities were largely absent from depictions of GIs in the 1940s. See Linderman, *World within War*, 300–44; Fussell, *Boys' Crusade*, 9–10; Kindsvatter, *American Soldiers*, 256–66. Russell Weigley has argued more broadly that the very "cultures" of civilian and military life have been at odds since the founding of the United States. See Weigley, "American Civil-Military Cultural Gap," 218.

71. Merrill, *Norman Mailer*, 26, 153.

72. *New York Times*, December 20, 1948, 23.

73. Quoted in *New York Times Book Review*, May 22, 1949, 8.

74. *New York Times*, May 24, 1949, 33.

75. MacDonald, "Novels of World War II," 42–43.

76. Gallup, *Gallup Poll*, 1:679, 723, 726–77.

77. *Nation*, June 26, 1948, 723.

78. Wecter, *When Johnny Comes Marching Home*, 6.

79. *Saturday Evening Post*, January 31, 1948, 86.

CHAPTER 4

1. *Time*, July 31, 1950, 17. Although "Kilroy was here" was the most popular piece of graffiti of World War II, the identity of Kilroy remained a mystery. In 1945 *Newsweek* claimed he was Sgt. Frank Kilroy, while in 1962 the Associated Press maintained he was James Kilroy of Bethlehem Steel Company. In that version

Kilroy allegedly scrawled his name on pieces of equipment for the war that he inspected, and then the slogan caught on among GIs. See Holsinger, *War and American Popular Culture*, 275–76.

2. Just one example was *Atlantic Monthly*, February 1946, 48–53. See also coverage of such concerns among student-GIs in Chapter 2.

3. *Time*, July 17, 1950, 23–24; *Newsweek*, July 17, 1950, 14; *Life*, July 10, 1950, 28–29.

4. In 2001 Peter Filene made the provocative argument that as the 1950s progressed, "ordinary Americans" became less and less concerned with the Cold War, while elites and policy makers remained obsessed with it. Nonetheless, Filene granted that in the late 1940s and early 1950s many Americans were worried about the prospect of war with the Soviet Union, a claim supported by polling data. See Filene, "'Cold War Culture,'" 156–74.

5. *New Republic*, July 3, 1950, 5. Emphasis in original.

6. Based on newly opened Soviet archives, John Lewis Gaddis asserted in 1997 that authorizing the assault on South Korea was one of Stalin's gravest blunders of the Cold War, mainly because he underestimated the American willingness to intervene. In fact, it seems Stalin was more prone to miscalculation than historians (or American cold warriors) ever allowed. For this information and other material in this paragraph, see Gaddis, *We Now Know*, 62–82, 96–99; LaFeber, *America, Russia, and the Cold War*, 99–124.

7. Oakley, *God's Country*, 80.

8. Administrator for Veterans Affairs, *Annual Report, 1946*, 1.

9. See Alexander, *Korea*, 49.

10. According to John Mueller's important study of the subject, popular opposition to the Korean War was comparable to later opposition to the Vietnam War and increased alongside American casualties in both cases. *Vocal* antiwar sentiment, however, was greater during the 1960s for a variety of reasons, including the general thawing of the Cold War and the absence of a fiercely anticommunist atmosphere like that of the early 1950s. During the Korean War anyone publicly opposing the conflict risked being labeled a communist. See Mueller, *War, Presidents and Public Opinion*, 42–65.

11. Consistent casualty figures are surprisingly difficult to find. Often cited is the figure of 33,000 American dead, but that number does not include nonbattle deaths. My numbers are compiled from Alexander, *Korea*, 483; Hermes, *United States Army*, 501; Edwards, *Korean War*, 7.

12. *New Republic*, July 24, 1950, 11.

13. *Nation*, July 22, 1950, 74.

14. Alexander, *Korea*, 46–52.

15. Higgins, *War in Korea*, 85.

16. Appleman, *United States Army*, 110, 264.

17. Flynn, *Lewis B. Hershey*, 162–89.

18. Alexander, *Korea*, 46–52.

19. In her book on combat photography, Susan Moeller has noted, "Korea was clearly the midway point between the 'partner' relationship of the press and the military in World War II and the 'adversary' relationship of the two during the Vietnam War." See Moeller, *Shooting War*, 273–81.

20. *Newsweek*, July 17, 1950, 13.

21. *Life*, July 17, 1950, 33.

22. *Time*, July 31, 1950, 16.

23. See, for example, Universal Newsreel, "New Aid Rushed to Korea," July 31, 1950; Vol. 23, Reel 374; Universal Newsreels, Record Group 200; National Archives at College Park, College Park, Md. (hereafter NACP).

24. *Time*, July 17, 1950, 17.

25. Ibid., July 24, 1950, 20–21.

26. Higgins, *War in Korea*, 84.

27. *Newsweek*, August 7, 1950, cover; *Time*, August 21, 1950, 20.

28. "Time for Defense," July 25, 1950, Sound Recording 330-TFD-39, Records of the Office of the Secretary of Defense, Record Group 330. NACP. *Time* magazine reported that "millions of radio listeners" heard the broadcast but printed much of it anyway. See *Time*, August 7, 1950, 20.

29. Countering such mythology of World War II combat motivation were scholars of the late 1940s, who found that GIs in that war had been driven by comradeship rather than patriotism—surely the case in the Korean War as well. See Stouffer et al., *Studies in Social Psychology*; Marshall, *Men Against Fire*.

30. Duncan, *This Is War!* no page numbers.

31. *Time*, August 28, 1950, 22.

32. *Life*, September 18, 1950, 41–47. The Duncan pictures would figure heavily in his own book, *This Is War!* and the Museum of Modern Art's photographic exhibit Faces of Korea, both of which appeared in 1951 and are discussed in detail later in this chapter.

33. Quoted in Moeller, *Shooting War*, 300.

34. On September 30, 1950, army strength in Korea was 103,601 men, while marine strength was 21,525. See Appleman, *United States Army*, 605–6.

35. *Life*, July 10, 1950, 19.

36. Ibid., July 17, 1950, 34–35.

37. For discussion of the shift in World War II imagery, see Roeder, *Censored War*, 24–25, 27–42.

38. According to George Roeder, the *Combat Bulletin* series was aimed at soldiers in training. See ibid., 51.

39. *Combat Bulletin* 101, "Battle for Time," 1950, Motion Picture 111-CB-101, Records of the Office of the Chief Signal Officer, Record Group 111, NACP.

40. See, for example, Universal Newsreels, "Decisive Battle Rages," August 14, 1950, Vol. 23, Reel 378; "The Korea Story," August 17, 1950, Vol. 23, Reel 379; "On the Korea Front," August 31, 1950, Vol. 23, Reel 383, Universal Newsreels, Record Group 200, NACP.

41. As Susan Moeller has written, "Finally, by Korea, American visions of the glory of war were being superseded by images of the sadness of it." See Moeller, *Shooting War*, 310.

42. See Engelhardt, *End of Victory Culture*.

43. See Mueller, *War, Presidents and Public Opinion*, 65, 155.

44. Quoted in Roeder, *Censored War*, 174 n. 22.

45. Quoted in *Time*, September 25, 1950, 26.

46. Appleman, *United States Army*, 264, 382.

47. Alexander, *Korea*, 133–54.

48. Quoted in *Newsweek*, October 30, 1950, 30.

49. For the information in these paragraphs see Alexander, *Korea*, 194–210, 219–39.

50. *Newsweek*, October 9, 1950, cover.

51. *Combat Bulletin* 102, "Turning the Tide," 1950, Motion Picture 111-CB-102, Records of the Office of the Chief Signal Officer, Record Group 111, NACP.

52. *Combat Bulletin* 103, "UN Offensive," 1950, Motion Picture 111-CB-103, Records of the Office of the Chief Signal Officer, Record Group 111, NACP.

53. *Newsweek*, October 16, 1950, 19.

54. Ibid., October 9, 1950, 24.

55. Ibid., October 23, 1950, 2.

56. The "price of victory" picture resurfaced in 1951 in Edward Steichen's photographic exhibit, Faces of Korea, discussed later in this chapter. See "American Infantryman is comforted after death of his friend while man methodically fills out casualty tags," Check and Installation List for Faces of Korea, MoMA Exhibit #470; Record II.1/56 (12), pp. 1–4; Museum of Modern Art Archives, Department of Circulating Exhibitions, New York, N.Y. (hereafter MoMA Archives).

57. *Combat Bulletin* 103, "UN Offensive," 1950, Motion Picture 111-CB-103, Records of the Office of the Chief Signal Officer, Record Group 111, NACP.

58. *Time*, October 9, 1950, 33.

59. *New York Times*, November 3, 1950, 4.

60. *Newsweek*, October 16, 1950, 21.

61. Ibid., October 9, 1950, 21.

62. Ibid., November 6, 1950, 4–6.

63. See *New Republic*, August 14, 1950, 8. For a brief, personal look at black service in Korea, see Banks, "Korean Conflict."

64. Foner, *Blacks and the Military*, 189–94.

65. *Newsweek*, July 31, 1950, 13.

66. *Time*, August 21, 1950, 19.

67. *New Republic*, November 6, 1950, 11–12.

68. *Crisis*, October 1950, 579.

69. *Nation*, September 2, 1950, 216.

70. For discussion of Cold War race relations, see Dudziak, *Cold War Civil Rights*.

71. *Crisis*, May 1951, 297.

72. *New York Times*, November 3, 1950, 4.

73. *Crisis*, December 1950, 715.

74. Ibid., October 1950, 578–79.

75. *New York Times*, November 3, 1950, 4.

76. See, for example, *Saturday Evening Post*, June 16, 1951, 31, discussed later in this chapter.

77. An early example appeared in *Life* magazine in August 1950, when several black soldiers were shown creeping through a rice paddy alongside a large photo of another black GI, Cpl. Ollie Linn. His gear proved that he was a combat soldier, not a member of a supply unit. See *Life*, August 21, 1950, 18–19.

78. See Mueller, *War, Presidents and Public Opinion*, 50–52.

79. In March 1951 Truman informed MacArthur that Washington would ask China and North Korea for a cease-fire along the thirty-eighth parallel. MacArthur, ever frustrated by his inability to conquer North Korea and take on the Chinese, released a statement disparaging the Chinese army and threatening to expand the war to China unless that country sued for peace, effectively throttling Truman's delicate efforts to end the war. See Alexander, *Korea*, 240–48, 299–367, 405–13.

80. Universal Newsreel, "Out of the Trap!" December 14, 1950, Vol. 23, Reel 413, Universal Newsreels, Record Group 200, NACP.

81. *Combat Bulletin* 105, "UN Forces Escape Trap," 1950, Motion Picture III-CB-105, Records of the Office of the Chief Signal Officer, Record Group 111, NACP.

82. *Newsweek*, January 15, 1951, cover, 1.

83. *Time*, January 1, 1951, cover.

84. Ibid., 16–23.

85. *Newsweek*, January 29, 1951, 30.

86. *Combat Bulletin* 107, "UN Forces Move North," 1951, Motion Picture III-CB-107, Records of the Office of the Chief Signal Officer, Record Group 111, NACP. Emphasis added.

87. George Roeder has agreed that during World War II official images of American soldiers suggested that battle would "harden" them. This picture persisted despite a secret report from the Office of the Surgeon General that found the average infantryman could go two hundred days before experiencing mental breakdown. See Roeder, *Censored War*, 16.

88. *Newsweek*, March 19, 1951, 30.

89. *Saturday Evening Post*, June 23, 1951, 26–27, 111–13, 116.

90. *Crisis*, May 1951, 297–305, 350–55.

91. *Saturday Evening Post*, June 16, 1951, 141.

92. Ibid., 31, 139, 141.

93. Ibid., 139.

94. See Foner, *Blacks and the Military*, 176–200; *Crisis*, October 1953, 510.

95. Just a few examples of black soldiers appearing favorably in popular magazines, on radio, and in film include *Time*, February 25, 1952, 26–27; *Combat Bulletin* 108, "Combat Activities in Korea," 1951, Motion Picture 111-CB-108, Records of the Office of the Chief Signal Officer, Record Group 111; "Time for Defense," October 1, 1951, Sound Recording 330-TFD-67; "Time for Defense," April 7, 1952, Sound Recording 330-TFD-87, Records of the Office of the Secretary of Defense, Record Group 330, NACP.

96. *Combat Bulletin* 113, "Stalemate in Korea," 1951, Motion Picture 111-CB-113, Records of the Office of the Chief Signal Officer, Record Group 111, NACP.

97. Hermes, *United States Army*, 513.

98. See Mueller, *War, Presidents and Public Opinion*, 50–52.

99. Alexander, *Korea*, 477–83; Hermes, *United States Army*, 401–97.

100. Check and Installation List for Faces of Korea, MoMA Exhibit #470, Record II.1/56 (12), pp. 1–4, MoMA Archives.

101. Itineraries for Faces of Korea, MoMA Exhibit #470, Record II.1/56 (12), MoMA Archives.

102. Check and Installation List for Faces of Korea, MoMA Exhibit #470, Record II.1/56 (12), pp. 1–4, MoMA Archives. These titles were used by museum personnel and were not included with the photos in the exhibit hall.

103. Caption List for Faces of Korea, MoMA Exhibit #470, Record II.1/56 (12), pp. 1–4, MoMA Archives.

104. See Duncan, *This Is War!* and "After jeep accident—men driving on," Check and Installation List for Faces of Korea, MoMA Exhibit #470, Record II.1/56 (12), pp. 1–4, MoMA Archives.

105. *Life*, September 18, 1950, 41.

106. Duncan, *This Is War!*

107. "Corporal Leonard Hayworth sees his picture in September 18 *Life* story," Check and Installation List for Faces of Korea, MoMA Exhibit #470, Record II.1/56 (12), pp. 1–4, MoMA Archives. Duncan dedicated *This Is War!* to Leonard Hayworth and a critically wounded sergeant named Leonard Young.

108. "Capt. 'Ike' Fenton learns he is out of ammunition," Check and Installation List for Faces of Korea, MoMA Exhibit #470, Record II.1/56 (12), pp. 1–4, MoMA Archives.

109. For a detailed discussion of The Family of Man, along with a picture of Fenton's photograph in the exhibit hall, see Staniszewski, *Power of Display*, 235–59.

110. *New York Times Book Review*, June 24, 1951, 3.

111. *New York Times*, June 25, 1951, 17. Another reviewer, Jacob Deschin, made similar comments in ibid., June 24, 1951, 12.

112. *Cavalier Daily, University of Virginia*, September 22, 1951; *Miami Herald*, August 26, 1951.

113. Press Release for Faces of Korea, MoMA Exhibit #470, Record II.1/56 (12), MoMA Archives. Emphasis added.

114. Steichen quotes from Niven, *Steichen*, 633.

115. Publicity Report, Faces of Korea, MoMA Exhibit #470, Record II.1/56 (12), pp. 1–4, MoMA Archives.

116. Steichen, *Life in Photography*, third page after plate 225.

117. For his part, Edward Steichen believed that all three of these exhibitions had "presented war in all its grimness," according to his autobiography. Yet even the most casual look at his three war-related shows reveals a progression from the sanitized Road to Victory to the graphic and disturbing Faces of Korea. See Steichen, *Life in Photography*, third page after plate 225.

118. Mauldin, *Bill Mauldin in Korea*, 10.

119. "Longines Chronoscope," October 26, 1951, Motion Picture LW-LW-23, Former Record Group 200, NACP. The Longines Chronoscope television program was sponsored by the watch company Longines-Wittnauer, and aired three times a week on CBS. The media executives that generally hosted the show included Ansel E. Talbert and Donald I. Rogers, editors of the *New York Herald Tribune*, and William Bradford Huie, editor of *American Mercury*.

120. Ibid.

121. "Longines Chronoscope," November 16, 1951, Motion Picture LW-LW-28, Former Record Group 200, NACP.

122. *Saturday Evening Post*, May 10, 1952, 19.

123. Michener, *World Is My Home*, 215, 217.

124. *Saturday Evening Post*, May 10, 1952, 19.

125. Ibid., 126.

126. Mueller, *War, Presidents and Public Opinion*, 44–50.

127. *Saturday Evening Post*, May 10, 1952, 128.

128. Ibid., 20, 128.

129. Michener, *Bridges at Toko-Ri*, 41. The *Life* magazine version sold 5 million copies in July 1953. See Appy, "'We'll Follow the Old Man,'" 91.

130. *Saturday Evening Post*, May 10, 1952, 20.

131. See Alexander, *Korea*, 483; Hermes, *United States Army*, 501; Edwards, *Korean War*, 7.

132. Caplow, Hicks, and Wattenberg, *First Measured Century*, 208.

133. On American masculinity in the decades after World War II, see Devlin, *Relative Intimacy*; Cuordileone, *Manhood and American Political Culture*; Faludi,

Stiffed; Gibson, *Warrior Dreams*; Gilbert, *Men in the Middle*; Kimmel, *Manhood in America*; Jarvis, *Male Body at War*; Nye, "Western Masculinities"; Traister, "Academic Viagra"; Mickenberg, "Men on the Suburban Frontier."

134. Historian David Blight has identified a similar valorization of suffering and victimhood in Civil War veterans, North and South, in speeches of the nineteenth century. See Blight, *Race and Reunion*, 90–92.

CHAPTER 5

1. Appy, *Working-Class War*, 18.
2. Administrator for Veterans Affairs, *Annual Report, 1954*, 1.
3. Gilpatrick, *Hero Next Door*.
4. Korean War figure from Caplow, Hicks, and Wattenberg, *First Measured Century*, 208.
5. For instance, novelist James Jones would write in 1962 of the "special qualities which the name Guadalcanal evoked for my generation." See Jones, *Thin Red Line*, "Special Note." All forthcoming page numbers from the 1991 paperback edition.
6. *New York Times Magazine*, May 28, 1950, 47.
7. O'Sheel and Cook, *Semper Fidelis*, vii, 160–61.
8. On reflections of the ambiguities of 1950s culture in efforts to commemorate the Korean War, see Piehler, *Remembering War the American Way*, 154–64.
9. For discussion of these crises, see, in order, Patterson, *Brown v. Board of Education*, 86–117; Kenneth T. Jackson, *Crabgrass Frontier*, 289–90; Schrecker, *Many Are the Crimes*; Oakley, *God's Country*, 95–110; Severo and Milford, *Wages of War*, 317–44.
10. Gallup, *Gallup Poll*, 2:963, 964, 1000, 1037, 1102. See also Mueller, *War, Presidents and Public Opinion*.
11. Ike's approval ratings are recorded in Gallup, *Gallup Poll*, 2:1116, 1269, 1522, 1552, 1570; for the "most admired man" polls, see 2:875, 963, 1038, 1111, 1113, 1296, 1462, 1536, 1584.
12. *Saturday Evening Post*, January 17, 1953, 97–98.
13. Gallup, *Gallup Poll*, 2:932, 934, 958, 1268, 1302. Universal military training, of course, never came to pass in the United States.
14. Ibid., 2:1018, 1118, 1241, 1255, 1346, 1376, 1447, 1514–15, 1570.
15. Engelhardt, *End of Victory Culture*, 86–87; Brinkley, "Illusion of Unity."
16. Appy, "'We'll Follow the Old Man,'" 76–78. Benjamin L. Alpers has argued that during World War II, government propagandists and producers of popular culture consistently, though inaccurately, portrayed the army as democratic. In many ways this chapter charts the breakdown of the democratic image in the 1950s, even if it uses different language. See Alpers, "This Is the Army."

17. For a useful synthesis of this process and its causes, see Hall, *Crossroads*, 50–58.
18. On combat films of the 1950s, see Suid, *Guts and Glory*, 116–228; Doherty, *Projections of War*, 265–315; Beidler, *Good War's Greatest Hits*; Basinger, *World War II Combat Film*, 156–70; Landon, "New Heroes"; Appy, "'We'll Follow the Old Man.'"
19. *Time*, June 19, 1950, 92.
20. See Suid, *Guts and Glory*, 116–60.
21. Appy, "'We'll Follow the Old Man,'" 82.
22. When a video version of *The Steel Helmet* appeared in 1997, the jacket showed how enduring the image of Korean War veterans as "forgotten" still was in the late twentieth century. Language on the video case almost commanded viewers to remember: "We will never forget the Korean War. One of the reasons is that Sam Fuller's gritty exploration of that war and day to day combat survival of the foot soldier won't let us. You will never forget *The Steel Helmet* just as you will never forget the Korean War."
23. See *Newsweek*, December 4, 1950, 82.
24. Fuller told an interviewer years later, at the beginning of the war in Vietnam, "I do not believe in the law of war. That is why I made the film. War is natural for animals. In the methods with which we are fighting, we are lower than animals." See *New York Times Magazine*, February 28, 1965, 43.
25. All quotations are from *The Steel Helmet*, dir. Samuel Fuller (Lippert, 1951).
26. *Variety*, January 3, 1951, 67. The technique of focusing on small units dominated films, novels, and television shows about war for decades after World War II, from Norman Mailer's *The Naked and the Dead* (1948) to Steven Spielberg's *Saving Private Ryan* (1998).
27. My analysis of *The Steel Helmet* largely agrees with a brief statement by Jeanine Basinger in her book on World War II combat pictures: "With the Korean War, we begin to see an increased cynicism about fighting wars, a questioning of whether or not we should let ourselves be talked into it. This is demonstrated most dramatically by stories which frequently question military leadership and which often present weak, frightened, or unreliable people in command of troops." Other scholars have lumped the film in with World War II combat movies. See Basinger, *World War II Combat Film*, 161; Doherty, *Projections of War*, 276; Suid, *Guts and Glory*, 137. Suid has written that soldiers in the film "differed not at all from the soldiers who had defeated Hitler and Tojo."
28. Two other films of the postwar era also exposed racial tensions in the U.S. military. In *Home of the Brave* (1949), produced by Stanley Kramer, GIs abuse an African American soldier. *Go For Broke!* (1951) celebrated the Japanese Ameri-

can 442nd Regimental Combat Team of World War II but featured a racist commander in charge of the Nisei. See Doherty, *Projections of War*, 277; Suid, *Guts and Glory*, 154.

29. This scene represented a strikingly early reference to the internment of Japanese Americans during World War II. Indeed, only in the 1970s did Gerald Ford officially apologize for the abuses, and reparation checks would not flow to camp survivors until 1990. See Daniels, *Concentration Camps*, 195–200.

30. In his brief discussion of *The Steel Helmet*, film historian Thomas Doherty has downplayed the difficulties exposed by these encounters with the prisoner: neither Edwards nor Loo "succumbs to a wily North Korean officer who attempts to subvert their patriotism with a recitation of an undeniable American history of unconstitutional detention and abiding bigotry." This statement minimizes the doubts awakened in each character by the prisoner's questioning. See Doherty, *Projections of War*, 276.

31. For one of many scholarly discussions of interethnic and interracial harmony and teamwork in World War II culture, see Alpers, "This Is the Army," 143–47.

32. *Newsweek*, January 29, 1951, 91.

33. Ehrhart and Jason, *Retrieving Bones*, 187. According to Jason, in the novel *Your Own Beloved Sons* (1956) Americans kill Koreans wantonly. See Jason, "Vietnam War Themes," 114.

34. Reprinted in Hedin, *Old Glory*, 255.

35. See Holsinger, *War and American Popular Culture*, 353. A similar fate befell the Korean War movie *One Minute to Zero* in 1952, when the army denied approval of the film over a sequence showing artillerymen firing at Korean refugees whose ranks had been permeated by communist soldiers. See Suid, *Guts and Glory*, 137.

36. Mauldin, *Bill Mauldin in Korea*, 10.

37. See Doherty, *Projections of War*, 278.

38. All quotations are from *To Hell and Back*, dir. Jesse Hibbs (Universal International, 1955).

39. *New York Times*, September 25, 1955, II, 5.

40. *Newsweek*, September 19, 1955, 120.

41. One scholar of postwar films has chosen to stress the connections between these plot devices and those of Westerns, while another has commented only on the film's widescreen battle footage. Neither pays much attention to images of soldiers and officers in the film, despite its heavy focus on those figures. See Basinger, *World War II Combat Film*, 156–59; Doherty, *Projections of War*, 278–79.

42. *Variety*, July 20, 1955, 6.

43. *New York Times*, September 23, 1955, 21.

44. *Newsweek*, September 19, 1955, 120.

45. *New York Times*, September 25, 1955, II, 5.

46. *Time*, October 17, 1955, 118.

47. Ibid.

48. *New York Times*, September 23, 1955, 21.

49. Ibid.

50. See Suid, *Guts and Glory*, 136–60; Hall, *Crossroads*, 54.

51. All quotations are from *Men in War*, dir. Anthony Mann (United Artists, 1957).

52. Telotte, *Voices in the Dark*, 2. See also Dimendberg, *Film Noir*.

53. *New York Times*, March 20, 1957, 32.

54. Such scenes led *Variety* to comment, "Footage graphically depicts the horror that is war." The trade journal recommended *Men in War* to theater owners as "saleable to young male audiences." *Variety*, January 23, 1957, 6.

55. Not surprisingly, critics have challenged the view, dominant in popular imagery of World War II, that the army was democratic. See Alpers, "This Is the Army," 129–63; Adams, *Best War Ever*, 69–90.

56. *Time*, April 8, 1957, 92.

57. Michener, *Bridges at Toko-Ri*, 122.

58. For these Korean War short stories, poetry, and a brief treatment of the isolation theme, see Ehrhart and Jason, *Retrieving Bones*, xxviii; for Korean War poetry, see Hedin, *Old Glory*, 235–59.

59. Ehrhart and Jason, *Retrieving Bones*, 181.

60. McCann, "Our Forgotten War," 82. For similar views of Korean War literature, see Axelsson, *Restrained Response*, 59–109; Hedin, *Old Glory*, xxiv–xxv. For discussion of the ways Korean War literature anticipated the literature of Vietnam, see Jason, "Vietnam War Themes," 109–21.

61. *Time*, April 8, 1957, 94. A "Section Eight" was an army discharge for various forms of mental instability, later made famous as the object of Klinger's efforts in the television series *M*A*S*H* in the 1970s. Presumably, the author of the article used the phrase "buying a Section Eight" to mean losing one's mind in combat, although during World War II military officials added homosexuality to the list of "undesirable habits" that could lead to the provision being invoked. See Bérubé, *Coming Out under Fire*, 139.

62. *Newsweek*, March 4, 1957, 101; *New York Times*, March 20, 1957, 32.

63. Quoted in Suid, *Guts and Glory*, 201.

64. *Variety*, May 6, 1959, 6.

65. All quotations are from *Pork Chop Hill*, dir. Lewis Milestone (United Artists, 1959).

66. Kerry was a member of the group Vietnam Veterans Against the War (VVAW). Quoted in Nicosia, *Home to War*, 138.
67. Ehrhart and Jason, *Retrieving Bones*, 164.
68. Ibid., 176.
69. Hedin, *Old Glory*, xxv.
70. On the postwar reshaping of negative Japanese stereotypes in American culture, see Dower, *War without Mercy*, 301–11.
71. *Variety*, May 6, 1959, 6.
72. A film that confronted the issue of racial integration in the military, but which seems to have garnered little attention in its own time or from scholars, was *All the Young Men* (1960), starring Sidney Poitier.
73. Other films of the era that depicted the futility of combat included *War Hunt* (1962), *The Victors* (1963), and *The War Lover* (1964), according to Suid, *Guts and Glory*, 202.
74. *The Thin Red Line* inspired a film of the same name in 1964, shot in Spain without the endorsement of the American military. Much later, in 1998, another version appeared in theaters but paled in comparison to that year's hit *Saving Private Ryan*. See Suid, *Guts and Glory*, 637.
75. Neither *The Thin Red Line* nor *Catch-22* was a top-ten bestseller. See Hackett and Burke, *80 Years of Best Sellers*, 183–86. Heller quote from Whitfield, "Still the Best Catch," 183.
76. Jones, *Thin Red Line*, dedication page.
77. Indeed, as Lawrence Suid has documented thoroughly, Jones's *From Here to Eternity* changed from a somewhat antimilitary novel to a Pentagon-sponsored film. See Suid, *Guts and Glory*, 142–51.
78. As the contemporary critic Edmond L. Volpe put it, *The Thin Red Line* was set "during World War II, but its attitudes and theme belong to the 1960s." This statement not only supports the notion that the novel departed from tones of World War II culture but also recognizes a distinctive cynicism associated with the 1960s *before* the Vietnam War. See Moore, *Contemporary American Novelists*, 107.
79. Jones, *Thin Red Line*, 181.
80. Ibid., 198.
81. Ibid., 209.
82. Ibid., 222–23. Emphasis added.
83. *New York Times Book Review*, September 9, 1962, 1.
84. Jones, *Thin Red Line*, 238.
85. Ibid., 229.
86. Moore, *Contemporary American Novelists*, 110. Emphasis added.
87. *New York Times*, September 17, 1962, 29.

88. Jones, *Thin Red Line*, 257.

89. Ibid., 166.

90. Kirstein, *Rhymes of a PFC*, 84–86, 113–16.

91. Nemerov, *War Stories*, 29.

92. Jones, *Thin Red Line*, 242.

93. Ibid., 259.

94. Anthologies call the poem "Fox Hole," though as originally published in 1964 it had no individual title. See Shapiro, *Collected Poems*, 204.

95. Jones, *Thin Red Line*, 354.

96. Oppen, *Collected Poems*, 60.

97. Pritchard, *Randall Jarrell*, 10–11.

98. Stokesbury, *Articles of War*, 114.

99. Hugo, *Making Certain It Goes On*, 121–24.

100. See Fussell introduction in Stokesbury, *Articles of War*, xxviii.

101. Jones, *Thin Red Line*, 307.

102. Ibid., 311.

103. Ibid., 328.

104. On such race hatred during World War II, see Dower, *War without Mercy*.

105. Jones, *Thin Red Line*, 124–28.

106. For discussion of such tensions regarding homosexuality during World War II, see Sherry, *In the Shadow of War*, 104–5. According to Allan Bérubé, despite new, stronger screening aimed at excluding gays from the military, during World War II manpower requirements, flaws in the screening process, and gays' desire to serve "led thousands [of homosexuals] into combat zones around the world." Some heterosexual soldiers, Bérubé reports, engaged in the "situational" gay sex described in *The Thin Red Line*—and were regarded by military officialdom as different from "confirmed perverts," just as the novel suggests. On such official typologies for judging homosexuality see Bérubé, *Coming Out under Fire*, 140, 176, 192; Canaday, "Building a Straight State," 941–42.

107. Castleman and Podrazik, *Watching TV*, 106, 159.

108. Davidsmeyer, *Combat!*, 13.

109. Like many depictions of World War II from the 1950s and early 1960s, *Combat!* often has been described as simply an extension of classic wartime themes. In Thomas Doherty's estimation, "*Combat* was a weekly reiteration of the tropes of the classical WWII combat film and the shooting script for a thousand adolescent war games." My view is that *Combat!* blended classic themes with newer ones ascendant in the 1950s and was not merely a "reiteration." See Doherty, *Projections of War*, 304. For a similar view, see Basinger, *World War II Combat Film*, 182.

110. *TV Guide*, June 15, 1963, 6, 9; *New York Times*, December 4, 2006.

111. See Davidsmeyer, *Combat!*, 51; *Combat!*, "Cat and Mouse," dir. Robert Altman (ABC, aired December 4, 1962).

112. On the theme of absurdity in Korean War fiction, see Axelsson, *Restrained Response*, 109.

113. All quotes are from *Combat!*, "Bridge at Chalons," dir. Ted Post (ABC, aired September 17, 1963).

114. See Davidsmeyer, *Combat!*, 128, 159; *Combat!*, "Hills Are for Heroes," dir. Vic Morrow (ABC, aired March 1 and 8, 1966).

115. See Davidsmeyer, *Combat!*, 62, 71, 73, 87, 95, 116, 124, 129.

116. See Goulden, *Best Years*; O'Neill, *American High*; Matusow, *Unraveling of America*; O'Neill, *Coming Apart*.

117. Jerry Lembcke dismantles the "spat-upon" myth surrounding Vietnam veterans in *Spitting Image*.

118. John F. Kennedy, *Inaugural Address*.

119. See Caputo, *Rumor of War*; Santoli, *To Bear Any Burden*; Donovan, *Once a Warrior King*.

120. See Appy, "'We'll Follow the Old Man'"; Engelhardt, *End of Victory Culture*; Whitfield, "Still the Best Catch."

121. Quote from Alpers, "This Is the Army," 163. For similar views see Beidler, *Good War's Greatest Hits*, 3; Adams, *Best War Ever*, 14; Suid, *Guts and Glory*, 159–60.

122. Gerald Nicosia has also reported that he grew up on "gung-ho Hollywood movies" of the 1950s, while film scholar Michael Anderegg has discussed other invocations of Wayne by Vietnam veterans. See Caputo, *Rumor of War*, 6; Nicosia, *Home to War*, 2; Anderegg, "Hollywood and Vietnam." For a discussion of how sanitized accounts of war have helped thrust young men into battle, see Kindsvatter, *American Soldiers*, 285–93.

123. Military historian Lawrence Suid, in a revised edition of his classic book on war movies, has expressed succinctly a different perspective from my own. As he has put it, "Not until the growing disenchantment with the Vietnam conflict did Americans begin to explore their long-standing love of the martial spirit and their previously unquestioned respect for the military establishment." Before that, most combat pictures of the 1950s "simply imitated the seminal works, retelling the same stories of both World War II and the Korean War, with few new insights into the nature of men in combat." Besides the films I have discussed in this chapter, others—including *Home of the Brave* (1949), *Battleground* (1949), *From Here to Eternity* (1953), *The Caine Mutiny* (1954), *The Bridges at Toko-Ri* (1954), *Attack!* (1956), *The Bridge on the River Kwai* (1957), *Run Silent, Run Deep* (1958), *War Hunt* (1962), *The Victors* (1963), and *The War Lover* (1964)—show that if grim portraits of war were not dominant in the 1950s and early 1960s, they certainly represented a significant undercurrent. See Suid, *Guts and Glory*, 2, 160, 202–3.

1. For a detailed account of this escalation, see Herring, *America's Longest War*, 147–61; Logevall, *Choosing War*. On recent literature see the Organization of American Historians roundtable, "Interchange: Legacies of the Vietnam War."

2. Quoted in Karnow, *Vietnam*, 384.

3. Taped conversations from the Johnson White House show defense secretary Robert McNamara's eagerness to provoke a second attack, as well as his careful selection of targets in North Vietnam before any such attack occurred. At the same time, though LBJ's advisers were hasty to accept reports of the phantom assault, they seem genuinely to have believed it happened. McNamara became convinced otherwise by North Vietnamese officials only in the 1990s. See Beschloss, *Taking Charge*, 495–505.

4. Quoted in Hallin, *"Uncensored War,"* 19.

5. See Herring, *America's Longest War*, 145.

6. See Mascaro, "Peril of the Unheeded Warning," 186.

7. *Newsweek*, January 18, 1965, 28. On *Newsweek*'s politics see Landers, *Weekly War*.

8. Arlen, *Living-Room War*, xi.

9. Ibid.

10. See Pach, "And That's the Way It Was."

11. Moeller, *Shooting War*, 387.

12. See for example, CBS, August 23, 1965, Reel A-3; *Weekly News Summary*, Assistant Secretary of Defense (Public Affairs); Records of the Department of Defense, Record Group 330; National Archives at College Park, College Park, Md. (hereafter DOD *Weekly News Summary*, NACP).

13. Quoted in Moeller, *Shooting War*, 365.

14. For a description of these methods of censorship, see Hammond, *Reporting Vietnam*, 42–43; Moeller, *Shooting War*, 363–66; Pach, "And That's the Way It Was," 92–95; Hallin, *"Uncensored War,"* 130.

15. Just a few contributions to the vast literature on media coverage of Vietnam include Clarence Wyatt, *Paper Soldiers*; Knightley, *First Casualty*, 409–68; Hammond, *Reporting Vietnam*; Braestrup, *Big Story*; Arlen, *Living-Room War*; Pach, "And That's the Way It Was"; Moeller, *Shooting War*, 323–413; Hallin, *"Uncensored War"*; Culbert, "Television's Visual Impact"; Landers, *Weekly War*; Mascaro, "Peril of the Unheeded Warning"; Schmitz, *Tet Offensive*.

16. Quoted in *Time*, June 10, 1966, 59.

17. *Newsweek*, for example, declared prophetically, "Those Americans who lead and shape public opinion are beginning to feel the first serious stirrings of doubt about the manner in which the Administration is handling the Vietnamese war. . . . If past experience is any guide, those doubts will in time transmit themselves in magnified form to the public at large." See *Newsweek*, January

18, 1965, 34. Daniel Hallin and William Hammond have described similar misgivings in the editorials of the *New York Times* and magazines around the country in early 1965. See Hallin, *"Uncensored War,"* 81–87; Hammond, *Reporting Vietnam*, 35.

18. In sharp contrast to later years of the war, 28 percent of respondents declared that they had "no opinion" on what the United States should do next in Vietnam. See Gallup, *Gallup Poll*, 3:1934.

19. DeBenedetti and Chatfield, *American Ordeal*, 105.

20. *Life*, July 23, 1965, 57.

21. See Herring, *America's Longest War*, 164–65; Flynn, *Lewis B. Hershey*, 234.

22. Quoted in *Look*, November 30, 1965, 34.

23. *Newsweek*, August 2, 1965, 17.

24. One statistic used to quantify the proportion of draftees to volunteers was the percentage of battle deaths. In 1965, when 1,369 Americans died in Vietnam, 16 percent of them were draftees. This figure would increase dramatically over the course of the war, rising to 43 percent in 1970 and even higher later. By 1970 or so it was common for fully two-thirds of combat units to be comprised of draftees. See Appy, *Working-Class War*, 28–29.

25. See Landers, *Weekly War*, 271–73.

26. *Time*, April 23, 1965, 22–26; Hallin, *"Uncensored War,"* 175.

27. *Time*, April 23, 1965, 25.

28. *Newsweek*, July 5, 1965, 32.

29. *Time*, April 23, 1965, 26.

30. NBC, November 26, 1965, Reel A-17, DOD *Weekly News Summary*, NACP.

31. ABC, November 26, 1965, Reel A-17, DOD *Weekly News Summary*, NACP.

32. *Newsweek*, July 12, 1965, 34.

33. *Life*, July 23, 1965, 57.

34. *Newsweek*, August 16, 1965, 32.

35. ABC, November 30, 1965, Reel A-17, DOD *Weekly News Summary*, NACP.

36. Safer quoted in Pach, "And That's the Way It Was," 102.

37. Johnson quoted in ibid.

38. Engelhardt, *End of Victory Culture*, 189.

39. *Newsweek*, August 16, 1965, 30; *Life*, July 23, 1965, 57; *Look*, November 30, 1965, 29.

40. *Look*, November 30, 1965, 39.

41. O'Neill, *Coming Apart*, 325.

42. *Newsweek*, September 13, 1965, 36.

43. For a look at how such paternalistic images of GIs appeared in government films, see Springer, "Military Propaganda."

44. CBS, August 23, 1965, Reel A-3, DOD *Weekly News Summary*, NACP.

45. See Pach, "And That's the Way It Was," 103; Safer quote from CBS, August 20, 1965, Reel A-3, DOD *Weekly News Summary*, NACP. Beyond whatever impact LBJ's tirade had, Daniel Hallin has ascribed the limitations on journalistic criticism to "ideological assumptions journalists shared with officials" and other broad, "impersonal" forces. See Hallin, *"Uncensored War,"* 132–34.

46. NBC, August 25, 1965, Reel A-3, DOD *Weekly News Summary*, NACP.

47. NBC, August 30, 1965, Reel A-4, DOD *Weekly News Summary*, NACP.

48. *Time*, October 22, 1965, 28.

49. Poll cited in DeBenedetti and Chatfield, *American Ordeal*, 123.

50. *Time*, January 7, 1966, 20. Later census data (referenced by Christian Appy) revealed, in fact, that 1,369 Americans died in Vietnam during 1965. See Appy, *Working-Class War*, 29.

51. CBS, November 29, 1965, Reel A-17, DOD *Weekly News Summary*, NACP.

52. See Karnow, *Vietnam*, 495–98.

53. See Herring, *America's Longest War*, 186.

54. See Gallup, *Gallup Poll*, 3:1993, 2027.

55. *Newsweek*, April 25, 1966, 21; *Time*, February 25, 1966, 21.

56. *Time*, June 3, 1966, 21. The draft drew disproportionately from the working class until it was reformed in 1967 and 1969. See Appy, *Working-Class War*, 36.

57. *Newsweek*, August 1, 1966, 30.

58. *Time*, January 7, 1966, 19.

59. *Life*, April 8, 1966, cover, 91–100.

60. CBS, October 28, 1966, Reel A-65, DOD *Weekly News Summary*, NACP.

61. See CBS, November 9, 1966, Reel A-66; ABC, November 14, 1966, Reel A-68; DOD *Weekly News Summary*, NACP.

62. *Look*, March 8, 1966, 30–35.

63. It was true that blacks suffered approximately 20 percent of combat deaths through 1967, compared to their 11 percent portion of the American population. Thanks to the efforts of civil rights activists, the Department of Defense took steps in 1967 to reduce the number of black combat casualties. Over the course of the entire war the proportion of black fatalities leveled out at 12.5 percent, just slightly higher than the percentage of blacks in the American population. See Appy, *Working-Class War*, 20–21.

64. Quotes from *Look*, October 18, 1966, 30; *Time*, December 23, 1966, 22.

65. Quotes from *Life*, May 6, 1966, 32; *Newsweek*, May 2, 1966, 18.

66. *Newsweek*, August 22, 1966, 46–48; *Time*, December 23, 1966, 22.

67. *Newsweek*, August 22, 1966, 48.

68. CBS, January 13, 1966, Reel A-23, DOD *Weekly News Summary*, NACP.

69. Figure cited in Patterson, *Grand Expectations*, 618.

70. CBS, November 21, 1966, Reel A-69, DOD *Weekly News Summary*, NACP.

71. *Time*, September 2, 1966, 23.

72. *Look*, March 8, 1966, 34.

73. Paul Fussell outlines one such tragedy of World War II, and censorship of it, in *Boys' Crusade*, 43–52.

74. See *Life*, July 2, 1965, cover.

75. See ibid., February 11, 1966, cover, 24D; ibid., October 28, 1966, cover. Strikingly similar images of wounded soldiers would reappear on the covers of magazines in 2003, during the third week of the war against Iraq. See *Time*, April 7, 2003; *Newsweek*, April 7, 2003.

76. *Newsweek*, April 18, 1966, 30. For coverage of Duncan's photos, see Chapter 4.

77. See, for example, ABC, November 11, 1966, Reel A-68; NBC, November 14, 1966, Reel A-68; DOD *Weekly News Summary*, NACP.

78. Moeller, *Shooting War*, 407.

79. CBS, January 13, 1966, Reel A-23, DOD *Weekly News Summary*, NACP.

80. *Look*, December 13, 1966, 27.

81. See *Time*, May 6, 1966, 29; ibid., January 21, 1966, 25A.

82. NBC, November 15, 1966, Reel A-68, DOD *Weekly News Summary*, NACP.

83. Figure on combat deaths from Appy, *Working-Class War*, 29.

84. *Look*, December 13, 1966, 27.

85. *Life*, January 21, 1966, 15.

86. See Karnow, *Vietnam*, 516–27.

87. Gallup, *Gallup Poll*, 3:2074, 2087, 2109.

88. Quoted in Baker, *Nam*, 15.

89. See Landers, *Weekly War*, 271–73.

90. Demonstrating the enduring impact of Morley Safer's dispatch from Cam Ne, King also spoke of watching television reports of blacks and whites "in brutal solidarity burning the huts of a poor village, but we realize that they would hardly live on the same block in Chicago." See Carson and Shepard, *Call to Conscience*, 139–64.

91. CBS, April 10, 1967, Reel A-90, DOD *Weekly News Summary*, NACP.

92. Statistic from Appy, *Working-Class War*, 22.

93. CBS, April 10, 1967, Reel A-90, DOD *Weekly News Summary*, NACP.

94. Quotes from *Time*, May 26, 1967, 19; *Newsweek*, November 20, 1967, 41; *Time*, May 26, 1967, 17–18.

95. *Time*, May 26, 1967, 15–16.

96. "Same Mud Same Blood" quoted in *Newsweek*, December 4, 1967, 90.

97. *Time*, May 26, 1967, 15.

98. See Frazier, *Negro Family*; Elkins, *Slavery*; Clark, *Dark Ghetto*.

99. Lemann, *Promised Land*, 177.

100. *Time*'s language recalled Moynihan's lament that "the largest percentage of

Negro families are dominated by the wife." See U.S. Department of Labor, *Negro Family*, 31.

101. *Time*, May 26, 1967, 19; *Newsweek*, November 20, 1967, 41.

102. CBS, April 11, 1967, Reel A-90, DOD *Weekly News Summary*, NACP.

103. CBS, September 25, 1967, Reel A-114, DOD *Weekly News Summary*, NACP.

104. CBS, July 5, 1967, Reel A-102, DOD *Weekly News Summary*, NACP.

105. CBS, September 28, 1967, Reel A-114, DOD *Weekly News Summary*, NACP.

106. See Hallin, *"Uncensored War,"* 163–67.

107. CBS, September 25, 1967, Reel A-114, DOD *Weekly News Summary*, NACP. In November an article in *Newsweek*, "Whose Benefit? Whose Doubt?" similarly reported on the distrust growing between the press and brass. See *Newsweek*, November 13, 1967, 68.

108. See *Time*, October 6, 1967, cover.

109. Quotes originally appeared in Michael Arlen's article, "A Day in the Life," in the September 30, 1967, issue of the *New Yorker*. Reprinted in Arlen, *Living-Room War*, 90, 92.

110. CBS, September 28, 1967, Reel A-114, DOD *Weekly News Summary*, NACP.

111. *Newsweek*, November 13, 1967, 68.

112. In his detailed account of television reporting of Con Thien, Daniel Hallin has briefly described imagery of soldiers in a similar fashion: "In this period, for the first time, soldiers interviewed on the news can be heard expressing less than enthusiasm for the war. . . . The troops who were the 'bait' in this war of attrition found themselves on the defensive for long periods, an unusual situation for American troops in Vietnam, and often taking high casualties for pieces of ground which were of little significance in themselves." Such imagery bore striking similarities to coverage of the Korean War and films about it in the 1950s. See Hallin, *"Uncensored War,"* 166.

113. CBS, April 12, 1967, Reel A-90, DOD *Weekly News Summary*, NACP.

114. Quoted in *Newsweek*, January 1, 1968, 17.

115. CBS, September 28, 1967, Reel A-114, DOD *Weekly News Summary*, NACP. Casualty figure from Appy, *Working-Class War*, 29.

116. *Newsweek*, December 25, 1967, 75. For a discussion of John Wayne's war movies and their role in filling young men's heads with images of glory, see Kindsvatter, *American Soldiers*, 285–93.

117. Peter Braestrup has argued that journalists overreacted to the offensive and inaccurately suggested that the Americans were losing. My own research, as well as the work of Chester Pach, suggests a more complicated story. Although publications such as *Time* and *Newsweek*, for instance, showed bloody and discouraging pictures, their text indicated that the Americans had effectively repelled the assault. See Braestrup, *Big Story*; Pach, "And That's the Way It Was," 110.

118. Polling data from Hammond, *Reporting Vietnam*, 122.

119. Karnow, *Vietnam*, 536; Engelhardt, *End of Victory Culture*, 205.

120. As Daniel Hallin has put it, "Tet was less a turning point than a crossover point, a moment when trends that had been in motion for some time reached balance and began to tip the other way." See Hallin, *"Uncensored War,"* 168.

121. NBC, February 2, 1968, Reel A-133, DOD *Weekly News Summary*, NACP.

122. *Life*, February 9, 1968, cover. Other such images appeared in *Newsweek*, January 1, 1968, 29; *Time*, February 9, 1968, 32; *Newsweek*, February 19, 1968, 40; *Time*, February 23, 1968, 32; *Look*, March 19, 1968, 39, 42.

123. NBC, February 12, 1968, Reel A-134, DOD *Weekly News Summary*, NACP.

124. *Time*, February 23, 1968, 5.

125. Quoted in ibid., January 5, 1968, 31–32.

126. *Newsweek*, February 19, 1968, 37, 39; *Life*, February 16, 1968, 28; *Look*, March 19, 1968, 45.

127. *Newsweek*, February 19, 1968, 39.

128. NBC, February 15, 1968, Reel A-134, DOD *Weekly News Summary*, NACP.

129. *Newsweek*, January 1, 1968, cover.

130. See, for example, ibid., February 5, 1968, 39; *Time*, February 9, 1968, following p. 22; *Newsweek*, February 12, 1968, 31; ibid., February 19, 1968, 35, 42; *Look*, March 19, 1968, 38.

131. CBS, February 13, 1968, Reel A-134, DOD *Weekly News Summary*, NACP.

132. *Time*, February 9, 1968, 15, and following p. 22; *Newsweek*, February 19, 1968, 36; *Life*, February 23, 1968, 24.

133. *Time*, February 16, 1968, 7; ibid., February 23, 1968, 5.

134. Cronkite broadcast reprinted in *Reporting Vietnam, Part One*, 581.

135. LBJ quote from Dallek, *Flawed Giant*, 506.

136. Appy, *Working-Class War*, 29.

137. LBJ quotations from Berman, *Lyndon Johnson's War*, 183; Dallek, *Flawed Giant*, 286–87.

138. See, for example, Lewy, *America in Vietnam*; Elegant, "How to Lose a War"; on military and diplomatic critiques of the press, see Hammond, "Press in Vietnam," 312–13; Carruthers, *Media at War*, 108–20; on an "oppositional" tone in media of the Vietnam era, see Hallin, "Media, the War in Vietnam, and Political Support."

139. Lewy, *America in Vietnam*, 433–44.

140. Baker, *Nam*, xv. Emphasis added.

141. See Herman and Chomsky, *Manufacturing Consent*, 169–252; Hammond, "Press in Vietnam"; Clarence Wyatt, *Paper Soldiers*; Hallin, *"Uncensored War"*; Engelhardt, *End of Victory Culture*, 192–93; Arlen, *Living-Room War*; Lichty, "Comments on the Influence of Television." For a useful overview of this literature, see Hallin, "Media and War."

142. Hallin, *"Uncensored War,"* 9; Hammond, "Press in Vietnam," 316.

143. In just one of the many compelling examples he uses, Tom Engelhardt has discussed the popularity of GI Joe action figures in the early 1960s. In 1966, there appeared a "Negro Joe." The inclusion of a black soldier in the realm of this highly macho toy—Hasbro never called them dolls—mirrored the phenomenon I am describing here. See Engelhardt, *End of Victory Culture*, 175–77.

144. See Faludi, *Stiffed*, 291–358; Bly, "Vietnam War." On the theme of "crisis" in masculinity studies, see Traister, "Academic Viagra"; Mickenberg, "Men on the Suburban Frontier"; Gilbert, *Men in the Middle*.

145. Baker, *Nam*, 5.

CHAPTER 7

1. The margin was narrow indeed, 46 percent to 44 percent in October 1967. See Gallup, *Gallup Poll*, 3:2087.

2. For discussion of these demonstrations see Small, *Antiwarriors*, 95–158; Gitlin, *Sixties*, 379, 394, 410–11.

3. Quoted in Small, *Antiwarriors*, 143.

4. See Kutler, *Wars of Watergate*, 158.

5. Quoted in Michener, *Kent State*, 436.

6. See *Nation*, June 15, 1970, 712–19.

7. Gallup, *Gallup Poll*, 3:2190, 2291, 2309.

8. For these figures, which reflect troop levels at the end of each year, see Herring, *America's Longest War*, 182.

9. Appy, *Working-Class War*, 29.

10. Appy, *Patriots*, 351.

11. Bilton and Sim, *Four Hours in My Lai*, 101. Much of my description in these paragraphs relies on this book.

12. See Olson and Roberts, *My Lai*, 99.

13. Ibid., 88–89.

14. Quoted in Bilton and Sim, *Four Hours in My Lai*, 254.

15. Olson and Roberts, *My Lai*, 27. Jay Roberts later admitted to *Life* magazine that he had "played [My Lai] up like it was a big success." See *Life*, December 5, 1969, 44.

16. Olson and Roberts, *My Lai*, 148.

17. See Bilton and Sim, *Four Hours in My Lai*, 247–54.

18. For television broadcasts see Reels A-226, A-227, A-228, A-229; *Weekly News Summary*, Assistant Secretary of Defense (Public Affairs); Records of the Department of Defense, Record Group 330; National Archives at College Park, College Park, Md. (hereafter DOD *Weekly News Summary*, NACP).

19. *New York Times*, November 26, 1969.

20. See Bilton and Sim, *Four Hours in My Lai*, 253–61, 315–21.

21. *Life*, December 5, 1969, 36–45.

22. Ibid., December 12, 1969, 46–47.

23. Quoted in Bilton and Sim, *Four Hours in My Lai*, 337.

24. NBC, March 29, 1971, Reel A-297, DOD *Weekly News Summary*, NACP.

25. NBC, April 3, 1971, Reel A-298, DOD *Weekly News Summary*, NACP.

26. "Press Release: Statement of Vietnam Veterans Against the War," April 1, 1971; Publicity, Press Releases and Statements, 1969–1972; Box 17, Folder 24; Records of the Vietnam Veterans Against the War, 1967–1979; Wisconsin Historical Society, Archives Division, Madison, Wisc. (hereafter VVAW Records, WHS).

27. ABC, March 30, 1971, CBS, March 31, 1971, Reel A-297, DOD *Weekly News Summary*, NACP.

28. Quoted in Bilton and Sim, *Four Hours in My Lai*, 340–41.

29. See Gershen, *Destroy or Die*, 10, 298–99; Hersh, *My Lai 4*, 181.

30. Polling data cited in Faludi, *Stiffed*, 347.

31. *Time*, April 19, 1971, 4–5, 13; ibid., April 26, 1971, 4.

32. *Look*, June 1, 1971, 76–77.

33. *Psychology Today*, June 1972, 81. Emphasis in original.

34. See Engelhardt, *End of Victory Culture*, 224; Faludi, *Stiffed*, 347; Bilton and Sim, *Four Hours in My Lai*, 340.

35. Quoted in Stacewicz, *Winter Soldiers*, 235.

36. For general accounts of VVAW, see Nicosia, *Home to War*; Hunt, *Turning*; Moser, *New Winter Soldiers*; Stacewicz, *Winter Soldiers*.

37. See Nicosia, *Home to War*, 49–55.

38. Hunt, *Turning*, 39, 68, 143.

39. For SDS membership figure see Small, *Antiwarriors*, 8.

40. Though Moser's figure is difficult to test, there is little doubt that large numbers of GIs and vets turned against the war. See Moser, *New Winter Soldiers*, 3.

41. See Letters to Al Hubbard, Summer 1970, Correspondence, Operation Rapid American Withdrawal, July–October 1970, Box 7, Folder 5, VVAW Records, WHS.

42. Waiver for RAW participants, Summer 1970, Programs, Operation Rapid American Withdrawal, September 1970, Box 15, Folder 7, VVAW Records, WHS. Emphasis added.

43. Other objectives involved exposing the racist elements of the war, demanding an end to American involvement, and bringing together a coalition of antiwar veterans from all services. See "Operation Raw," undated VVAW memo, Correspondence, Memoranda to Coordinators, 1968–1972, n.d., Box 6, Folder 14, VVAW Records, WHS.

44. "Operation RAW," undated VVAW memo, Correspondence, Memoranda to Coordinators, 1968–1972, n.d., Box 6, Folder 14, VVAW Records, WHS.

45. Untitled plan for Operation RAW, September 4, 1970, Programs, Operation Rapid American Withdrawal, September 1970, Box 15, Folder 7, VVAW Records, WHS.

46. For accounts of such excessive acting, see Nicosia, *Home to War*, 65; Hunt, *Turning*, 50.

47. "A U.S. Infantry Company Just Came Through Here," leaflet for Operation RAW, Programs, Operation Rapid American Withdrawal, September 1970, Box 15, Folder 7, VVAW Records, WHS.

48. "Ambushes Maim or Kill G.I.s in Vietnam Everyday," leaflet for Operation RAW, Programs, Operation Rapid American Withdrawal, September 1970, Box 15, Folder 7, VVAW Records, WHS.

49. Bob Greene has collected many of these stories in *Homecoming*. Jerry Lembcke has called into question the frequency of such episodes in *The Spitting Image*.

50. Untitled leaflet of Operation RAW, Programs, Operation Rapid American Withdrawal, September 1970, Box 15, Folder 7, VVAW Records, WHS.

51. Quotes and my account of Valley Forge derive from Nicosia, *Home to War*, 68–73.

52. A similar march in May 1971 from Concord to Bunker Hill, the reverse of Paul Revere's ride, culminated in the mass arrest of VVAW members and their supporters when they tried to camp on the village green in Lexington, Massachusetts. That march has been vividly depicted in the documentary film, *An Unfinished Symphony*, dir. Mike Majoros and Bestor Cram (Northern Light Productions, 2000).

53. See Nicosia, *Home to War*, 62–63.

54. Quoted in Vietnam Veterans Against the War (VVAW), *Winter Soldier Investigation*, 1.

55. "Call to the Winter Soldier Investigation," Fall 1970, Correspondence, Memoranda to Coordinators, 1968–1972, n.d., Box 6, Folder 14, VVAW Records, WHS. Emphasis in original.

56. Letter from C. Scott Moore to Edward M. Sloan, December 24, 1970, Correspondence, Winter Soldier Investigation, 1970–1971, Box 7, Folder 11, VVAW Records, WHS. Emphasis in original.

57. Undated proposal for WSI film, Programs, Winter Soldier Investigation, 1971, Publicity, Box 16, Folder 19, VVAW Records, WHS. Emphasis added.

58. Letter to VVAW members, November 18, 1970, Correspondence, Winter Soldier Investigation, 1970–1971, Box 7, Folder 11, VVAW Records, WHS.

59. Letters to potential WSI supporters, January 20, 1971, Correspondence, Winter Soldier Investigation, 1970–1971, Box 7, Folder 11, VVAW Records, WHS.

60. Although *images* of Vietnam veterans with PTSD were increasingly common, psychiatrists in the 1970s found that soldiers in World War II and Korea had experienced mental breakdown at comparable or higher rates. For a summary of

the literature on this subject, see Karsten, "'New' American Military History." Several works identify PTSD as a universal experience, no matter the war, including Dean, *Shook over Hell*; Talbott, "Soldiers, Psychiatrists, and Combat Trauma." Other authors grant the timelessness of PTSD in soldiers, but argue that the moral and political ambiguities of the Vietnam War made postwar readjustment more difficult for Vietnam veterans. A prominent work in this vein is Shay, *Achilles in Vietnam*.

61. VVAW, *Winter Soldier Investigation*, 1–2.

62. Ibid., 30–31, 36–37, 55.

63. Ibid., 14, 40, 47–48, 149–50.

64. Quote from *An Unfinished Symphony*, dir. Mike Majoros and Bestor Cram (Northern Light Productions, 2000). Emphasis added.

65. VVAW, *Winter Soldier Investigation*, 5, 151, 157, 162–63. Emphasis added. Writing in the *New Yorker* in July 2004, Dan Baum described how military psychiatrists in the twenty-first century still largely neglected the psychological costs of killing. See *New Yorker*, July 12 and 19, 2004, 44–52.

66. VVAW, *Winter Soldier Investigation*, 58, 154. On such displays of "hypermasculinity" during the Vietnam War, see Kimmel, *Manhood in America*, 263.

67. VVAW, *Winter Soldier Investigation*, 167. Emphasis added.

68. These included Representatives Bella Abzug, Robert Drinan, and Michael Harrington, as well as Senators George McGovern and Mark Hatfield. See Hunt, *Turning*, 73–74.

69. See CBS, January 31, 1971, Reel A-289, DOD *Weekly News Summary*, NACP.

70. For an account of media coverage of WSI, see Hunt, *Turning*, 73.

71. *New York Times*, February 7, 1971; *New York Daily World*, January 26, 1971; *New Republic*, February 27, 1971.

72. "V.V.A.W. Newsletter '71 #1," March 1971, Programs, Dewey Canyon III, April 1971, General Information, Box 13, Folder 10, VVAW Records, WHS.

73. *Life*, June 27, 1969, 20–32; Ibid., May 22, 1970, 24–33; *Newsweek*, January 11, 1971, 29–37.

74. My description here relies on Hunt, *Turning*, 94–119.

75. On May 6, 2001, John Kerry appeared on NBC's *Meet the Press* and denounced his earlier charge that American officials were war criminals as "the words of an angry young man." The original Kerry quotes are from "Statement of John Kerry," April 22, 1971, Programs, Winter Soldier Investigation, 1971, General Information, Box 16, Folder 13, VVAW Records, WHS. Emphasis added.

76. See Hunt, *Turning*, 110.

77. Quote from *An Unfinished Symphony*, dir. Mike Majoros and Bestor Cram (Northern Light Productions, 2000). This episode highlights the fact that hundreds of thousands of medals were awarded in Vietnam, some hastily, to fight low morale among the troops. As Christian Appy has pointed out, more bronze

stars were awarded to the 3 million Americans in Vietnam than to the 12 million troops serving abroad during World War II. See Appy, *Working-Class War*, 247.

78. Dewey Canyon III also drew the scrutiny of the Nixon administration, which had always feared the organization and tried to subvert it with undercover informants and other dirty tricks. In the midst of Dewey Canyon III Nixon's people arranged for the leader of the Veterans of Foreign Wars to charge publicly that many participants in the demonstration were not really veterans. The accusation fell apart when scores of VVAWers came forward with documentation of their service; one vet introduced his glass eye as evidence of combat experience. See Small, *Antiwarriors*, 141.

79. *Akron Beacon Journal*, April 26, 1971; *Christian Science Monitor*, April 22, 1971.

80. See "Dewey Canyon III," collection of news clippings and headlines, Programs, Dewey Canyon III, April 1971, General Information, Box 13, Folder 10, VVAW Records, WHS.

81. Quotes from, in order, CBS, April 18, 19, 20, 1971, Reel A-300, DOD *Weekly News Summary*, NACP. Emphasis added.

82. "Statement of John Kerry," April 22, 1971, Programs, Winter Soldier Investigation, 1971, General Information, Box 16, Folder 13, VVAW Records, WHS. This question approximated the theme of 1959's Korean War film *Pork Chop Hill*.

83. *Newsweek*, January 11, 1971, 34.

84. CBS, March 26, 1971, Reel A-297; CBS, April 19, 1971, Reel A-300; ABC, January 5, 1971, Reel A-285; DOD *Weekly News Summary*, NACP.

85. *Time*, March 1, 1971, 15.

86. "Jimi Hendrix—A Brother Veteran," press release, September 1970, Publicity, Press Releases and Statements, 1969–1972, Box 17, Folder 24, VVAW Records, WHS.

87. Terry, *Bloods*, xvi–xvii.

88. *Newsweek*, January 11, 1971, 34, 37.

89. NBC, January 27, 1971, Reel A-288, DOD *Weekly News Summary*, NACP.

90. Taylor, *Vietnam and Black America*, 234–35.

91. *Newsweek*, January 11, 1971, 37.

92. ABC, January 4, 1971, Reel A-285, DOD *Weekly News Summary*, NACP.

93. VVAW, *Winter Soldier Investigation*, 152–55.

94. *Newsweek*, January 11, 1971, 30, 34.

95. Desertion figure cited in King and Karabell, *Generation of Trust*, 22.

96. *Time*, April 5, 1971, 25. Emphasis added.

97. *Newsweek*, January 11, 1971, 34.

98. Figures from Appy, *Working-Class War*, 246–47; quote from Gettleman et al., *Vietnam and America*, 327.

99. CBS, April 20, 1971, Reel A-300, DOD *Weekly News Summary*, NACP.

100. ABC, January 12, 1971, Reel A-286, DOD *Weekly News Summary*, NACP.

101. NBC, January 27, 1971, Reel A-288, DOD *Weekly News Summary*, NACP.

102. Caputo, *Rumor of War*, 137; Whitman quoted in Blight, *Race and Reunion*, 22.

103. Christian Appy has written of this "victim posture" marking American culture since the Vietnam War: "The mere survivors of ordeals by agents of state power—veterans, POWs, hostages—have, since Vietnam, been automatically defined as heroes." Looking further back in history, David Blight has found orators in the post–Civil War era who held up Confederate veterans as the "suffering victims of fate," admirable simply for their devotion even to a lost cause. See the Organization of American Historians roundtable, "Interchange: Legacies of the Vietnam War," 487; Blight, *Race and Reunion*, 90.

104. On the inadequacy of Vietnam-era GI benefits, see Severo and Milford, *Wages of War*, 347–71.

105. Works charting military breakdown include Hauser, *America's Army in Crisis*; Gabriel and Savage, *Crisis in Command*; Cincinnatus, *Self-Destruction*.

106. All quotations from Veterans Administration, *Myths and Realities*, 63, 79–80, 157.

CHAPTER 8

1. See *Boston Globe*, October 26, 2005, F1. Television critics cited viewer saturation with Iraq War news, as well as the show's reluctance to take a strong political stand on the conflict, for its low ratings and subsequent cancellation.

2. For these figures see Devine, *Vietnam at 24 Frames*, xi. The Green Berets—the Special Forces troops of the U.S. Army created in the 1950s, named for their headgear and famously championed by John Kennedy—occupied a position of special cultural prominence during the war. By the fall of 1965 seventy-five newspapers were running the daily comic strip, "Tales of the Green Beret." In 1966 Special Forces member Barry Sadler recorded "The Ballad of the Green Berets," and by December it was the best-selling record of the year. Young boys owned Green Beret trading cards, board games, uniforms, toy guns, and of course, hats. In 1968 John Wayne used "Ballad" as the theme song to his movie *The Green Berets*, but by that point the increasingly unpopular war had rendered even the glamorous Special Forces a touchy subject. According to *Newsweek*, as early as 1966 many readers found the "Tales of the Green Beret" comic strip uncomfortably bombastic. Many papers cut "Tales" from their pages, and most war-related comic books continued to use World War II as a setting. See Holsinger, *War and American Popular Culture*, 365–66; *Newsweek*, September 12, 1966, 66, 71.

3. Anderegg, "Hollywood and Vietnam," 15.

4. See Hall, *Crossroads*, 181.

5. The book was a phenomenal success in 1965, selling 100,000 copies in hard-

cover and over a million in paperback. See Hackett and Burke, *80 Years of Best Sellers*, 195–96.

6. See Kolpacoff, *Prisoners of Quai Dong*; Eastlake, *Bamboo Bed*; O'Brien, *If I Die*; Kovic, *Born on the Fourth*; Caputo, *Rumor of War*; Herr, *Dispatches*; O'Brien, *Going after Cacciato*; Ehrhart, *Vietnam-Perkasie*; O'Brien, *Things They Carried*; Karlin, Paquet, and Rottmann, *Free Fire Zones*. For discussion of the "canon" of Vietnam War literature, see Bates, *Wars We Took to Vietnam*; Neilson, *Warring Fictions*.

7. See Rottmann, Barry, and Paquet, *Winning Hearts and Minds*; Barry and Ehrhart, *Demilitarized Zones*; Ehrhart, *Carrying the Darkness*; Ehrhart, *Unaccustomed Mercy*; Balaban, *After Our War*; Ehrhart, *To Those Who Have Gone*; Komunyakaa, *Dien Cai Dau*; Bowen, *Playing Basketball*. *Winning Hearts and Minds*, *Demilitarized Zones*, *After Our War*, and a good deal of other Vietnam War poetry may be found in the Harris Collection of American Poetry and Plays, John Hay Library, Brown University, Providence, R.I.

8. See Ehrhart, *Unaccustomed Mercy*, 1.

9. See Suid, *Guts and Glory*, 2; John Clark Pratt preface in Ehrhart, *Unaccustomed Mercy*, ix–x.

10. See Chapter 5 for a detailed discussion of these films.

11. Malo and Williams, *Vietnam War Films*, 33. On the "Vietnamization" of World War II in American culture, see Jarvis, *Male Body at War*, 190.

12. Less than a decade later, the esteemed British military historian John Keegan's first book would argue that fear was the abiding experience of the foot soldier. See Keegan, *Face of Battle*. See Chapter 5 for discussion of fear in World War II poetry.

13. All quotations are from *Beach Red*, dir. Cornel Wilde (United Artists, 1967).

14. Promotional Material, *Beach Red* (call no. PN1997.B422 A1 1967); Archive of Imaginative Representations of the Viet Nam War, Connelly Library, La Salle University, Philadelphia, Pa. (hereafter VN Archives, La Salle).

15. Eastlake, *Bamboo Bed*, 40. Human depravity also had been a prominent theme of Cord Meyer's prize-winning short story of 1946, "Waves of Darkness." In that work Meyer wrote of the marine-protagonist, "For a moment it appeared impossible to him that what was about to take place could actually occur. Adult human beings of the civilized world did not slaughter one another. There must be some mistake which could be corrected before it was too late." See Meyer, "Waves of Darkness," 20.

16. Rottmann, Barry, and Paquet, *Winning Hearts and Minds*, 39.

17. Promotional Material, *Beach Red* (call no. PN1997.B422 A1 1967), VN Archives, La Salle.

18. I survey two other violent films of the period later in this chapter: *Soldier Blue* (1970) and *Ulzana's Raid* (1972). See Lopez, *Films By Genre*, 362–63.

19. *New York Times*, August 4, 1967, 18.

20. One film critic has written that such scenes "depersonalize the soldiers themselves, turning the victims of war into a collection of organs and bloodied flesh among whom the doctors crack jokes and leer at the nurses." In my view, while the wounded GIs in the film are certainly anonymous, the bloody operating room scenes nonetheless make a potent antiwar statement. See Malo and Williams, *Vietnam War Films*, 269.

21. *New York Times*, January 26, 1970, 26.

22. All quotations are from *M*A*S*H*, dir. Robert Altman (Twentieth-Century Fox, 1970).

23. Ring Lardner, who wrote the screenplay for *M*A*S*H*, defended the film against charges that it was antireligious, writing in the *New York Times*, "People who sense an attack on religion per se were missing the point about the peculiar inappropriateness of religious sentiment in the combat zone. War is such a distinctly man-made institution it seems quite unfair to involve God at all." See *New York Times*, June 14, 1970, 11.

24. One unimpressed critic wrote of Major Houlihan's transformation: "The movie's idea of redemption is to turn her, and all the other women in the outfit, into affable imbeciles who are only to be trusted with passing the scalpel, cheerleading at a ball game, and acting as acquiescent bedmates." See *New York Times*, March 22, 1970, II, 19.

25. Quoted in Suid, *Guts and Glory*, 279.

26. See Mauldin, *Bill Mauldin in Korea*.

27. Promotional Material, *The Dirty Dozen* (call no. PN1997.D5775 A1 1967), VN Archives, La Salle.

28. Promotional Material, *Kelly's Heroes* (call no. PN1997.K444 A1 1970), VN Archives, La Salle.

29. All of these books are available for study at the La Salle University archives in Philadelphia. See Melvin, *Sorry 'Bout That!*; Melvin, *"Be Nice!"*; Abood and Ranfone, *How to Live in Vietnam*. Other satirical works had general audiences, including a collection of Doonesbury cartoons: Trudeau, *But This War Had Such Promise*; and a novel touted as a "savage, steamy M*A*S*H": Maitland, *Only War We've Got*.

30. Melvin, *Sorry 'Bout That!*, 19.

31. Melvin, *"Be Nice!"*, front and back covers.

32. Hodgson, *With Sgt. Mike in Vietnam*, back cover.

33. One encyclopedia of television history has called the final episode "a national event"; another has claimed that 77 percent of Americans watching TV on February 28, 1983, tuned their sets to that show. See Brown, *Les Brown's Encyclopedia of Television*, 340–41; Lackman, *20th-Century American Television*, 224–25.

34. For one account of public cynicism about the military after the Vietnam War—

and of the subsequent *increase* of trust in that institution—see King and Kara-bell, *Generation of Trust*.

35. Eastlake, *Bamboo Bed*, 23. On frontier themes in Vietnam War literature see Bates, *Wars We Took to Vietnam*, Chapter 1.

36. Malo and Williams, *Vietnam War Films*, 394–95. For contemporary reviews see *Newsweek*, August 24, 1970, 65; *New York Times*, September 20, 1970, II, 13.

37. All quotations are from *Soldier Blue*, dir. Ralph Nelson (Avco Embassy Pictures, 1970).

38. Students for a Democratic Society (SDS) was a radical campus group of the 1960s. See *Newsweek*, August 24, 1970, 65.

39. See *Time*, February 2, 1970, 71; *Newsweek*, August 24, 1970, 65; *New York Times*, August 13, 1970, 29. Another critic, Dotson Rader of the *New York Times*, seemed quite alone in praising the film. He wrote, "'Soldier Blue' must be numbered among the most significant, the most brutal and liberating, the most honest American films ever made." See *New York Times*, September 20, 1970, II, 13.

40. William Calley described the tortured American GI in Sack and Calley, *Lieutenant Calley*, 126. See my Chapter 7 for detailed coverage of My Lai.

41. In his Vietnam War novel *The Bamboo Bed* (1969), William Eastlake drew the same parallel between American atrocities in Southeast Asia and the Sand Creek Massacre. See Eastlake, *Bamboo Bed*, 35–36. On the interplay of photographs and motion pictures see Sontag, *Regarding the Pain of Others*, 77–78.

42. Promotional Material, *Soldier Blue* (call no. PN1997.S599 A1 1970), VN Archives, La Salle.

43. Rottmann, Barry, and Paquet, *Winning Hearts and Minds*, v.

44. On the ubiquity of atrocity in Vietnam War literature—and the difficulty writers had in tackling the subject—see Balaban et al., "Carrying the Darkness."

45. Rottmann, Barry, and Paquet, *Winning Hearts and Minds*, 101.

46. Ehrhart, *To Those Who Have Gone*, 20; originally published in 1975 in *A Generation of Peace*.

47. Komunyakaa, *Dien Cai Dau*, 17, 19–20.

48. See Chapter 7 for discussion of this policy, which replaced American soldiers with South Vietnamese troops.

49. All quotations are from *Ulzana's Raid*, dir. Robert Aldrich (Universal, 1972).

50. Promotional Material, *Ulzana's Raid* (call no. PN1997.U499 A1 1972), VN Archives, La Salle.

51. Eastlake, *Bamboo Bed*, 28, 35. Some indeterminate (though surely small) number of American GIs collected ears from Vietnamese dead.

52. *New York Times*, December 3, 1972, II, 1. Emphasis added.

53. Quoted in Malo and Williams, *Vietnam War Films*, 450.

54. Eastlake, *Bamboo Bed*, 35.

55. For coverage of public cynicism in the mid-1970s, see Schulman, *Seventies*, 121–43; Carroll, *It Seemed Like Nothing Happened*, 207–32.

56. A sampling of this literature includes MacPherson, *Long Time Passing*; Egendorf, *Healing from the War*; Lifton, *Home from the War*; Greene, *Homecoming*.

57. All quotations are from *The Boys in Company C*, dir. Sidney J. Furie (Golden Harvest, 1978). For a similarly harsh portrait of a DI—and of the hinted homoeroticism I discuss later in the section—see *Full Metal Jacket*, dir. Stanley Kubrick (Warner Brothers, 1987).

58. *Newsweek*, February 6, 1978, 89.

59. Layne, *How Audie Murphy Died*, no page numbers.

60. O'Brien, *If I Die*, 156.

61. For critics who equated the film with World War II movies, see *New York Times*, February 2, 1978, C15; ibid., February 19, 1978, II, 1. A reviewer for *Newsweek* said the opposite, writing, "When it's good, the film gives a fresh and harrowing reading of a struggle so chaotic and irrational that it approached the climate of hallucination." See *Newsweek*, February 6, 1978, 89.

62. Komunyakaa, *Dien Cai Dau*, 16.

63. Ibid., 32. For a vivid account of a liaison with a prostitute, see Caputo, *Rumor of War*, 144–45.

64. Barry and Ehrhart, *Demilitarized Zones*, 20.

65. For drug use see O'Brien, *Things They Carried*, 20; Herr, *Dispatches*.

66. *New York Times*, February 16, 1978, C20.

67. For these critiques see ibid., February 16, 1978, C20; *Time*, February 20, 1978, 68; *Newsweek*, February 20, 1978, 89–90; Suid, *Guts and Glory*, 325–30.

68. All quotations are from *Coming Home*, dir. Hal Ashby (United Artists, 1978).

69. Jones, *Whistle*, 4.

70. Susan Jeffords has made a similar argument, writing in an encyclopedia of Vietnam films, "*Coming Home* remains basically a male-hero film, in which the hero is redefined as non-phallic and non-dominating." In a different context, Peter Novick has excoriated the replacement of stoicism with sensitivity in this era. See Malo and Williams, *Vietnam War Films*, 93; Novick, *Holocaust in American Life*, 8.

71. *New York Times*, February 19, 1978, II, 13.

72. O'Brien, *Things They Carried*, 130.

73. On sexual tension in *Best Years* see Gerber, "Heroes and Misfits," 87–88.

74. As one reviewer commented, "Luke's passionate lovemaking is glibly contrasted to the mechanical bedroom manner of Sally's husband." See *Time*, February 20, 1978, 68.

75. See Suid, *Guts and Glory*, 329: "The filmmakers tried to have their cake and eat it, suggesting from the way they shot the scene that Luke and Sally were actually making love."

76. *Newsweek*, February 20, 1978, 90.

77. In his discussion of the Vietnam War novels and memoirs emerging in the late 1970s, Peter C. Rollins has identified this idea of war's negative, transformative effect. Referring to works by Ron Kovic and Philip Caputo, Rollins has written, "The protagonist leaves a healthy, civilian environment to become immersed in a war that leaves him physically or psychically wounded." See Rollins, "Vietnam War," 422.

78. O'Brien, *If I Die*, 146.

79. *New York Times*, December 3, 1972, II, 1.

80. In addition to those surveyed here was a fourth Vietnam War film, *Go Tell the Spartans*.

81. *Time* called the sequence "one of the most gut-wrenching ever," while *Newsweek* agreed that it was "one of the most frightening, unbearably tense sequences ever filmed." See *Time*, December 18, 1978, 86; *Newsweek*, December 11, 1978, 113.

82. Perhaps unaware of the subtle ways Vietnam westerns had done this earlier, one contemporary critic said of the film, "*The Deer Hunter* is the first film to look at Vietnam not politically, but as the manifestation of an endemic murderousness." See *Newsweek*, December 11, 1978, 113.

83. *Newsweek*, December 11, 1978, 115.

84. All quotations are from *The Deer Hunter*, dir. Michael Cimino (Universal, 1978).

85. Barry and Ehrhart, *Demilitarized Zones*, 65.

86. Ibid., 13.

87. Ibid., 52. For the dream/nightmare trope see also, in that volume, Frank A. Cross Jr., "Rice Will Grow Again," 19–20; Landon Thorne, "Hand to Hand Combat, A Recurring Dream," 81; Jan Barry, "Sleeping with a Light On," 106.

88. See Devine, *Vietnam at 24 Frames*, xi. More in line with my thinking is Michael Anderegg, who has written in an article on Vietnam War films, "Several Korean War films of the mid to late fifties prefigure the narrative and ideological ambiguities characteristic of Hollywood's Vietnam." See Anderegg, "Hollywood and Vietnam," 3.

89. George quote from Maraniss, *They Marched into Sunlight*, 11; Kerry quote from *Atlantic Monthly*, December 2003, 49, excerpted from Douglas Brinkley, *Tour of Duty*.

CONCLUSION

1. Historian Kurt Piehler has suggested more broadly that the Cold War's untraditional and anxious nature, without great moments of victory, inhibited monument building in those decades. See Piehler, *Remembering War the American Way*, 186.

2. For images of and information about the Vietnam Veterans Memorial, see <<http://www.nps.gov/vive/>>; for a description of it (and the "black gash" quote), see Hass, *Carried to the Wall*, 14–20. In 1993 a Vietnam Women's Memorial, commemorating the work of nurses, joined the three soldiers in the vicinity of the Wall.

3. In historian John Bodnar's words, the soldier statues "appear fearful that they could be killed or hurt at any moment." See Bodnar, "*Saving Private Ryan*."

4. See <<http://www.nab.usace.army.mil/projects/WashingtonDC/korean .html>>. For the National Park Service site see <<http://www.nps.gov/kowa/>>. Emphasis added.

5. Douglas Brinkley has contended that Ronald Reagan's speech on the fortieth anniversary of D-Day, in 1984, catalyzed the resurgence of World War II nostalgia; see Douglas Brinkley, *Boys of Pointe du Hoc*. Popular works of the 1990s contributing to the veneration of the World War II cohort included the film *Saving Private Ryan* (1998); Tom Brokaw's nonfiction account *Greatest Generation*; and books by Stephen E. Ambrose such as *Band of Brothers*, *D-Day*, and *Citizen Soldiers*. Following on the heels of these works were the World War II films *Pearl Harbor* (2001), *Hart's War* (2002), *Windtalkers* (2002), and *Flags of Our Fathers* (2006). To one commentator the works of the 1990s and the WWII memorial all aim "to honor that generation rather than put it under an historical microscope." See Mills, *Their Last Battle*, 218.

6. See <<http://www.wwiimemorial.com/default.asp?page=overview.asp& subpage=intro>>. Emphasis added.

7. For images of the World War II memorial see <<http://www.wwiimemorial. com/>>; Mills, *Their Last Battle*.

8. Maya Lin's design satisfied the wishes of Jan Scruggs and others that the memorial emphasize "the soldiers rather than the federal government," as one scholar of the Vietnam Veterans Memorial has put it. See Hass, *Carried to the Wall*, 11.

9. On the masculinity "crisis" of the postwar period, see Gilbert, *Men in the Middle*; Traister, "Academic Viagra"; Mickenberg, "Men on the Suburban Frontier"; Kimmel, *Manhood in America*, 291–328.

10. Novick, *Holocaust in American Life*, 8.

11. See Brokaw, *Greatest Generation*.

12. It is hardly possible to cite the wide array of critics aiming these attacks at American society. Such critiques are part of the wider "culture wars" raging in American civic life since at least the 1960s. See, among others, Hunter, *Culture Wars*.

13. See, for example, *New York Times*, June 14, 2003; *San Francisco Chronicle*, December 27, 2003.

14. *New York Times*, July 9, 2003; Lutz, *Crying*, 230–35.

15. See the Organization of American Historians roundtable, "Interchange: Legacies of the Vietnam War," 490.
16. Beidler, *Good War's Greatest Hits*, 3. See Coser, *Maurice Halbwachs*. Works invoking his theory of collective memory in relation to the Second World War include Torgovnick, *War Complex*, 3; Novick, *Holocaust in American Life*, 3–4.
17. Paul Fussell, long a critic of sentimental imagery of World War II, wrote in 2003, "Now, almost sixty years after the horror, there has been a return, especially in popular culture, to military romanticism." See Fussell, *Boys' Crusade*, xiii.
18. *New York Times*, October 20, 2006.

BIBLIOGRAPHY

ARCHIVAL COLLECTIONS
Boston, Mass.
    John F. Kennedy Library
        John F. Kennedy Personal Papers
        Papers of the National Veterans Housing Conference, 1948
        Pre-Presidential Papers
College Park, Md.
    National Archives
        March of Time Productions
        Paramount Newsreels
        Records of the Department of Defense
        Records of the Department of the Army
        Records of the Department of the Treasury
        Records of the Office of the Chief Signal Officer
        Records of the Office of War Information
        Universal Newsreels
Madison, Wis.
    Wisconsin Historical Society
        Papers of Vietnam Veterans Against the War
New York, N.Y.
    Museum of Modern Art Archives
        Records of the Department of Circulating Exhibits
Philadelphia, Pa.
    La Salle University Library
        Archive of Imaginative Representations of the Viet Nam War
Providence, R.I.
    John Hay Library, Brown University
        Harris Collection of American Poetry and Plays
Washington, D.C.
    National Archives
        Records of the Veterans Administration

PERIODICALS

Akron Beacon Journal　　　　*Army Times Vet-Letter*
American Mercury　　　　*Atlantic Monthly*

Bangor (Maine) News
Boston Globe
Boston American
Bronx (N.Y.) Home News
Cavalier Daily, University of Virginia
Chicago Herald-American
Chicago Sun
Chicago Tribune
Christian Science Monitor
Cleveland Plain Dealer
Cleveland Press
Collier's
Commonweal
Congressional Quarterly Almanac
Crisis
Detroit Free Press
Future: The Magazine for Young Men
Harper's Magazine
Jackson (Mich.) Citizen Patriot
Kalamazoo (Mich.) Gazette
Ladies' Home Journal
Life
Look
Madison (Wis.) Capital Times
Memphis Press-Scimitar
Miami Herald

Military Affairs
Monterey (Calif.) Herald
Nation
Nation's Business
Negro History Bulletin
New Republic
Newsweek
New York Daily World
New York Times
New Yorker
Phylon
Providence (R.I.) Journal
Psychology Today
Public Opinion Quarterly
Rotarian
San Francisco Chronicle
Saturday Evening Post
Springfield (Mass.) Daily News
St. Louis Globe-Democrat
Time
TV Guide
Variety
Veterans' News
Washington Post
Woodstock (Vt.) Standard

PUBLISHED PRIMARY SOURCES

Abood, Ken, and Tony Ranfone. *How to Live in Vietnam for Less than 10 Cents a Day . . . and Other Glimpses of the Lighter Side of War.* Tokyo: Wayward Press, 1967.

Administrator for Veterans Affairs. *Annual Report, 1946.* Washington, D.C.: Government Printing Office, 1947.

———. *Annual Report, 1954.* Washington, D.C.: Government Printing Office, 1955.

Appy, Christian G. *Patriots: The Vietnam War Remembered from All Sides.* New York: Viking Press, 2003.

Baker, Mark. *Nam: The Vietnam War in the Words of the Men and Women Who Fought There.* New York: Cooper Square Press, 1981.

Balaban, John. *After Our War.* Pittsburgh: University of Pittsburgh Press, 1974.

Barry, Jan, and W. D. Ehrhart, eds. *Demilitarized Zones: Veterans after Vietnam.* Perkasie, Pa.: East River Anthology, 1976.

Bolté, Charles G. *The New Veteran.* New York: Reynal and Hitchcock, 1945.

Bowen, Kevin. *Playing Basketball with the Viet Cong*. Willimantic, Conn.: Curbstone Press, 1994.

Bowker, Benjamin C. *Out of Uniform*. New York: W. W. Norton, 1946.

Braceland, Francis J. *The Retraining and Re-Education of Veterans: A Lecture Delivered on the Nellie Heldt Lecture Fund*. Oberlin, Ohio: Oberlin College, 1945.

Brown, Harry. *A Walk in the Sun*. New York: Knopf, 1944.

Burns, John Horne. *The Gallery*. 1947. Reprint, New York: New York Review of Books, 2004.

Caplow, Theodore, Louis Hicks, and Ben J. Wattenberg, eds. *The First Measured Century: An Illustrated Guide to Trends in America, 1900–2000*. Washington, D.C.: AEI Press, 2001.

Caputo, Philip. *A Rumor of War*. New York: Rinehart and Winston, 1977.

The Civil War: A Centennial Exhibition of Eyewitness Drawings. Washington, D.C.: National Gallery of Art, 1961.

Congressional Quarterly. Vol. 2, no. 2, 1946. Washington: Government Printing Office, 1946.

Congressional Record. 79th Cong., 1st sess. Vol. 91. Washington, D.C.: Government Printing Office, 1945.

———. 79th Cong., 2nd sess. Vol. 92. Washington, D.C.: Government Printing Office, 1946.

Corwin, Norman. *This Is War! A Collection of Plays about America on the March*. New York: Dodd, Mead, 1942.

———. *Untitled, and Other Radio Dramas*. New York: Henry Holt, 1946.

Crespi, Leo P., and G. Schofield Shapleigh. "'The' Veteran—A Myth." *Public Opinion Quarterly* 10 (Autumn 1946): 361–72.

Donovan, David. *Once a Warrior King: Memories of an Officer in Vietnam*. New York: McGraw-Hill, 1985.

Duncan, David Douglas. *This Is War! A Photo Narrative in Three Parts*. New York: Harper, 1951.

———. *Photo Nomad*. New York: W. W. Norton, 2003.

Dupuy, Colonel R. Ernest, and Lt. Colonel Herbert L. Bregstein, eds. *Soldiers' Album*. Boston: Houghton Mifflin, 1946.

Eastlake, William. *The Bamboo Bed*. New York: Simon and Schuster, 1969.

Ehrhart, W. D. *Vietnam-Perkasie: A Combat Marine Memoir*. Jefferson, N.C.: McFarland, 1983.

———. *To Those Who Have Gone Home Tired: New and Selected Poems*. New York: Thunder's Mouth Press, 1984.

———. *Unaccustomed Mercy: Soldier-Poets of the Vietnam War*. Lubbock: Texas Tech University Press, 1989.

———, ed. *Carrying the Darkness: American Indochina—The Poetry of the Vietnam War*. New York: Avon Books, 1985.

Ehrhart, W. D., and Philip K. Jason, eds. *Retrieving Bones: Stories and Poems of the Korean War*. New Brunswick, N.J.: Rutgers University Press, 1999.

Ellis, John. *World War II: A Statistical Survey*. New York: Facts on File, 1993.

Gallup, George H. *The Gallup Poll: Public Opinion, 1935–1971*. 3 vols. New York: Random House, 1972.

Gellhorn, Martha. *The Face of War*. London: Rupert Hart-Davis, 1959.

Gettleman, Marvin E., Jane Franklin, Marilyn B. Young, and H. Bruce Franklin, eds. *Vietnam and America: A Documented History*. New York: Grove Press, 1995.

Giangreco, D. M., ed. *Dear Harry: Truman's Mailroom, 1945–1953*. Mechanicsburg, Pa.: Stackpole Books, 1999.

Gilpatrick, Kristin. *The Hero Next Door: Stories from Wisconsin's World War II Veterans*. Oregon, Wis.: Badger Books, 2000.

Greene, Bob, ed. *Homecoming: When the Soldiers Returned from Vietnam*. New York: Putnam, 1989.

Grinker, Roy G., and John P. Spiegel. *Men under Stress*. Philadelphia: Blakiston, 1945.

Hedin, Robert, ed. *Old Glory: American War Poems from the Revolutionary War to the War on Terrorism*. New York: Persea Books, 2004.

Heller, Jonathan, ed. *War and Conflict: Selected Images from the National Archives, 1765–1970*. Washington, D.C.: National Archives and Records Administration, 1990.

Herr, Michael. *Dispatches*. New York: Knopf, 1977.

Hersh, Seymour M. *My Lai 4: A Report on the Massacre and Its Aftermath*. New York: Random House, 1970.

Higgins, Marguerite. *War in Korea: The Report of a Woman Combat Correspondent*. Garden City, N.Y.: Doubleday, 1951.

Hodgson, Michael T. *With Sgt. Mike in Vietnam*. Washington, D.C.: Army Times, 1970.

Hugo, Richard. *Making Certain It Goes On: The Collected Poems of Richard Hugo*. New York: W. W. Norton, 1984.

Jones, James. *The Thin Red Line*. 1962. Reprint, New York: Dell Publishing, 1991.
———. *Whistle*. New York: Delacorte Press, 1978.

Karlin, Wayne, Basil T. Paquet, and Larry Rottmann, eds. *Free Fire Zones: Short Stories by Vietnam Veterans*. New York: McGraw-Hill, 1973.

Kennedy, John F. *The Inaugural Address of John Fitzgerald Kennedy, President of the United States: Delivered at the Capitol, Washington, January 20, 1961*. Worcester, Mass.: Achille J. St. Onge, 1961.

Kirstein, Lincoln. *Rhymes of a PFC*. Boston: David R. Godine, 1981.

Kolpacoff, Victor. *The Prisoners of Quai Dong*. New York: New American Library, 1967.

Komunyakaa, Yusef. *Dien Cai Dau*. Middletown, Conn.: Wesleyan University Press, 1988.

Kovic, Ron. *Born on the Fourth of July*. New York: McGraw-Hill, 1976.

Layne, McAvoy. *How Audie Murphy Died in Vietnam*. Garden City, N.Y.: Anchor Books, 1973.

Leinbaugh, Harold P., and John D. Campbell. *The Men of Company K: The Autobiography of a World War II Rifle Company*. New York: Morrow, 1985.

MacDonald, Charles B. "Novels of World War II: The First Round." *Military Affairs* 13 (Spring 1949): 42–46.

Mailer, Norman. *The Naked and the Dead*. New York: Rinehart, 1948.

Maitland, Derek. *The Only War We've Got*. New York: Morrow, 1970.

Marshall, S. L. A. *Men Against Fire: The Problem of Battle Command in Future War*. Washington, D.C.: Combat Forces Press, 1947.

Mauldin, Bill. *Up Front*. New York: Henry Holt, 1945.

———. *Bill Mauldin in Korea*. New York: W. W. Norton, 1952.

Mays, Benjamin E. "Veterans: It Need Not Happen Again." *Phylon* 6 (Third Quarter 1945): 205–11.

Melvin, Ken. *Sorry 'Bout That!: Cartoons, Limericks, and Other Diversions of GI Vietnam*. Tokyo: Wayward Press, 1966.

———. *"Be Nice!"* Tokyo: Wayward Press, 1967.

Meyer, Cord, Jr. "Waves of Darkness." In *"The Secret Sharer" and Other Great Stories*, edited by Abraham H. Lass and Norma L. Tasman, 11–30. New York: Penguin Books, 1969.

Michener, James A. *The Bridges at Toko-Ri*. New York: Random House, 1953.

———. *Kent State: What Happened and Why*. New York: Random House, 1971.

———. *The World Is My Home: A Memoir*. New York: Random House, 1992.

Murphy, Audie. *To Hell and Back*. New York: Henry Holt, 1949.

Nemerov, Howard. *War Stories: Poems about Long Ago and Now*. Chicago: University of Chicago Press, 1987.

O'Brien, Tim. *If I Die in a Combat Zone*. New York: Dell, 1973.

———. *Going after Cacciato*. New York: Delacorte Press, 1978.

———. *The Things They Carried: A Work of Fiction*. Boston: Houghton Mifflin, 1990.

Oppen, George. *The Collected Poems of George Oppen*. New York: New Directions, 1975.

Orwell, George. *Homage to Catalonia*. New York: Harcourt, Brace, 1952.

O'Sheel, Patrick, and Gene Cook, eds. *Semper Fidelis: The U.S. Marines in the Pacific—1942–1945*. New York: William Sloane Associates, 1947.

Pritchard, William H., ed. *Randall Jarrell: Selected Poems*. New York: Farrar, Straus, and Giroux, 1990.

Pyle, Ernie. *Here Is Your War*. New York: Henry Holt, 1943.

———. *Brave Men*. New York: Henry Holt, 1944.

Rampersad, Arnold, ed. *The Collected Poems of Langston Hughes*. New York: Knopf, 2000.

Rogers, Carl R., and John L. Wallen. *Counseling with Returned Servicemen*. New York: McGraw-Hill, 1946.

Rottmann, Larry, Jan Barry, and Basil T. Paquet, eds. *Winning Hearts and Minds: War Poems by Vietnam Veterans*. Brooklyn, N.Y.: First Casualty Press, 1972.

Sack, John, and William Calley. *Lieutenant Calley: His Own Story*. New York: Viking Press, 1971.

Santoli, Al. *To Bear Any Burden: The Vietnam War and Its Aftermath in the Words of Americans and Southeast Asians*. New York: Dutton, 1985.

Schlesinger, Arthur M., Jr. *A Life in the Twentieth Century: Innocent Beginnings, 1917–1950*. New York: Houghton Mifflin, 2000.

Shapiro, Karl. *Collected Poems, 1940–1978*. New York: Random House, 1978.

Stacewicz, Richard. *Winter Soldiers: An Oral History of Vietnam Veterans Against the War*. London: Twayne Publishers, 1997.

Stallworthy, Jon. *Wilfred Owen: The Complete Poems and Fragments*. Vol. 1. London: Chatto and Windus, 1983.

Steichen, Edward. *A Life in Photography*. Garden City, N.Y.: Doubleday, 1963.

Steinbeck, John. *Once There Was a War*. New York: Viking Press, 1958.

Stokesbury, Leon, ed. *Articles of War: A Collection of American Poetry about World War II*. Fayetteville: University of Arkansas Press, 1990.

Stouffer, Samuel, et al. *Studies in Social Psychology during World War II: The American Soldier*. 4 vols. Princeton: Princeton University Press, 1948–52.

Taylor, Clyde, ed. *Vietnam and Black America: An Anthology of Protest and Resistance*. Garden City, N.Y.: Anchor Press, 1973.

Terkel, Studs. *"The Good War": An Oral History of World War Two*. New York: New Press, 1984.

Trudeau, G. B. *But This War Had Such Promise*. New York: Holt, Rinehart and Winston, 1973.

U.S. Bureau of the Census. *Historical Statistics of the United States: Colonial Times to 1970*. Washington, D.C.: U.S. Department of Commerce, 1975.

U.S. Department of Labor. *The Negro Family: The Case for National Action*. 1965. Reprint, Westport, Conn.: Greenwood Press, 1981.

U.S. House Committee on Veterans' Affairs. *Legislative Programs of Veterans' Organizations for 1948*. 80th Cong., 2nd sess., 1948. Washington, D.C.: Government Printing Office, 1948.

———. *Laws Relating to Veterans and their Dependents Enacted on and after September 16, 1940 and through September 30, 1950*. 81st Cong., 2nd sess., 1950. Washington, D.C.: Government Printing Office, 1950.

U.S. Senate Committee on Military Affairs. *Superseniority Rights of Veterans*. 79th
Cong., 2nd sess., 1946. Washington, D.C.: Government Printing Office, 1946.

Veterans Administration. *Myths and Realities: A Study of Attitudes Toward Vietnam
Era Veterans*. Washington, D.C.: Government Printing Office, 1980.

Vietnam Veterans Against the War (VVAW). *The Winter Soldier Investigation: An
Inquiry into American War Crimes*. Boston: Beacon Press, 1972.

Waller, Willard. *The Veteran Comes Back*. New York: Dryden Press, 1944.

Wecter, Dixon. *When Johnny Comes Marching Home*. Boston: Houghton Mifflin,
1944.

Wells, Stanley, and Gary Taylor, eds. *William Shakespeare: The Complete Works*.
New York: Clarendon Press, 1988.

Wilbur, Richard. *The Beautiful Changes And Other Poems*. New York: Harcourt,
Brace, 1947.

Wyatt, Wilson W., Sr. *Whistle Stops: Adventures in Public Life*. Lexington: University
Press of Kentucky, 1985.

SECONDARY SOURCES

Adams, Michael C. C. *The Best War Ever: America and World War II*. Baltimore:
Johns Hopkins University Press, 1994.

Aichinger, Peter. *The American Soldier in Fiction, 1880–1963: A History of Attitudes
toward Warfare and the Military Establishment*. Ames: Iowa State University
Press, 1975.

Aldgate, Anthony. *Cinema and History: British Newsreels and the Spanish Civil War*.
London: Scolar Press, 1979.

Alexander, Bevin. *Korea: The First War We Lost*. 1986. Rev. ed., New York:
Hippocrene Books, 2000.

Alpers, Benjamin L. "This Is the Army: Imagining a Democratic Military in World
War II." *Journal of American History* 85 (June 1998): 129–63.

Ambrose, Stephen E. *Band of Brothers: E Company, 506th Regiment, 101st Airborne:
From Normandy to Hitler's Eagle's Nest*. New York: Simon and Schuster, 1992.

———. *D-Day, June 6, 1944: The Climactic Battle of World War II*. New York: Simon
and Schuster, 1994.

———. *Citizen Soldiers: The U.S. Army from the Normandy Beaches to the Bulge
to the Surrender of Germany, June 7, 1944–May 7, 1945*. New York: Simon and
Schuster, 1997.

Anderegg, Michael. "Hollywood and Vietnam: John Wayne and Jane Fonda as
Discourse." In *Inventing Vietnam: The War in Film and Television*, edited by
Michael Anderegg, 15–32. Philadelphia: Temple University Press, 1991.

Appleman, Roy E. *United States Army in the Korean War: South to the Naktong,
North to the Yalu (June–November 1950)*. Washington, D.C.: Department of the
Army, 1961.

Appy, Christian G. *Working-Class War: American Combat Soldiers and Vietnam.* Chapel Hill: University of North Carolina Press, 1993.

———. "'We'll Follow the Old Man': The Strains of Sentimental Militarism in Popular Films of the Fifties." In *Rethinking Cold War Culture*, edited by Peter J. Kuznick and James Gilbert, 74–105. Washington, D.C.: Smithsonian Institution Press, 2001.

Arlen, Michael J. *Living-Room War.* New York: Viking Press, 1969.

Astor, Gerald. *The Right to Fight: A History of African Americans in the Military.* Novato, Calif.: Presidio, 1998.

Axelsson, Arne. *Restrained Response: American Novels of the Cold War and Korea, 1945–1962.* Westport, Conn.: Greenwood Press, 1990.

Bacevich, Andrew J. *The New American Militarism: How Americans Are Seduced by War.* New York: Oxford University Press, 2005.

Balaban, John, W. D. Ehrhart, Wayne Karlin, and Basil Paquet. "Carrying the Darkness: Literary Approaches to Atrocity." In *Facing My Lai: Moving Beyond the Massacre*, edited by David L. Anderson, 77–93. Lawrence: University Press of Kansas, 1998.

Banks, Samuel L. "The Korean Conflict." *Negro History Bulletin* 36 (October 1973): 131–32.

Barber, Lucy G. *Marching on Washington: The Forging of an American Political Tradition.* Berkeley: University of California Press, 2002.

Baritz, Loren. *Backfire: A History of How American Culture Led Us into Vietnam and Made Us Fight the Way We Did.* New York: William Morrow, 1985.

Basinger, Jeanine. *The World War II Combat Film: Anatomy of a Genre.* 1986. Rev. ed., Middletown, Conn.: Wesleyan University Press, 2003.

Bates, Milton J. *The Wars We Took to Vietnam: Cultural Conflict and Storytelling.* Berkeley: University of California Press, 1996.

Baughman, James L. "Who Read *Life*? The Circulation of America's Favorite Magazine." In *Looking at "Life" Magazine*, edited by Erika Doss, 41–51. Washington, D.C.: Smithsonian Institution Press, 2001.

Beattie, Keith. *The Scar That Binds: American Culture and the Vietnam War.* New York: New York University Press, 1998.

Beidler, Philip D. *The Good War's Greatest Hits: World War II and American Remembering.* Athens: University of Georgia Press, 1998.

Bérubé, Allan. *Coming Out under Fire: The History of Gay Men and Women in World War Two.* New York: Free Press, 1990.

Berman, Larry. *Lyndon Johnson's War: The Road to Stalemate in Vietnam.* New York: W. W. Norton, 1989.

Beschloss, Michael R., ed. *Taking Charge: The Johnson White House Tapes, 1963–1964.* New York: Simon and Schuster, 1997.

Bilton, Michael, and Kevin Sim. *Four Hours in My Lai.* New York: Viking, 1992.

Blight, David. *Race and Reunion: The Civil War in American Memory.* Cambridge: Harvard University Press, 2001.

Blum, John Morton. *V Was for Victory: Politics and American Culture during World War II.* New York: Harcourt Brace Jovanovich, 1976.

Bly, Robert. "The Vietnam War and the Erosion of Male Confidence." In *The Vietnam Reader,* edited by Walter Capps, 82–86. New York: Routledge, 1991.

Bodnar, John. "*Saving Private Ryan* and Postwar Memory in America." *American Historical Review* 106 (June 2001): 805–17.

Boggs, Carl, and Tom Pollard. *The Hollywood War Machine: U.S. Militarism and Popular Culture.* Boulder, Colo.: Paradigm Publishers, 2007.

Braestrup, Peter. *Big Story: How the American Press and Television Reported and Interpreted the Crisis of Tet 1968 in Vietnam and Washington.* 1977. Abgd. ed., New Haven: Yale University Press, 1983.

Brinkley, Alan. "The Illusion of Unity in Cold War Culture." In *Rethinking Cold War Culture,* edited by Peter J. Kuznick and James Gilbert, 61–73. Washington, D.C.: Smithsonian Institution Press, 2001.

Brinkley, Douglas. *Tour of Duty: John Kerry and the Vietnam War.* New York: William Morrow, 2004.

———. *The Boys of Pointe du Hoc: Ronald Reagan, D-Day, and the U.S. Army 2nd Ranger Battalion.* New York: William Morrow, 2005.

Brokaw, Tom. *The Greatest Generation.* New York: Random House, 1998.

Brown, Les. *Les Brown's Encyclopedia of Television.* 3rd ed. Detroit: Gale Research, 1992.

Bruscino, Thomas A., Jr. "Bringing Together Social Histories." *Reviews in American History* 33 (December 2005): 581–86.

Canaday, Margot. "Building a Straight State: Sexuality and Citizenship under the 1944 G.I. Bill." *Journal of American History* 90 (December 2003): 935–57.

Carroll, Peter N. *It Seemed Like Nothing Happened: The Tragedy and Promise of America in the 1970s.* New York: Holt, Rinehart and Winston, 1982.

Carruthers, Susan L. *The Media at War: Communication and Conflict in the Twentieth Century.* New York: St. Martin's Press, 2000.

Carson, Clayborne, and Kris Shepard, eds. *A Call to Conscience: The Landmark Speeches of Dr. Martin Luther King, Jr.* New York: Warner Books, 2001.

Castleman, Harry, and Walter J. Podrazik. *Watching TV: Four Decades of American Television.* New York: McGraw-Hill, 1982.

Cincinnatus. *Self-Destruction: The Disintegration and Decay of the United States Army during the Vietnam Era.* New York: W. W. Norton, 1981.

Clark, Kenneth B. *Dark Ghetto: Dilemmas of Social Power.* New York: Harper and Row, 1965.

Cole, Garold. "Home from the War: The Popular Press Views the Veteran Problem, 1944–1948." *North Dakota Quarterly* 46 (Summer 1978): 41–61.

Coser, Lewis A., ed. *Maurice Halbwachs: On Collective Memory*. Chicago: University of Chicago Press, 1992.

Cripps, Thomas, and David Culbert. "The Negro Soldier (1944): Film Propaganda in Black and White." *American Quarterly* 31 (Winter 1979): 616–40.

Culbert, David. "Television's Visual Impact on Decision-making in the USA, 1968: The Tet Offensive and Chicago's Democratic National Convention." *Journal of Contemporary History* 33 (July 1998): 419–49.

Cullen, Jim. *The Civil War in Popular Culture: A Reusable Past*. Washington, D.C: Smithsonian Institution Press, 1995.

Cuordileone, K. A. *Manhood and American Political Culture in the Cold War*. New York: Routledge, 2005.

Dallek, Robert. *Flawed Giant: Lyndon Johnson and His Times, 1961–1973*. New York: Oxford University Press, 1998.

Daniels, Roger. *Concentration Camps, North America: Japanese in the United States and Canada During World War II*. Malabar, Fla.: Krieger, 1993.

Davidsmeyer, Jo. *Combat! A Viewer's Companion to the Classic TV Series*. Hillside, Ill.: R&G Productions, 1997.

Dean, Eric T. *Shook over Hell: Post-Traumatic Stress, Vietnam, and the Civil War*. Cambridge: Harvard University Press, 1997.

DeBenedetti, Charles, and Charles Chatfield. *An American Ordeal: The Antiwar Movement of the Vietnam Era*. Syracuse, N.Y.: Syracuse University Press, 1990.

Deutsch, James I. "Coming Home From 'The Good War': World War II Veterans as Depicted in American Film and Fiction." Ph.D. diss., George Washington University, 1991.

Devine, Jeremy M. *Vietnam at 24 Frames a Second: A Critical and Thematic Analysis of Over 400 Films about the Vietnam War*. Jefferson, N.C.: McFarland, 1995.

Devlin, Rachel. *Relative Intimacy: Fathers, Adolescent Daughters, and Postwar American Culture*. Chapel Hill: University of North Carolina Press, 2005.

Dick, Bernard F. *The Star-Spangled Screen: The American World War II Film*. Lexington: University Press of Kentucky, 1985.

Diggins, John P. "The American Writer, Fascism and the Liberation of Italy," *American Quarterly* 18 (Winter 1966): 611–14.

Dimendberg, Edward. *Film Noir and the Spaces of Modernity*. Cambridge: Harvard University Press, 2004.

Dittmer, John. *Local People: The Struggle for Civil Rights in Mississippi*. Urbana: University of Illinois Press, 1994.

Doherty, Thomas. *Projections of War: Hollywood, American Culture, and World War II*. 1993. Rev. ed., New York: Columbia University Press, 1999.

Dower, John W. *War without Mercy: Race and Power in the Pacific War*. New York: Pantheon Books, 1986.

Dudziak, Mary L. *Cold War Civil Rights: Race and the Image of American Democracy.* Princeton: Princeton University Press, 2000.

Edwards, Paul M., ed. *The Korean War: An Annotated Bibliography.* Westport, Conn.: Greenwood Press, 1998.

Egendorf, Arthur. *Healing from the War: Trauma and Transformation after Vietnam.* Boston: Houghton Mifflin, 1985.

Egerton, John. *Speak Now Against the Day: The Generation Before the Civil Rights Movement in the South.* New York: Knopf, 1994.

Elegant, Robert. "How to Lose a War: Reflections of a Foreign Correspondent." *Encounter* 57 (August 1981): 73–90.

Elkins, Stanley M. *Slavery: A Problem in American Institutional and Intellectual Life.* Chicago: University of Chicago Press, 1959.

Engelhardt, Tom. *The End of Victory Culture: Cold War America and the Disillusioning of a Generation.* New York: Basic Books, 1995.

Faludi, Susan. *Stiffed: The Betrayal of the American Man.* New York: William Morrow, 1999.

Filene, Peter. "'Cold War Culture' Doesn't Say it All." In *Rethinking Cold War Culture,* edited by Peter J. Kuznick and James Gilbert, 156–74. Washington, D.C.: Smithsonian Institution Press, 2001.

Flynn, George Q. *Lewis B. Hershey, Mr. Selective Service.* Chapel Hill: University of North Carolina Press, 1985.

Foner, Jack. *Blacks and the Military in American History: A New Perspective.* New York: Praeger, 1974.

Franklin, H. Bruce. *Vietnam and Other American Fantasies.* Amherst: University of Massachusetts Press, 2000.

Frazier, E. Franklin. *The Negro Family in the United States.* Chicago: University of Chicago Press, 1939.

Frydl, Kathleen Jyll. "The GI Bill." Ph.D. diss., University of Chicago, 2000.

Fussell, Paul. *The Great War and Modern Memory.* New York: Oxford University Press, 1975.

———. *Wartime: Understanding and Behavior in the Second World War.* New York: Oxford University Press, 1989.

———. *The Boys' Crusade: The American Infantry in Northwestern Europe, 1944–1945.* New York: Modern Library, 2003.

Gabriel, Richard A., and Paul L. Savage. *Crisis in Command: Mismanagement in the Army.* New York: Hill and Wang, 1978.

Gaddis, John Lewis. *We Now Know: Rethinking Cold War History.* New York: Oxford University Press, 1997.

Gerber, David A. "Heroes and Misfits: The Troubled Social Reintegration of Disabled Veterans in *The Best Years of Our Lives.*" In *Disabled Veterans in History,* edited by David A. Gerber, 70–95. Ann Arbor: University of Michigan Press, 2000.

Gershen, Martin. *Destroy or Die: The True Story of My Lai.* New Rochelle, N.Y.: Arlington House, 1971.

Giangreco, D. M. "'Spinning' the Casualties: Media Strategies During the Roosevelt Administration." *Passport* 35 (December 2004): 22–30.

Gibson, James William. *Warrior Dreams: Paramilitary Culture in Post-Vietnam America.* New York: Hill and Wang, 1994.

Gilbert, James. *Men in the Middle: Searching for Masculinity in the 1950s.* Chicago: University of Chicago Press, 2005.

Gitlin, Todd. *The Sixties: Years of Hope, Days of Rage.* New York: Bantam Books, 1987.

Goulden, Joseph C. *The Best Years: 1945–1950.* New York: Atheneum, 1976.

Hackett, Alice Payne, and James Henry Burke, *80 Years of Best Sellers, 1895–1975.* New York: R. R. Bowker, 1977.

Hale, Barbara Skluth. "The Representation of the Veteran in American Film, 1945–1950." Ph.D. diss., New York University, 1996.

Hall, Mitchell K. *Crossroads: American Popular Culture and the Vietnam Generation.* Lanham, Md.: Rowman and Littlefield, 2005.

Hallin, Daniel C. "The Media, the War in Vietnam, and Political Support: A Critique of the Thesis of an Oppositional Media." *Journal of Politics* 46 (February 1984): 2–24.

———. *The "Uncensored War": The Media and Vietnam.* New York: Oxford University Press, 1986.

———. "The Media and War." In *International Media Research: A Critical Survey,* edited by John Corner, Philip Schlesinger, and Roger Silverstone, 206–31. New York: Routledge, 1997.

Hallin, Daniel C., and Todd Gitlin. "The Gulf War as Popular Culture and Television Drama." In *Taken By Storm: The Media, Public Opinion, and U.S. Foreign Policy in the Gulf War,* edited by W. Lance Bennett and David L. Paletz, 149–63. Chicago: University of Chicago Press, 1994.

Hammond, William M. "The Press in Vietnam as Agent of Defeat: A Critical Examination." *Reviews in American History* 17 (June 1989): 312–23.

———. *Reporting Vietnam: Media and Military at War.* Lawrence: University Press of Kansas, 1998.

Hannavy, John. *The Camera Goes to War: Photographs from the Crimean War, 1854–56.* Edinburgh: Scottish Arts Council, 1974.

Harari, Yuval Noah. "Martial Illusions: War and Disillusionment in Twentieth-Century and Renaissance Military Memoirs." *Journal of Military History* 69 (January 2005): 43–72.

Harris, Brayton. *Blue & Gray in Black & White: Newspapers in the Civil War.* Washington, D.C.: Brassey's, 1999.

Hart, Sue. "Madison Avenue Goes to War: Patriotism in Advertising During World War II." In *Visions of War: World War II in Popular Literature and Culture,* edited by M. Paul Holsinger and Mary Anne Schofield, 114–26. Bowling Green, Ky.: Bowling Green State University Popular Press, 1992.

Hass, Kristin Ann. *Carried to the Wall: American Memory and the Vietnam Veterans Memorial.* Berkeley: University of California Press, 1998.

Hastings, Max. *Armageddon: The Battle for Germany, 1944–1945.* New York: Knopf, 2004.

Hauser, William L. *America's Army in Crisis: A Study in Civil-Military Relations.* Baltimore: Johns Hopkins University Press, 1973.

Hellmann, John. *American Myth and the Legacy of Vietnam.* New York: Columbia University Press, 1986.

Herman, Edward S., and Noam Chomsky. *Manufacturing Consent: The Political Economy of the Mass Media.* 1988. Rev. ed., New York: Pantheon Books, 2002.

Herman, Ellen. *The Romance of American Psychology: Political Culture in the Age of Experts.* Berkeley: University of California Press, 1995.

Hermes, Walter G. *United States Army in the Korean War: Truce Tent and Fighting Front.* Washington, D.C.: Government Printing Office, 1966.

Herring, George C. "Vietnam Remembered." *Journal of American History* 73 (June 1986): 152–64.

———. *America's Longest War: The United States and Vietnam, 1950–1975.* 4th ed. New York: McGraw-Hill, 2002.

Hoganson, Kristin L. *Fighting for American Manhood: How Gender Politics Provoked the Spanish-American and Philippine-American Wars.* New Haven: Yale University Press, 1998.

Holsinger, M. Paul. *War and American Popular Culture: A Historical Encyclopedia.* Westport, Conn.: Greenwood Press, 1999.

Horten, Gerd. "'Propaganda Must Be Painless': Radio Entertainment and Government Propaganda During World War II." *Prospects* 21 (1996): 373–95.

Hunt, Andrew E. *The Turning: A History of Vietnam Veterans Against the War.* New York: New York University Press, 1999.

Hunter, James Davison. *Culture Wars: The Struggle to Define America.* New York: Basic Books, 1991.

Ibson, John. "Masculinity under Fire: *Life's* Presentation of Camaraderie and Homoeroticism before, during, and after the Second World War." In *Looking at "Life" Magazine,* edited by Erika Doss, 179–99. Washington, D.C.: Smithsonian Institution Press, 2001.

Isaacs, Arnold R. *Vietnam Shadows: The War, Its Ghosts, and Its Legacy.* Baltimore: Johns Hopkins University Press, 1997.

Jackson, Kenneth T. *Crabgrass Frontier: The Suburbanization of the United States.* New York: Oxford University Press, 1985.

Jackson, Martin A. "The Uncertain Peace: *The Best Years of Our Lives* (1946)." In *American History/American Film: Interpreting the Hollywood Image,* edited by John E. O'Connor and Martin A. Jackson, 147–65. New York: Ungar, 1979.

Jarvis, Christina S. *The Male Body at War: American Masculinity during World War II.* DeKalb, Ill.: Northern Illinois University Press, 2004.

Jason, Philip K. "Vietnam War Themes in Korean War Fiction." *South Atlantic Review* 61 (Winter 1996): 109–21.

Jeffords, Susan. *The Remasculinization of America: Gender and the Vietnam War.* Bloomington: Indiana University Press, 1989.

Kamalipour, Yahya R., and Nancy Snow, eds. *War, Media, and Propaganda: A Global Perspective.* Lanham, Md.: Rowman and Littlefield, 2004.

Kaplan, Richard L. "American Journalism Goes to War, 1898–2001: A Manifesto on Media and Empire." *Media History* 9 (2003): 209–19.

Karnow, Stanley. *Vietnam: A History.* New York: Viking Press, 1983.

Karsten, Peter. "The 'New' American Military History: A Map of the Territory, Explored and Unexplored." *American Quarterly* 36, no. 3 (1984): 389–418.

Keegan, John. *The Face of Battle.* New York: Viking Press, 1976.

Keene, Jennifer D. *Doughboys, the Great War, and the Remaking of America.* Baltimore: Johns Hopkins University Press, 2001.

Kellner, Douglas. *The Persian Gulf TV War.* Boulder, Colo.: Westview Press, 1992.

Kennedy, David M. *Over Here: The First World War and American Society.* New York: Oxford University Press, 1980.

Kershaw, Alex. *Blood and Champagne: The Life and Times of Robert Capa.* New York: Thomas Dunne Books, 2003.

Kimble, James J. *Mobilizing the Home Front: War Bonds and Domestic Propaganda.* College Station: Texas A&M University Press, 2006.

Kimmel, Michael. *Manhood in America: A Cultural History.* New York: Free Press, 1996.

Kindsvatter, Peter S. *American Soldiers: Ground Combat in the World Wars, Korea, and Vietnam.* Lawrence: University Press of Kansas, 2003.

King, David C., and Zachary Karabell. *The Generation of Trust: Public Confidence in the U.S. Military since Vietnam.* Washington, D.C.: AEI Press, 2003.

Knightley, Phillip. *The First Casualty: The War Correspondent as Hero and Myth-Maker from the Crimea to Kosovo.* 1975. Rev. ed., Baltimore: Johns Hopkins University Press, 2000.

Koppes, Clayton R., and Gregory D. Black. "What to Show the World: The Office of

War Information and Hollywood, 1942–1945." *Journal of American History* 64 (June 1977): 87–105.

———. "Blacks, Loyalty, and Motion-Picture Propaganda in World War II." *Journal of American History* 73 (September 1986): 383–406.

———. *Hollywood Goes to War: How Politics, Profits, and Propaganda Shaped World War II Movies.* New York: Free Press, 1987.

Kutler, Stanley I. *The Wars of Watergate: The Last Crisis of Richard Nixon.* New York: W. W. Norton, 1990.

Lackman, Ron. *The Encyclopedia of 20th-Century American Television.* New York: Checkmark Books, 2003.

LaFeber, Walter. *America, Russia, and the Cold War, 1945–1990.* 1967. Rev. ed., New York: McGraw-Hill, 1991.

Landers, James. *The Weekly War: Newsmagazines and Vietnam.* Columbia: University of Missouri Press, 2004.

Landon, Philip J. "New Heroes: Post-War Hollywood's Image of World War II." In *Visions of War: World War II in Popular Literature and Culture,* edited by M. Paul Holsinger and Mary Anne Schofield, 18–26. Bowling Green, Ky.: Bowling Green State University Popular Press, 1992.

Langman, Larry, and Ed Borg. *Encyclopedia of American War Films.* New York: Garland, 1989.

Lee, Wayne E. "Mind and Matter—Cultural Analysis in American Military History: A Look at the State of the Field." *Journal of American History* 93 (March 2007): 1116–1142.

Lemann, Nicholas. *The Promised Land: The Great Black Migration and How It Changed America.* New York: Vintage Books, 1992.

Lembcke, Jerry. *The Spitting Image: Myth, Memory, and the Legacy of Vietnam.* New York: New York University Press, 1998.

Leuchtenburg, William F. *The Perils of Prosperity, 1914–1932.* 2nd ed. Chicago: University of Chicago Press, 1993.

Lewy, Guenter. *America in Vietnam.* New York: Oxford University Press, 1978.

Lichty, Lawrence W. "Comments on the Influence of Television on Public Opinion." In *Vietnam as History: Ten Years after the Paris Peace Accords,* edited by Peter Braestrup, 158–60. Washington, D.C.: University Press of America, 1984.

Lifton, Robert Jay. *Home from the War: Vietnam Veterans: Neither Victims nor Executioners.* New York: Basic Books, 1985.

Linderman, Gerald F. *The World within War: America's Combat Experience in World War II.* Cambridge: Harvard University Press, 1997.

Logevall, Fredrik. *Choosing War: The Lost Chance for Peace and the Escalation of War in Vietnam.* Berkeley: University of California Press, 1999.

Lopez, Daniel. *Films by Genre: 775 Categories, Styles, Trends and Movements Defined, with a Filmography for Each.* Jefferson, N.C.: McFarland, 1993.

Loss, Christopher P. "'The Most Wonderful Thing Has Happened to Me in the Army': Psychology, Citizenship, and American Higher Education in World War II." *Journal of American History* 92 (December 2005): 864–91.

Lubow, Arthur. *The Reporter Who Would Be King: A Biography of Richard Harding Davis.* New York: Scribner, 1992.

Lundberg, David. "The American Literature of War: The Civil War, World War I, and World War II." *American Quarterly* 36, no. 3 (1984): 373–88.

Lutz, Tom. *Crying: The Natural and Cultural History of Tears.* New York: W. W. Norton, 1999.

Lynn, John A. "The Embattled Future of Academic Military History." *Journal of Military History* 61 (October 1997): 777–89.

MacCann, Richard Dyer. *The People's Films: A Political History of U.S. Government Motion Pictures.* New York: Hastings House, 1973.

MacDonald, J. Fred. *Don't Touch That Dial! Radio Programming in American Life, 1920–1960.* Chicago: Nelson-Hall, 1979.

MacGregor, Morris J. *Integration of the Armed Forces, 1940–1965.* Washington, D.C.: Government Printing Office, 1981.

MacPherson, Myra. *Long Time Passing: Vietnam and the Haunted Generation.* Garden City, N.Y.: Doubleday, 1984.

Magder, Ted. "Watching What We Say: Global Communication in a Time of Fear." In *War and the Media: Reporting Conflict 24/7,* edited by Daya Kishan Thussu and Des Freedman, 28–44. London: Sage Publications, 2003.

Malo, Jean-Jacques, and Tony Williams, eds. *Vietnam War Films: Over 600 Feature, Made-for-TV, Pilot and Short Movies, 1939–1992, from the United States, Vietnam, France, Belgium, Australia, Hong Kong, South Africa, Great Britain and other Countries.* Jefferson, N.C.: McFarland, 1994.

Maraniss, David. *They Marched into Sunlight: War and Peace, Vietnam and America, October 1967.* New York: Simon and Schuster, 2003.

Margolis, Jon. *The Last Innocent Year: America in 1964.* New York: William Morrow, 1999.

Martin, Andrew. *Receptions of War: Vietnam in American Culture.* Norman: University of Oklahoma Press, 1993.

Martin, Russell. *Picasso's War: The Destruction of Guernica, and the Masterpiece That Changed the World.* New York: Dutton, 2002.

Mascaro, Thomas A. "The Peril of the Unheeded Warning: Robert F. Rogers's 'It's a Mad War.'" *Journalism History* 28 (Winter 2003): 182–90.

Matusow, Allen J. *The Unraveling of America: A History of Liberalism in the 1960s.* New York: Harper and Row, 1986.

McCann, David R. "Our Forgotten War: The Korean War in Korean and American Popular Culture." In *America's Wars in Asia: A Cultural Approach to History* and Memory, edited by Philip West, Steven I. Levine, and Jackie Hiltz, 65–83. Armonk, N.Y.: M. E. Sharpe, 1998.

McEnaney, Laura. "Nightmares on Elm Street: Demobilizing in Chicago, 1945–1953." Journal of American History 92 (March 2006): 1265–91.

Mermin, Jonathan. Debating War and Peace: Media Coverage of U.S. Intervention in the Post-Vietnam Era. Princeton: Princeton University Press, 1999.

Merrill, Robert. Norman Mailer. Boston: Twayne Publishers, 1978.

Mickenberg, Julia L. "Men on the Suburban Frontier: Rethinking Midcentury Masculinity." Reviews in American History 34 (December 2006): 529–36.

Miller, David. "Information Dominance: The Philosophy of Total Propaganda Control?" In War, Media, and Propaganda: A Global Perspective, edited by Yahya R. Kamalipour and Nancy Snow, 7–16. Lanham, Md.: Rowman and Littlefield, 2004.

Mills, Nicolaus. Their Last Battle: The Fight for the National World War II Memorial. New York: Basic Books, 2004.

Moeller, Susan D. Shooting War: Photography and the American Experience of Combat. New York: Basic Books, 1989.

Molotsky, Irvin. The Flag, the Poet, and the Song: The Story of the Star-Spangled Banner. New York: Dutton, 2001.

Moore, Harry T., ed. Contemporary American Novelists. Carbondale: Southern Illinois University Press, 1964.

Moser, Richard R. The New Winter Soldiers: GI and Veteran Dissent during the Vietnam Era. New Brunswick, N.J.: Rutgers University Press, 1996.

Mosse, George L. Fallen Soldiers: Reshaping the Memory of the World Wars. New York: Oxford University Press, 1990.

Mueller, John E. War, Presidents and Public Opinion. New York: John Wiley and Sons, 1973.

Musicant, Ivan. Empire by Default: The Spanish-American War and the Dawn of the American Century. New York: Henry Holt, 1998.

Nalty, Bernard, and Morris J. MacGregor, eds. Blacks in the Military: Essential Documents. Wilmington, Del.: Scholarly Resources, 1981.

Nam, Charles B. "Impact of the 'GI Bills' on the Educational Level of the Male Population." Social Forces 43 (October 1964): 26–32.

Neilson, Jim. Warring Fictions: Cultural Politics and the Vietnam War Narrative. Jackson: University Press of Mississippi, 1998.

Nicosia, Gerald. Home to War: A History of the Vietnam Veterans' Movement. New York: Crown Publishers, 2001.

Niven, Penelope. Steichen: A Biography. New York: Clarkson Potter, 1997.

Novick, Peter. The Holocaust in American Life. New York: Houghton Mifflin, 1999.

Nye, Robert A. "Western Masculinities in War and Peace." *American Historical Review* 112 (April 2007): 417–38.

Oakley, J. Ronald. *God's Country: America in the Fifties.* New York: W. W. Norton, 1986.

Olson, James S., and Randy Roberts, eds. *My Lai: A Brief History with Documents.* Boston: Bedford Books, 1998.

Olson, Keith W. *The GI Bill, the Veterans, and the Colleges.* Lexington: University Press of Kentucky, 1974.

O'Neill, William L. *Coming Apart: An Informal History of America in the 1960s.* Chicago: Quadrangle Books, 1971.

———. *American High: The Years of Confidence, 1945–1960.* New York: Free Press, 1986.

Organization of American Historians (roundtable). "Interchange: The Practice of History." *Journal of American History* 90 (September 2003): 576–611.

———. "Interchange: Legacies of the Vietnam War." *Journal of American History* 93 (September 2006): 452–90.

O'Toole, G. J. A. *The Spanish War: An American Epic—1898.* New York: W. W. Norton, 1984.

Pach, Chester J., Jr. "And That's the Way It Was: The Vietnam War on the Network Nightly News." In *The Sixties: From Memory to History,* edited by David Farber, 90–118. Chapel Hill: University of North Carolina Press, 1994.

Patterson, James T. *Grand Expectations: The United States, 1945–1974.* New York: Oxford University Press, 1996.

———. *Brown v. Board of Education: A Civil Rights Milestone and Its Troubled Legacy.* New York: Oxford University Press, 2001.

Piehler, G. Kurt. *Remembering War the American Way.* Washington, D.C.: Smithsonian Institution Press, 1995.

Reporting Vietnam, Part One: American Journalism, 1959–1969. New York: Library of America, 1998.

Roberts, Randy, and James S. Olson. *John Wayne: American.* Lincoln: University of Nebraska Press, 1995.

Robertson, Linda R. *The Dream of Civilized Warfare: World War I Flying Aces and the American Imagination.* Minneapolis: University of Minnesota Press, 2003.

Roeder, George H., Jr. *The Censored War: American Visual Experience during World War Two.* New Haven: Yale University Press, 1993.

Rollins, Peter C. "The Vietnam War: Perceptions through Literature, Film, and Television." *American Quarterly* 36, no. 3 (1984): 419–32.

Rollyson, Carl. *The Lives of Norman Mailer: A Biography.* New York: Paragon House, 1991.

Rosenthal, Marilyn. *Poetry of the Spanish Civil War.* New York: New York University Press, 1975.

Sachsman, David B., S. Kittrell Rushing, and Debra Reddin van Tuyll, eds. *The Civil War and the Press*. New Brunswick, N.J.: Transaction Publishers, 2000.

Sanderson, Rena, ed. *Blowing the Bridge: Essays on Hemingway and "For Whom the Bell Tolls."* New York: Greenwood Press, 1992.

Sandweiss, Martha A., ed. *Photography in Nineteenth-Century America*. Fort Worth, Tex.: Amon Carter Museum, 1991.

Savage, Barbara Dianne. *Broadcasting Freedom: Radio, War, and the Politics of Race, 1938–1948*. Chapel Hill: University of North Carolina Press, 1999.

Schecter, Danny. *Media Wars: News at a Time of Terror*. Lanham, Md.: Rowman and Littlefield, 2003.

Schmitz, David F. *The Tet Offensive: Politics, War, and Public Opinion*. Lanham, Md.: Rowman and Littlefield, 2005.

Schrecker, Ellen. *Many Are the Crimes: McCarthyism in America*. Boston: Little, Brown, 1998.

Schrijvers, Peter. *The GI War against Japan: American Soldiers in Asia and the Pacific during World War II*. New York: New York University Press, 2002.

Schulman, Bruce J. *The Seventies: The Great Shift in American Culture, Society, and Politics*. New York: Free Press, 2001.

Seelye, John. *War Games: Richard Harding Davis and the New Imperialism*. Amherst: University of Massachusetts Press, 2003.

Severo, Richard, and Lewis Milford. *The Wages of War: When America's Soldiers Came Home—From Valley Forge to Vietnam*. New York: Simon and Schuster, 1989.

Shafer, Michael D., ed. *The Legacy: The Vietnam War in the American Imagination*. Boston: Beacon Press, 1990.

Shay, Jonathan. *Achilles in Vietnam: Combat Trauma and the Undoing of Character*. New York: Atheneum, 1994.

Sherry, Michael. *In the Shadow of War: The United States since the 1930s*. New Haven: Yale University Press, 1995.

Sitkoff, Harvard. *The Struggle for Black Equality, 1954–1980*. New York: Hill and Wang, 1981.

———. "African American Militancy in the World War II South: Another Perspective." In *Remaking Dixie: The Impact of World War II on the American South*, edited by Neil McMillen, 70–92. Jackson: University Press of Mississippi, 1997.

Small, Melvin. *Antiwarriors: The Vietnam War and the Battle for America's Hearts and Minds*. Wilmington, Del.: Scholarly Resources, 2002.

Sontag, Susan. *On Photography*. New York: Picador, 1977.

———. *Regarding the Pain of Others*. New York: Picador, 2003.

Sparrow, James T. "Fighting Over the American Soldier: Moral Economy and National Citizenship in World War II." Ph.D. diss., Brown University, 2002.

Springer, Claudia. "Military Propaganda: Defense Department Films from World War II and Vietnam." In *The Vietnam War and American Culture,* edited by John Carlos Rowe and Rick Berg, 95–114. New York: Columbia University Press, 1991.

Staniszewski, Mary Anne. *The Power of Display: A History of Exhibition Installations at the Museum of Modern Art.* Cambridge: MIT Press, 1998.

Stoler, Mark A. "The Second World War in U.S. History and Memory." *Diplomatic History* 25 (July 2001): 383–92.

Suid, Lawrence H. *Guts and Glory: The Making of the American Military Image in Film.* 1978. Rev. ed., Lexington: University Press of Kentucky, 2002.

Susman, Warren. "Did Success Spoil the United States? Dual Representations in Postwar America." In *Recasting America: Culture and Politics in the Age of Cold War,* edited by Lary May, 19–37. Chicago: University of Chicago Press, 1989.

Sweeney, Michael S. *Secrets of Victory: The Office of Censorship and the American Press and Radio in World War II.* Chapel Hill: University of North Carolina Press, 2001.

Talbott, John E. "Soldiers, Psychiatrists, and Combat Trauma." *Journal of Interdisciplinary History* 27 (Winter 1997): 437–54.

Tansey, Richard G., and Fred S. Kleiner. *Gardner's Art Through the Ages.* 10th ed. Fort Worth, Tex.: Harcourt Brace College Publishers, 1996.

Taylor, D. J. *Orwell: The Life.* New York: Henry Holt, 2003.

Taylor, Philip M. *War and the Media: Propaganda and Persuasion in the Gulf War.* Manchester, U.K.: Manchester University Press, 1998.

Telotte, J. P. *Voices in the Dark: The Narrative Patterns of Film Noir.* Urbana: University of Illinois Press, 1989.

Terry, Wallace. *Bloods: An Oral History of the Vietnam War by Black Veterans.* New York: Random House, 1984.

Thomas, Gareth. *The Novel of the Spanish Civil War (1936–1975).* Cambridge, U.K.: Cambridge University Press, 1990.

Thussu, Daya Kishan, and Des Freedman, eds. *War and the Media: Reporting Conflict 24/7.* London: Sage Publications, 2003.

Tobin, James. *Ernie Pyle's War: America's Eyewitness to World War II.* New York: Free Press, 1997.

Torgovnick, Marianna. *The War Complex: World War II in Our Time.* Chicago: University of Chicago Press, 2005.

Traister, Bryce. "Academic Viagra: The Rise of American Masculinity Studies." *American Quarterly* 52 (June 2000): 274–304.

Valleau, Marjorie A. *The Spanish Civil War in American and European Films.* Ann Arbor, Mich.: UMI Research Press, 1982.

Van Ells, Mark D. *To Hear Only Thunder Again: America's World War II Veterans Come Home.* Lanham, Md.: Lexington Books, 2001.

Varley, Paul. *Japanese Culture.* 4th ed. Honolulu: University of Hawaii Press, 2000.

Wanke, Paul. "American Military Psychiatry and Its Role Among Ground Forces of World War II." *Journal of Military History* 63 (January 1999): 127–46.

Weigley, Russell F. "The American Civil-Military Cultural Gap: A Historical Perspective, Colonial Times to the Present." *In Soldiers and Civilians: The Civil-Military Gap and American National Security,* edited by Peter D. Feaver and Richard H. Kohn, 215–46. Cambridge: MIT Press, 2001.

Whitfield, Stephen J. "Still the Best Catch There Is: Joseph Heller's *Catch-22.*" In *Rethinking Cold War Culture,* edited by Peter J. Kuznick and James Gilbert, 175–200. Washington, D.C.: Smithsonian Institution Press, 2001.

Williams, Bruce A. "The New Media Environment, Internet Chatrooms, and Public Discourse after 9/11." In *War and the Media: Reporting Conflict 24/7,* edited by Daya Kishan Thussu and Des Freedman, 176–89. London: Sage Publications, 2003.

Wills, Garry. *John Wayne's America: The Politics of Celebrity.* New York: Simon and Schuster, 1997.

Wilson, Edmund. *Patriotic Gore: Studies in the Literature of the American Civil War.* New York: Oxford University Press, 1962.

Winkler, Allan M. *The Politics of Propaganda: The Office of War Information, 1942–1945.* New Haven: Yale University Press, 1978.

———. *Home Front U.S.A.: America During World War II.* Arlington Heights, Ill.: H. Davidson, 1986.

Winter, Jay. "Film and the Matrix of Memory." *American Historical Review* 106 (June 2001): 857–64.

Wyatt, Clarence R. *Paper Soldiers: The American Press and the Vietnam War.* New York: W. W. Norton, 1993.

Zangrando, Robert L. *The NAACP Crusade Against Lynching, 1909–1950.* Philadelphia: Temple University Press, 1980.

TEXT CREDITS

INDEX

China, 97, 98, 114, 119, 127, 130; soldiers from, 99, 104, 107, 108, 113,
148
Chomsky, Noam, 10, 204
Chosin Reservoir, 114, 132
Cimino, Michael, 266
Citizens' Committee of Inquiry into
War Crimes in Indochina (CCI),
223, 224, 227
Civilians: insensitivity toward soldiers
of, 90, 127–29, 263; relations with
soldiers and veterans, 21, 22, 27, 34,
36, 47–48, 50, 59, 69, 75, 239–40,
291 (n. 76); as sacrificing on home
front, 22, 41, 134. See also Public
opinion
Civil rights movement, 45, 47, 52–53,
133, 134, 137, 152, 185, 231, 292
(n. 95). See also African Americans
Civil War, 4, 5, 237, 242, 251
Cleveland Plain Dealer, 213
Cold War, 97, 119, 127, 128, 133, 151,
166, 172, 174; and American culture,
133–35, 167; nature of, 281; and news
media, 106, 204
Collier's, 5, 52, 59, 62
Columbia Broadcasting System (CBS),
173, 179–202 passim, 213, 227, 230,
236
Combat: as damaging to soldiers, 6, 12,
65, 71, 84–92, 116–17, 129–30, 143,
145, 167, 214, 226, 244–46, 255–56,
262–70, 276, 278–79; as dehumanizing, 244–46, 255–56, 266, 276,
278, 325 (n. 15); futility of, 73, 150,
157, 163, 164–65, 194–98, 271, 310
(n. 73); as hardening soldiers, 16,
18, 22, 25, 26, 36, 48, 70, 78, 86;
as honorable, 3, 125, 130, 138, 184;
murky ethics of, 139–40, 147, 161,
213, 236, 246, 256; nature of, dur-

ing Korean War, 98–99, 100–105,
106–10, 113–17, 119–29; nature of,
during Vietnam War, 172, 176, 186,
217, 221–22; nature of, during World
War II, 17–18, 39, 65, 78
Combat!, 162–65, 193, 266, 277
Combat Bulletin, 105, 108, 114, 116, 119,
301 (n. 38)
Coming Home (1978), 241, 262–66, 279
Committee on Public Information
(CPI), 19
Commonweal, 63
Con Thien, 194–96, 197 (ill.)
Corwin, Norman, 48
Crane, Stephen, 4, 5
Creel, George, 19
Crisis, 45–47, 53, 112, 113
Cronkite, Walter, 173, 174, 182, 195–96,
202–3, 230, 231, 236, 283 (n. 2)
Crying, 280; in long 1950s, 105, 108,
109 (ill.), 116, 121, 122, 123 (ill.), 130,
142, 195, 277; in Vietnam era, 186,
200, 202, 230, 264, 266, 270; in
World War II era, 26, 83, 85
Cynicism. See Public opinion: and
cynicism

Davis, Richard Harding, 5
Day without End (1949), 144
D-Day (June 6, 1944), 6, 32, 37, 39, 66,
73, 132, 138, 274
Deer Hunter, The (1978), 241, 262,
266–70, 279
Demilitarized Zone (DMZ), Vietnam,
182, 186, 189, 194–97
Democratic values, 146; in military,
167, 291 (n. 75), 306 (n. 16)
De Niro, Robert, 267
Desegregation of military, 110, 113,
117–19, 120 (ill.), 184, 191
Desertion, 165, 233–35

Gitlin, Todd, 8, 11
Goulden, Joseph, 47
Grainger, Edmund, 78
Great Britain, 4, 5, 7, 21, 37, 47, 91; and
    World War I memoirs, 6
Great Depression, 15, 37, 49, 57, 60, 68,
    141
Greatest generation mythology, 68,
    279–80, 281–82, 330 (n. 5)
Green Berets, The (film, 1968), 241,
    257
Green Berets, The (novel, 1965), 241
Grinker, Roy, 33–34
Guadalcanal, 53, 128, 132, 154
Guerrilla theater, 221, 228–29
Gulf War (1991), 10

Haeberle, Ronald, 173, 213, 252–53
Hagopian, Patrick, 280
Halberstam, David, 173, 174
Halbwachs, Maurice, 280
Hallin, Daniel, 8, 11, 178, 195, 204,
    283 (n. 2)
Hammond, William, 204
Hanks, Tom, 136
Harari, Yuval Noah, 3, 284 (n. 24)
Harper's, 4, 5, 50, 51, 65, 69, 89
Harris polls. *See* Public opinion
Hayworth, Leonard, 122, 123 (ill.)
Hedin, Robert, 151
Heller, Joseph, 153–54
Hemingway, Ernest, 6, 7
Herr, Michael, 242, 257, 261
Hersey, John, 84, 88
Hersh, Seymour, 213, 215, 246
Hershey, Lewis, 100
Higgins, Marguerite, 99, 101
Hines, Frank T., 21
Hinojosa, Rolando, 151
Hitler, Adolf, 48, 98
Ho Chi Minh Trail, 171

Hollywood. *See* Film
Homosexuality, 87–88, 154, 162, 248,
    258–59, 285 (n. 34), 298 (n. 55), 309
    (n. 61), 311 (n. 106)
House Committee on Veterans' Affairs,
    63
Hughes, Langston, 43
Hugo, Richard, 160
Humphrey, Hubert, 207
Huntley, Chet, 172, 173
Huston, John, 82

Infantrymen. *See* Soldiers, depictions of
Into the Valley (1943), 88
Iraq War, 241, 280
Italy, 5, 38, 39, 73, 84–88, 113, 132, 141
Iwo Jima, 108, 205; American fighting
    on, 21, 24, 132; in film, 77–80

Japan, 98, 99, 101, 106, 117, 130; defeat
    of, 47; fighting against, 77–80, 88–
    89, 154; leadership of, 15, 18, 128;
    planned U.S. invasion of, 21; soldiers
    from, 34, 88, 92, 245
Japanese Americans: in films, 136,
    137–38, 149–51, 307 (n. 28); intern-
    ment of, 17, 137, 308 (n. 29); racism
    toward, in Vietnam era, 234; World
    War II service of, 17, 137–38
Jarrell, Randall, 85, 160
Jarvis, Christina, 32
Jennings, Peter, 173
Johnson, Lyndon, 127, 175, 178, 184;
    approval ratings of, 172, 182–83,
    190, 198, 243; and credibility gap,
    196, 198, 202–3, 207, 238; declines
    to run in 1968, 207; and news me-
    dia, 180, 181, 189–90, 203; scales
    back Vietnam War, 207; and Viet-
    nam War escalation, 171–73, 179,
    182

News media, 4; and bias, 11, 173–74; and federal government, 10–11, 106, 173–74, 204, 286 (nn. 45–46); and identification with soldiers, 11–12, 106, 174–75, 186, 238, 276, 277; and Korean War, 11, 97–131; and Office of War Information, 20; and Spanish-American War, 5; and Vietnam War, 10, 11, 173–206, 213–17, 222, 227–28, 230–37; and World War I, 5; and World War II, 11, 18, 19–23, 27–43, 45, 50–69, 129–30. *See also* Censorship; War correspondents; *and specific news outlets*

Newspapers, 3–4, 5, 37, 155, 173. *See also* News media; *and specific newspapers*

Newsreels, 7, 45, 61, 64, 67, 75, 101, 105, 113, 114, 126, 142

Newsweek (magazine): and Korean War, 97, 101, 107, 108, 115, 116, 149; and Vietnam War, 172–202 passim, 228, 231, 232, 234, 235, 265, 268; and World War II, 27, 29, 32, 34, 47, 55, 76, 79, 143. *See also* News media; War correspondents

New York Daily World, 227

New Yorker, 173, 175

New York Herald, 4

New York Illustrated News, 4

New York Journal, 5

New York Times, 4, 15, 163, 280, 282; and Korean War, 108, 112, 113, 125, 149; and Vietnam War, 173, 212, 213, 222, 224, 227; and World War II, 33, 37, 47, 51, 52, 76, 79, 88, 90, 143

New York Times Magazine, 76

New York Tribune, 4

New York World, 5

Ngo Dinh Diem, 171, 182

Nguyen Cao Ky, 182

Nguyen Khanh, 171

Nguyen Ngoc Loan, 199

Nixon, Richard, 166, 207; and antiwar movement, 207–9, 218, 323 (n. 78); approval ratings of, 209; and management of Vietnam War, 207–8, 254; and My Lai massacre, 213, 215, 216

North Africa, 17, 38, 53

Novick, Peter, 279

Nuclear weapons, 98

O'Brien, Tim, 242, 257, 261, 264, 265

Office of Censorship, 19–20

Office of War Information (OWI), 19–20, 38, 41, 75, 81–82, 83, 275; and Bureau of Motion Pictures, 23, 45; and Hollywood, 20; idealism of, 19; and *The Negro Soldier*, 45–47; and news media, 20–23; and photographic exhibits, 15; and radio, 20; and other wartime agencies, 19–20. *See also* Propaganda

Officers: African Americans among, 46, 118, 190, 191; and conflicts with soldiers, 41, 73, 89, 138–39, 144–47, 154, 164, 167, 234–37, 238, 258–61; and cooperation with soldiers, 142; ineptitude of, 42; insensitivity of, 41, 167, 258; resentment of military brass, 147, 150–51, 155–56, 196, 260

Okinawa, 21, 53, 83, 132

Olejarz, Lenny, 261

Operation Dewey Canyon III, 228–31

Operation Rapid American Withdrawal (RAW), 219–22

Operation Rolling Thunder, 172

Oppen, George, 159

Orwell, George, 7

Pach, Chester, 181, 317 (n. 117)

Panmunjom, Korea, 119, 149

Paramount. *See* Newsreels

Pathé. *See* Newsreels

Paths of Glory (1957), 143

Patriotism: during long 1950s, 128, 141, 142, 165; during Vietnam era, 193, 206, 222, 251, 267; during World War II era, 73, 79, 134, 163, 276

Patton, George, 39, 41; film about, 241

Peace Comes to America (1945), 26

Pearl Harbor, 15, 45, 50, 98, 128, 141, 153, 161, 172, 225, 274

Peleliu, 29, 30 (ill.), 34, 35 (ill.)

Pentagon. *See* U.S. Department of Defense

Philippines, 5, 21, 47

Photography, 4, 5, 6–7; during Korean War, 101–31 passim; during Vietnam era, 173–206 passim, 212, 213; during World War II era, 15–16, 20, 27, 28 (ill.), 29, 31 (ill.), 65–67, 70–71

Physical casualties: cheerfulness of, 27, 67; as dependent, 21, 76; as independent, 76, 81; during long 1950s, 97–126 passim, 158–59, 164, 165; official desires for depiction of, 21, 24; portrayal of, in film, 74–77, 78, 80–82, 244, 247, 262–70; portrayal of, in literature, 158–59; portrayal of, in news media, 27–32, 38, 51, 65–67, 97–126 passim, 174, 178–79, 186, 187 (ill.), 188, 193–94, 195–98, 200, 201 (ill.), 202; portrayal of, on television programs, 164, 165; rehabilitation of, 80–82, 93, 262–70; stoicism of, 29, 67; during Vietnam era, 174, 178–79, 186, 187 (ill.), 188, 193–94, 195–98, 200, 201 (ill.), 202, 219, 220 (ill.); and virility, 75–76, 263, 265; during World War II, 17, 21,

28 (ill.), 30 (ill.), 31 (ill.). *See also* Casualty figures; Soldiers, depictions of: as wounded; Veterans, depictions of: as wounded

Picasso, Pablo, 6

Pilots: in film, 142; during Korean War, 105, 127–29; in literature, 85, 129, 158, 160; during Vietnam War, 180, 181, 186, 188; during World War II era, 8, 18, 32, 58, 85. *See also* U.S. Air Force; U.S. Navy

Pirosh, Robert, 163

Platke, Stan, 244, 253

Poetry: and Korean War, 139–40, 148, 151; and Vietnam War, 253–54, 256, 258–59, 261, 268–69; and World War I, 6; and World War II, 18, 84, 85, 87, 157–61

Pork Chop Hill (1959), 149–53, 154, 155, 163, 164, 167, 185, 196, 234, 279

Post-traumatic stress disorder (PTSD), 82, 83, 224, 321 (n. 60)

Power in the Pacific (1945), 70–71, 72 (ill.), 121, 125

Prescott, Orville, 90, 125, 157

Press. *See* News media

Prisoners of war (POWs): American, 64, 108, 119, 129, 133, 161, 181, 200; German, 39, 40 (ill.), 43, 48; Italian, 43; Japanese, 88, 159, 161; North Korean, 107, 108, 110, 119, 137–38; Vietnamese, 180–81, 184, 188–89, 199

Propaganda, 16, 19–20; in official World War II films, 26; during World War I, 19, 142. *See also* Office of War Information

Prostitution, 86–87, 261

Psychiatric casualties: during long 1950s, 107, 116–17, 125, 142, 145, 147, 148–49, 154, 159–61, 165, 167, 276;

Soldiers, depictions of—in Vietnam
  era, *continued*
  as exhausted, 189; and feelings of
  guilt, 180, 224, 242, 253, 264, 266;
  as fierce, 192; and fragging, 210, 231,
  234–36, 257, 261, 278; as frightened,
  178, 194–97, 244; and hatred of
  officers or sergeants, 210, 234–37,
  238, 258–61, 278; as hostile toward
  home front, 195, 242; as heroes, 175,
  184, 192, 205, 216, 267; and inadvertent harm to civilians, 180; as
  individuals, 171–271 passim; and low
  morale, 209–10, 231–37; as patriots,
  193, 206, 251; as programmed to
  kill, 214–15, 219–22, 225–26, 243,
  278; and psychological trauma, 178,
  190, 221, 223–24, 226, 244, 262–
  70; as resentful of military brass,
  190, 196, 238, 291 (n. 73); as skilled
  professionals, 175, 176, 177 (ill.), 178,
  183–84, 192–93, 204; as sorrowful,
  199; as stoic, 188, 194–98, 256; and
  "support" of, 217; as team players,
  176, 178, 181, 204; as undisciplined,
  209–10, 225, 231–37, 258; as victims,
  181, 186, 194–98, 205, 210, 215, 219–
  40 passim, 243, 250, 260, 277, 278;
  and war crimes, 181, 204, 210–18,
  219–28, 252–53, 278; as wounded,
  174, 178–79, 186, 187 (ill.), 188,
  193–94, 195–98, 200, 201 (ill.),
  202, 244, 247
—in World War II era, 15–93; as abusive, 88; and camaraderie, 139, 163;
  as courageous, 42, 48; as cynics,
  38, 41, 42, 73, 78–79, 84–92; as
  damaged by combat, 65, 71, 84–92;
  deceased, 29, 31–32, 66, 71, 78, 79,
  85; as disillusioned, 84–92; as exhausted, 38, 39, 40 (ill.), 48, 66; as
  expendable, 39, 84–85, 89; as fierce,
  15; as forgotten by home front, 34; as
  frightened, 38, 39, 42; as gripers, 38,
  42; as hardened by combat, 16, 18,
  22, 36, 48, 70, 78, 303 (n. 87); and
  hatred of officers or sergeants, 41,
  73, 77–78, 89; as heroes, 15, 16, 18,
  27, 36, 46, 48, 49, 71, 103, 134, 138,
  175; as hostile toward home front,
  22, 41, 49, 84, 86, 89–90; as humble, 15, 48; as individuals, 12, 41, 49,
  71, 84–92, 276; as isolated, 86, 90;
  and motivation, 142–43, 301 (n. 29);
  as patriots, 79, 134, 163, 276; and
  psychological trauma, 35 (ill.), 38, 39,
  73, 84, 88; as resentful of military
  brass, 41, 84–92; as sorrowful, 38; as
  stoic, 27, 29, 38, 42; as team players,
  12, 18, 49, 66, 71, 78, 86, 92, 128,
  130, 136, 163, 216, 276; as undisciplined, 77, 79–80; as victims, 34, 41,
  48, 49, 71, 85, 89, 276; as wounded,
  29, 30 (ill.), 31 (ill.), 32, 38, 78
—*See also* Physical casualties; Psychiatric casualties; Veterans, depictions of
Soviet Union, 21, 97, 119, 133
Spain, 1, 5, 6–7, 202
Special Forces, 324 (n. 2)
Stalin, Joseph, 97, 98, 99, 119
Stanton, Frank, 180
Stars and Stripes, 37, 41, 190
Steel Helmet, The (1951), 136–40, 142,
  144, 147, 149, 150, 154, 163, 167,
  234, 243, 256; video version of,
  307 (n. 22)
Steichen, Edward, 15, 70, 121, 125, 126,
  130
Stewart, Ed, 49
Story of G.I. Joe, The (1945), 73–74, 143
Supreme Court, 52–53, 58
Susman, Warren, 50